Small Business Services

Dear Cardmember:

We appreciate your Cardmembership and consider you one of our most valued Cardmembers. So, it gives me great pleasure to present you with the 2001 Zagat Survey of America's Top Restaurants, a guide to the most-celebrated restaurants in the country.

Refer to Zagat's Survey throughout the year whenever you plan business lunches and dinners, out-of-town meetings, or evenings with friends. It's our way of thanking you for being a loyal Cardmember.

From all of us here at Small Business Services, we wish you the best as you ring in the new year.

Sincerely,

Jim Blann
General Manager
Small Business Services

The Corporate Card from American Express Small Business Services.

Flexible business solutions to help you write your own success story.

Expense Management & Information

- *Quarterly Management Report*
- *Information and Advice*
- *No Preset Spending Limit**
- *Online Access to Daily Account Activity*
- *Express Cash*

Insurance Programs

- *Car Rental Loss and Damage Insurance*
- *Travel Accident Insurance*
- *Baggage Insurance*
- *Buyer's Assurance Plan*
- *Purchase Protection Plan*

Savings & Rewards

- *Exclusive Everyday Savings*
- *Complimentary Hertz #1 Club Gold Membership*
- Membership Rewards® *Program*

* Your purchases are approved based on a variety of factors, including your account history, credit record and personal resources.

Unparalleled Cardmember Services

- *24-Hour Customer Service*
- *Over 1,700 Travel and Foreign Exchange Service Locations, Worldwide*
- *Emergency Card Replacement*
- *Guaranteed Reservations*

Financial Services

- *BusinessFlex*
- *Line of Credit*
- *Credit Cards*

Small Business Services

ZAGATSURVEY®

2001
AMERICA'S TOP
RESTAURANTS

Editors: Catherine Bigwood with
Gail Hall Zarr and Lorraine Mead

Published and distributed by
ZAGAT SURVEY, LLC
4 Columbus Circle
New York, New York 10019
Tel: 212 977 6000
E-mail: americastop@zagat.com
Web site: www.zagat.com

Acknowledgments

Our special thanks to the thousands of surveyors who have shared their views with us and made this nationwide *Survey* possible. We would also like to thank our editors and coordinators in each city: Nichole Bernier Ahern, Angela Allen, Andrew Berk, Karen Berk, Marlene Berlow, Arlene Blut, Olga Boikess, Margaret Briggs, Mark Brown, Nikki Buchanan, Teresa Byrne-Dodge, Suzi Forbes Chase, Jon Christensen, Providence Cicero, Jane Cisneros, Andrea Clurfeld, Pat Denechaud, Victoria Pesce Elliott, Carrie Floyd, Hal Foster, Jeanette Foster, William Fox, Connie Frost, Randy Fuller, Norma Gottlieb, Meesha Halm, Barbara Herring, Suzanne Hough, Marty Katz, Michael Klein, Sandy Kupfer, Gretchen Kurz, Nancy Leson, Sharon Litwin, John Long, Myrna Marston, John Martellaro, John McDermott, Carolyn McGuire, Colleen Moore, Maryanne Muller, Kelley Nakamura, David Nelson, Kristine Nickel, Sharon Niederman, Cynthia Nims, Ann Orton, Ann Lemons Pollack, Joe Pollack, June Naylor Rodriguez, Susan Safronoff, Shelley Skiles Sawyer, John Schell, Maura Sell, Merrill Shindler, Victoria Spencer, Mary Stagaman, Muriel Stevens, Bill St. John, Steve Stover, Paul Uhlmann III, Jill Van Cleave, Ann Verme, Phil Vettel, Carla Waldemar, Cheryl Walsh, Julie Wilson, Kay Winzenried, Sue Zelickson and Nancy Zimmerman.

This guide would not have been possible without the exacting work of our staff:

Phil Cardone, Larry Cohn, Erica Curtis, Liz Daleske, Carol Diuguid, Laura du Pont, Audrey Farolino, Jeff Freier, Curt Gathje, Sarah Kagan, Sinting Lai, Natalie Lebert, Mike Liao, Dave Makulec, Jefferson Martin, Andrew O'Neill, Bernard Onken, Benjamin Schmerler, Troy Segal, Robert Seixas, Zamira Skalkottas, LaShana Smith and Yoji Yamaguchi.

Contents

About This Survey

Here are the results of our *2001 Zagat Survey of America's Top Restaurants,* covering some 1,279 restaurants in 44 US cities and states. This book represents a compilation of the best restaurants selected by thousands of local *Survey* participants. For each area, we have included a list of the top restaurants (based on the results of our most recent *Surveys* in that area) as well as a list of "Additional Note-worthy Places" chosen by our local editors.

The cities covered were chosen mainly because they are leading culinary centers. However, this is still a "work in progress." Each year we add more areas of the country, but we still have more to cover.

By regularly surveying large numbers of local restaurant-goers across the country, we think we have achieved a uniquely reliable guide. We hope you agree. On the assumption that most people want a "quick fix" on the places at which they are considering eating, we've tried to be concise, and have provided a handy cuisine index.

Knowing that the quality of this *Survey* is the direct result of their voting and commentary, we sincerely thank each participant. They include numerous professionals, business executives and just plain folks – food lovers all. We also thank our local editors. It was they who helped us choose the restaurants to be surveyed and edited the *Survey* results.

We invite you to be a reviewer in our city *Restaurant Surveys* or in our *Hotels, Resorts & Spas Surveys*. So that we can contact you at the time of the next *Survey*, send a stamped, self-addressed, business-size envelope to ZAGAT SURVEY, 4 Columbus Circle, New York, NY 10019 indicating the *Survey* in which you would like to participate, e.g. "LA" or "Hotel", or e-mail us at americastop@zagat.com, so that we will be able to contact you. Each participant will receive a free copy of the resulting *Survey* when it's published.

Your comments, suggestions and criticisms of this *Survey* are also solicited. There is always room for improvement – with your help.

New York, New York
November 6, 2000

Nina and Tim Zagat

Foreword

As we raise our forks to a new millennium, one thing is clear: Americans have some remarkably fine dining ahead. We continue to enjoy the fruits of a culinary revolution that in the span of a generation has transformed the country's restaurants, bringing a level of quality and diversity that would have been unimaginable a quarter of a century ago.

Peruse these pages and it's hard not to be struck by the sheer variety of eateries they encompass. As befits a nation of immigrants, our restaurants reflect us, proffering cuisines from every culinary capital. While most of the entries that appear here are decidedly upscale – after all, this is a compendium of the *crème de la crème* – others aren't the least bit fancy but embody in some way the cities that they serve (for instance, New York City is devoted to its delis, while Kansas City is synonymous with its barbecue).

Fine dining's coming of age is also due to diners themselves: Americans are better traveled and educated than at any time before and their worldliness translates into higher culinary expectations. With dozens of TV shows, books, magazines and Web sites devoted to gastronomy, the public is more informed about food and their standards rise as their knowledge grows.

The amazing array of ingredients now available also contributes to the elevated state of the art. Where once a button mushroom would do, for example, now there are morels, *matsutakes* and dozens of varieties in between. Local producers customize their crops to suit the needs of chefs, allowing them to build seasonal menus around regional produce, while improvements in technology and transportation enable ever-more exotic perishables to cross the country and arrive almost as fresh as the moment they were harvested.

Chefs have changed, too. Increasingly today our top toques have been trained in the U.S., where the leading culinary schools rank second to none. And while once upon a time career-minded women couldn't wait to get out of the kitchen, now a new generation – of both women and men – views a culinary profession as a worthy aspiration. With such an infusion of young blood into the industry and an unprecedentedly vibrant economy, we anticipate more dynamic developments in the decades to come.

This *2001 Zagat Survey of America's Top Restaurants* is a celebration of our country's current culinary vitality. We hope you'll visit us at our Web site – zagat.com – to give us your feedback and vote for your own favorites in over 40 cities, both in America and abroad.

New York, New York
November 6, 2000

Nina and Tim Zagat

Dining Tips

Over our 20-plus years of surveying restaurant-goers, we've heard from hundreds of thousands of people about their dining-out experiences. Most of their reports are positive – proof of the ever-growing skill and dedication of the nation's chefs and restaurateurs. But inevitably, we also hear about problems.

Obviously, there are certain basics that everyone has the right to expect when dining out: 1. Courteous, hospitable, informative service; 2. Clean, sanitary facilities; 3. Fresh, healthful food; 4. Timely honoring of reservations; and 5. Smoke-free seating.

Sadly, if these conditions aren't met, many diners simply swallow their disappointment, assuming there's nothing they can do. However, the truth is that diners have far more power than they may realize. Every restaurateur worth his or her salt wants to satisfy customers, since happy clients equal a successful business. Rather than the adversaries they sometimes seem to be, diners and restaurateurs are natural allies – both want the same outcome, and each can help the other achieve it. Toward that end, here are a few simple but sometimes forgotten tips that every restaurant-goer should bear in mind:

1. Speak up: If dissatisfied by any aspect of your experience – from the handling of your reservation to the food, service or physical environment – tell the manager. Most problems are easy to resolve at the time they occur – but not if management doesn't know about them until afterward. The opposite is also true: if you're pleased, speak up.

2. Spell out your needs ahead of time: If you have specific dietary requests, wish to bring your own wine, want a smoke-free (or smoking) environment, or have any other special needs, you can avoid disappointment by calling ahead to make sure the restaurant can satisfy you.

3. Do your part: A restaurant's ability to honor reservations, for example, is largely dependent on diners honoring reservations and showing up on time. Make it a point to cancel reservations you're unable to use and be sure to notify the restaurant if you'll be late. The restaurant, in turn, should do its best to seat parties promptly, and, if there are delays, should keep diners informed (a free drink doesn't hurt either).

4. Vote with your dollars: Most people tip 15 to 19%, and often 20% or more at high-end restaurants. Obviously, you have the right not to tip at all if unhappy with the service; but in that case, many simply leave 10% to get the message across. If you like the restaurant, it's worth accompanying the low tip with a word to the management. Of course, the ultimate way to vote with your dollars is not to come back.

5. Put it in writing: Like it or not, all restaurants make mistakes. The best ones distinguish themselves by how well they acknowledge and handle mistakes. If you've expressed your complaints to the restaurant management but haven't gotten a satisfactory response, write to your local restaurant critic, with a copy to the restaurant, detailing the problem. That really gets the restaurateur's attention. Naturally, we also hope you'll express your feelings, pro and con, by voting on zagat.com.

Key to Ratings/Symbols

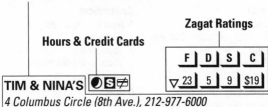

Name, Address & Phone Number

Zagat Ratings

Hours & Credit Cards

F	D	S	C
▽23	5	9	$19

TIM & NINA'S ◐ 🆂 ⊄
4 Columbus Circle (8th Ave.), 212-977-6000

◢ Open 24/7, this "crowded", "over popular" joint started the "Swedish-Mexican craze" (i.e. herring or lox on tiny tacos with mole or chimichurri sauce); though it looks like a "garage" and T & N "never heard of credit cards or reservations" – yours in particular – "dirt cheap" tabs for "*muy bien* eats" draw demented "debit-account" diners to this "deep dive."

Review with surveyors' comments in quotes

Before each review a symbol indicates whether responses were uniform ■ or mixed ◢.

Hours: ◐ serving after 11 PM
🆂 open on Sunday

Credit Cards: ⊄ no credit cards accepted

Ratings: Food, Decor and Service are rated on a scale of **0** to **30**. The Cost (C) column reflects our surveyors' estimate of the price of a meal including one drink.

F Food	D Decor	S Service	C Cost
23	5	9	$19

0–9 poor to fair	**20–25** very good to excellent
10–15 fair to good	**26–30** extraordinary to perfection
16–19 good to very good	▽ low response/less reliable

A place listed without ratings is either an important **newcomer** or a popular **write-in**. For such places, the estimated cost is indicated by the following symbols.

I	$15 and below	**E**	$31 to $50
M	$16 to $30	**VE**	$51 or more

Top Five Food Rankings by Area

Atlanta
1. Bacchanalia
2. Ritz-Carlton Buck. Din. Rm.
3. Soto
4. Brasserie Le Coze
5. Seeger's

Atlantic City
1. Le Palais
2. White House
3. Savaradio
4. Tre Figlio
5. Chef Vola's

Baltimore/Annapolis
1. Lewnes' Steakhouse
2. Prime Rib
3. Hampton's
4. Antrim 1844
5. Inn at Perry Cabin

Boston
1. L'Espalier
2. Aujourd'hui
3. Olives
4. Hamersley's Bistro
5. Caffe Bella

Chicago
1. Le Français
2. Carlos'
3. Ritz-Carlton Din. Rm.
4. TRU
5. Ambria

Cincinnati
1. Maisonette
2. Palace
3. Chez Alphonse
4. BonBonerie
5. Precinct

Cleveland
1. Johnny's Bar
2. Phnom Penh
3. Johnny's Downtown
4. Lola
5. Hyde Park Grille

Columbus
1. Handke's Cuisine
2. Refectory
3. L'Antibes
4. Rigsby's
5. Hyde Park

Connecticut
1. Restaurant du Village
2. Cavey's
3. Jean-Louis
4. Thomas Henkelmann
5. La Colline Verte

Dallas
1. French Room
2. Riviera
3. Mansion on Turtle Creek
4. Pyramid Grill
5. Cafe Pacific

Denver/Mountain Resorts
1. Papillon
2. Highlands Garden Cafe
3. Sweet Basil
4. Renaissance
5. Keystone Ranch

Fort Lauderdale
1. Eduardo de San Angel
2. Darrel & Oliver's Cafe
3. Armadillo Cafe
4. Mark's Las Olas
5. Black Orchid Cafe

Fort Worth
1. Cacharel
2. Del Frisco's
3. Saint-Emilion
4. Bistro Louise
5. Railhead Smokehouse

Honolulu
1. Alan Wong's
2. La Mer
3. Roy's
4. Hoku's
5. Ruth's Chris

Houston
1. DeVille
2. Rotisserie/Beef & Bird
3. Chez Nous
4. Cafe Annie
5. La Réserve

Kansas City
1. Cafe Allegro
2. American Restaurant
3. Tatsu's
4. Ruth's Chris
5. Metropolis

Las Vegas
1. Andre's
2. Michael's
3. Steak House
4. Emeril's New Orleans
5. Drai's

Long Island
1. Mill River Inn
2. Mirabelle
3. Peter Luger
4. Kotobuki
5. La Piccola Liguria

Los Angeles
1. Matsuhisa
2. Sushi Nozawa
3. L'Orangerie
4. Chinois on Main
5. Belvedere, The

Miami
1. Norman's
2. Osteria del Teatro
3. Chef Allen's
4. Tropical Chinese
5. Palm

Minneapolis/St. Paul
1. Goodfellow's
2. D'Amico Cucina
3. Bayport Cookery
4. Manny's Steakhouse
5. Lucia's

New Jersey
1. Jeffrey's
2. Saddle River Inn
3. Sagami
4. Scalini Fedeli
5. Ryland Inn

New Orleans
1. Bayona
2. Brigtsen's
3. Gabrielle
4. Grill Room
5. Artesia

New York City
1. Le Bernardin
2. Chanterelle
3. Nobu
4. Sugiyama
5. Peter Luger

Orange County
1. Aubergine
2. Troquet
3. Pascal
4. Pinot Provence
5. Five Feet

Orlando
1. Victoria & Albert's
2. La Coquina
3. Del Frisco's
4. Le Coq au Vin
5. California Grill

Palm Beach
1. Four Seasons
2. Maison Janeiro
3. La Vieille Maison
4. Kathy's Gazebo
5. Morton's of Chicago

Philadelphia
1. Le Bec-Fin
2. Fountain
3. Le Bar Lyonnais
4. Swann Lounge
5. Susanna Foo

Phoenix/Scottsdale
1. Mary Elaine's
2. Marquesa
3. Vincent Guerithault
4. T. Cook's
5. RoxSand

Portland
1. Genoa
2. Paley's Place
3. Couvron
4. Heathman
5. Tina's

Salt Lake City Area
1. Fresco Italian Cafe
2. Grapevine
3. Mariposa
4. New Yorker
5. Glitretind

San Diego
1. El Bizcocho
2. WineSellar & Brasserie
3. Mille Fleurs
4. Sushi Ota*
5. Azzura Point

---

* Tied with the restaurant listed directly above it.

San Francisco Bay Area
1. French Laundry
2. Gary Danko
3. Chez Panisse
4. Masa's
5. Ritz-Carlton Din. Rm.

Santa Fe
1. Old House
2. Geronimo
3. Santacafe
4. Cafe Pasqual's
5. Ristra

Seattle
1. Rover's
2. Campagne
3. Tosoni's
4. Fullers
5. Shiro's Sushi

So. New York State
1. Xaviar's
2. Xaviar's at Piermont
3. Freelance Cafe
4. La Panetière
5. La Crémaillère

St. Louis
1. Fio's La Fourchette
2. Tony's
3. Trattoria Marcella
4. Dominic's
5. Café de France

Tampa Bay/Sarasota
1. Mise en Place
2. Beach Bistro
3. Bern's Steak House
4. Blue Heron
5. Euphemia Haye

Tucson
1. Ventana Room
2. Dish
3. Janos
4. Cafe Poca Cosa
5. Le Rendez-Vous

Washington, D.C.
1. Inn at Little Washington
2. Makoto
3. Kinkead's
4. Citronelle
5. Gerard's Place

Most Popular by Area

Atlanta
1. Bacchanalia
2. Brasserie Le Coze
3. Bone's
4. Canoe
5. Seeger's

Atlantic City
1. Ram's Head Inn
2. Le Palais
3. Chef Vola's
4. White House
5. Girasole

Baltimore/Annapolis
1. Prime Rib
2. Tio Pepe
3. Charleston
4. Linwood's
5. Ruth's Chris

Boston
1. Aujourd'hui
2. Olives
3. Hamersley's Bistro
4. Elephant Walk
5. Rialto

Chicago
1. Charlie Trotter's
2. Ambria
3. TRU
4. Everest
5. Le Français

Cincinnati
1. Maisonette
2. Precinct
3. Golden Lamb
4. Palace
5. Phoenix

Cleveland
1. Sans Souci
2. Johnny's Bar
3. Hyde Park Grille
4. Blue Pointe Grill
5. Baricelli Inn

Columbus
1. Refectory
2. Lindey's
3. Rigsby's Cuisine Volatile
4. Handke's Cuisine
5. Mitchell's

Connecticut
1. Thomas Henkelmann
2. Jean-Louis
3. Mayflower Inn
4. Elms
5. Da Pietro's

Dallas
1. Mansion on Turtle Creek
2. Cafe Pacific
3. Riviera
4. Star Canyon
5. French Room

Denver/Mountain Resorts
1. Papillon Cafe
2. Barolo Grill
3. Aubergine Cafe
4. Flagstaff House
5. Highlands Garden Cafe

Fort Lauderdale
1. Mark's Las Olas
2. Darrel & Oliver's Cafe
3. Brooks
4. Armadillo Cafe
5. Burt & Jack's

Fort Worth
1. Bistro Louise
2. Del Frisco's
3. Reata
4. La Piazza
5. Saint-Emilion

Honolulu
1. Alan Wong's
2. Hoku's
3. Roy's
4. 3660 on the Rise
5. Indigo

Houston
1. Cafe Annie
2. Brennan's
3. Anthony's
4. Rotisserie/Beef & Bird
5. Ruggles Grill

Kansas City
1. Cafe Allegro
2. American Rest.
3. Grand St. Cafe
4. Garozzo's
5. JJ's

Las Vegas
1. Andre's
2. Spago
3. Emeril's New Orleans
4. P.F. Chang's
5. Palm Rest.

Long Island
1. Peter Luger
2. Mill River Inn
3. Mirabelle
4. Bryant & Cooper
5. Panama Hatties

Los Angeles
1. Cafe Bizou
2. Campanile
3. Spago Bev. Hills
4. Hotel Bel-Air
5. Patina

Miami
1. Norman's
2. Joe's Stone Crab
3. Chef Allen's
4. Forge, The
5. Pacific Time

Minneapolis/St. Paul
1. Goodfellow's
2. D'Amico Cucina
3. Kincaid's
4. Palomino
5. Manny's

New Jersey
1. Ryland Inn
2. Saddle River Inn
3. Scalini Fedeli
4. Cafe Panache
5. Fromagerie

New Orleans
1. Commander's Palace
2. Galatoire's
3. Bayona
4. Brigtsen's
5. Grill Room

New York City
1. Union Square Cafe
2. Gramercy Tavern
3. Gotham Bar & Grill
4. Aureole
5. Le Bernardin

Orange County
1. Troquet
2. Ritz
3. Pinot Provence
4. Gustaf Anders
5. Pascal

Orlando
1. California Grill
2. Le Coq au Vin
3. Pebbles
4. Maison et Jardin
5. Enzo's on the Lake

Palm Beach
1. La Vieille Maison
2. Cafe L'Europe
3. Four Seasons
4. Cafe Chardonnay
5. Max's Grille

Philadelphia
1. Le Bec-Fin
2. Fountain
3. Buddakan
4. Brasserie Perrier
5. Susanna Foo

Phoenix/Scottsdale
1. Lon's at the Hermosa
2. RoxSand
3. T. Cook's
4. Vincent Guerithault
5. Ruth's Chris

Portland
1. Genoa
2. Higgins
3. Paley's Place
4. Wildwood
5. Cafe des Amis

Salt Lake City Area
1. New Yorker
2. Fresco Italian Cafe
3. Log Haven
4. Tuscany
5. Metropolitan

San Diego
1. George's at the Cove
2. Mille Fleurs
3. Laurel
4. Pamplemousse Grille
5. WineSellar/Brasserie

San Francisco Bay Area
1. Boulevard
2. French Laundry
3. Jardinière
4. Aqua
5. Gary Danko

Santa Fe
1. Geronimo
2. Santacafe
3. Cafe Pasqual's
4. Coyote Cafe
5. Old House

Seattle
1. Wild Ginger
2. Dahlia Lounge
3. Campagne
4. Rover's
5. Canlis

So. New York State
1. La Panetière
2. Xaviar's at Piermont
3. Crabtree's Kittle House
4. Xaviar's
5. La Crémaillère

St. Louis
1. Fio's La Fourchette
2. Tony's
3. Sidney Street Cafe
4. Trattoria Marcella
5. Harvest

Tampa Bay/Sarasota
1. Michael's on East
2. Bern's Steak House
3. Bijou Café
4. Mise en Place
5. Café L'Europe

Tucson
1. Ventana Room
2. Janos
3. Cafe Poca Cosa
4. Anthony's/Catalinas
5. Cafe Terra Cotta

Washington, D.C.
1. Kinkead's
2. L'Auberge Chez François
3. Inn at Little Washington
4. Galileo
5. DC Coast

Alphabetical Directory of Restaurants

Atlanta

TOP 20 FOOD RANKING

Restaurant	Cuisine Type
28 Bacchanalia	New American
Ritz-Carlton Buck. Din. Rm.	New French/Med.
27 Soto	Japanese
Brasserie Le Coze	New French
Seeger's	Continental
Chops	Steakhouse/Seafood
Pano's & Paul's	Continental
La Grotta	N/S Italian
26 Sushi Huku	Japanese
Bone's	Steakhouse
Nikolai's Roof	Classic French/Russian
Park 75	New American
Ritz-Carlton Buck. Café	Continental/French
Sia's	Asian/Southwestern
Tamarind	Thai
25 Hashiguchi	Japanese
Nava	Southwestern
dick and harry's	New American
Food Studio	New American
Floataway Cafe	French Bistro/Italian

ADDITIONAL NOTEWORTHY PLACES

Abruzzi	N/S Italian
Aria	New American/Southern
Atlanta Fish Market	Seafood
Babette's Cafe	International
BluePointe	New American
Buckhead Diner	New American
Canoe	New American
Chopstix	Chinese
Eno	Mediterranean
Harvest	Southern
Kamogawa	Japanese
Morton's of Chicago	Steakhouse
Mumbo Jumbo	New American
103 West	New French/Continental
Prime	Steakhouse/Seafood
South City Kitchen	Southern
Tierra	Latin American
Van Gogh's	New American
Veni Vidi Vici	N/S Italian
Watershed	New American

Abruzzi
24 | 19 | 24 | $44

Peachtree Battle Shopping Ctr., 2355 Peachtree Rd. (Peachtree Battle Ave.), 404-261-8186

■ "Buckhead matrons" at lunch and a "who's who" of "regulars" at dinner patronize this "warm" and "clubby" "upscale" Italian for "excellent" fare and "old-fashioned", "gracious" service by a "professional staff" and "delightful" owner; for those who found the decor a bit "sparse", a remodeling job in the past year should help fill in the blanks.

Aria
– | – | – | M

490 E. Paces Ferry Rd. (Maple Dr.), 404-233-7673

In its third major transformation in just as many years, this jewel box of a space in Buckhead may have finally found its groove with this stylish and upscale yet casual spot that smartly sports tiered leather walls and metal drapery; diners can tell that Gerry Klaskala is back in the kitchen after just one taste of his succulent slow-roasted dishes from the New American menu with a Southern twist.

Atlanta Fish Market 🅂
23 | 20 | 20 | $32

265 Pharr Rd. (bet. Peachtree & Piedmont Rds.), 404-262-3165

■ Packed to the gills, this "first-class" Buckhead seafood palace is so "busy" that some worry "they'll single-handedly deplete the ocean"; the "impressive case" displays "many choices" of the "freshest" fish, each "always cooked just right"; though some carp "the menu could use an update", most attest it's "worth it" because "if I were a fish, I'd want to be prepared here."

Babette's Cafe 🅂
24 | 20 | 22 | $28

471 N. Highland Ave. (bet. Colquitt Ave. & Freedom Pkwy.), 404-523-9121

■ "Pity one can't book a reservation" lament loyalists of this "charming all around" Poncey-Highlands International bistro that offers a "unique menu" of "fabulous", "classy European comfort food" served by a "knowledgeable" staff in a "romantic" ambiance; but scores of devotees promise it's "worth the trip" to "delight" in this "wonderful" "gem."

Bacchanalia
28 | – | 26 | $59

1198 Howell Mill Rd. (14th St.), 404-365-0410

■ Ranked once again as Atlanta's Most Popular restaurant, this "heavenly" New American that's "in a class by itself" is "where Bacchus himself would eat" swear disciples; also rated No. 1 for Food, the "incredible" cuisine, accompanied by an "extraordinary wine list", combines with "seamless" service to create the "best magic in town"; N.B. a post-*Survey* move to new digs in West Midtown transformed the mood from intimate Victorian to cutting-edge warehouse chic.

BluePointe 🅂
– | – | – | E

3455 Peachtree Rd. (Lenox Rd.), 404-237-9070

Blue bloods, businessmen and Buckhead Life Group boosters eager for a bite of this white-hot scene stream into a soaring space where sensuous curves and flattering lighting soften the immensity of the room; courtesy of co-owner Kevin Rathbun (of Nava), chef Ian Winslade and sushi wizard 'Taka-san' come an assortment of New American dishes accented with Asian flavors; if you can put up with the crush, this big-city spot is worth the wait.

Bone's S   26 | 22 | 25 | $47

3130 Piedmont Rd. (Peachtree Rd.), 404-237-2663

■ "When money and cholesterol are no object", "old Atlanta" heads to this "essential Buckhead power center" for "huge portions" of some of the "best steaks anywhere", teamed with "great side dishes"; expect "lavish service", as well as a "he-man" ambiance and lots of "cigar smoke"; though a few quibble that it's "too clubby", "regulars" are more than happy to keep up this "favorite" "tradition."

Brasserie Le Coze   27 | 24 | 24 | $38

Lenox Sq., 3393 Peachtree Rd. (Lenox Rd.), 404-266-1440

■ "You could be in Paris" at this "sophisticated", "first-rate" New French bistro in Buckhead, where the seasonal menu is simply "exceptional"; as it's run by the same owners as NYC's top-rated Le Bernardin, it's no surprise that the seafood here is "just perfect"; along with "stunning" decor and "professional service" (that's "not stuffy or arrogant"), it adds up to a "memorable" experience that'll make diners "forget they're at Lenox Square."

Buckhead Diner S   23 | 22 | 21 | $29

3073 Piedmont Rd. (Pharr Rd.), 404-262-3336

☑ Whether you're there to "see and be seen" or to impress "your out-of-town guests", this "upscale" Buckhead New American diner has long been a "favorite" thanks to its "creative menu", "glitzy atmosphere" and "marvelous service"; but even loyalists are frustrated with the "no-reservations" policy, while critics accuse it of "living on its past reputation."

Canoe S   24 | 26 | 22 | $38

Vinings on the River, 4199 Paces Ferry Rd. (I-75), 770-432-2663

☑ Romantics love to stroll in the garden at this "bucolic" "delight" "on the banks of the Chattahoochee River" in Vinings, which showcases vaulted ceilings and ironwork by a local artisan that are as "beautiful" as its "gorgeous landscaping"; factor in the "outstanding" New American dishes with a Southern twist and "excellent" service, and the result is an "impressive" "class act", but critics detect "way too much attitude" and warn that it can be "incredibly noisy."

Chops S   27 | 25 | 25 | $47

Buckhead Plaza, 70 W. Paces Ferry Rd. (Peachtree Rd.), 404-262-2675

■ Upstairs at this Buckhead standout is a "hearty men's-club steakhouse" (ranked the top meatery in Atlanta) that delivers "great" beef and an "excellent wine list" to a "power" business crowd eager to "make an impression"; downstairs at the Lobster Bar is a "glitzy scene" and an arched white-tile ceiling that makes for "romantic grotto" dining over sublime seafood; a few spoilers sniff about "snooty" service, but for most it's all a "real treat."

Chopstix S   25 | 19 | 22 | $31

Chastain Sq., 4279 Roswell Rd. (Wieuca Rd.), 404-255-4868

■ "Even if you hate Chinese, you'll love this" "upscale" Buckhead eatery where "gourmet" ingredients are turned into "innovative" dishes; details like flickering candles and soft piano music add a touch of "formality" and "romance"; factor in a "stellar" staff and the result is a "not-to-be-missed" experience.

dick and harry's
25 | 20 | 22 | $36

Holcomb Woods Village, 1570 Holcomb Bridge Rd. (½ mi. east of GA 400), Roswell, 770-641-8757

■ A "culinary adventure" awaits at the Marmulstein brothers "refreshing" New American "destination", which is definitely "worth a trip" to Roswell for the "exceptional", "trendsetting menu" that guarantees "incredible" "flavor combinations" (the "seafood is a must"); the "upscale, modern interior" makes an ideal backdrop for the chef's "innovative presentations", and even if it can get "noisy to a fault", this is still a "suburban delight."

Eno S
– | – | – | E

800 Peachtree St. (5th St.), 404-685-3191

In an up-and-coming area of Midtown, which is on the verge of trendy, accomplished chef Jamie Adams (ex Veni Vidi Vici) turns out zesty Med fare – bar nibbles, appetizers and entrees – that's perfectly backed up by the well-stocked wine cellar; it's a prime pick for a romantic dinner or a pre-theater meal.

Floataway Cafe
25 | 21 | 21 | $37

1123 Zonolite Rd. (bet. Briarcliff & Johnson Rds.), 404-892-1414

☑ Bacchanalia's "funky little sister", this "edgy" yet "sophisticated" French-Italian bistro set in a "converted warehouse" near Emory sports polished metals and airy cloud paintings; the less enchanted "don't like" the "cold" surroundings or the "servers with way too much attitude", but just about everyone appreciates the "amazing" cuisine; be warned, though, of the decibel level – "how does great food make so much noise?"

Food Studio S
25 | 26 | 23 | $38

King Plow Art Center, 887 W. Marietta St. (bet. Ashby St. & Howell Mill Rd.), 404-815-6677

■ "Feast your eyes and your mouth" at this "stunning" New American in a turn-of-the-century West Midtown loft; old brick walls and flickering candlelight create a "hyper-romantic" mood in which to savor the "inventive", "awesome" menu of chef Christopher Brandt, complemented by a wine list that's "nothing short of perfect."

Harvest S
24 | 22 | 22 | $30

853 N. Highland Ave. (St. Charles Ave.), 404-876-8244

■ Delighted diners shovel heaps of praise on this "romantic" Va-Highlands Southern "gem" tucked in a "cozy" old house "enhanced" by "great" Arts and Crafts details and six working fireplaces; admirers savor "generous portions" of "imaginative", "exceptional" cuisine crafted with "loving attention to detail", and since the service is "friendly" to boot, this "true joy" "has all the bases covered"; P.S. don't miss the "scrumptious" Sunday brunch.

Hashiguchi
25 | 18 | 20 | $24

The Terrace, 3000 Windy Hill Rd. (Powers Ferry Rd.), Marietta, 770-955-2337

Hashiguchi Jr.

3400 Wood Dale Dr. (Peachtree St.), 404-841-9229

■ Boosters bow in honor of this Japanese duo that showcases "first-rate sushi and sashimi" (one of the "best deals we've found"), as well as "pleasing" cooked dishes, in a "simple" (or is that "bland"?) setting; factor in a "nice" staff and it's easy to see why they're "authentic" "favorites" for many "regulars."

F	D	S	C

Kamogawa [S]

F	D	S	C
24	23	20	$36

Grand Hyatt Atlanta, 3300 Peachtree Rd. NE (Piedmont Rd.), 404-841-0314

■ "Wonderful Japanese food", including some of the "best sushi in the Southeast", is the hallmark of this South Buckhead "classic" in the Grand Hyatt Atlanta; it's "pricey", but the "outstandingly fresh" fish proffered by a "great" staff in a refined setting is "perfect, just perfect."

La Grotta

F	D	S	C
27	22	26	$44

2637 Peachtree Rd. (bet. Lindbergh Dr. & W. Wesley Rd.), 404-231-1368

Crowne Plaza Ravinia Hotel, 4355 Ashford Dunwoody Rd. (Hammond Dr.), 770-395-9925

■ Once again ranked as the No. 1 Italian in Atlanta, this "lovely" duo promises "one of the finest dining experiences anywhere" since it "maintains its standards year after year"; while the Buckhead flagship is most "romantic", the Dunwoody offshoot is "delightful" too and both showcase "incredible" "classic" dishes that "just get even better with time"; complemented by a "superb" staff that's "professional all the way", the impeccable reputation of this "Atlanta mainstay" is clearly "well deserved."

Morton's of Chicago [S]

F	D	S	C
24	21	22	$45

3379 Peachtree Rd. (Lenox Rd.), 404-816-6535

303 Peachtree Ctr. Ave. (Baker St.), 404-577-4366

◪ "You expect the best and you get it" at the Downtown and Buckhead outposts of these "upper-class" steakhouses, "the best of the chains by far" according to partisans, where "great meat" and "outsized portions" are the norm; loyal locals who prefer other "high-priced" beef barns insist that it's "overrated" and "brutally overpriced", but if you "go on someone else's ticket", it's easier to "enjoy."

Mumbo Jumbo [S]

F	D	S	C
22	24	19	$35

89 Park Pl. (Auburn Ave.), 404-523-0330

◪ "Splashy", "modern" decor sets the stage at this "hip", "high-energy" New American with a "great bar" and "superb" food from chef Shaun Doty, whose presentations "deserve photographing" (the dishes "taste as good as [they] look"); but dissenters find it "uneven" and even fans who dub it the "best Downtown" mumble that they need to "lose the 'tude."

Nava [S]

F	D	S	C
25	27	23	$37

Buckhead Plaza, 3060 Peachtree Rd. (W. Paces Ferry Rd.), 404-240-1984

■ "This sexy Southwestern success" is "still inventive and fun" cheer admirers of chef Kevin Rathbun's "spicy", "imaginative" cooking, backed up by "fine service" and a "gorgeous" theme that only adds to the "wonderful experience"; and though a few grumble that it's just "another overrated Buckhead spot", the overwhelming majority likes being "in the hands of someone who knows what he's doing": "there's not an 'ok' thing on the menu – it's all superb."

Nikolai's Roof ⓢ | 26 | 26 | 26 | $64 |

Atlanta Hilton, 255 Courtland St., 30th fl. (bet. Baker & Harris Sts.), 404-221-6362

☑ It's "hard to top the view" from this rooftop French with a Russian flair at Downtown's Atlanta Hilton, where "tourists", "expense-account crowds" and celebrants enjoy one of the "best dining experiences" in the city, from the "excellent" old-world service to the iced vodkas, silver domes and "great food", including classics such as piroshkis, borscht and caviar (but of course!); though many moan it's "horribly overpriced", it's "a treat" and thus, "you have to go at least once."

103 West | 24 | 23 | 25 | $49 |

103 W. Paces Ferry Rd. (Peachtree Rd.), 404-233-5993

☑ Renowned for its "romantic" "Victorian" setting appointed with "rococo furnishings", this "old-world charmer" is where Buckhead celebrates "special occasions"; even though the New French–Continental cuisine is "superb" (especially the "exceptional" "fried lobster tails") and "beautifully served", detractors find it at once a "bit too formal" and "gaudy"; still, loyalists laud the "lavish" experience.

Pano's & Paul's | 27 | – | 25 | $50 |

W. Paces Ferry Shopping Ctr., 1232 W. Paces Ferry Rd. (Northside Pkwy.), 404-261-3662

■ "Consistently excellent for two decades", this "elegant" Buckhead "patriarch endures" thanks to "classic Continental cuisine" that's simply "exquisite" (don't miss the "famous fried lobster tail"), proffered by a "friendly and efficient" staff; better "take $$$", but for a "romantic" "special-occasion" "treat", this "exceptional" "experience" is hard to beat; N.B. post-*Survey,* the room was redone and now sports a sleek art deco look.

Park 75 ⓢ | 26 | 26 | 25 | $50 |

Four Seasons Atlanta, 75 14th St. (bet. Peachtree & W. Peachtree Sts.), 404-253-3840

■ A "favorite" of fans who crown it "the best new restaurant in a long time", this New American showplace at the Four Seasons Atlanta in Midtown is among the "most exciting" in town; the "smoking menu" designed by chef Brooke Vosika is "wonderful" (the "delightfully innovative" dim sum–style Sunday brunch is a must), service is just about "perfect" and the "great" decor mixes together palm trees, beautiful fabrics and oil paintings.

Prime ⓢ | 24 | 22 | 21 | $38 |

Lenox Sq., 3393 Peachtree Rd. (Lenox Rd.), 404-812-0555

■ "Can you believe this place is in a mall?" marvel boosters of this Lenox Square "hot spot" that offers "something for everyone" in a "beautiful" room that melds manly clubhouse with a light-filled Asian feel; an eager clientele gathers for "prime" cuts of meats, "fabulous sushi" and some of the "best fish you'll ever eat in a steakhouse"; it may be "much too noisy" (and some would add "overpriced"), but most just sigh "sublime!"

Ritz-Carlton Buckhead Café 🗗   26 | 26 | 26 | $39
Ritz-Carlton Buckhead, 3434 Peachtree Rd. (Lenox Rd.), 404-237-2700
■ "When you want to act grown-up", go straight to this "beautiful", "first-class" Continental with a French flair at the Ritz-Carlton Buckhead where "great food, service and dancing" are the norm, and where they "set the standard for Sunday brunch"; despite quibbles that it's "a bit stuffy", the majority maintains it's a veritable "model to emulate."

Ritz-Carlton Buckhead   28 | 27 | 27 | $64
Dining Room
Ritz-Carlton Buckhead, 3434 Peachtree Rd. (Lenox Rd.), 404-237-2700
■ Take a breath and just count the accolades awarded this "superlative" main room of the Ritz-Carlton Buckhead – No. 1 for Decor and Service and for both its New French and Mediterranean cuisines, as well as tops for hotel dining in Atlanta; put yourself "in the hands of an artist", chef Joel Antunes, whose "exquisite" dishes are proffered by an "attentive" staff that makes patrons "feel like royalty"; devotees are convinced that "heaven can't get much better" than this "memorable" "experience."

Seeger's   27 | 26 | 26 | $77
111 W. Paces Ferry Rd. (E. Andrews Dr.), 404-846-9779
☑ "What fine dining is all about, from top to bottom" cheer acolytes of this "world-class restaurant" in Buckhead housed in a "sophisticated" space that's an ideal backdrop for the modern Continental creations of "Atlanta's resident culinary genius", Guenter Seeger; grumps gripe about "minute servings for a king's ransom" and "snobby service to boot", but loyalists laud this "incomparable" experience as "fabulous in every respect."

Sia's   26 | 24 | 25 | $41
The Shoppes of St. Ives, 10305 Medlock Bridge Rd. (Wilson Dr.), Duluth, 770-497-9727
■ "Finally, a classy place outside the perimeter" of the city, this "suburban star" in Duluth is the "beautiful" brainchild of Sia Moshk (ex general manager of the renowned 103 West); in a "modern" cobalt-and-tangerine-colored room, chef Scott Serpas' "superb" Asian-Southwestern creations are brought to table on silver trays by an "attentive" staff; keep an eye on this "outstanding" gem.

Soto ◑   27 | 14 | 15 | $34
Kroger Shopping Ctr., 3330 Piedmont Rd. (Peachtree Rd.), 404-233-2005
■ Ranked once again as the No. 1 Japanese in Atlanta, this "modest" winner in Buckhead is renowned for the "best sushi on the East Coast", crafted by one of the "most skilled and inventive chefs in the city"; the interior may be "unappealing" and you might want to "bring a book" (the "service is sooooo slow"), but the "exquisite" fare – when it arrives – compensates for all.

South City Kitchen 🗗   23 | 22 | 21 | $31
1144 Crescent Ave. (14th St.), 404-873-7358
■ "They've led the way in new Southern cuisine" according to admirers of this "terrific" Midtown pioneer set in a "wonderful", "unique house" where "inside or out", the beautiful people engage in "sophisticated dining"; the "innovative" dishes prepared by chef Jay Swift "never cease to amaze", but beware that "you have to put up with the noise" "to get the great food."

Sushi Huku 🅂   26 19 23 $32

Powers Ferry Landing, 6300 Powers Ferry Rd. (Northside Dr.),
770-956-9559

■ "Feel like you've traveled to Japan" after a dinner at this Northside establishment that showcases not only some of "the best sushi in Atlanta" – "fresh and well-prepared" – but also "authentic" cooked dishes, including "excellent tempura and teriyaki"; most of the customers are Japanese, but the "friendly" staff makes everyone feel welcome.

Tamarind 🅂   26 21 22 $26

80 14th St. (bet. Spring & Williams Sts.), 404-873-4888

■ "Clearly the leader" in "gourmet" Siamese, the No. 1 Thai in Atlanta attracts a following that likes to "relax" in the "beautiful", "peaceful" room while nibbling on "unusual", "flavorful" and "well-presented" fare; a "family-run" establishment, it also earns nods for "courteous service" – small wonder it's at the "top of the heap."

Tierra 🅂   23 19 20 $28

1425-B Piedmont Ave. (Westminster Dr.),
404-874-5951

■ "Terrific Latin American fusion at the edge of Piedmont Park" is creating a stir among aficionados of this "interesting concept" from chef-owners Ticha and Dan Krinsky, who employ "fresh, unique ingredients" to interpret the "flavors of the Americas"; the "charming" interior and "nice patio" provide pleasant backdrops for the "great food" and "reasonably priced wine" – all reasons fans fear that "crowds will overwhelm" this "tiny", "bright" spot.

Van Gogh's 🅂   24 23 22 $34

70 W. Crossville Rd. (Crabapple Rd.), Roswell,
770-993-1156

■ "Gogh, gogh, gogh!" urge boosters of this New American "gourmet delight" as they paint a glowing picture of the "creative" cuisine, "charming" atmosphere and "wonderful service"; ever a "trendsetter", it remains one of the "best in Roswell" and well "worth the drive"; N.B. a post-*Survey* renovation outdates the above decor score.

Veni Vidi Vici 🅂   23 23 22 $36

41 14th St. (bet. Spring & W. Peachtree Sts.), 404-875-8424

🔳 "They've conquered" the market for "upscale" Italian at this Midtowner with the Buckhead Life Group; the "beautiful" art nouveau interior draws a "trendy, loud" crowd that proclaims "every course" of the "sophisticated" fare a "memorable and savory experience"; yet the disgruntled few who advise "bring earplugs" ask "does the attitude make it better?"

Watershed   23 20 19 $22

406 W. Ponce de Leon Ave. (Commerce Dr.), Decatur,
404-378-4900

■ "How creative can you get?" marvel adventurous admirers of this "fabulous" New American set in a "cool" renovated garage in Decatur; let the "knowledgeable" staff advise on the "unique" menu designed by chef Scott Peacock, who employs "smart ingredients" to craft his "divine" dishes, which are paired with a "top-notch wine selection"; though a few nitpick that it's "expensive for what you get", most simply savor this "breath of fresh air."

Atlantic City

TOP 10 FOOD RANKING

Restaurant	Cuisine Type
27 Le Palais	New French
26 White House	Deli/Sandwich Shop
Savaradio	Eclectic
25 Tre Figlio	N/S Italian
24 Chef Vola's	N/S Italian
Brighton Steak House	Steakhouse
Little Saigon*	Vietnamese
Ram's Head Inn*	Traditional American
23 Cousin's	N/S Italian
Girasole	N/S Italian

F	D	S	C

Brighton Steak House 🅂

24	23	23	$44

Sands Hotel & Casino, Indiana Ave. (Brighton Park), 609-441-4300
■ "Succulent steaks, nicely served" is the MO at this AC beef
parlor in the Sands; those enviously eyeing all the comped diners
remark that it's a "typical, pricey meat place", though a recent
renovation draws applause.

Chef Vola's 🅂⊅

24	11	22	$37

111 S. Albion Pl. (Pacific Ave.), 609-345-2022
☑ Enthusiasts of this AC "hideaway" in a "cramped" basement
say it's like "dining with the perfect Italian family you never had"
and undergo reservations hell for entry: leave a message for owner
Louise Esposito, wait several months or secure a last-minute
cancellation, grab cash and vino then hightail it over for "plentiful
portions" of "excellent" food and a "one-of-a-kind" experience.

Cousin's 🅂

23	15	21	$28

104 Asbury Ave. (1st Ave.), Ocean City, 609-399-9462
■ "No trip to the Shore is complete without a meal" at this "great
little Italian restaurant in the basement of an old house", serving
"home-cooked gourmet meals with flair"; Ocean City is a dry town,
so don't expect liquor with your lusty Mediterranean-accented
supper, though you can take home the *Cousin's Cookbook* to keep
you warm in the off-season.

Girasole 🅂

23	21	20	$35

*Ocean Club Condos, 3108 Pacific Ave. (bet. Chelsea & Montpelier Aves.),
609-345-5554*
■ "Beautiful people like to be seen" and "see the clothes" of other
"chic" patrons at this "trendy" AC Italian at the Ocean Club Condos,
an "always hopping", gorgeous setting for "yummy food" like
pastas and "tuna carpaccio to die for"; a few puff about "attitude",
though even casino employees tout this nongambling option.

---

* Tied with the restaurant listed directly above it.

Le Palais [S] 27 | 27 | 27 | $49

Resorts Casino & Hotel, 1133 Boardwalk (North Carolina Ave.), 609-340-6400

■ This "top-notch" New French in the Resorts Hotel showcases "outstanding cuisine" and "elegant decor" to create a casino restaurant that's "one of this gambling town's most sophisticated dining experiences" and rated No. 1 for Food, Decor and Service in AC; the "utter indulgence" includes a pianist who helps fuel the "romantic" atmosphere.

Little Saigon [S]⊭ 24 | 10 | 20 | $20

2801 Arctic Ave. (Iowa Ave.), 609-347-9119

■ "Excellent Vietnamese" that's "the real deal" is the skinny on this AC BYO where "attentive service" and a "delightful, caring" chef enhance an eatery that's unusual for South Jersey; N.B. vegetarians will find plenty to munch on.

Ram's Head Inn, The [S] 24 | 26 | 24 | $42

9 W. White Horse Pike (bet. Garden State Pkwy. S. & Rte. 30), Absecon, 609-652-1700

■ The "stately, old-world aura" of this Absecon spot, voted the Most Popular restaurant in the AC *Survey*, makes it a "destination" that diners feel they "must do once a year", especially around Christmas; expect "white-glove" service, fireplaces and candlelit tables that bring a glow to the seasonal Traditional American menu, even though a few glower that it's "living off its reputation."

Savaradio [S]⊭ 26 | 18 | 22 | $31

5223 Ventnor Ave. (Little Rock Ave.), Ventnor, 609-823-2110

■ Chef-owner Lisa Savage creates "sophisticated and unique" Eclectic dishes along with "great specials" at this Ventnor BYO, which has moved to art-filled, slightly "larger quarters" with a "sparse, modern look"; the infatuated tout the "best coffee and desserts" around, as well as the $16.95 prix fixe dinner, available during the off-season.

Tre Figlio [S] 25 | 20 | 22 | $35

500 W. White Horse Pike (bet. Pomona Ave. & Tilton Rd.), Egg Harbor City, 609-965-3303

■ "Be very hungry when you go" to "this little bit of South Philly" in Egg Harbor City that offers "high-quality Italian food" (the "best veal chop ever", an "excellent" early-bird prix fixe) as well as "attentive", "friendly" service in a "warm" setting; N.B. don't miss the award-winning wine list.

White House [S]⊭ 26 | 9 | 16 | $12

2301 Arctic Ave. (Mississippi Ave.), 609-345-1564

■ Some of "the best subs in the USA" emerge from this James Beard Award–winning sandwich landmark (since 1946) and are the "choice of a last meal" for many as well as the No. 1 Bang for the Buck in AC; not only do "Hollywood stars have the subs shipped to them", but fans add that the "only thing better than the food and the prices are the aromas."

Baltimore/Annapolis

TOP 10 FOOD RANKING

Restaurant	Cuisine Type
28 Lewnes' Steakhouse/A*	Steakhouse
Prime Rib	Steakhouse
Hampton's	New American
27 Antrim 1844	New American
Inn at Perry Cabin/A	Continental
Charleston	Traditional American
Rudys' 2900	Continental/New American
26 Linwood's	New American
208 Talbot/A	New American
Boccaccio	Northern Italian

ADDITIONAL NOTEWORTHY PLACES

Black Olive	Greek/Seafood
Bo Brooks	Seafood
Helmand	Afghan
Milton Inn	Regional American
Petit Louis	French Bistro
Pierpoint	Seafood
Polo Grill	Regional American
Ruth's Chris	Steakhouse
Samos	Greek
Tio Pepe	Spanish/Continental

F	D	S	C

Antrim 1844 Country Inn S   27 | 28 | 27 | $55
30 Trevanion Rd. (Rte. 140), Taneytown, 410-756-6812
■ "Perfect in every way" gush visitors to this pre–Civil War mansion near Gettysburg that's graced with "magnificent" gardens; inside, the "opulent" dining rooms filled with "many roaring fires and 19th-century period pieces" set the mood for "superb" prix fixe New American meals; no wonder couples find it ideal for the seduction, the engagement and the wedding itself, even if the budget-minded may be discouraged by the "very expensive" prices.

Black Olive S   25 | 18 | 21 | $41
814 S. Bond St. (bet. Shakespeare & Thames Sts.), 410-276-7141
◪ "*The* place to go for fresh fish" is this "sophisticated" Fells Point Greek taverna where a "charming" family gives a "pick-your-own" "tour" of exotic seafood offerings (including "fish we've never heard of!") that are then cooked simply and paired with fine Greek wines; despite the "exceptional" quality, though, some quip it's "cheaper to cruise Greece" than pay premium prices for what they see as "plain" fare served in a "casual" atmosphere.

---

* A = Annapolis/Eastern Shore

Bo Brooks Crab House S
21 | 9 | 17 | $26

Baltimore Marine Ctr., 2701 Boston St. (Lakewood Ave.), 410-558-0202

■ "Show me the crabs, no time for salads and such" say fans who need not go to the Northeast for their crustaceans anymore, as this seafooder has relocated to spacious waterfront digs in Canton (not yet reflected in the above decor rating); while it may have lost some of its "real Baltimore" feel in the move, it still delivers "large crabs seasoned just right" and the "best cream of crab soup."

Boccaccio S
26 | 24 | 24 | $44

925 Eastern Ave. (bet. Exeter & High Sts.), 410-234-1322

■ "It's hard to be the best", but this *primo* Little Italy Northern Italian "power" place has proven yet again that it "can't be beat" by continuing to showcase "first-class" food "impeccably served" in an "elegant" setting; if they started "honoring reservation times", they might win even greater accolades.

Charleston S
27 | 26 | 26 | $47

1000 Lancaster St. (bet. Central & Exeter Sts.), 410-332-7373

■ "Baltimore's answer to NYC and SF" – and that's not just local pride talking – is Inner Harbor East's "fabulous" Traditional American "gem" owned by chef Cindy Wolf and her husband, Tony Forman; in "handsome" surroundings, her "innovative" Southern-accented cuisine is "queen", while his "monumental wine cellar" and expertise are "king"; add on the "pampering" service proffered by an intelligent staff and the result is a dining experience that "wows" just about everyone; "worth" the "splurge"? – you bet.

Hampton's S
28 | 29 | 27 | $58

Harbor Court Hotel, 550 Light St. (bet. Conway & Lee Sts.), 410-347-9744

■ "Never less than excellent", Baltimore's "best" hotel dining establishment is rated No. 1 for Service in the *Baltimore/Annapolis Survey* and ranks among the top three vote-getters for Food and Decor; "world-class" treatment, a "gorgeous" room and "beautiful harbor views" complement the "top-notch" seasonal New American fare, making this Charm City's foremost site for "special occasions"; in sum, it's "almost perfect."

Helmand, The S
26 | 21 | 23 | $23

806 N. Charles St. (Madison St.), 410-752-0311

■ Combine a "wonderful" adventure for "bored taste buds", intriguing "ambiance", a "helpful staff" and "reasonable prices" and you'll usually wind up with a "full house", like at this popular Mt. Vernon Afghan; it "wins over" most anyone who wants to break timid friends into "exotic" dining, "delight" a date or dig into the "best rack of lamb."

Inn at Perry Cabin S
27 | 29 | 26 | $60

308 Watkins Ln. (Talbot St.), St. Michaels, 410-745-2200

■ Rated No. 1 for Decor in the *Baltimore/Annapolis Survey*, this luxurious Eastern Shore retreat is "an elegant experience from start to finish"; everyone's treated like a "celebrity" (they come here too, quietly) and a meal in its modern Continental restaurant is "one that you won't forget"; though a few quibble about "pretentious" pampering, most just wish they lived "closer" so they could "visit more"; P.S. be sure to have the "wonderful" formal tea served on the lovely patio, which boasts a spectacular view of the water.

Lewnes' Steakhouse S | 28 | 23 | 26 | $45 |
401 Fourth St. (Severn Ave.), Annapolis, 410-263-1617
■ Proving beyond any doubt that diners still love to go out for "prime steaks" and "great wines", this "gentlemen's club" in Eastport is ranked No. 1 for Food in the *Baltimore/Annapolis Survey*; well-hooved carnivores gather here for hefty portions of "really outstanding beef", accompanied by traditional sides; yes, it's "pricey", but it's well "worth it", as it's "excellent on all fronts."

Linwood's S | 26 | 26 | 25 | $43 |
McDonough Crossroads, 25 Crossroads Dr. (McDonough & Reisterstown Rds.), Owings Mills, 410-356-3030
■ Linwood Dame "gets it all right" at his "prestigious" Owings Mills New American, delivering a "creative" menu in a "clubby, cozy" setting that works equally well for casual bar dining (quite the see-and-"be-seen" scene) or "special occasions" when elegant "ambiance and service count"; though it's too "pricey" and "stuffy" to some, the "worldly" set lauds it as a "class act" with "city sophistication."

Milton Inn S | 25 | 27 | 24 | $48 |
14833 York Rd. (3 mi. north of Shawan Rd.), Sparks, 410-771-4366
■ "Class and character", plus "excellent" Regional American fare with a Continental accent served up in a *"Masterpiece Theatre"* manor setting, sum up this "special-occasion" mecca in North Baltimore County; though it's "expensive", few places anywhere can match its "romantic" ambiance, and most laud the owners for "improving" its "quality"; P.S. the $30 dinner prix fixe Sundays–Fridays means you can dine here without taking out a "bank loan."

Petit Louis S | – | – | – | E |
4800 Roland Ave. (Upland Ave.), 410-366-9393
Charleston's boisterous sibling in Roland Park features polished renditions of classic Parisian bistro fare in the former Morgan Millard landmark space; a top-flight wine list complements such dishes as *croque monsieur* and braised veal shank.

Pierpoint S | 24 | 16 | 20 | $37 |
1822 Aliceanna St. (bet. Ann & Wolfe Sts.), 410-675-2080
■ "Fells Point at its best" rave fans of chef-owner Nancy Longo's "hip and sophisticated" "small bistro with big seafood" flavor; expect "innovative", reinterpreted Maryland classics and a "relaxing atmosphere" "tucked behind" an ordinary row house "facade"; while the "humble" surroundings are in keeping with the area's low-key sensibility, critics object to the "close" seating.

Polo Grill S | 26 | 25 | 24 | $47 |
Inn at the Colonnade, 4 W. University Pkwy. (bet. Canterbury Rd. & N. Charles St.), 410-235-8200
■ "Baltimore's 'who's who'" and "new money" head for this "handsome" Homewood "public club" "to be seen", as well as to enjoy the "wonderful" takes on Regional American cooking (including a "great fried lobster tail") while being cosseted by the "veteran" staff; the unconvinced complain about the "serious $$" and a "noise" level that drowns out conversation, but most would agree "if someone else is buying, I'm there!"

Prime Rib ●S   28 | 26 | 27 | $51

Horizon House, 1101 N. Calvert St. (Chase St.), 410-539-1804
■ Voted the Most Popular restaurant in the *Baltimore/Annapolis Survey* (and ranked No. 2 for Food), this Downtown retro supper club with a "swank", big-city feel proves that dressing up for a great evening of martinis and red meat has enduring appeal; while setting "the standard" for beef and seafood (its crab dishes are as notable as the signature prime rib), its "superior" service and "'50s-era" "glamour" also make any occasion "special."

Rudys' 2900 S   27 | 22 | 25 | $42

2900 Baltimore Blvd. (Rte. 91), Finksburg, 410-833-5777
■ "Way, way out" in Finksburg, this Continental-American has cultivated a discriminating coterie that's willing to make the trip to enjoy the "consistent" excellence of the "Rudy and Rudy twosome" (chef-owner Rudy Speckamp cooks up "inspired" "gourmet and regional favorites" that please both "steak-and-potato guys" and lovers of haute cuisine, while co-owner Rudy Paul provides "great personal attention"); though it has a "nice country ambiance", it could possibly use a third Rudy to do some "redecorating."

Ruth's Chris Steak House S   25 | 23 | 23 | $47

600 Water St. (bet. Gay St. & Market Pl.), 410-783-0033
1777 Reisterstown Rd. (Hooks Ln.), Pikesville, 410-837-0033
■ No "need to ask where's the beef" at this "clubby", Big Easy–style steakhouse chain – it's drenched in butter and sizzling on your plate, hauled out by "courteous" servers; but while these "top-drawer" "guy" havens are beacons for travelers elsewhere, they rank just below the Prime Rib in the Baltimore area's power stakes.

Samos ⊅   25 | 9 | 19 | $15

600 S. Oldham St. (Fleet St.), 410-675-5292
■ Voted the top Greek restaurant in the *Baltimore/Annapolis Survey,* this modest corner eatery serves an "enormous variety" of "authentic" dishes at prices that make it "value-driven eating"; good news: owner Nick Georgales and his "friendly" crew gained "some breathing room" with an expansion and renovation (not reflected in the above decor rating).

Tio Pepe S   25 | 22 | 23 | $42

10 E. Franklin St. (bet. Charles & St. Paul Sts.), 410-539-4675
◪ Perennially popular, this Downtown Spanish-Continental with an "underground mystique" (it's housed in a "noisy cellar") is a "happy-occasion" fiesta for many aficionados, who "go back" (and back) for the "excellent" paella, suckling pig and other "rich", "decadent" dishes (and "don't-miss sangria"); but despite the "professional service", lots of complaints surface about the "ridiculous" "waits, even with reservations", as well as the feeling that "rudeness rules" if you're not a regular.

208 Talbot S   26 | 23 | 24 | $45

208 N. Talbot St. (bet. Dodson Ave. & North St.), St. Michaels, 410-745-3838
■ Join the Shore's "upper crust" at this "romantic" New American "hideaway" in St. Michaels, where the "beautiful presentations" of "innovative" dishes (based on local seafood and produce) amount to "art on your plate"; "extremely well-run", it's definitely a "worthy" "destination" in this charming maritime town.

Boston

TOP 20 FOOD RANKING

Restaurant	Cuisine Type
28 L'Espalier	New French
Aujourd'hui	New American
27 Olives	Mediterranean
Hamersley's Bistro	French/New American
26 Caffe Bella	Mediterranean
Julien	New French
Il Capriccio	Northern Italian
Radius	New French
Saporito's	N/S Italian
Rialto	Mediterranean
Lumière	New French
Sage	Californian/Italian
Icarus	New American
Blue Ginger	Asian/Eclectic
Clio	New French
25 Silks	New French
Maurizio's	Italian/Mediterranean
Ginza	Japanese
Terramia	N/S Italian
La Campania	N/S Italian

ADDITIONAL NOTEWORTHY PLACES

Ambrosia on Huntington	Asian/French
Anago	New American
Aquitaine	French Bistro
Biba	New American
Blue Room	Eclectic
East Coast Grill & Raw Bar	Barbecue/Seafood
Elephant Walk	Cambodian/New French
Grill 23 & Bar	Steakhouse
Harvest	Traditional American
Jasper White's	Seafood
KingFish Hall	Seafood
Legal Sea Foods	Seafood
Maison Robert	Classic French
Mistral	French Provençal
Ritz-Carlton Dining Room	Classic French
Rowes Wharf	Regional American
Salamander	Asian/Eclectic
Sel de la Terre	French Bistro
Tremont 647	New American
Truc	French Bistro

Ambrosia on Huntington [S] 24 24 23 $50

116 Huntington Ave. (bet. Dartmouth & Newton Sts.), 617-247-2400

◪ This "flashy" Back Bay spot "hits the mark" with "great eye appeal" and a "chic, sophisticated ambiance"; equally noteworthy is its "inventive" Asian-French cuisine that some call a "tasty but precious" example of "fusion intrusion" – the "ingredients sometimes seem strangely combined" and the desserts look like "architectural projects"; still, the service is "attentive" (if "pretentious") and the "sexy bar" attracts a "glitzy" clientele.

Anago [S] 24 23 22 $49

Lenox Hotel, 65 Exeter St. (Boylston St.), 617-266-6222

◪ Since moving from Cambridge to the "trendy" Lenox Hotel in the Back Bay, this little red room has become quite the "happening scene" with a "young, professional crowd" that "feels quite regal" dining on "innovative" New American cuisine; dissenters, however, find it "overrated", "overpriced" and "snooty" and wonder "what all the fuss is about."

Aquitaine [S] 23 22 20 $42

569 Tremont St. (Clarendon St.), 617-424-8577

◪ Bringing "France to the South End", this "beautiful" "find" features "quintessential bistro fare" prepared with "flair" (notably "great steak frites"), accompanied by an "excellent wine list"; while critics grumble that it's "overrated", "pretentious" and staffed by an unusually "loud" bunch, devotees insist it's "warm and welcoming, and we could stay all night", then come back for brunch.

Aujourd'hui [S] 28 28 28 $64

Four Seasons Hotel, 200 Boylston St. (bet. Arlington & S. Charles Sts.), 617-351-2071

■ "Heaven's main dining room", according to disciples, is in the "luxurious" Four Seasons Hotel where pampered diners are virtually guaranteed "an elegant", "world-class" evening; in a "magnificent" space with "regal decor" and a stellar view of the Public Garden, an "impeccable" staff proffers "glorious" New American cuisine layered with French and Asian accents; Boston's Most Popular restaurant, it also ranks as the city's No. 2 for Food.

Biba [S] 25 24 22 $52

272 Boylston St. (bet. Arlington & S. Charles Sts.), 617-426-7878

◪ Among the city's premier "power-dining spots", this "oh-so-chic" Back Bay New American boasts a "fantastic view of the Public Garden" from the "fabulous" Adam Tihany–designed room and "inspired", "innovative" dishes from chefs Lydia Shire and Susan Regis that are admittedly "sometimes weird"; but even if the "menu is too avant-garde, this is still one of Boston's best tables"; P.S. the "buzzing" bar is a "good place to eat and people-watch."

Blue Ginger 26 22 23 $41

583 Washington St. (Rte. 16), Wellesley, 781-283-5790

■ "Good luck getting reservations" at "brilliant chef" Ming Tsai's "casually elegant" "gem" in Wellesley, "but if you do, you're in for a treat" because his "exciting" Asian-Eclectic cuisine is "uniquely" "exquisite", infused with an "outstanding blend of flavors" (don't miss his "awesome" signature sake-marinated Chilean sea bass); despite some negative marks for the "hard-edged decor", most "welcome" it as a "first-class" "oasis in the Western suburbs."

F | D | S | C

Blue Room, The [S] 24 | 20 | 22 | $36

1 Kendall Sq. (bet. Broadway & Portland St.), Cambridge, 617-494-9034

◪ In Kendall Square, this "upbeat", "always satisfying" experience seems to "get even better every year"; chef Steve Johnson's "fabulous" Eclectic menu (with "Asian touches") is "innovative and flavorful, based on unexpected combinations that work", and it's matched with a "killer wine list"; the "attractive, relaxed" surroundings make this an "all-around great hangout", and "you'll leave as happy" as Julia Child (this "jewel" is one of her favorites).

Caffe Bella 26 | 19 | 22 | $34

19 Warren St. (bet. Main St. & Rte. 139), Randolph, 781-961-7729

■ Set in a strip mall in Randolph, this "unbelievable" Med gem is the "South Shore's culinary trophy"; "genius" chef-owner Patrick Barnes Jr.'s "perfectly prepared" dishes with "wonderful flavors" are accompanied by an "incredible wine list"; it's "too loud" and "crowded", with "squishy seating" and "ridiculous waits", but even so, devotees "could dine here nightly"; "don't miss this one."

Clio [S] 26 | 26 | 24 | $57

Eliot Suite Hotel, 370A Commonwealth Ave. (Mass Ave.), 617-536-7200

■ "Swanky" and "romantic", this petite Eliot Suite Hotel dining room in the Back Bay is "where the chic eat" surrounded by "plush" appointments like cushy banquettes and a leopard-print carpet; "brilliant" chef Ken Oringer "gets it just right", turning out "divine" New French cuisine; admirers only wish they'd "consider serving lunch" – and lower the "astronomical" prices.

East Coast Grill & Raw Bar [S] 24 | 18 | 20 | $32

1271 Cambridge St. (Prospect St.), Cambridge, 617-491-6568

■ Chris Schlesinger's Inman Square "seafood thriller" continues to sizzle with "finger-licking 'cue" and "sensory-overload sides" delivered in an "exuberant" room with a "funky" vibe; heat-chasers urge "come on 'hotter-than-hell' nights" when the "spicy" food is notched up yet a few more degrees; despite a "jammed" site and "long waits", these masters of the grill "know their smoky stuff" – in fact, it's ranked the No. 1 BBQ in Boston.

Elephant Walk [S] 23 | 21 | 20 | $30

900 Beacon St. (Park Dr.), 617-247-1500

2067 Mass Ave. (bet. Hadley & Russell Sts.), Cambridge, 617-492-6900

◪ Hordes "stampede" to Kenmore and Porter Squares for this duo's "wonderful juxtaposition" of Cambodian and New French cuisines, which "deliciously" results in "eclectic" dishes such as "phenomenal" *loc lac* (lime-cured beef); the "classy" ambiance is made "exotic" with elephant figurines along the ceiling, and despite "long waits", most urge "run, don't walk" to get in on this "unique" experience.

Ginza [S] 25 | 17 | 18 | $29

16 Hudson St. (bet. Beach & Kneeland Sts.), 617-338-2261 ◐

1002 Beacon St. (St. Mary's St.), Brookline, 617-566-9688

■ Rated the No. 1 Japanese in Boston, this "bit of Tokyo" in Chinatown and Brookline will "make you wonder why food should ever be cooked" after just one bite of its "amazing", "artistically presented" sushi; the "late-night" Hudson Street flagship is "hip and crowded", despite somewhat "sterile" surroundings, so expect "long waits."

Grill 23 & Bar [S] 25 | 23 | 24 | $49

161 Berkeley St. (Stuart St.), 617-542-2255

■ "Movers and shakers" gather at this "manly" steakhouse in the Back Bay to "relax and indulge" in chef Jay Murray's "superb" menu, which goes "beyond beef" to highlight "excellent" seafood; the historic building boasts a "beautiful", "soaring interior", and thanks to an ongoing expansion, doubled seating on a second floor.

Hamersley's Bistro [S] 27 | 24 | 24 | $51

553 Tremont St. (Clarendon St.), 617-423-2700

■ Gordon Hamersley's South End namesake is a "stylish yet understated" French–New American "phenomenon", with a "versatile", "consistently excellent" seasonal menu offering the likes of bouillabaisse and "jaw-droppingly good" roast chicken to the city's power brokers; along with "impeccable decor", "attentive service" and an "interesting wine list", it "remains a classic" and "every visit reinforces" its rep.

Harvest [S] 23 | 22 | 22 | $43

44 Brattle St. (Church St.), Cambridge, 617-868-2255

■ Now run by the Grill 23 & Bar management team, this revived "Cambridge relic" in Harvard Square is "clubbier and more mature" than before, with an "outstanding" Traditional American menu showcasing striped bass, grilled rack of lamb and "one mean chowder"; the "tasteful" layout features subdued wood with taupe tones, a "lovely courtyard" and the perfect bar for a "sophisticated drink"; the verdict: "reincarnation works."

Icarus [S] 26 | 24 | 24 | $47

3 Appleton St. (bet. Arlington & Berkeley Sts.), 617-426-1790

■ When it's time for a "splurge", the well-heeled wing it to this "sophisticated" South Ender, a "class act" where "superb", "inventive" New American fare is delivered by an "A+ staff" amid "stunning decor"; most agree it "lives up to its well-deserved reputation" as a "formal" standout where the extras include live jazz Friday nights and valet parking.

Il Capriccio 26 | 21 | 23 | $45

888 Main St. (Prospect St.), Waltham, 781-894-2234

■ "Why go to Boston?" suburbanites wonder when there's a "first-class" Northern Italian right in Waltham serving "delicious, innovative" handmade pastas (and a "sublime" porcini soufflé), matched with a "great wine list"; pros claim it "elegant", if "noisy", and its status as "Waltham's best" means it can be "difficult to get in."

Jasper White's Summer Shack [S] – | – | – | M

149 Alewife Brook Pkwy. (Sterling St.), Cambridge, 617-520-9500

Fin fans dive into casual seafood at lobster czar Jasper White's kitschy newcomer in the Alewife area, where the family-friendly menu offers everything from chowder and baked stuffed lobster to corn dogs and fresh-fruit snow cones; booths and picnic tables fill a huge space featuring corrugated-tin walls, a raw bar and a giant lobster tank.

Julien
26 | 27 | 26 | $57

Le Meridien Hotel, 250 Franklin St. (bet. Oliver & Pearl Sts.), 617-451-1900

☑ "Civility" defines this "elegant", "formal" New French in Le Meridien Hotel where diners savor "perfection" in "every bite"; look forward to a "wonderful wine list", "great" "European-style" service and a "relaxing" ambiance; overall, it's an "awesome place" for a "quiet" "celebration" or a "power lunch", but then again, it "should be at these prices."

KingFish Hall ⓢ
– | – | – | M

Faneuil Hall Mktpl., South Market Bldg., 617-523-8862

Chef-owner Todd English continues to scatter loaves and fishes, now at this new seafooder in Faneuil Hall; selections range from sushi to a raw bar to whole fish cooked on a 'fish dancer' rotisserie, plus nonaquatic options like rib eye and quail satay, all served in a David Rockwell–designed room where dangling mobiles stick to the marine theme.

La Campania
25 | 22 | 22 | $35

504 Main St. (bet. Cross & Heard Sts.), Waltham, 781-894-4280

■ Run by a "gracious", "hardworking" family that's "devoted to its food and customers", this "Waltham hot spot" with "charming country decor" wins raves for its "gourmet and traditional" Italian offerings, backed by a 300-bottle wine list; the only complaint is that its 40 seats are clearly "not enough."

Legal Sea Foods ⓢ
21 | 15 | 18 | $30

Long Wharf, 255 State St. (Court St.), 617-227-3115
Prudential Ctr., 800 Boylston St. (bet. Fairfield & Gloucester Sts.), 617-266-6800
Copley Pl., 100 Huntington Ave. (bet. Dartmouth & Exeter Sts.), 617-266-7775
26 Park Sq. (Columbus Ave.), 617-426-4444
South Shore Plaza, 250 Granite St., Braintree, 781-356-3070
Burlington Mall, 1131 Middlesex Tpke. (Rte. 128), Burlington, 781-270-9700
Kendall Sq., 5 Cambridge Ctr. (bet. Ames & Main Sts.), Cambridge, 617-864-3400
43 Boylston St. (Hammond Pond Pkwy.), Chestnut Hill, 617-277-7300
Miltons Plaza, 1400 Worcester Rd. (bet. Rte. 126 & Speen St.), Natick, 508-820-1115
Northshore Mall, Rtes. 114 & 128, Peabody, 978-532-4500

☑ A "local legend" that's "gone national", Roger Berkowitz's ever-expanding fleet of fish houses owes its "hall-of-fame" status to "impeccably fresh" seafood; while detractors carp about "pricey" yet "boring" preparations and "plain" settings, they're outvoted by schools of fin fans.

L'Espalier
28 | 27 | 27 | $69

30 Gloucester St. (bet. Commonwealth Ave. & Newbury St.), 617-262-3023

■ Count the accolades: Frank McClelland's "world-class" Back Bay New French ranks No. 1 for Food, No. 2 for Decor and No. 3 for Service in the *Boston Survey*; revel in "sheer bliss" with a "sumptuous" three-course prix fixe or seven-course dégustation menu served in a "gorgeous" townhouse setting by a "gracious" staff; the tab is definitely "not for the faint of heart", but this is a "perfect experience from coat check to goodbye."

Lumière 🆂
26 24 25 $44

1293 Washington St. (Waltham St.), West Newton,
617-244-9199

■ "The brightest light" in the suburbs may well be this "small", cozy New French bistro in West Newton that turns out "straightforward", "absolutely delicious" cuisine, paired with a "dynamite" wine list and served by an "excellent" staff; the "upbeat" interior features cream-colored walls, whimsical light fixtures and an open kitchen that "radiates warmth."

Maison Robert
24 24 24 $48

Old City Hall, 45 School St. (bet. Tremont & Washington Sts.),
617-227-3370

☑ "C'est magnifique!" declare devotees of this Old City Hall Classic French where Jacky Robert crafts "top-notch" preparations, the "professional" staff "pampers" all and the "magnificent" peach-colored, crystal chandelier–graced "formal" room exudes pure "elegance"; dissenters cite a "stodgy" ambiance, but they're far outvoted by those who relish it as a special-occasion "favorite."

Maurizio's 🆂
25 16 21 $30

364 Hanover St. (Clark St.), 617-367-1123

■ "Bring a date" to this "first-rate" North End Italian-Med where chef Maurizio Loddo prepares the "world's best bruschetta" and appetizers "so huge you have to make room" for his "terrific Sardinian" specialties; it's "cramped", but the "attentive" staff helps compensate, and they "accept reservations."

Mistral 🆂
25 25 23 $54

223 Columbus Ave. (Berkeley St.), 617-867-9300

☑ Straddling the Back Bay and the South End, this "electric" French Provençal is often "filled at midnight on a Wednesday" with a "trendy", "power" crowd, thanks to a room that's "one of the most beautiful in Boston", as well as "excellent" cuisine from "talented chef" Jamie Mammano; so "dress to impress", "bring $$$" and prepare for a major "people-watching" "scene."

Olives
27 22 22 $48

10 City Sq. (bet. Main & Park Sts.), Charlestown,
617-242-1999

☑ "Every bite introduces something new" at the Charlestown headquarters of chef Todd English, whose unique brand of Med cooking involves an "enormous menu" of "complex combinations", resulting in "layers and layers of flavors" that most call "exquisite" but a few find "over the top"; the "casual", "beautiful" room is another crowd-pleaser, though even devotees are irked by the "no-reservations" policy (for parties fewer than six) that creates "mob-scene" waits.

Radius
26 25 25 $57

8 High St. (bet. Federal & Summer Sts.), 617-426-1234

■ Among "the best places in town" is this Financial District "power scene" where chef-partner Michael Schlow makes his mark with "daring", "indescribably delicious" New French fare, "magnificently presented" and served by one of "the best staffs in the city" in an "amazing space" with an "energized atmosphere"; even though it's "obscenely expensive", most rave that "everything is wonderful."

Rialto S

26 | 25 | 24 | $53

Charles Hotel, 1 Bennett St. (Harvard Sq.), Cambridge, 617-661-5050

■ Chef "Jody Adams' jewel", this Cambridge "heavyweight" boasts an "elegant setting that's a perfect foil for the bold flavors" of her "dynamite" Mediterranean interpretations; a "beautiful" venue that's as "high energy" as it is "formal" makes it "the ultimate" "special-event destination"; though it's "getting to be an expense-account type of restaurant", most insist the sheer "bliss" is "worth every penny."

Ritz-Carlton Dining Room S

25 | 27 | 27 | $59

Ritz-Carlton, 15 Arlington St. (Newbury St.), 617-536-5700

■ An "old Boston" legacy lives on at this bastion of Back Bay society dining, which reaches "the pinnacle" of haute French cuisine; the "world-class" fare, matched with an "outstanding" wine list, is proffered by an "extraordinary" staff in a "country-club setting" that provides a "great view of the Public Garden", as well as a glimpse into how "the other half lives"; in sum, most purr "it's the Ritz – what do you expect except the best?"

Rowes Wharf S

24 | 27 | 24 | $53

Boston Harbor Hotel, 70 Rowes Wharf (Atlantic Ave.), 617-439-3995

■ In a "beautiful" space with "magnificent waterfront views", this "fabulous" restaurant in the Boston Harbor Hotel showcases the works of "remarkable chef Daniel Bruce", "a great interpreter of New England–style cuisine" (don't miss the "awesome brunch"); it's "very expensive, but what a treat!", and in the summertime, the outdoor cafe is a swell spot to "watch the yachts go by."

Sage

26 | 18 | 23 | $35

69 Prince St. (Salem St.), 617-248-8814

■ An "adorable", "surprisingly sophisticated" "little place" in the North End with a "limited menu" of "innovative" Californian-Italian specialties "cooked to order" ("homemade pastas are the way to go") and served by a "delightful staff"; seating is "limited" too, and it's always "crowded", so "reservations are a must."

Salamander

– | – | – | E

Trinity Pl., 25 Huntington Ave. (Dartmouth St.), 617-451-2150

Chef-owner Stan Frankenthaler is on the move from Cambridge to Copley Square, where his creative Asian-Eclectic fare is due to find a new home this fall in the luxury residential development Trinity Place; the standout kitchen will retain its focus on locally grown organic produce, and the room will see the addition of a satay bar and private dining spaces beneath its 14-foot ceilings.

Saporito's S

26 | 17 | 23 | $37

11 Rockland Circle (George Washington Blvd.), Hull, 781-925-3023

■ It's a "small, plain beach cottage" "far off the beaten path" in Hull, but reviewers report this "creative" Italian is "worth the drive from anywhere" for its "tasty, fresh, carefully prepared dishes" and "excellent daily specials" at "half the price of in-town restaurants"; enthusiasts are convinced it's an "institution in the making."

Sel de la Terre 🅂
255 State St. (Atlantic Ave.), 617-720-1300

A Gallic haven on the waterfront, this French bistro is the new offspring of chef-partners Frank McClelland (L'Espalier) and Geoff Gardner, who match their Provençal cooking with artisanal homemade breads (also sold in the vestibule boulangerie); although it's nestled near ground zero of the Big Dig project, the interior sets a tranquil tone with a slate tile floor, wrought-iron chandeliers and leather banquettes.

Silks 🅂
25 25 25 $52

Stonehedge Inn, 160 Pawtucket Blvd. (Rte. 113), Tyngsboro, 978-649-4400

■ It's "worth the ride" to this "lavish country manor" in Tyngsboro, a "special" inn restaurant boasting a "superbly prepared", if "limited", New French menu; "knockout wine list", "lovely decor" and "marvelous service"; a few feel it's "pretentious", but many more deem it "dining at its finest" – "Four Seasons North."

Terramia 🅂
25 16 20 $38

98 Salem St. (Parmenter St.), 617-523-3112

■ "Put yourself in the hands of Mario Nocera" advise the many fans of this "intimate North End" Italian that's "as good as it gets", with "fresh, delicate, creative" fare and a staff "right out of central casting"; the sweet of tooth moan about the lack of desserts, but others "go out for cannoli" afterward and stretch their legs after sitting in a room that "walks a fine line between cozy and cramped."

Tremont 647 🅂
22 19 20 $37

647 Tremont St. (W. Brookline St.), 617-266-4600

■ The "grill is the centerpiece" of chef-owner Andy Husbands' "cutting-edge" New American in the South End where "imaginative" fare prepared "with zip" and an outstanding wine list are proffered by an "accommodating staff"; a handful feels the food is "uneven" and "overpriced", but the majority maintains it's a "real treat."

Truc
23 20 21 $44

560 Tremont St. (Clarendon St.), 617-338-8070

☑ "Within the French bistro craze, Truc gets it right" rave Francophiles who flock to this subterranean "South End charmer" sporting a "small but well-executed" and "wonderfully inventive" menu; reviewers also talk up the "romantic" "back-room greenhouse" that's like a "winter garden"; N.B. they no longer serve brunch, but they do take reservations.

Chicago

TOP 20 FOOD RANKING

Restaurant	Cuisine Type
29 Le Français	Classic French
28 Carlos'	New French
Ritz-Carlton Dining Room	New French
Tru	New American
Ambria	New French
27 Seasons	New American
Everest	New French
Le Titi de Paris	Classic French
Trio	Eclectic
Charlie Trotter's	New American
Tallgrass*	New French
Topolobampo	Mexican
Les Nomades	Classic French
26 Arun's	Thai
302 West	New American
Spiaggia	N/S Italian
Courtright's	New American
Mk	New American
Gabriel's	Italian/New French
Frontera Grill	Mexican

ADDITIONAL NOTEWORTHY PLACES

Atlantique	Seafood
Aubriot	New French
Blackbird	New American
Brasserie Jo	New French
Crofton on Wells	Regional American
D & J Bistro	French Bistro
Gibsons Steakhouse	Steakhouse
Grace	New American
Ixcapuzalco	Mexican
Mirai Sushi	Japanese
Mod.	New American
Morton's of Chicago	Steakhouse
Nine	Steakhouse/Seafood
Nomi	Classic French/International
one sixtyblue	New American
Pasteur	Vietnamese
Shaw's	Seafood
Va Pensiero	N/S Italian
Vong	Thai/French
Zealous	New American

* Tied with the restaurant listed directly above it.

Ambria 28 | 26 | 27 | $68

Belden Stratford Hotel, 2300 N. Lincoln Park W. (Belden Ave.), 773-472-5959

■ "As always", this Lincoln Park New French is a "romantic" "oasis of luxury" where chef Anselmo Ruiz's "superb" cuisine is matched with "impeccable service" in an art nouveau room that manages to be "elegant" without the "pretense"; in sum, "a heavenly dining experience": "when I die, I want to go to Ambria."

Arun's [S] 26 | 23 | 25 | VE

4156 N. Kedzie Ave. (bet. Belle Plaine & Berteau Aves.), 773-539-1909

◩ "Master chef" Arun Sampanthavivat "is an artist" whose "exquisite" presentations of "top-notch" Thai entice the faithful to this "out-of-the-way" North Side "class act"; ordering is easy because a "breathtaking" $75 tasting menu is the only option, and if some are "alienated" by the "excessive" cost, aficionados agree there's "no better Thai" anywhere – "and that includes Thailand."

Atlantique [S] 24 | 19 | 23 | $40

5101 N. Clark St. (bet. Carmen & Foster Aves.), 773-275-9191

■ Chef-owner Jack Jones launches "another winner" at this "ambitious" "nautical newcomer" in Andersonville, where "the freshest seafood" makes for a "mouthwatering" meal served by a "welcoming" staff; marine mavens deem it "excellent", and high ratings buoy their claims.

Aubriot [S] 22 | 19 | 22 | $50

1962 N. Halsted St. (Armitage Ave.), 773-281-4211

◩ There's "not a scene" at this Lincoln Park "gastronomic gem", just an "inventive" New French menu courtesy of "rising star" Eric Aubriot; "fabulous food" is served "without the attitude", though a few complain of "high prices" for "tiny portions"; N.B. dinner only.

Blackbird 24 | 19 | 21 | $47

619 W. Randolph St. (bet. Desplaines & Jefferson Sts.), 312-715-0708

◩ Contrasting "minimalist decor" with "maximal flavor", this "chic" West Loop New American "would be at home in TriBeCa or South Beach"; "the beautiful people" flock in to peck at "stellar", "innovative" dishes amid "stark" surroundings, though phobes pass on the "pretentious" scene and seating that's "too close for comfort."

Brasserie Jo [S] 20 | 21 | 20 | $34

59 W. Hubbard St. (bet. Clark & Dearborn Sts.), 312-595-0800

◩ When he's not overseeing the acclaimed Everest or fine-tuning Las Vegas' Eiffel Tower, chef Jean Joho brings his dizzying talents to his River North New French namesake; loyalists label it an "all-around pleasant experience" with a "great art deco" look and "imaginative" food, though the disgruntled size it up as "once great, now just popular."

Carlos' [S] 28 | 25 | 27 | $69

429 Temple Ave. (bet. Green Bay & Half Day Rds.), Highland Park, 847-432-0770

■ Rated No. 2 for Food in the *Chicago Survey,* this New French "North Shore dining temple" boasts "the ultimate hosts" in Carlos and Debbie Nieto and "outstanding food and service" "despite chef changes"; *amis* agree the "exquisite presentations", "professional" staff and "intimate setting" add up to "truly magnificent dining" that's "worth every penny."

	F	D	S	C
Charlie Trotter's	27	26	27	VE

816 W. Armitage Ave. (Halsted St.), 773-248-6228

■ Once again voted Most Popular in the *Chicago Survey*, this "world-class" Lincoln Park New American offers "exquisite" tasting menus (priced from $90 to $150) that exhibit the "limitless creativity" and "magnificent" flavor palette of "artistic" chef-owner Charlie T.; detractors decry it as "pricey" and "pretentious", but consensus still says "on a scale of 1 to 10, this is a 20."

	F	D	S	C
Courtright's [S]	26	26	25	$45

8989 S. Archer Ave. (Willow Springs Rd.), Willow Springs, 708-839-8000

■ A "surprise in the Southwest Suburbs", this "exquisite" New American is proof that "brains and taste" can flourish in the outskirts; the "truly gourmet" cuisine (including an "excellent degustation" menu) backed by an "exceptional" wine list is as captivating as the "elegant" room, which offers a "photo-op" view of a garden and "forest preserve."

	F	D	S	C
Crofton on Wells	24	20	21	$46

535 N. Wells St. (bet. Grand Ave. & Ohio St.), 312-755-1790

■ Chef-owner Suzy Crofton's "brilliance shines through" at this "outstanding" Regional American in River North; an "innovative menu" of "consistently high-quality" seasonal dishes served in a stylish, "intimate" setting makes it a "winner", though hedgers hint "lighten up on the attitude."

	F	D	S	C
D & J Bistro [S]	25	21	23	$35

466 S. Rand Rd. (Rte. 22), Lake Zurich, 847-438-8001

■ Voted the best bistro in the *Chicago Survey*, this "fetching" French is a "hard-to-find" "treasure" in a Far Northwest strip mall that's built its rep with a "terrific", "innovative menu" and "charming" service; the three-course, $24 prix fixe deal is nominated "best value in the metro area" – "wish it were in the city."

	F	D	S	C
Everest	27	27	27	$76

One Financial Place, 440 S. La Salle St., 40th fl. (Congress Pkwy.), 312-663-8920

■ The "dining is almost as spectacular as the view" at this 40th-floor New French in the Loop, where chef Jean Joho's "ethereal and beautiful" creations (backed by a "marvelous wine selection") set a culinary "standard"; with its "breathtaking" setting and "flawless" service, it's a "pinnacle of haute cuisine."

	F	D	S	C
Frontera Grill	26	22	22	$33

445 N. Clark St. (bet. Hubbard & Illinois Sts.), 312-661-1434

■ "Rick Bayless is a master" according to admirers who say "olé" to his "amazing" River North Mexican, "a feast for the eyes and mouth" that ranks among the "best in the USA"; it's a "perennial fave" for "unbeatable", "zesty" food and "margaritas from heaven", and though there's "always a wait", it "sure beats Taco Bell!"

	F	D	S	C
Gabriel's	26	23	25	$53

310 Green Bay Rd. (Highwood Ave.), Highwood, 847-433-0031

■ In the eyes of jealous urbanites, Gabriel Viti's namesake is "too good for the 'burbs", though North Shore natives are tickled to call this "elegantly understated" "French-Italian crossover" their own; "spectacular food" and "meticulous service" make it an "occasion place" where patrons pay "out-of-sight prices" to "feel like a million bucks."

| F | D | S | C |

Gibsons Steakhouse ●S

| 25 | 20 | 22 | $47 |

1028 N. Rush St. (Bellevue Pl.), 312-266-8999
Doubletree Hotel, 5464 N. River Rd. (bet. Balmoral & Bryn Mawr Aves.), Rosemont, 847-928-9900

■ As a "hometown favorite", this Gold Coast steakhouse-seafooder gives the "beautiful people" a chance to "see and be seen" while indulging in "fabulous", "Flintstone-size" "hunks of meat" delivered by a "professional" staff; it's "bedlam", but the "best steaks" are "worth the chaos"; N.B. the Rosemont offshoot opened post-*Survey*.

Grace

| 24 | 20 | 21 | $45 |

623 W. Randolph St. (bet. Desplaines & Jefferson Sts.), 312-928-9200

■ "Created with the hip in mind", this "marvelous" West-of-Loop New American with a "suave menu" offers "exotic meats" ("be game and try some") and "inventive desserts"; the "cordial" service and "dark, sexy" room enhance the "cool vibe."

Ixcapuzalco S

| 24 | 18 | 17 | $32 |

2919 N. Milwaukee Ave. (Diversey Pkwy.), 773-486-7340

☑ Winning olés for its "excellent moles", this "gourmet" Logan Square Mexican showcases "creative" cooking from chef-owner Geno Bahena (ex Frontera Grill and Topolobampo), who turns every meal into a "culinary adventure"; "slow service" is a common complaint, but even those who have trouble with the "tough name" pronounce it otherwise "wonderful."

Le Français

| 29 | 27 | 28 | $76 |

269 S. Milwaukee Ave. (bet. Dundee & Willow Rds.), Wheeling, 847-541-7470

■ Once again voted No. 1 in the *Chicago Survey* for Food and Service, this "phenomenal" Wheeling destination is still "the best French restaurant west of Paris"; fans hail the return after a decade's absence of founding chef and owner Jean Banchet ("long live the king!"), who "hasn't lost a step" in creating "amazing, wonderful" cuisine that ranks with "the finest in all respects."

Les Nomades

| 27 | 24 | 26 | $69 |

222 E. Ontario St. (bet. Fairbanks Ct. & St. Clair St.), 312-649-9010

■ Having relinquished control of Le Français, Roland and Mary Beth Liccioni's principal business is now this "elegant" Classic French in Streeterville that boasts "flawless haute cuisine", "exemplary" service and "subtle" "Parisian ambiance"; it's a jacket-required "bastion of civility", and if some find it "a tad snooty", all agree it's "a refined dining experience."

Le Titi de Paris

| 27 | 25 | 26 | $58 |

1015 W. Dundee Rd. (Kennicott Ave.), Arlington Heights, 847-506-0222

■ "Toques off" to owner Pierre Pollin and chef Michael Maddox for some of the "best-value haute French in Chicagoland" at this "charmer" in the Northwest, where the food is "masterful" and the wine is "outstanding"; that this "jewel" can thrive in its "dull suburban setting" is proof that a prime "location isn't always imperative."

Mirai Sushi S

▽ | 26 | 22 | 22 | $35 |

2020 W. Division St. (Damen Ave.), 773-862-8500

■ "A worthy competitor to the established sushi" emporia, this West Side Japanese has trendsetters labeling it "*the* place" for "delish" fish, including several "unusual" varieties, all "fresh" and "beautifully presented"; there's also a loungey upstairs that "caters to the 'in' crowd."

Mк S
26 | 25 | 24 | $52

868 N. Franklin St. (bet. Chicago Ave. & Oak St.), 312-482-9179
■ Michael Kornick's "creative and cultured" Near North New American is "memorable" as a "hip place" that "doesn't take itself too seriously"; the "superb" cuisine perfectly complements the "sleek", "very chichi" setting and "trendy", black-clad clientele; P.S. "there is nothing better than dessert" here, so "save room."

Mod. S
– | – | – | E

1520 N. Damen Ave. (North Ave.), 773-252-1500
Wicker Park's trendy set congregates at this New American over upscale, Alice Waters–inspired cooking courtesy of chef Kelly Courtney; the space-age setting features perforated wall dividers, futuristic furnishings and a riot of color, and those trapped in the present are grateful for free parking in the adjacent lot.

Morton's of Chicago S
26 | 20 | 22 | $51

Newberry Plaza, 1050 N. State St., lower level (Maple St.), 312-266-4820
9525 W. Bryn Mawr Ave. (River Rd.), Rosemont, 847-678-5155
1 Westbrook Corporate Ctr. (22nd St. & Wolf Rd.), Westchester, 708-562-7000
■ It's "first class all the way" at these "meat-and-potato paradises", once again voted the "best steak experience" in the *Chicago Survey*; the "succulent beef" and "awesome" service are the "epitome" of "old-world sophistication", and even the "second-mortgage" tabs "live up to" every expectation.

Nine
– | – | – | E

440 W. Randolph St. (bet. Canal St. & Wacker Dr.), 312-575-9900
"A contender for your beef dollar", this West-of-Loop entry is a mod version of a steak-and-seafooder, with über-hip decor and a champagne bar that attracts an "'in' crowd."

Nomi S
– | – | – | VE

Park Hyatt Chicago, 800 N. Michigan Ave. (Chicago Ave.), 312-335-1234
As the showpiece of the Park Hyatt on the Mag Mile, this luxe French-International pulls out all the stops with a Tony Chi–designed dining room, stunning views, a 3,000-bottle wine cellar and (lest anyone forget) picture-perfect cuisine from chef Sandro Gamba; those with any attention to spare can focus on the polished-steel display kitchen.

one sixtyblue
24 | 25 | 22 | $53

160 N. Loomis St. (Randolph St.), 312-850-0303
■ Bringing together a "beautiful" Adam Tihany–designed space and "brilliant cooking" courtesy of chef Patrick Roberston, this West Side New American is "a perfect blend" of food and mood; it offers "stylish" "dining at the highest level" and yet "another reason to love Michael" (silent partner Michael Jordan, that is).

Pasteur S
23 | 22 | 19 | $31

5525 N. Broadway (Bryn Mawr Ave.), 773-878-1061
■ Quite a few call this "beautiful and romantic" Edgewater "gem" "the best Vietnamese in the area", citing "delicious" food delivered by a "pleasant" staff; the "pretty room" features wicker chairs and slow-spinning ceiling fans ("just like Saigon, right?"), but some warn the "intimate" space may grow "very noisy."

Ritz-Carlton Dining Room S
28 | 27 | 28 | $66

Ritz-Carlton Hotel, 160 E. Pearson St. (Michigan Ave.), 312-573-5223

■ Chicago's showcase for hotel dining continues to "impress in every way": chef Sarah Stegner's "stellar" New French cuisine "never ceases to amaze", the "opulent" room (voted No. 1 for Decor in the *Chicago Survey*) is an "experience in luxe" and service is "superb"; here's a chance to feel "pampered" over an "outstanding" dinner or Sunday brunch.

Seasons S
27 | 27 | 27 | $61

Four Seasons Hotel, 120 E. Delaware Pl., 7th fl. (bet. Michigan Ave. & Rush St.), 312-649-2349

■ "Want to impress"?; this "gracious" Michigan Avenue New American is "a delight for all the senses", where chef Mark Baker's "superb" cuisine is "so delicious you'll lick the plate clean"; with its "magnificent room" and "exceptional" service, it's an "elaborate" "tribute to Chicagoland dining", and the Sunday brunch is just "out of this world."

Shaw's Crab House & Blue Crab Lounge S
23 | 19 | 20 | $36

21 E. Hubbard St. (bet. State St. & Wabash Ave.), 312-527-2722

Shaw's Seafood Grill S
22 | 18 | 21 | $34

660 W. Lake Cook Rd. (bet. Pfingsten & Waukegan Rds.), Deerfield, 847-948-1020

■ These "bustling" seafooders "aim to please", serving such "terrific", "consistent" fin fare that "it's hard to believe they aren't on the coast"; the city location's "lively" Blue Crab Lounge is favored for the "best oysters and martinis" around, but the suburban sib is a "better value", especially given its "great" early-bird deal.

Spiaggia S
26 | 27 | 25 | $60

One Magnificent Mile Bldg., 980 N. Michigan Ave., 2nd fl. (Oak St.), 312-280-2750

■ With the departure of chef Paul Bartolotta, it's now up to successor Tony Mantuano to maintain this "elegant" Gold Coast Italian's "superb" standards in the kitchen; the "superior" service is still in place, along with the "breathtaking" room and view that "alone make it outstanding" – just bring "lotsa lire"; N.B. the chef change is not reflected in the above food score.

Tallgrass S
27 | 24 | 26 | $62

1006 S. State St. (10th St.), Lockport, 815-838-5566

■ In the "exurban destination" of Lockport, this "charming" New French is a showcase for chef Robert Burcenski's "innovative", "picture-perfect" culinary creations; the setting is an "intimate" Victorian dining room, and the menu typically offers a choice of "excellent" three-, four- or five-course prix fixe spreads that are "well worth the long ride" (and the "pricey" tab); N.B. jacket required.

302 West
26 | 24 | 25 | $47

302 W. State St. (3rd St.), Geneva, 630-232-9302

■ Sited in an "old bank building" turned New American in the Far Western 'burbs, this low-lit, "high-class" dinner spot is a "very romantic" "gem" where there's "always something great" on the "creative" seafood-leaning menu; "delicious desserts" and an all-American wine list featuring "small vineyards" leave admirers feeling like a million.

Topolobampo | 27 | 23 | 25 | $46 |

445 N. Clark St. (bet. Hubbard & Illinois Sts.), 312-661-1434

■ "Unique and outstanding" flavors qualify Rick Bayless' "gourmet Mexican" in River North as "best of breed"; the "fancy" counterpart to Frontera Grill (with which it shares a kitchen), it offers "haute cuisine versions" of regional dishes (including a $55 tasting menu that's "worth every penny") in a "high-class" room – just call it 'Tops' for short.

Trio [S] | 27 | 25 | 27 | $70 |

Homestead Hotel, 1625 Hinman Ave. (Davis St.), Evanston, 847-733-8746

■ "Daring food combinations" offer devotees a taste of "gourmet heaven" at this "magnificent" Eclectic on the North Shore; it's a "refined experience" all around, where "cuisine as art" meets "superb" service in an "elegant" yet "serene" setting; deep-pocketed regulars report the "tasting menu is the way to go" – "each course is spectacular."

TRU | 28 | 27 | 27 | $88 |

676 N. St. Clair St. (Huron St.), 312-202-0001

■ Truly "lush and luscious", Rick Tramonto and Gale Gand's "exciting" Streeterville companion to Trio is "already established as one of the best in town"; the New American cuisine elevates "food to an art form" (the signature caviar staircase leads "to heaven"), with "spectacular decor" and "excellent service" to match; it may be a "wallet-breaker", but true believers observe "perfection" rarely comes cheap.

Va Pensiero [S] | 25 | 22 | 23 | $42 |

Margarita Inn, 1566 Oak Ave. (Davis St.), Evanston, 847-475-7779

■ Consistently one of Chicago's most popular spots, this "treasure of the North Shore" is "excellent in every detail", with "sophisticated" Italian food from Jeff Muldrow and "fabulous attention" from a professional staff; the "quiet, romantic" environment works for everything from a "low-key supper to a classy celebration", and if they "insist on offering only Italian wines", they do offer 250 of them.

Vong [S] | 23 | 23 | 21 | $51 |

6 W. Hubbard St. (State St.), 312-644-8664

◪ Most folks feel that "you can't go Vong" at the Loop branch of Jean-Georges Vongerichten's Thai-French fusion concept, raving about an "elegant symphony of hot and mild tastes" – especially the "to-die-for" seven-course tasting menu; critics carp about the "postage stamp–size portions" and note "creative food may require creative financing."

Zealous ▽ | 23 | 20 | 21 | $52 |

419 W. Superior St. (Chicago Ave.), 312-475-9112

■ "Brilliant cooking without a safety net" is how supporters sum up the New American cuisine of Charlie Trotter protégé Michael Taus, who's flying high after a move from Elmhurst to River North; thanks to a substantial "no-expense-spared" upgrade, there's "dramatic decor" (purple suede and bamboo trees) to match food that simply "rocks", even if a handful of detractors are less than zealous about the "undersized portions."

Cincinnati

TOP 10 FOOD RANKING

Restaurant	Cuisine Type
28 Maisonette	New French
Palace	New American
27 Chez Alphonse	Classic French
26 BonBonerie	Bakery/Tearoom
Precinct	Steakhouse
25 Phoenix	New American
China Gourmet	Chinese
Barresi's	N/S Italian
Morton's of Chicago	Steakhouse
Scalea's	N/S Italian

ADDITIONAL NOTEWORTHY PLACES

Brown Dog Cafe	New American
Daveed's at 934	New American
Dee Felice Cafe	Cajun/Creole
Golden Lamb	Traditional American
Grand Finale	New American
Iron Horse Inn	New American
Jo An	Japanese
Montgomery Inn	Barbecue
Nicola's	Northern Italian
Pacific Moon Cafe	Chinese/Pan-Asian

F	D	S	C

Barresi's Italian Restaurant
25	20	23	$34

4111 Webster Ave. (Blue Ash Rd.), Deer Park, 513-793-2540
■ "Excellent" Italian cuisine served in "huge portions" plus a candlelit, "white-tablecloth" interior, a "no-rush" ambiance and "very attentive" service draw a "low-key" crowd to this family-run "celebration" venue in Deer Park; while it may be "expensive", boosters suggest that this multiroom "hidden gem" is perhaps the only Cincinnati restaurant in its category that "could keep its doors open in NYC"; P.S. the new bar area is a "nice" option for solo dining.

BonBonerie
26	16	18	$12

2030 Madison Rd. (O'Bryon St.), 513-321-3399
■ "Outstanding pastries" and "pretty-as-a-picture" cakes that earn nods as "the best" in town (especially the "amazing" opera cream version) keep a well-heeled crowd addicted to this O'Bryonville bakery, which is lauded for using "real butter and fresh fruit"; busy bees may opt for takeout, but there's also a tea room (complete with creaky old chairs and a novelty teapot collection) that's ideal for "coffee, scones and the morning paper" or for a light lunch.

www.zagat.com 45

F | D | S | C

Brown Dog Cafe
23 | 17 | 20 | $27

Pfeiffer Commons, 5893 Pfeiffer Rd. (bet. I-71 & Kenwood Rd.), Blue Ash, 513-794-1610

■ Set in a suburban Blue Ash strip mall and decorated with a few well-placed antiques and art-glass fixtures that add punch to the otherwise "spartan" "California-style" decor, this "great little bistro" attracts a label-conscious clientele with "imaginative" New American cuisine, middle-of-the-road prices, "solicitous" service and "personal attention" from chef-owner Mary Swortwood.

Chez Alphonse
27 | 21 | 25 | $48

654 Highland Ave. (Grand Ave.), Ft. Thomas, KY, 859-442-5488

◪ You've got to go "off the beaten path" to find this Ft. Thomas–based, big-ticket Classic French destination, which supporters call a "very proper" "class act" and "the best northern Kentucky has to offer", citing "excellent" food ("wonderful duck"), "friendly but not intrusive" service and a wine list strong on Alsatians; dissenters call it a "Maisonette wanna-be" with "somber" decor, but ratings back up the boosters.

China Gourmet
25 | 18 | 24 | $30

3340 Erie Ave. (Marburg Ave.), 513-871-6612

■ Regulars know to "toss away the menu and eat the specials" (especially any whole fish) recommended by the "friendly" Moy family at this "absolutely superb" "high-end" Chinese, which easily "sets the standard for local Asian creativity"; tucked into a white-and-maroon basement hideaway in Hyde Park and stocked with rosewood chairs imported from China, this 23-year-old vet continues to be a "local favorite."

Daveed's at 934 [S]
– | – | – | E

934 Hatch St. (Louden St.), 513-721-2665

Owners David and Liz Cook are making waves at this chic, pricey Mt. Adams New American with International influences; set on the first floor of an artfully renovated townhouse, it attracts a tony clientele with its big-city feel (apricot cream walls, black lacquer–framed artwork), sophisticated cuisine, food-friendly wine list and knowledgeable staff; signature dishes feature trendy ingredients such as seared foie gras.

Dee Felice Cafe [S]
23 | 21 | 21 | $27

529 Main St. (6th St.), Covington, KY, 859-261-2365

■ For a "touch of New Orleans in Kentucky", consider this "authentic" Cajun-Creole standby in Covington featuring tin ceilings and marble floors from its former days as a pharmacy, as well as "great" food, solid service and "reasonable" prices; it's a favorite place to "go with a group" or "bring out-of-towners" because of the "wonderful" nightly jazz.

Golden Lamb, The [S]
21 | 24 | 21 | $25

The Golden Lamb Inn, 27 S. Broadway St. (Main St.), Lebanon, 513-932-5065

◪ Tourists and locals alike are drawn to this "one of a kind" "historic" Lebanon inn where travelers, including Charles Dickens and several presidents, have lodged and dined since 1803; the moderately priced Traditional American fare is served in period rooms by the "gracious" longtime staff, and though a few complain that "the atmosphere outshines the food", most agree it's "year-round delicious" and "especially nice at holiday time."

Grand Finale [S] — 25 | 22 | 22 | $27

3 E. Sharon Ave. (Congress Ave.), Glendale, 513-771-5925

■ "Picturesque" Glendale is the setting for this "always pleasing" New American ensconced in a "charming", antiques-filled Victorian building that evokes the 1890s; the kitchen turns out "well-prepared" and "well-presented" edibles at all times, but voters save their superlatives for the "wonderful" Sunday brunch (best taken in the lovely garden) and "legendary", "unsurpassed" desserts.

Iron Horse Inn [S] — 23 | 23 | 20 | $28

40 Village Sq. (Sharon Rd.), Glendale, 513-771-4787

■ "A great renovation" of a circa 1858 trackside tavern has Glendale denizens debating which section of this attractive restaurant is more appealing: the "elegant" and subdued first floor, the hunter-green, ski lodge–like upstairs with a lively, cherrywood bar or the "nice outdoor patio"; the "accommodating" staff and "varied" New American menu earn kudos all around.

Jo An — ▽ 26 | 14 | 19 | $28

3940 Olympic Blvd. (Mineola Pike), Erlanger, KY, 859-746-2634

■ Toyota executives and other deep-pocketed diners pay top dollar for "fresh, authentic" Japanese food, including some of the "best sushi" in the Tristate, at this Kentucky outpost with a serene ambiance and somewhat tentative but gracious staff; there's a distinguished list of sakes to choose from, and owner Kotaro Nakamura is especially proud of his traditional multicourse *kaiseki* meals, which are available on 24-hours' notice.

Maisonette — 28 | 27 | 28 | $56

114 E. Sixth St. (bet. Main & Walnut Sts.), 513-721-2260

■ This Downtown Mediterranean-influenced Contemporary French grande dame turned 50 last year, but still managed a clean sweep of the Cincinnati *Survey* (No. 1 for Food, Decor, Service and Popularity) thanks to chef Jean-Robert de Cavel's "fabulous food", a 14,000-bottle wine list, "impeccable", "personalized" tableside service and "elegant", crystal-chandeliered, banquette-lined dining rooms filled with a fabulous collection of American Impressionist paintings – in sum, a class act all the way.

Montgomery Inn [S] — 22 | 19 | 21 | $24

9440 Montgomery Rd. (Cooper Rd.), Montgomery, 513-791-3482

◪ Droves of devotees declare that the "best ribs in the world" are served at this Montgomery shrine to BBQ, which looks like a giant sports bar (albeit a "nicely remodeled one") and attracts a sometimes rowdy crowd with "finger-lickin' good" babybacks and Saratoga chips; despite long waits, most find it "reliable" in every way, although a few heretics argue that it's "overrated" ("shows what good marketing will do").

Morton's of Chicago [S] — 25 | 23 | 23 | $46

Tower Pl. Mall, 28 W. Fourth St. (Race St.), 513-241-4104

■ Tucked under the Tower Place Mall, this Downtown chain steakhouse keeps "expense-account", "he-man" high rollers happy with gigantic portions of USDA Prime beef and one of the "best wine lists in town"; savvy regulars know that the efficient and solicitous staff won't penalize them for sharing what is "arguably, the best steak in Cincy."

Nicola's 23 | 22 | 21 | $33

1420 Sycamore St. (Liberty St.), 513-721-6200

■ "Truly fine Tuscan" could refer to Florentine owner Nicola Pietoso or to the cooking at his Over-the-Rhine "contemporary" Northern Italian, which turns out a "lobster ravioli that would make Julia Child drool", cannelloni to crow about and a "don't-miss seafood risotto"; moreover, the collection of large-faced clocks and landscape paintings makes "imaginative use" of the cavernous space, another reason why this is a romantic favorite before or after the theater or symphony.

Pacific Moon Cafe [S] 24 | 17 | 20 | $27

Market Place Complex, 8300 Market Place Ln. (Montgomery Rd.), Montgomery, 513-891-0091

■ "Excellent", "authentic" Chinese fare, a "huge" selection of veggie-friendly Pan-Asian offerings and spectacular dim sum on weekends prompt a loyal crowd to rate this Montgomery ethnic one of "the best" in its category; sure, you can get pad Thai elsewhere for less, but the colorful, upscale dining rooms should tell you that this isn't your mother's chop suey place.

Palace, The [S] 28 | 27 | 27 | $47

Cincinnatian Hotel, 601 Vine St. (6th St.), 513-381-6006

■ "Who said hotel food can't be great?" ask advocates of this "classy" Downtown New American where an "outstanding" seasonal menu is complemented by a 300-choice, domestic-focused wine list, "service fit for a king", live nightly music and a "gorgeous" terra-cotta dining room with mirrored panels, cozy banquettes and fresh orchids on every table; N.B. crab cakes are a highlight.

Phoenix, The Restaurant at the 25 | 25 | 25 | $37

812 Race St. (9th St.), 513-721-8901

■ "An undiscovered treasure" awaits explorers who head Downtown to this "classy" New American in an "old-world", lovingly restored men's club; despite the luxe surroundings (25-foot ceilings, oak-paneled walls, lots of marble and drapery) and well-dressed clientele, regulars consider it an "excellent fine-dining value"; P.S. "every restaurant should have its wine savvy."

Precinct, The [S] 26 | 21 | 23 | $41

311 Delta Ave. (Columbia Pkwy.), 513-321-5454

◪ Set in a former police station in Columbia-Tusculum, this "meat-eater's mecca" attracts "jocks" and other "manly" types with "hearty", "out-of-this-world" steaks and chops; while dissenters may take issue with the "noisy" "sports-bar atmosphere" and tables that are "too close together", few have any beefs with the "excellent" edibles.

Scalea's 25 | 21 | 21 | $34

318-20 Greenup St. (3rd St.), Covington, KY, 859-491-3334

■ "Inventive" "nouveau" Italian cooking is augmented by an all-Italian wine list and a "fabulous" staff at this "lovely", "well-designed" Kentucky destination set in a rehabbed 19th-century building whose Mediterranean decor extends to its patio and adjacent deli; popular items include the filet mignon Florentino, veal chop and saffron gnocchi.

Cleveland

TOP 10 FOOD RANKING

	Restaurant	Cuisine Type
28	Johnny's Bar	N. Italian/Continental
27	Phnom Penh	Cambodian/Vietnamese
	Johnny's Downtown	N. Italian/Continental
	Lola	Midwestern
	Hyde Park Grille	Steakhouse
	Sans Souci	New French/Mediterranean
26	Shuhei	Japanese/Pan-Asian
	Baricelli Inn	Continental
	Market Square Bistro	New American
	Chez François	Classic French

ADDITIONAL NOTEWORTHY PLACES

Blue Pointe Grill	Seafood
Fat Cats	New American/Italian
Kosta's	New American
Morton's of Chicago	Steakhouse
Moxie	New American
Napa Valley Grille	Californian
One Walnut	New American
Parker's	New French
Salvatore's	N/S Italian
Sergio's	International

	F	D	S	C
Baricelli Inn	26	26	25	$49

2203 Cornell Rd. (Murray Hill Rd.), 216-791-6500

■ A "beautiful, old" "converted mansion" on the outskirts of Little Italy is the setting for one of "Cleveland's most exclusive dining experiences", a "formal", big-night-out venue where "serious, ambitious" Continental cuisine (and a don't-miss cheese course) is served in one of seven distinct dining rooms; N.B. those on a budget should consider the less expensive outdoor garden bistro.

	F	D	S	C
Blue Pointe Grill [S]	26	25	23	$41

700 W. St. Clair Ave. (6th St.), 216-875-7827

■ "Casual but chic", this "sophisticated" "hot spot" in the historic Warehouse District boasts the "best seafood in town" – it's as if the "Atlantic Ocean moved to the Midwest"; sample "top-quality" raw oysters and the signature grouper sauté, paired with such sides as "excellent lobster mashed potatoes", in a "magnificent space" with exposed brick walls and gilded columns; this is "where the elite meet", so it's "always a scene."

Chez François S   26 | 27 | 26 | $48
555 Main St. (Liberty Ave.), Vermilion, 440-967-0630
■ "Worth the long drive" from Cleveland or Toledo, this romantic "special-occasion" destination in Vermilion rewards travelers with a "beautiful" room (rated No. 1 for Decor in the Cleveland area) and a "superb" Classic French cuisine; even if a few quibble that the "food sometimes doesn't measure up to the scenery", most regard it as a "favorite" and advise "pick the patio" seating to best take in the "great setting on the river"; N.B. it's closed from January–mid-March.

Fat Cats   25 | 18 | 22 | $28
2061 W. 10th St. (University Rd.), 216-579-0200
■ Located in a frame house in Tremont, this "hip" "out-of-the-way" "find" with a "wonderful view across the Flats of Downtown Cleveland" is a "funky, fun" place to "enjoy" an "eclectic menu" of "yummy", "unusual" New American–Italian fare; add a staff that's "eager to please", and it's no wonder that plenty of admirers just "love" this little "gem."

Hyde Park Grille   27 | 23 | 24 | $40
123 Prospect Ave. W. (W. 2nd St.), 216-344-2444 S
1825 Coventry Rd. (bet. Hampshire & Lancashire Rds.), Cleveland Hts., 216-321-6444
34205 Chagrin Blvd. (S. O. M. Ctr. Rd.), Moreland Hills, 216-464-0688 S
■ Once again the top steakhouse in Cleveland, this "wildly popular", "clubby" chain constantly "buzzes" with carnivores happily carving into "fantastic" "prime" cuts, notably the "superior" house specialty, a Kansas City strip; though it's "way too noisy" and the tabs are in the "expense-account" league, legions attest that this is a "beef-eater's paradise" (better "fast before going – the steaks are huge").

Johnny's Bar   28 | 23 | 25 | $43
3164 Fulton Rd. (Trent Ave.), 216-281-0055
■ This dark, art deco–style former tavern in a working-class West Side neighborhood is once again rated No. 1 for Food in Cleveland, thanks to "large portions" of "excellent" Northern Italian–Continental cuisine ("lots of veal dishes") complemented by a winning wine list; granted, it's "expensive" and "noisy", but "simply a great place", nonetheless.

Johnny's Downtown S   27 | 25 | 25 | $44
1406 W. Sixth St. (St. Clair Ave.), 216-623-0055
■ Where Cleveland's "celebrities" and "movers and shakers" gather, this hopping Downtown Northern Italian–Continental offshoot of the Fulton Road favorite has the same "outstanding food" and professional service, but adds a more "upscale", "inviting" setting, which is conducive to "business or romance."

Kosta's   24 | 23 | 23 | $36
2179 W. 11th St. (Fairfield Ave.), 216-622-0011
■ Voters gush that "rising star" chef Brandt Evans' "excellent", "innovative" New American cuisine has "vastly improved" this "trendy Tremont" art deco restaurant, which sports a "great" mahogany and bird's-eye maple bar and spiffy outdoor terrace; signature dishes include the lobster, crawfish-and-tomato bisque, and polenta-crusted calamari.

Lola Bistro & Wine Bar ◐ [S] 27 23 25 $41

900 Literary Rd. (Professor Rd.), 216-771-5652

■ Savvy foodies "book months ahead" for a prime-time weekend table at this "trendy" Tremont "knockout" where "outstanding" chef (and co-owner) Michael Symon uses local ingredients to spin "imaginative" twists on Midwestern comfort foods; dig into his "unusual and delicious" menu in "mod" (if "very loud") surroundings appointed with an open kitchen, lots of stainless steel, tin ceilings and "groovy" but "uncomfortable" leopard-skin seats.

Market Square Bistro [S] 26 19 19 $32

16725 Chillicothe Rd. (E. Washington St.), Bainbridge Twp., 440-543-5115

■ "To-die-for meat loaf" and bread pudding that's dubbed the "best dessert in town" elicit ecstatic groans from patrons of this "casual" Frank Lloyd Wright–themed New American bistro in a strip mall outside of Chagrin Falls; but while no one disputes the "large portions" of "wonderful food" from its open kitchen, there are scattered complaints about "rushed" service and a high decibel level.

Morton's of Chicago [S] 25 23 24 $49

The Avenue at Tower City Ctr., 1660 W. Second St. (Prospect Ave.), 216-621-6200

◪ "Expense-account" diners love to "entertain clients" over "obscene" portions ("suitable for a farm laborer") of "consistently" "fantastic" steaks at this Downtown chain beef shrine with lamps on every table and a dark, clubby ambiance; those paying their own way feel a "hurting on the wallet" but still find a few extra bucks for the Grand Marnier soufflé and Godiva chocolate cake.

Moxie [S] 26 23 23 $41

3355 Richmond Rd. (Chagrin Blvd.), Beachwood, 216-831-5599

■ Local celebs, "beautiful people" and "classy" types from the neighborhood know to "wear black" when mingling at the happening bar or sitting in the earth-toned, brick dining room (check out the massive dining-themed mural) of this "large", "trendy" New American where chef Jonathan Bennett turns out "excellent" seasonal cuisine; P.S. while still "upbeat", it's no longer "extremely noisy" due to the installation of sound-absorbing material.

Napa Valley Grille [S] 24 24 22 $36

Beachwood Pl. Mall, 26300 Cedar Rd., upper level (Richmond Rd.), Beachwood, 216-514-8686

■ "Surprisingly good for a mall restaurant", especially one that's a chain, is a frequent take on the Californian cuisine served at this charming, adobe-style Beachwood outlet, a "comfortable", "cool oasis" "to pop into while shopping" for an "interesting salad", salmon Napoleon and glass of pinot noir; N.B. call ahead about the monthly wine dinners, which draw on a 350-choice list.

One Walnut – – – VE

1 Walnut Ave. (bet. 9th & 12th Sts.), 216-575-1111

Veteran Cleveland chef Marlin Kaplan is behind the stove at this elegant newcomer to the Financial District, where suits on expense accounts can feast their eyes (there's a dark cherrywood bar, a large mural of city life, an open kitchen and beautiful art deco–style light fixtures) while pampering their palates on seasonal New American fare such as grilled rack of lamb, slow-roasted chicken and pan-seared tuna.

Parker's Restaurant & Bistro Bar S 26 22 23 $45
2801 Bridge Ave. (W. 28th St.), 216-771-7130

◪ "Inspired" Contemporary French cuisine that "highlights local produce" and pasture-raised poultry garners kudos for chef-owner Parker Bosley at this "charming" Downtown hideaway, which is decorated with etchings of old European buildings; N.B. those looking for less expensive, lighter fare should consider eating in the bar area.

Phnom Penh S⊅ 27 10 22 $16
13124 Lorain Ave. (W. 131st St.), 216-251-0210

■ Just overlook the plain "storefront" setting of this "tiny" West Side Asian because the kitchen delights the palate with a "different kind" of taste sensation, showcasing a "super variety" of "intensely wonderful" and "spicy" Cambodian and Vietnamese dishes; moreover, prices are rock-bottom "low", it's BYO, and the staff is "helpful" and "courteous", so "come with a group" and explore the "totally divine" treats at this "total dive."

Salvatore's S 24 18 21 $29
2181 Murray Hill Rd. (Cornell Rd.), 216-231-7670

■ Situated in Little Italy and decorated with old photographs of the owner's family, this "cute" Italian storefront is hailed as a neighborhood "favorite" for "to-die-for calamari", "the best pizza" and winning pasta dishes such as spaghetti *alla madda* (mixed seafood); while it's "hard to get into on weekends", there's extra space during warm weather when sidewalk seating is added.

Sans Souci S 27 27 26 $41
Cleveland Renaissance Hotel, 24 Public Sq. (Superior Ave. & W. 3rd St.), 216-696-5600

◪ Once again voted the Most Popular restaurant in town, this "pride of Cleveland" housed in Downtown's Renaissance Hotel showcases "exquisite" New French–Mediterranean cuisine served by a "first-class" staff (ranked tops in town) in a "beautiful" room graced with Provençal-themed murals and hearthside seating; despite "high marks", a vocal contingent expresses "disappointment" in the kitchen's "uneven" execution, resulting in "expensive" tabs that are "not always worth it."

Sergio's in University Circle 25 19 23 $35
1903 Ford Dr. (Bellflower Rd.), 216-231-1234

■ Potent caipirinhas start the meal with "a wow" at this "wonderful" University Circle eatery, a "perfect pre–Cleveland Orchestra" spot that serves "interesting" Brazilian-influenced International cuisine highlighted by beef tenderloin with black beans and shrimp *baiana*; since the "converted carriage house" setting is "tiny" and "very noisy", many prefer the "charming" outdoor patio.

Shuhei Restaurant of Japan S 26 20 23 $31
23360 Chagrin Blvd. (Green Rd.), Beachwood, 216-464-1720

■ The "best sushi in Cleveland" ("by far"), traditional Japanese dishes such as tempura and sukiyaki, and Pan-Asian offerings along the lines of garlic-marinated steaks and roast duck in plum wine sauce garner rave reviews for this "friendly" and tastefully decorated (antique wood carvings, Edo-period screens) destination on the lower level of an East Side office complex; N.B. reservations are strongly recommended.

TOP 10 FOOD RANKING

Restaurant	Cuisine Type
28 Handke's Cuisine	Eclectic
Refectory	Classic French
27 L'Antibes	Classic French
Rigsby's	Eclectic
Hyde Park	Steakhouse
Trattoria Roma	N/S Italian
26 Ruth's Chris	Steakhouse
Restaurant Japan	Japanese
Mitchell's	Steakhouse
Lindey's	New American

ADDITIONAL NOTEWORTHY PLACES

Alana's Food & Wine	Eclectic
Bexley's Monk	Eclectic
Braddock's Grandview	Southern
Cameron's	New American
Figlio Wood-Fired Pizza	Pizza
Giuseppe's Ritrovo	Southern Italian
G. Michael's	Italian/New American
Out on Main	Eclectic/Regional American
Scali Ristorante	N/S Italian
Starliner Diner	Diner/Eclectic

F | D | S | C |

– | – | – | M |

Alana's Food & Wine
2333 N. High St. (W. Patterson Ave.), 614-294-6783
This "fabulous new place" with a spacious patio just north of
Ohio State University is thrilling palates with chef-owner Alana
Shock's "imaginatively prepared" Eclectic cuisine; the menu is
ever changing, but it's always composed with an "emphasis on
good [locally purveyed] ingredients" and it pairs beautifully with
the extensive (and surprisingly low-priced) wine list.

Bexley's Monk 🖸
25 | 23 | 24 | $29 |

Bexley Sq., 2232 E. Main St. (College Ave.), Bexley,
614-239-6665
🔲 "Bexley's answer to *Cheers*", this "comfy" and "always busy"
"neighborhood spot" with a "cozy atmosphere" and "the best piano
bar" is a time-honored "tradition" for great food at "reasonable
prices"; friends and families "depend" on it for "impeccably"
executed Eclectic dishes (notably "exceptional pastas" and
"consistently excellent fish") brought by "well-trained servers",
even if detractors find it "boring."

F	D	S	C

Braddock's Grandview [S]

25	22	23	$28

1470 Grandview Ave. (Ida St.), 614-487-0077

■ "They know fish" and "outstanding" Low Country cooking at this "wonderful new addition to the local scene" in Grandview, where the "innovative dishes" ("terrific tuna") provide a refreshing, upscale Southern "break from the usual Columbus fare"; while it has to "work out a few bugs" (the staff, for example, is "friendly" but "needs some seasoning"), it has made a "promising start" and enthusiasts "hope it lasts."

Cameron's [S]

25	21	24	$27

2185 W. Dublin-Granville Rd. (Linworth Rd.), Worthington, 614-885-3663

■ "Cameron [Mitchell] knows how to manage his operations", as proven by the "high standards" still maintained by the eponymous Worthington flagship of his restaurant group; the "creative" New American menu, executed with "flair", "changes frequently" but always offers an "outstanding variety" of choices, and the staff is "knowledgeable"; so even if some beg "remodel *now*" and gripe that it's "too loud", legions regard it as a "sentimental favorite."

Figlio Wood-Fired Pizza

24	20	22	$21

1369 Grandview Ave. (bet. 3rd & 5th Aves.), 614-481-8850
3712 Riverside Dr. (Fishinger Rd.), Upper Arlington, 614-459-6575

■ "Everyone's doing wood-fired pizzas", but partisans insist "they do it best" at this pair of "happy places" in Grandview and Upper Arlington; while the tables may be "too close" together, it's worth "rubbing elbows as you eat" because these "gourmet" pies are "yummy" and "unique" with "an incredible variety" of toppings; the menu also offers "excellent" salads and "wonderful pastas", all delivered by "friendly" servers ; loyal followers "love" these "homey spots" where the "owners really take pride" in their work.

Giuseppe's Ritrovo Italian Café

25	17	21	$21

2268 E. Main St. (Drexel Ave.), Bexley, 614-235-4300

■ "Everyone raves about" this "wonderful family kitchen" in Bexley, "a real success story" due to the efforts of Calabrian-bred Giuseppe Mangano, the "great chef-owner" who prepares "rich", "delicious" regional Italian specialties that are "authentic" yet "creative"; "warm" and "pleasant", this "tiny gem" is imbued with such a "personal touch" that admirers only "wish it were larger"; N.B. good news: a much needed expansion is underway.

G. Michael's Italian-American Bistro & Bar [S]

25	24	22	$27

595 S. Third St. (E. Willow St.), 614-464-0575

■ Blessed with a "great location" on the cobblestone streets of quaint German Village, this "delightful" newcomer "stepped right up to the top" of many gourmands' lists as soon as it opened; and no wonder – the "superb", "innovative" Italian–New American dishes burst with "fresh flavors" and the menu is so "interesting" "we want to eat our way through it"; what's more, its historic townhouse setting is "romantic" without being "stuffy" and the tabs are quite "affordable."

Handke's Cuisine 28 25 25 $39

520 S. Front St. (bet. Beck & Blenkner Sts.), 614-621-2500

◪ "Master chef" (and owner) Hartmut Handke possesses an "extraordinary dedication to food" and it's clearly evident in every creation in his "spectacular" Eclectic repertoire – from the barbecued oysters to the buffalo tenderloin to "the best crème brûlée in the country"; with a No. 1 ranking for food in the Columbus *Survey*, a dinner here is "a celebration in itself"; but while some praise its setting in a vaulted rathskeller in the Brewery District as "one of a kind", a few grumble about "dining in a dungeon."

Hyde Park Grille [S] 27 24 25 $36

1615 Old Henderson Rd. (Larwell Dr.), Upper Arlington, 614-442-3310

Hyde Park Chop House

6360 Frantz Rd. (off Rte. 161, east of I-270), Dublin, 614-717-2828

■ This "atmospheric" Upper Arlington "old reliable" (with a spin-off in Dublin) is still pulling in herds of cow lovers with its "fabulous" "specialty steak" dishes named after Ohio sports legends, sizzled up at the "best price-to-value" ratio in an appropriately "smoky, dark and noisy" setting (with live "cool jazz" Tuesday–Saturday).

L'Antibes 27 22 26 $40

772 N. High St. (Warren Ave.), 614-291-1666

◪ "Top-drawer all the way" declare devotees of this "romantic" Classic French in the Short North that's a "small, elegant and quiet" destination where "every meal is handcrafted" by chef-owner Dale Gussett; dissenters, however, find it "overrated", targeting a "limited" menu, "expensive, tiny" portions and a "barren room", but they're outvoted.

Lindey's [S] 26 25 25 $32

169 E. Beck St. (Mohawk St.), 614-228-4343

■ "Crowded and chaotic but fun", this "winning" New American bistro set in a "well-maintained" "old house" is still the "'in' place to be" in German Village, say scenesters; the "inventive cooking" is "always delicious", the service "pleasant", the people-watching "excellent" and the "classy-yet-informal" atmosphere "unbeatable", making it "an all-time favorite for all reasons and seasons"; P.S. there's "good jazz on Thursdays."

Mitchell's Steakhouse [S] 26 28 25 $40

45 N. Third St. (bet. Gay & Lynn Sts.), 614-621-2333

■ "Columbus' hottest steakhouse", this "chic and sophisticated" homage to meat (from the Cameron Mitchell restaurant group) set in a renovated bank with "very high ceilings" "has it all" and thus "raises the bar" Downtown, not least with its "gorgeous" "art deco" look that's rated No. 1 for Decor in the Columbus *Survey*; nearly equal to the "beautiful room" is the "excellent" beef, accompanied by an impressive wine list; awash in "big-city style", this "see-and-be-seen" "expense-account" magnet is "like being in NYC."

Out on Main S　　　　　26 | 23 | 25 | $28
122 E. Main St. (bet. 3rd & 4th Sts.), 614-224-9510

■ Surely, "Liberace would have come out to eat" at this "daringly different" Downtown Eclectic–Regional American, and "if you're comfortable with your sexual orientation", consider joining the "hip, artsy crowd" here because the "creative" food is "surprisingly good", prepared by "one of Columbus' finest chefs" (don't miss a sampling of the appetizers, particularly the "wonderful crawfish cakes", or the "terrific brunch items" on Sundays); while it's "gay-themed", the "excellent" staff "caters to all" and makes everyone feel comfortable.

Refectory　　　　　28 | 26 | 26 | $40
1092 Bethel Rd. (Kenny Rd.), 614-451-9774

■ Once again voted Columbus' Most Popular restaurant, this "awesome" Northwest French "grande dame" housed in a "beautiful old church" is a "classy", "romantic" destination for an "impeccable" "gourmet" dinner crafted by chef Richard Blondin, matched with a "nationally renowned wine list" and proffered by an "outstanding" staff (ranked the "best in the city"); yes, it's "expensive", but it's "worth it" for a "special evening" because "they don't make mistakes" here; P.S. the midweek dinners offered in the cocktail lounge are "a little-known bargain" (a three-course menu for $17).

Restaurant Japan S　　　　26 | 19 | 21 | $25
1173 Old Henderson Rd. (Kenny Rd.), Upper Arlington, 614-451-5411

■ Follow the Asian hordes to this Upper Arlington "favorite" if you have a yen for the "best Japanese food in the city", from "killer sushi" that "never misses" to "great", "authentic" cooked specialties including tempura and udon dishes; though there's "not much atmosphere" and service is "sometimes slow", the "prettily presented" fare and moderate prices compensate.

Rigsby's Cuisine Volatile　　　27 | 24 | 25 | $36
698 N. High St. (Lincoln Rd.), 614-461-7888

■ Aptly located in the lively Short North arts district, this "trendy" "place to be seen" is "always a big treat" because chef-owner "Kent [Rigsby] does a great job"; the "open kitchen" turns out "superb", "sophisticated" Eclectic fare (starting with the "best bread in town"), paired beautifully with an "innovative wine list" and delivered by an "accommodating" staff in a "chic setting"; on nights when there's live piano music, it's even more "winning."

Ruth's Chris Steak House S　　　26 | 25 | 24 | $44
7550 High Cross Blvd. (E. Campus View Blvd.), 614-885-2910

◪ "Plush and comfortable", this "clubby" chain chophouse in Crosswoods is an "unbeatable choice for steaks" according to many carnivores; detractors gripe it's "too rich" (in every sense) and "overrated", but most surveyors feel you "can't go wrong" at this "meat-lover's paradise" "if you have the bucks"; P.S. expect "large portions" of everything, so "don't forget to split the sides."

Scali Ristorante
25 | 16 | 23 | $22

Livingston Ctr., 1901 Rte. 256 (Livingston Ave.), Reynoldsburg, 614-759-7764

■ At this Reynoldsburg Italian imbued with a "warm" "family feel", "mama checks on the customers" in the dining room while her son prepares "wonderful", "home-cooked" meals in the kitchen; there's nothing fancy or cutting-edge here, but many locals "love this place" because the pastas are "perfectly" made, the atmosphere is "friendly" and the prices are a "good value."

Starliner Diner S
25 | 17 | 20 | $15

5240 Cemetery Rd. (east of Main St.), Hilliard, 614-529-1198

■ "Full of kitsch" and "funky to the max", this "strange and wonderful" Hilliard diner is "a hoot", slinging "huge portions" of eats at "tremendous value" amid "garage-sale" trappings; while "all the dishes" on the globe-trotting Eclectic menu are "very flavorful", the Cuban dishes have particular "flair"; even if a few find that it "tries too hard to be original", there's "nothing else like it" in town; P.S. it boasts one of the "best breakfasts ever."

Trattoria Roma
27 | – | 22 | $27

1447 Grandview Ave. (W. 5th Ave.), 614-488-2104

■ Now in larger, more formal digs in Grandview, this former Northeast strip center "hidden treasure" once again earns nods as the "best Italian in Columbus"; fans rave over the "fabulous" cooking ("the real thing") and heap more praise on the "intelligent" staff and "unpretentious" ambiance – in short, a "real gem" that should acquire even more polish in its new location.

Connecticut

Restaurant	Cuisine Type
28 Restaurant du Village	New French
Cavey's	N. Italian/French
27 Jean-Louis	Classic French
Thomas Henkelmann	Classic French
La Colline Verte	New French
26 Da Pietro's	N. Italian/French
Peppercorn's Grill	N/S Italian
Frog & The Peach	New American
Polo Grille & Wine Bar	N/S Italian
Sally's Apizza	Pizza
Frank Pepe Pizzeria	Pizza
Ondine	New French
Steve's Centerbrook	New American
Meson Galicia	Spanish
Rebeccas	New American
25 Gennaro's	N/S Italian
Max Downtown	New American
Max Amoré	Northern Italian
Stonehenge	Continental
Copper Beech Inn	Country French

ADDITIONAL NOTEWORTHY PLACES

Ann Howard's Apricots	Regional American
Aux Delices	New French
Beacon	Seafood/Steakhouse
Bee & Thistle Inn	Traditional American
Carbone's	Northern Italian
Carmen Anthony Steakhouse	Steakhouse
Carole Peck	New American
Elms	New American
Golden Lamb Buttery	Traditional American
Habana	Cuban
Jeffrey's	New American/Continental
Max a Mia	Northern Italian
Mayflower Inn	Regional American
Mediterranean Grill	Mediterranean
Morton's of Chicago	Steakhouse
Piccolo Arancio	N/S Italian
Quattro's	N/S Italian
Roger Sherman Inn	Classic French
Union League Cafe	French Bistro
West Street Grill	New American

Ann Howard's Apricots S
24 | 22 | 22 | $37

1593 Farmington Ave. (Rte. 4), Farmington, 860-673-5405

■ As if its "beautiful setting" on the Farmington River weren't enough, this perennially popular (and "pricey") American classic remains "the best New England dining experience in New England", with "elegantly simple food", "plenty of choices", "outrageous desserts", an "excellent wine selection" and "fine service"; P.S. "drinks on the patio before dinner are a delight."

Aux Delices Foods by Debra Ponzek
24 | 16 | 18 | $28

1075 E. Putnam Ave. (Riverside Ln.), Greenwich, 203-698-1066 S

■ "Whether take-out or eat-in", Debra Ponzek's New French food is "the greatest" agree NY visitors who "wish she'd return to Manhattan" and locals who gloat that the chef "has found a home" in Greenwich; "Paris prices" don't deter those who drop in for "morning pastry and coffee", lunch or tea, or those who leave with what they say is "the best catered food in CT" – just remember to "hide the container before claiming credit for the meal."

Beacon S
– | – | – | VE

183 Harbor Dr. (Shippan Ave.), Stamford, 203-327-4600

A Stamford outpost of Waldy Malouf's Manhattan flagship, this new marina side seafooder-steakhouse shines its light on open-fire cooking – wood-roasting lobsters, spit-roasting ducks and grilling steaks, all under the aegis of chef de cuisine Mark LeMoult; outdoor deck dining is a fair-weather plus.

Bee & Thistle Inn S
23 | 25 | 23 | $40

100 Lyme St./Rte. 1 (I-95, exit 70), Old Lyme, 860-434-1667

■ "Lovely Victorian" inn in Old Lyme that works its magic with a "warm", "romantic", "old-money" atmosphere that includes Saturday night harp music; "yummy [Traditional American] food" that relies on "herbs and veggies from the garden" and "caring" service make for an evening so "wonderful that we slept over" and enjoyed the "elegant Sunday brunch."

Carbone's Ristorante
24 | 21 | 22 | $34

588 Franklin Ave. (Goodrich St.), Hartford, 860-296-9646

■ Three generations of Hartford pols and just plain folks have called this family-owned "classical" Northern Italian "one of the best on the East Coast" for "superb food" and "excellent service" in an "elegant setting"; anniversaries and special occasions here are "special indeed!"

Carmen Anthony Steakhouse S
24 | 20 | 23 | $39

496 Chase Ave. (Nottingham Terrace), Waterbury, 203-757-3040

■ "Fun, fattening and expensive" say surveyors about this steakhouse on the outskirts of Waterbury, where "buttery, melt-in-your-mouth" meats meet in a macho atmosphere of dark-wood paneling and cigar nights; N.B. large live lobsters are also offered.

Carole Peck's Good News Cafe S
25 | 17 | 19 | $33

694 Main St. S. (Rtes. 6 & 64), Woodbury, 203-266-4663

■ The eponymous chef-owner describes her fare as 'global cuisine with a healthy twist'; our voters dub it "Nouvelle American" with "cutting-edge", "oddball combinations that taste great" and are "always a treat"; whatever they call it, crowds crowd into this "colorful", "easygoing" Woodbury "gem" in the Litchfield Hills.

Cavey's   28 | 24 | 26 | $44
45 E. Center St. (Main St.), Manchester, 860-643-2751
■ Airy Northern Italian upstairs, formal French downstairs – it's the "best of both worlds" according to our surveyors, who voted chef-owner Steve Cavagnaro's Midtown Manchester mecca No. 2 for Food and No.1 for Service in the *CT Survey*; cooking that's "consistently excellent year after year" (since 1932), award-winning wine lists, a "courteous" staff and "elegant surroundings" make it a "fabulous" "special-date place."

Copper Beech Inn S   25 | 26 | 24 | $46
46 Main St. (Rte. 9, exit 3), Ivoryton, 860-767-0330
■ For "top-of-the-line" Country French cuisine with a "soft-edged New England mise-en-scène" and "fabulous service", reviewers recommend this acclaimed Ivoryton auberge; expect "no tricks" but such "tons of charm" that you may want to linger and "spend the weekend" in one of the "exquisite guestrooms."

Da Pietro's   26 | 19 | 23 | $47
36 Riverside Ave. (bet. Boston Post Rd. & Cross St.), Westport, 203-454-1213
◪ Those who love this "postage stamp–size" Westport Northern Italian–French chef-owned spot sing its praises for "consistently marvelous" food that's a "culinary experience"; however, a few wallet-watchers whine that it's "too pricey" to dine in quarters so "cramped" that "you can eat off a stranger's plate without moving."

Elms Restaurant & Tavern S   25 | 22 | 23 | $44
Elms Inn, 500 Main St./Rte. 35 (Gilbert St.), Ridgefield, 203-438-9206
■ "Cutting-edge in the country" sums up chef-owner Brendan Walsh's "fresh" "[New] American fare at its best" as it's served in this "atmospheric" 1799 Ridgefield inn; there's "excellent service" in the "quiet", "comfortable" formal dining room (open for dinner only, Wednesday–Sunday), but many find the "authentically rustic New England" tavern "more fun" and less costly.

Frank Pepe Pizzeria S⊄   26 | 13 | 15 | $16
157 Wooster St. (bet. Brown & Olive Sts.), New Haven, 203-865-5762
■ New Haven "legend" (since 1925) that devotees declare makes the "best pizza in the USA", although it was edged out by arch-rival Sally's as the No. 1 pizzeria in the *CT Survey*; "expect to wait" ("bring the Sunday paper to read on line") for an order of the "great white clam pie", but it's definitely "worth the hassle"; though there's "no decor" and "service is erratic", surveyors sigh "I hope my last meal" will be here; N.B. closed Tuesdays.

Frog & The Peach, The S   26 | 19 | 23 | $37
160 Albany Tpke. (Rte. 44), Canton, 860-693-6345
■ Plum Canton New American with "elegant", "delicious, innovative food"; while the "atmosphere is delightful", a number of admirers wish this "tiny place" in an old Victorian cottage had "more elbow room"; N.B. reservations recommended.

Gennaro's Ristorante d'Amalfi   25 | 21 | 22 | $34
937 State St. (bet. Bishop & Humphrey Sts.), New Haven, 203-777-5490
■ Disciples declare "you can't go wrong" with this "family-run" New Haven Italian, a "stranger-friendly" spot in Midtown, where veal dishes and ravioli are conspicuous among the "authentic" pleasures; living up to its rep, it remains a standout "in a town brimming" with competitors.

Golden Lamb Buttery, The ✍　24 | 24 | 22 | $46
499 Wolf Den Rd. (Bush Hill Rd.), Brooklyn, 860-774-4423
■ Hayrides precede cocktails in the barn at this "one-of-a-kind" Brooklyn Traditional American where husband-and-wife team Bob and Jimmie Booth have been presenting "magical" meals spiked with garden herbs since 1963; the setting on a 1,000-acre Northeast Corner farm is "quintessential Connecticut" and well "worth the long drive."

Habana 🖂　23 | 20 | 19 | $35
70 N. Main St. (Marshall St.), South Norwalk, 203-852-9790
■ Rumba under the ceiling fans while you wait for a seat at this "trendy" SoNo hot spot, home to "superior Cuban cuisine that Castro never tasted"; crowds, noise and a "tropical aura" add authentic flavor, and "handy definitions on the menu" help the neophyte navigate new territory.

Jean-Louis　27 | 23 | 26 | $59
61 Lewis St. (bet. Greenwich Ave. & Mason St.), Greenwich, 203-622-8450
■ "If you can't get to Paris", chef-owner Jean-Louis Gerin's "elegant", "truly cosmopolitan" Classic French awaits just off Greenwich Avenue; diners with deep pockets style it "Lutèce North", and even those who find the formality "intimidating" sigh "a pro is in the kitchen", so the experience is "close to perfect."

Jeffrey's　24 | 21 | 23 | $32
501 New Haven Ave. (Old Gate Ln.), Milford, 203-878-1910
■ "Yes, there is a Jeffrey" at this waterside Milford New American–Continental, and admirers attest owner Jeff Johnson "knows his business" – that is, overseeing an "exciting", "top-of-the-line" seasonal menu and a "well-trained", "accommodating" staff; converts call this "class act" "a pleasant surprise."

La Colline Verte 🖂　27 | 25 | 26 | $49
Greenfield Hill Shopping Ctr., 75 Hillside Rd. (Bronson Rd.), Fairfield, 203-256-9242
■ To experience "Provence in Connecticut", Francophiles head for this "charming, cheerful" New French in an incongruous Fairfield mall locale; the "sophisticated crowd" gathered over "excellent food" cries "bravo to [owner] Jean-Pierre Rudaz" for providing a "luxurious" but "not pretentious" setting and "fine service"; a very few warn of "tiny portions" and sizable tabs.

Max a Mia 🖂　24 | 20 | 21 | $29
70 E. Main St./Rte. 44 (Rte. 10), Avon, 860-677-6299
■ Supporters signal "thumbs way up" for this "red-curtain" Avon trattoria where the "delicious" Northern Italian spread takes it to the max with the likes of brick-oven pizza and polenta cake, served in a suitably "snappy atmo"; it's "always hopping", so no one expects intimate conversation.

Max Amoré Ristorante 🖂　25 | 23 | 23 | $29
Somerset Sq., 140 Glastonbury Blvd. (Main St.), Glastonbury, 860-659-2819
■ A local "place to be", this "raucous", "upbeat" Northern Italian in a Glastonbury shopping center provides "city atmosphere in a small town"; from "Tuscan salad" to tiramisu, partisans proclaim it a spot for a "great meal" that turns on even "more charm than its [Max] brothers."

Max Downtown S   25 24 23 $39
185 Asylum St. (bet. Haynes & Trumbull Sts.), Hartford, 860-522-2530
■ Bring an expense account to Downtown Hartford and take in the "kissy-kissy scene" at this New American sophisticate where "the Mayor is always walking by your table"; it's a "terrific grill" known for "great flavor and seasonings", even if skeptics see it as "self-impressed."

Mayflower Inn, The S   25 28 25 $52
118 Woodbury Rd./Rte. 47 (Rte. 199), Washington, 860-868-9466
■ "Rolls-Royces abound" on the "gorgeous" grounds of this Litchfield County "classic" with a layout that "looks like an English lord's country estate", winning it the No. 1 Decor rating in the *CT Survey*; foodwise, the "superb" New England menu is matched with an "impressive wine list"; P.S. sybarites can book a room and "sleep in the fab beds."

Mediterranean Grill S   24 21 22 $39
Stop & Shop Plaza, 5 River Rd. (bet. Rte. 33 & Wolfpit Rd.), Wilton, 203-762-8484
■ For a "reliable, creative" Mediterranean meal, devotees drop in at this "trendy" Wilton offspring of Norwalk's Meson Galicia; the kitchen is "consistently excellent", and a "warm welcome" and "impeccable service" compensate for the shopping center locale.

Meson Galicia S   26 22 23 $41
10 Wall St. (bet. High & Knight Sts.), Norwalk, 203-866-8800
■ "Save the airfare to Spain", because this "authentic", "elegantly done" Norwalk Spaniard has its homegrown "yuppie clientele" crying "bravo"; the food is "creative and beautifully prepared", and the location in an old trolley barn lends a "robust and very informal" feel; neophytes note: an assortment of tapas may be "the best way to sample" this "extraordinary" cuisine.

Morton's of Chicago S   25 22 22 $52
Swiss Bank Ctr., 377 N. State St. (bet. Atlantic & Washington Sts.), Stamford, 203-324-3939
■ The Chicago stockyards roll into corporate Stamford via this "classic" chain steakhouse, with its trademark "gigantic portions at gigantic prices" and "men's club decor and atmo"; some sniff at the "Saran-Wrapped" presentation of the day's cuts, but beef eaters praise the "predictable" "all-around excellence", crying "damn the cholesterol" – this is "how steak used to taste."

Ondine S   26 24 24 VE
69 Pembroke Rd./Rte. 37 (Wheeler Dr.), Danbury, 203-746-4900
■ Earning "As across the board", this "fancy" New French outside Danbury proffers a "creative" prix fixe menu of five "rich" courses ("every one a delight") for $45; admirers reckon it the "best deal" around for "great food in a formal setting"; N.B. Sunday brunch is also prix fixe ($25).

Peppercorn's Grill   26 22 22 $36
357 Main St. (bet. Buckingham St. & Capital Ave.), Hartford, 860-547-1714
■ A contemporary Italian bedecked with modern Roman murals, this family-run sophisticate may be the "best in Downtown Hartford" according to admirers who marvel that it "keeps getting better"; the "first-rate", "beautifully presented" dishes include a "creative" swordfish and seared veal carpaccio.

Piccolo Arancio   25 | 22 | 22 | $36
819 Farmington Ave. (Rtes. 4 & 10), Farmington, 860-674-1224
■ This Farmington sib of Peppercorn's Grill aims to please with an "interesting" rustic Italian menu; the "excellent food" keeps it "very popular" and "noisy", but the warm, wood-toned interior is a "pleasing" antidote.

Polo Grille & Wine Bar 🖪   26 | 22 | 22 | $34
7 Elm St. (State St.), New Haven, 203-787-9000
■ New Haven Italian with "top-notch food and service", a wine bar with 36 selections by the glass and a "masculine" ambiance that includes cigar nights; it's "great for a business lunch" and holding up well in what was formerly a high-turnover location.

Quattro's 🖪   24 | 18 | 19 | $33
Strawberry Hill Plaza, 1300 Boston Post Rd. (opp. Bishop's Farm), Guilford, 203-453-6575
■ Though some snipe that the "same 10 trendy ingredients" show up in every dish, most love this Post Road "storefront" Italian with a "creative chef", where you can "make a meal" of the "stunning appetizers" alone or try the "great but expensive specials"; "plan way ahead" because it's "hard to get reservations."

Rebeccas 🖪   26 | 19 | 22 | $46
265 Glenville Rd. (Riversville Rd.), Greenwich, 203-532-9270
🗷 A "hot crowd" clamors to get into this "Manhattan-chic" New American on Glenville, where "awesome", "innovative" food is prepared in a glass-walled kitchen ("watch the crème brûlée being torched"); but while a "welcome addition" for the majority, cooler heads find it "pretentious" and "noisy", with "uncomfortable chairs" that remind many of "being back in grade school."

Restaurant du Village 🖪   28 | 25 | 26 | $48
59 Main St. (Maple St.), Chester, 860-526-5301
■ It's "always tops" at this "charming", chef-owned New French storefront classic (rated No. 1 for Food in the *CT Survey*) where the village is Chester but "you feel like you're in France"; devotees rave over the "great care [that] goes into each course" (the "bread is unforgettable") and sigh "just the aroma will make you salivate"; the "lovely setting" and "stellar service" are more reasons it's "worth the price"; N.B. dinner only, Wednesday–Sunday.

Roger Sherman Inn 🖪   23 | 25 | 23 | $46
195 Oenoke Ridge (Homewood Ln.), New Canaan, 203-966-4541
■ "A little tarnished" but still a "grand lady", this New Canaan landmark draws an "old-money crowd" for "elegant and formal" dining on Classic French cuisine ("try the soufflé"), "fine service", a piano bar and "lunch outside on a summer day"; regulars, citing a "turnabout", say "management has done a great job."

Sally's Apizza 🖪⊅   26 | 11 | 14 | $16
237 Wooster St. (Olive St.), New Haven, 203-624-5271
■ "Better make friends with Flo" (the "matriarch") because "privileged people don't wait in line" according to steamed observers who've cooled their heels waiting for "the best pizza in the world" at this Wooster Street grande dame; the drill: order a "sublime" white clam pie and listen to your neighbors argue whether it's "not quite Pepe's" or it "out Pepe's Pepe's."

Steve's Centerbrook Cafe §   26 | 22 | 24 | $38 |
78 Main St./Rte. 154 (Rte. 80), Centerbrook, 860-767-1277
■ Devotees call Steve Wilkinson "the best chef-host on the East Coast" for his "creative" New American dishes served in the "pretty setting" of a "friendly old home" in Centerbrook; "reasonable prices" make this twentysomething darling "one of the best deals in the Valley."

Stonehenge §   25 | 26 | 25 | $51 |
Stonehenge Inn, 35 Stonehenge Rd. (Rte. 7), Ridgefield, 203-438-6511
■ Admirers are rendered "speechless" by the "incredible lakeside" vistas, "fabulous" Continental cuisine and "elegant service" at this Ridgefield countryside "classic" that's been charming cognoscenti since 1946; all in all, it's the "perfect special-occasion" place and "worth a drive."

Thomas Henkelmann §   27 | 26 | 25 | $52 |
Homestead Inn, 420 Field Point Rd. (bet. Bush Ave. & Horseneck Ln.), Greenwich, 203-869-7500
■ "A special occasion deserves a special place", and this "romantic" Victorian "jewel" in Greenwich fits the bill, making it Connecticut's Most Popular restaurant; Thomas Henkelmann, chef-owner since '97, is "breathing new air" into this Classic French, a destination where "the well-heeled meet to eat" "world-class" cuisine; it's "a bit stuffy", maybe, but then again that's part of the "colonial charm."

Union League Cafe   24 | 25 | 23 | $37 |
1032 Chapel St. (bet. Crown & High Sts.), New Haven, 203-562-4299
■ "Fine French bistro food", including "magnificent soups" and "amazing desserts", is the draw at this Downtown "historic location" that's considered by many to be "New Haven's finest"; insiders advise: sit "near the fireplace" at one of the "widely spaced tables" in the "beautiful" dining room where service is "attentive" and "accommodating."

West Street Grill §   23 | 20 | 19 | $39 |
43 West St. (on the green), Litchfield, 860-567-3885
☑ "A lively, hip New Yorky sort of place" "to be seen", this "Litchfield goody" on the green pleases regulars with "light, tempting" New American cuisine served in a "sophisticated atmosphere"; but some feel it's "resting on its laurels", "needs some adrenaline" and charges "big prices" for "small portions."

TOP 20 FOOD RANKING

Restaurant	Cuisine Type
29 French Room	Classic French
28 Riviera	New French/Med.
Mansion on Turtle Creek	Southwestern
27 Pyramid Grill	Steakhouse/Seafood
Cafe Pacific	Seafood
Laurels	Eclectic
Bob's Steak & Chop Hse.	Steakhouse
York St.	New American
26 Del Frisco's	Steakhouse
Fogo de Chao	Brazilian/Steakhouse
Nana Grill	New American
Mediterraneo	Mediterranean
Hôtel St. Germain	French/Continental
Grape	Eclectic
Star Canyon	Texan/Southwestern
Green Room	New American
Chez Gerard	Country French/Bistro
25 Morton's of Chicago	Steakhouse
AquaKnox	Seafood
Lawry's	Steakhouse

ADDITIONAL NOTEWORTHY PLACES

Abacus	New American/Pacific Rim
Al Biernat's	Steakhouse/Seafood
Arc-en-Ciel	Chinese/Vietnamese
Capital Grille	Steakhouse/Seafood
Ciudad	Mexican
EatZi's	Eclectic
Il Sole	Mediterranean
Javier's	Mexican
Lombardi Mare	Italian/Seafood
Mi Piaci	Northern Italian
Nick & Sam's	Steakhouse
Palomino Euro Bistro	Mediterranean
Salve!	Northern Italian
Samba Room	Latin American/Fusion
Sevy's Grill	New American
Sonny Bryan's	Barbecue
Sullivan's	Steakhouse
Tramontana	French Bistro
Voltaire	New American
We Oui	French Bistro/Trad. American

Abacus
－ | － | － | E

4511 McKinney Ave. (Knox St.), 214-559-3111
Everything clicks at this Uptown jewel where the creative menu,
well-chosen wine list and sleek decor add up to some of the
city's most impressive dining; ever-popular chef/co-owner Kent
Rathbun crafts New American–Pacific Rim fare with flair – fans can
splurge on his eight-course tasting menu, which changes frequently.

Al Biernat's S
▽ 26 | 26 | 26 | $50

4217 Oak Lawn Ave. (bet. Herschel & Wycliff Aves.), 214-219-2201
■ Al Biernat, for many years the popular maitre d' of the Palm in
Dallas, now runs this eponymous Oak Lawn surf 'n' turfer in the
space that used to be the hip Joey's; his lobster salad is a hit, as
are his "awesome" sea bass and hefty cuts of beef; N.B. a lower-
priced menu now puts the above cost estimate into question.

AquaKnox S
25 | 26 | 23 | $48

3214 Knox St. (Cole Ave.), 214-219-2782
◪ "A must for seafood lovers" is the word on this "sophisticated"
Knox/Henderson standout; while the "gorgeous" decor is "worth"
seeing, what really draws the "chic clientele" is "impeccable",
imaginative aquatic fare from Stephan (Star Canyon) Pyles' "real
jewel" of a menu; N.B. the lounge area, christened Fish Bowl,
features light bites with an Asian twist.

Arc-en-Ciel S
21 | 9 | 16 | $14

3555 W. Walnut St. (Jupiter Rd.), Garland, 972-272-2188
■ This "huge" (1,600 seats), no-frills Garland Asian is "a bargain",
offering "possibly the best dim sum in town" ("get there early for
the best variety") along with a "wide menu" of other Chinese and
Vietnamese fare; service is "average" and there's not much decor,
but "even if you don't like Chinese food" it "makes you a believer."

Bob's Steak & Chop House
27 | 22 | 24 | $38

4300 Lemmon Ave. (Wycliff Ave.), 214-528-9446
■ This Uptown "classic" with the requisite "masculine, clubby"
look serves some of "the best steak in town (best value too)" and
is also lauded for its lamb chops and side dishes (it "wins the 'great
carrot' prize" for its honey-glazed version); grumblers cite "tight
quarters" and warn "don't breathe in the lounge – full of cigars",
but others find it the "most intimate", comfy steakhouse around.

Cafe Pacific
27 | 26 | 25 | $34

24 Highland Park Village (Mockingbird Ln. & Preston Rd.), 214-526-1170
■ "The best seafood in Dallas by far" rave fans of this "elegant"
Highland Park bistro that wows with "noteworthy" seviche and
the "best damn New England clam chowder west of Boston"; "old
money, old wine, new food" sums it up, and if a few complain of
waiters "direct from France", more cite "polished service" and
"people-watching" courtesy of the "Chanel/Escada/Hermès set."

Capital Grille S
－ | － | － | E

500 Crescent Ct. (bet. Cedar Springs Rd. & McKinney Ave.), 214-303-0500
This swank East Coast chain's Uptown surf 'n' turfer dazzles diners
with massive portions of prime beef and lobster; while the elegant
setting comes complete with the obligatory cigar lounge as well as
random celeb sightings and live jazz (Tuesday–Saturday), you
might want to check your corporate charge limit before entertaining.

Chez Gerard
26 | 22 | 23 | $34 |

4444 McKinney Ave. (1 block south of Knox St.), 214-522-6865

■ For "traditional Country French" dining, this "intimate, upscale" bistro on McKinney Avenue "still works every time", offering "outstanding" lamb, "terrific soufflés" and "great pommes frites" along with "excellent" service; it's thoroughly Gallic, right "down to the boutique wine list", and admirers rate it "one of the best French for the price", but even they don't like waiting despite reservations.

Ciudad S
– | – | – | M |

3888 Oak Lawn Ave. (Lemmon Ave.), 214-219-3141

Monica Greene is making many amigos with her casual, colorful Oak Lawn Mexican, which provides a new setting for the same food that turned her into a local celebrity; fans arrive ready to start off with a sprightly margarita and a plate of crispy duck flautas.

Del Frisco's Double Eagle Steak House
26 | 23 | 24 | $47 |

5251 Spring Valley Rd. (N. Dallas Pkwy.), 972-490-9000

☑ Legions of loyalists consider this "the best" steakhouse not just in North Dallas but "in the country" – "if my husband could pick his last meal on earth, this would be the place"; nitpickers fault "long" waits, sometimes "arrogant" service and "expense-account" prices ("everything à la carte"), but most think it's "steak heaven."

EatZi'S S
23 | 19 | 19 | $14 |

3403 Oak Lawn Ave. (Lemmon Ave.), 214-526-1515

■ "A lifesaver", "incredible takeout" and "the best grocery store ever" typify reactions to this Oak Lawn gourmet market/cafe offering a "fantastic selection of fresh, hard-to-get" provisions plus Eclectic prepared fare; it can be "chaotic" and "crowded", but fans say it's the "best thing to happen to Dallas since 'black gold'" – "wish there were more" (there are, but in other cities).

Fogo de Chao S
26 | 22 | 26 | $37 |

4300 Belt Line Rd. (Midway Rd.), Addison, 972-503-7300

■ "Wow!" – this "different" Brazilian steakhouse in Addison offers an unending parade of grilled meats and poultry presented on swords by gaucho-esque waiters; it's mostly a "meat-lovers' haven", but there's also a "gorgeous" salad bar and it's hard to beat for "great value and atmosphere"; "go hungry", and even then you may feel "like a goose being force-fed for foie gras."

French Room, The
29 | 29 | 28 | $61 |

Adolphus Hotel, 1321 Commerce St. (bet. Akard & Field Sts.), 214-742-8200

■ Rated No. 1 for Food, Decor and Service in Dallas, this "flawless" Downtown Classic French combines "incredible" cooking with a "beautiful, very formal" setting and "skilled service" to achieve the "ultimate dining experience" – this is "romance at its best" and, remarkably, most detect "no stuffy airs" ("I felt like a queen"); *très cher* it is, but such "very special" experiences rarely come cheap.

Grape, The ●S
26 | 22 | 23 | $26 |

2808 Greenville Ave. (bet. Monticello Ave. & Vickery Blvd.), 214-828-1981

■ Aging "like fine wine" say admirers of this Eclectic bistro on Greenville that's been going strong for over 25 years and remains "one of the most romantic restaurants around"; with its dark, "comfy, laid-back room", "nifty wine" list and blackboard menu featuring the likes of "terrific mushroom soup", it's an "all-time favorite."

Green Room, The 🅂

26 | 20 | 21 | $32

2715 Elm St. (Crowdus St.), 214-748-7666

■ "Funky" and "eclectic" describe both the ambiance and the "creative food" at this "hip" Deep Ellum New American; Marc Cassel (ex Star Canyon) runs the kitchen, and his nightly four-course 'Feed Me' prix fixe ($36 without wine, $58 with) is a popular "good deal"; the "wonderful open patio" is a plus on fine evenings.

Hôtel St. Germain

26 | 27 | 26 | VE

Hôtel St. Germain, 2516 Maple Ave. (bet. Cedar Springs Rd. & McKinney Ave.), 214-871-2516

■ The "exceptional European" ambiance of this Uptown Victorian home sets the stage for New and Classic French–Continental fare that most find "exquisite" and "a bargain" even at the prix fixe tab of $85; considered the "epitome of elegance", it's a "classy" place.

Il Sole 🅂

– | – | – | M

4514 Travis St. (Fitzhugh Ave.), 214-559-3888

Mi Piaci–bred owners Brian and Sonia Black and chef Tim Penn boast decades of restaurant experience among them, and it sure shows at their Mediterranean Uptown yearling; the interior is soothing, the wine list invites serious study and the food delights, from the satisfying honey-glazed chicken to the maple crème brûlée; N.B. their balcony is one of the best people-watching spots in town.

Javier's 🅂

25 | 24 | 23 | $26

4912 Cole Ave. (Harvard Ave.), 214-521-4211

■ "Excellent", "real Mexico City" eats, including the "best mole in Dallas" and "awesome black bean soup", are served in an "upscale" yet "low-key" ambiance at this North of Downtown "favorite"; it's "crowded and noisy", but "if you can get in, you can't go wrong"; N.B. the goat entree ranks as one of Dallas' best forkfuls.

Laurels

27 | 27 | 23 | $49

Westin Park Central Hotel, 12720 Merit Dr. (Coit Rd.), 972-851-2021

■ Commanding an "excellent view" from atop the Westin Park Central, this 'global fusion' specialist offers what some call "the ultimate dining in Dallas"; foodies love the "exciting", "innovative" Eclectic menu, which is served by a pro staff in an "elegant" ambiance – in sum, a "class operation."

Lawry's the Prime Rib 🅂

25 | 23 | 24 | $33

14655 Dallas Pkwy. (bet. Belt Line & Spring Valley Rds.), Addison, 972-503-6688

■ "Red-meat indulgence" is shamelessly alive at the Addison outpost of this beef emporium known for the "best prime rib around", "heavenly mashed potatoes" and "excellent Yorkshire pudding"; the "men's club" ambiance is backed up by "old-world service" and the sandwich bar is also a big draw.

Lombardi Mare 🅂

23 | 25 | 22 | $34

Village on the Parkway, 5100 Belt Line Rd. (Montfort Dr.), Addison, 972-503-1233

■ "The little black dress is alive and well" at this "chic", "very Uptown" Far North Italian seafooder, praised for its "excellent", "fresh" (albeit "a bit pricey") fare and "attentive service"; it's "worth a trip just to see" the place, especially the bar scene, which unfolds beneath goldfish swimming in bowls suspended overhead.

Mansion on Turtle Creek S
28 | 28 | 27 | $56

Mansion on Turtle Creek, 2821 Turtle Creek Blvd. (Gillespie St.), 214-559-2100

■ "Top class in every way", Dallas' Most Popular restaurant showcases the "awesome" Southwestern fare of Dean Fearing, who "sets the standard" with dishes like lobster tacos and tortilla soup; a "classy" Downtown setting and "knowledgeable" (a few say "stuffy") service are more reasons why it's "worth a splurge" – "when you hit the lottery, this is the place to celebrate!"

Mediterraneo S
26 | 25 | 24 | $38

18111 Preston Rd. (Frankford Rd.), 972-447-0066

☑ "One of the first great ones in Far North Dallas" say fans of this Mediterranean with "imaginative food", "understated elegance" and "some of the best service in town"; on the downside, it can get "noisy", but it's a place "to be seen", not necessarily heard.

Mi Piaci Ristorante S
24 | 24 | 21 | $32

14854 Montfort Rd. (Belt Line Rd.), Addison, 972-934-8424

■ This "elegant, sophisticated" Addison Northern Italian is "a great package", with a "romantic" setting and "excellent" fare, notably the osso buco and tortelloni fonduta; patrons appreciate the fact that they cure their own meats, grow their own herbs and bake their own bread.

Morton's of Chicago S
25 | 23 | 24 | $43

501 Elm St. (Houston St.), 214-741-2277
14831 Midway Rd. (Belt Line Rd.), Addison, 972-233-5858

■ For the last word in "excellent prime beef from the Midwest", old-school meat eaters turn to this Downtown and Addison steakhouse duo; they're "expensive", but the combination of "large portions", "attentive service" and elegant atmosphere (with muted lighting, dark wood and etched glass) is sure to "impress clients."

Nana Grill S
26 | 27 | 25 | $44

Wyndham Anatole Hotel, 2201 Stemmons Frwy. (I-35), 214-761-7470

■ With its "breathtaking" view of the Downtown skyline, this New American in the Wyndham Anatole offers some of the "most romantic" dining around; it's also an ideal place to "entertain", thanks to "excellent food", "terrific service" and "superb" wines, all of which justify the "expensive" tab.

Nick & Sam's S
– | – | – | E

3008 Maple Ave. (Oak Lawn Ave.), 214-871-7444

One never knows what to expect at this Uptown steakhouse where free caviar in the bar and a grand piano positioned right outside the open kitchen signal it's no mainstream meatery; but don't let the high style and the deafening decibels distract from the prime cuts served with 'damngood' (as the menu would have it) fries.

Palomino Euro Bistro S
23 | 26 | 23 | $32

Crescent Court, 500 Crescent Ct. (bet. Cedar Springs Rd. & Pearl St.), 214-999-1222

☑ "Beautiful" sums up the decor, the food and the clientele at this suave and "glitzy" Mediterranean at the Crescent Court; it follows through with "very good service" and "reasonable prices", but predictably, skeptics find it too "trendy" – the "cell-phone capital of the US."

Pyramid Grill [S] 27 27 27 $51
(fka Pyramid Room)
Fairmont Hotel, 1414 N. Akard St. (Ross Ave.), 214-720-5249
■ This "well-kept secret" offers "everything you'd want" in Downtown seafooder-steakhouse dining, i.e. a "classy, quiet" ambiance and "outstanding" food and service; celebrants proclaim this "*the* place for anniversaries, proposals, birthdays and clinching" deals; N.B. don't miss the lobster bisque.

Riviera, The 28 27 28 $57
7709 Inwood Rd. (Lovers Ln.), 214-351-0094
◪ Some of "the best food in the city" (rated No. 2 in Dallas) gives this Inwood New French–Med a strong start, and it goes the distance with a "suave" setting, a "primo" wine list and a staff that treats each patron as a "pampered guest"; however, it stumbles a bit in the eyes of critics who find the prices and the noise level too high.

Salve! [S] – – – E
2120 McKinney Ave. (Pearl St.), 214-220-0070
The authentic Tuscan experience is alive and well at this Uptown Italian newcomer where the chic meet and greet over classic cuisine matched with a sublime wine list; insiders know to rely on attentive maitre d' Wayne Broadwell, and to save room for pastry chef David Brawley's sweet sensations.

Samba Room, The ◐[S] – – – M
4514 Travis St. (Armstrong Ave.), 214-522-4137
Located in the heart of hip Knox/Henderson, this upscale yet relaxed Latin fusion stop features Italian marble floors, a cigar lounge, a patio and a kitchen turning out a moderately priced mix focusing on Cuban and Brazilian cuisines; after a taste of the seared tuna, you'll know you're on to the next big trend.

Sevy's Grill [S] 22 22 20 $27
8201 Preston Rd. (Sherry Ln.), 214-265-7389
◪ This New American on Preston Road is a "solid performer" that's considered "outstanding in its price range", with a "tasty" menu enhanced by "good wine selections"; "noise is a problem", but they're working on it, and the back room is ideal for groups in search of privacy.

Sonny Bryan's 21 11 15 $11
2202 Inwood Rd. (bet. Forest Park Rd. & Harry Hines Blvd.), 214-357-7120 [S]
Galleria Mall, 133-75 Dallas Pkwy. (bet. LBJ Frwy. & N. Dallas Tollway), 972-851-5131
4701 Frankford Rd. (bet. Dallas Pkwy. & Pear Ridge Rd.), 972-447-0102 [S]
302 N. Market St. (Pacific Ave.), 214-744-1610 [S]
Republic Towers, 325 N. St. Paul St. (bet. Bryan St. & Pacific Ave.), 214-979-0102
■ Texas reveres its BBQ, and to loyalists this "legend" is simply "the best BBQ in Dallas since dirt", especially the Inwood original; "no out-of-town guest should depart the state before eating this good meat", nor before learning to "love those onion rings"; hard-core connoisseurs need no encouragement to "put on some old clothes and go wallow" in the 'cue – and they never fail to "take home some sauce."

Star Canyon [S] 26 27 24 $41

3102 Oak Lawn Ave. (Cedar Springs Rd.), 214-520-7827

■ Sure, it's "hard to get reservations" at this Oak Lawn Texan-Southwestern, but that's because so many people think "Stephan Pyles does it best" when it comes to "interesting combinations of tastes and flavors" and "impeccable presentation"; "Texan elegant" decor and sharp service help make it a "true Texas feast" that's worth the expense and effort to get in; N.B. now open for lunch.

Sullivan's – – – E

17795 N. Dallas Pkwy. (Briargrove Ln.), 972-267-9393

This North Dallas offshoot of a chain steakhouse offers two cigar-friendly bars and a mammoth wine list, but deviates from the norm with a '40s theme, featuring a swing band Thursday–Saturday and impromptu dancing – even though there's no formal dance floor.

Tramontana – – – M

8220B Westchester Dr. (Northwest Hwy.), 214-368-4188

He's already a local favorite, and chef-owner James Neel (ex Al Biernat's) continues to work wonders at this welcoming Preston Center French bistro, which he took over a year ago; although Neel is building its rep with tasty Gallic favorites, he also turns out a top-notch burger, complete with skinny, crisp fries.

Voltaire – – – E

5150 Keller Springs Rd. (Dallas Pkwy.), 972-239-8988

Unveiled amid reports of a $12 million–plus price tag, this North Dallas New American is dressed to impress with its innovative lighting, minimalist design and museum-worthy glass sculptures courtesy of owner Scott Ginsburg; raves for the foie gras–topped tenderloin, the wine and dessert lists and the happening bar scene prove it has substance to match its enlightened style.

We Oui [S] – – – M

Hotel Crescent Court, 100 Crescent Court (McKinney Ave.), 214-220-3990

This vividly decorated Uptown upstart serves Traditional American food with a French accent – and French food with an American accent – at an attractive price; it draws a hip crowd with bistro standouts like the rotisserie chicken, meaty frogs' legs and (but of course) classic pommes frites.

York St. 27 22 26 $39

6047 Lewis St. (bet. Live Oak & Skillman Sts.), 214-826-0968

■ This "hidden gem" in Old East Dallas offers a "fabulous" New American menu, and there's "no friendlier staff in town than owner Felissa [Shaw]" and company; add a "romantic" setting and you have the ideal "date place" and "a real find."

Denver Area &
Mountain Resorts

TOP 20 FOOD RANKING

	Restaurant	Cuisine Type
28	Papillon Cafe	New French
	Highlands Garden Cafe	New American
	Sweet Basil	New American
27	Renaissance	Med./New American
	Keystone Ranch	New American
	Palace Arms	Continental/Trad. Amer.
	Splendido	New American
	Sushi Den	Japanese
	Wildflower	New American
	Tante Louise	French
	Grouse Mtn. Grill	Regional American
	Charles Court	Continental/New Amer.
	La Petite Maison	French
26	Briarwood Inn	Trad. American/Continental
	Alpenglow Stube	Regional American
	Cafe Brazil	Brazilian
	La Montaña	Mexican/Southwestern
	Barolo Grill	Northern Italian
	Piñons*	Regional American
	Del Frisco's	Steakhouse

ADDITIONAL NOTEWORTHY PLACES

Restaurant	Cuisine Type
Aubergine Cafe	French Bistro/Med.
Bang!	Traditional American
Beehive	Med./New American
Domo	Japanese
Flagstaff House	Continental/New Amer.
Jax Fish House	Seafood
Kevin Taylor	New American
Little Nell	New American
Manhattan Grill	Steakhouse/Trad. American
Mel's Bar & Grill	Californian/Med.
Ombra	N/S Italian
Potager	New American
Radex	New American
Roy's	Eurasian
Rue Cler	Eclectic
Sacre Bleu	New American
Strings	New American/Med.
240 Union	New American
Vesta Dipping Grill	Eclectic
Watercourse Foods	Vegetarian

* Tied with the restaurant listed directly above it.

Alpenglow Stube 🅂   26 | 28 | 26 | $56

Keystone Resort, 154 Soda Ridge Rd. (top of N. Peak Mtn.), Keystone, 970-496-4386

■ Diners yodel in favor of this Keystone Regional American, the country's highest restaurant at 12,000 feet, serving "terrific food in an unforgettable setting", backed up by "impeccable service"; it's "worth the money" for a "blowout celebration" – the gondola ride up and down "is the crème de la crème."

Aubergine Cafe 🅂   26 | 22 | 24 | $30

225 E. Seventh Ave. (bet. Grant & Sherman Sts.), Denver, 303-832-4778

■ For "true Mediterranean bistro food" in what some call the "most romantic setting" in Denver, fans head to this near-Downtown "friendly, comfortable and consistent" "little slice of heaven" with "innovative" cooking, a "carefully selected wine list" and a "knowledgeable staff"; but this "like-Provence" "gem" can be "a little crowded", so reserve early.

Bang!   25 | 14 | 17 | $14

3609 W. 32nd Ave. (bet. Lowell Blvd. & Meade St.), Denver, 303-455-1117

■ A "tiny", "bang-up" North Denver "hole-in-the-wall" serving "superb" "homestyle" Traditional American food ("wonderful soups", "great meat loaf") that's "exactly what mom should have cooked but couldn't"; despite "counter service", "fluorescent lighting" and the "competition to snag a table", addicts yearn for a "clone" in their nabe – though many also yearn for a liquor license.

Barolo Grill   26 | 25 | 24 | $37

3030 E. Sixth Ave. (bet. Milwaukee & St. Paul Sts.), Denver, 303-393-1040

■ "Go to Italy or go here" rave fans of the "scrumptious" cooking at this "lovely" East Denver Northern Italian where the "owner's attention to details shows", especially in the "best Italian wine list in the West"; although service, while "knowledgeable", strikes critics as "self-important", ratings support boosters who say it "gets better every year."

Beehive   – | – | – | M

606 Corona St. (E. 6th Ave.), Denver, 303-832-5766

One of the newer additions to Denver's Congress Park neighborhood, this hip Med–New American yearling combines the winning duo of Janice Henning (chef) and hubby Tim Elenteny (sommelier) for terrific, hearty eats and super (mostly imported) wines.

Briarwood Inn, The 🅂   26 | 27 | 26 | $40

1630 Eighth St. (Hwy. 58 & US 6), Golden, 303-279-3121

☑ "Don't eat the day before you dine here" advise patrons of this "lavish", "romantic" Traditional American–Continental in Golden known for "superb meals" served in an atmosphere of "absolute elegance"; though a few bicker it's "past its prime", it remains a "traditionalist's paradise" that's "expensive and worth it."

Cafe Brazil ⌀   26 | 17 | 23 | $25

3611 Navajo St. (W. 36th Ave.), Denver, 303-480-1877

■ The "smells will drive you crazy and make your tongue dance" gush admirers of the "fabulous food" you will "dream about and crave" at North Denver's "hip" Brazilian "hideaway"; it may be just a "hole-in-the-wall with style", but it's "homey", service is "charming" and oh, the grub – an "indescribable, wonderful melding of flavors"; N.B. reservations are "a must" – and so is hard cash.

Charles Court S | 27 | 27 | 26 | $46 |
Broadmoor Hotel, 1 Lake Ave., Colorado Springs, 719-634-7711
☑ The Broadmoor's fine dining room in Colorado Springs is a "formal" Continental–New American offering "the perfect getaway for a romantic evening", with a "beautiful view of Broadmoor Lake", an "elegant, comfortable setting" and "consistent, proven" food and service; although casual sorts find it too "costly" and "stuffy", ratings say it all for the majority: a "treat for special occasions."

Del Frisco's Double Eagle Steak House | 26 | 25 | 25 | $48 |
Denver Tech Ctr., 8100 E. Orchard Rd. (I-25), Greenwood Village, 303-796-0100
■ "Texas comes to Denver" at this "extremely expensive but excellent" Greenwood Villager, where a "top-notch" staff delivers "power dinners" of "great" martinis and mammoth hunks of seared steer in a "clubby setting" accented by a "fabulous cigar bar"; though many find it "incredibly enjoyable" (and rate it the top steakhouse in the Colorado *Survey*), a few beef "big is not always beautiful" and warn you'll "spend a bundle."

Domo | 25 | 28 | 21 | $23 |
1365 Osage St. (Colfax Ave.), Denver, 303-595-3666
■ "A joy to the palate and a delight to the eyes" gush devotees of this "unique" Denver Downtowner that's "like a Japanese country inn" with a "very traditional menu" ("no sushi, no sashimi") of "food you didn't even know existed"; but the "stunning" decor ("stone tables", "large Japanese garden") and unusual, "authentic" fare draw crowds, leading to "interminable waits" (no reserving), and "inept" service doesn't help matters.

Flagstaff House S | 26 | 27 | 25 | $48 |
1138 Flagstaff Rd. (on Flagstaff Mtn.), Boulder, 303-442-4640
■ Boulder's top "special-occasion" restaurant earns applause for its "elegant" and "imaginative" (albeit "pricey") Continental–New American dining, "amazing wine list" and, especially, for its "fantastic view" of the city below (it's the "best place to take out-of-state visitors" or "someone you love"); while most agree it has "few, if any, flaws", there are gripes about service that's "terribly impressed with itself."

Grouse Mountain Grill S | 27 | 26 | 25 | $47 |
Beaver Creek Resort, 141 Scott Hill Rd. (Village Rd.), Avon, 970-949-0600
■ "Gorgeous and delicious" sums up this "intimate, quiet" Beaver Creek Regional American with a "great view" of the Valley below and "extraordinary food, decor and service", plus a "top-notch wine selection", inside; though the "delicious, large portions could serve two people", save room for the "excellent desserts."

Highlands Garden Cafe | 28 | 27 | 26 | $33 |
3927 W. 32nd Ave. (bet. Osceola & Perry Sts.), Denver, 303-458-5920
■ "Open your eyes, it's not a dream" counsel enthusiasts of this North Denver New American (No. 2 for Food in the Colorado *Survey*), where two "lovely older homes" redone into softly lit dining rooms provide the setting for "one of Denver's very best" and well-priced menus; "if you eat inside, though, you've missed" the "fabulous gardens", so "dine by candlelight among the roses" at what may be the "most romantic restaurant in town."

F	D	S	C

Jax Fish House 🅂 | 24 | 19 | 20 | $27 |

1539 17th St. (Wazee St.), Denver, 303-292-5767

◪ The praise – and pans – come in waves for this "hip" Denver seafooder offering "proof that you can get great seafood without a nearby coast"; although the "fresh fish" is "perfectly prepared" and the "bustling atmosphere" strikes some as "vibrant" and "fun", others rail about the "deafening music", "rude yuppie crowds" and "no reservation" policy; your call.

Kevin Taylor | 25 | 26 | 25 | $54 |

Hotel Teatro, 1106 14th St. (Arapahoe St.), Denver, 303-820-2600

◪ Although star chef Kevin Taylor's Downtown Denver New American scores highly, diners report mixed reactions: aficionados point to the "elegant" food, "ethereal" space, "amazing wine list" and "superb ingredients", but foes retort it's "too expensive" ("my wallet hurts just thinking about it") and claim its "reach exceeds its grasp"; ratings, however, side with fans.

Keystone Ranch Restaurant 🅂 | 27 | 27 | 27 | $56 |

Keystone Ranch Resort (2½ mi. west of Hwy. 6), Keystone, 970-496-4386

◼ "Elegant, excellent but expensive" are the three Es at this "must-go" Summit County New American in the "best setting imaginable" – a "historic ranch home" with "superb views" of Keystone Valley; although "pricey", consensus is it's "worth it" for the "gourmet" "prix fixe" meals ("excellent game"), "impeccable service" and "world-class setting."

La Montaña 🅂 | 26 | 21 | 21 | $29 |

Village Ctr., 2500 Village Dr. (Après Ski Way), Steamboat Springs, 970-879-5800

◼ "Excellent", "upscale" Mexican-SW food is the deal at this "sizeable but cozy, second-story" Steamboat Springs beanery; "unusual combinations" and "pretty presentations" add up to "outstanding" eats, so "make reservations."

La Petite Maison | 27 | 25 | 27 | $34 |

1015 W. Colorado Ave. (bet. 10th & 11th Sts.), Colorado Springs, 719-632-4887

◼ Colorado Springs' oldest French restaurant, set in a "darling house", offers "excellent" "classical" and "innovative" cooking presented "with flair", plus a "nice wine list" and "very good individual service"; it's perfect "for a romantic dinner", although perhaps "a little too cutesy" for a few; P.S. insiders advise "try the pâté and try not to fill up on the bread."

Little Nell Restaurant 🅂 | 26 | 26 | 26 | $49 |

Little Nell Hotel, 675 E. Durant St. (Spring St.), Aspen, 970-920-6330

◼ It's "worth every dollar you will spend" purr enthusiasts of this "very cosmopolitan", "pricey" Aspen hotel dining room where, despite chef turnover, pampered sybarites continue to enjoy "fantastic" New American fare and a "great wine list" in a "gorgeous" setting; don't miss the "courtyard for an alfresco lunch."

Manhattan Grill 🅂 | – | – | – | E |

231 Milwaukee St. (bet. 2nd & 3rd Aves.), Denver, 303-333-6444

Already known for its super-tender, dry-aged Chicago beef, this Cherry Creek Traditional American newcomer also has a nice way with seafood and a 'town club' salad that's Denver's best and tastiest way to eat your vegetables; nightly jazz in a clubby atmosphere adds appeal.

Mel's Bar & Grill S   24 | 22 | 22 | $33 |
235 Fillmore St. (bet. 2nd & 3rd Aves.), Denver, 303-333-3979
☑ "Melvyn Master is an excellent host" at his Cherry Creek North Cal-Med, where the ambiance is "terrific" if "always slightly chaotic" (especially with the "singles scene" at the "smoky bar"); add a "frequently changing menu", "great wine list" and "hip" and "very loyal clientele" and you've got a "constant in Denver"; those who don't "feel part of the sophisticated family" gripe that this "Elaine's wanna-be" is "overrated."

Ombra   – | – | – | M |
300 Fillmore St. (3rd Ave.), Denver, 303-333-1133
At this Cherry Creek newcomer, mother and daughter Elena and Chiara Marzano (both hailing from the old country) feed you 'as Italians eat' in Mama Elena's words – 'no rock star chef, no complicated food, just simple'; it's as good an example of fine Italian dining as Denver has seen in years, and at reasonable prices to boot.

Palace Arms S   27 | 28 | 27 | $47 |
Brown Palace Hotel, 321 17th St. (bet. Broadway & Tremont Pl.), Denver, 303-297-3111
■ The top-drawer dining room of the 104-year-old Brown Palace Hotel, this Downtown Denver Traditional American–Continental is the "only superelegant, plush restaurant left", according to devotees who rave about its "old Denver" "class, class, class", "turn-of-the-century furnishings" and "impeccable" (if slightly "snooty") service; it may be "for the filthy rich", but it's "worth the price" to "feel like royalty"; N.B. jacket and tie required.

Papillon Cafe S   28 | 25 | 25 | $38 |
250 Josephine St. (bet. 2nd & 3rd Aves.), Denver, 303-333-7166
■ No. 1 for Food and Popularity in our Colorado *Survey*, this Denver New French with Asian accents offers chef-owner Radek Cerny's "outstanding" cuisine that's "as beautifully presented as it is delicious" (though wags warn you "could get vertigo" from the vertical constructions); "well-coached servers" and an "intelligent" wine list leave little room for complaint, though one diner tries: "I hate restaurants where everything on the menu is great."

Piñons S   26 | 25 | 26 | $54 |
105 S. Mill St. (Main St.), Aspen, 970-920-2021
■ "Go for the venison" say boosters of this "pricey" Aspen Regional American attracting an "older crowd" with "excellent game" and other "delicious" fare enhanced by "wonderful service" and "gorgeous" Western decor; though a few gripe that the "menu hasn't changed in 10 years", the majority applauds the fact that it "oozes consistency."

Potager   25 | 22 | 22 | $31 |
1109 Ogden St. (bet. 11th & 12th Aves.), Denver, 303-832-5788
☑ Most agree that this "airy", "hip, urban" Denver New American "addition to the Capitol Hill scene" does up a "clever menu" of "fab food in a funky" but "comfortable" setting (a former laundry in a newly urbanized area) where the "outdoor seating in the back is a great touch"; "inconsistent" service is the main complaint, though even fans admit the "adventurous", "changing" bill of fare is "sometimes too avant-garde."

Radex ◐ [S] — 25 | 23 | 23 | $29

100 E. Ninth Ave. (Lincoln St.), Denver, 303-861-7999

◩ "Wonderful martinis" and "interesting" New American food from "genius" chef-owner Radek Cerny draw the "beautiful people" to this younger and less expensive Papillon sib; admirers of this Denver hot spot gush it's "so cool, from the hip staff to the superchic interior" – though cynics claim the latter is "like unfinished South Beach"; N.B. live jazz is another draw.

Renaissance [S] — 27 | 25 | 26 | $57

304 E. Hopkins Ave. (bet. Mill & Monarch Sts.), Aspen, 970-925-2402

◩ "Well-heeled clients" shower encomiums on Aspen's toniest Med–New American, giving high marks to its "unbelievably professional staff" and "generally superb", "imaginative and creative" food in a "very elegant" setting that's good for "celebrity watching"; although a few cite occasional "misses" and find it a bit "pretentious", those who can handle the high tabs rate it one of the "best in the state" and a "favorite anywhere."

Roy's [S] — – | – | – | M

Cherry Creek Ctr., 3000 E. First Ave. (Fillmore St.), Denver, 303-333-9300

Cherry Creek's Eurasian outpost from star toque Roy Yamaguchi is already a zinger, with quick-on-the-heels service (among the best in Denver), a slew of fin and gill from the kitchen and sauces (aka 'reductions') that number into the 60s; the tony, suntanned crowd the area is famous for provides the perfect final touch to this Hawaiian-based import.

Rue Cler [S] — – | – | – | M

5575 E. Third Ave. (Holly St.), Denver, 303-355-3775

Chef Michael Degenhart just got tired one day after 12 years of *pâté de la maison* at restaurant Tante Louise, so he opened his own smashingly clean-lined East Denver eatery offering Eclectic fare that spans the northern hemisphere, such as quail tagine and braised lamb shank.

Sacre Bleu [S] — – | – | – | E

410 E. Seventh Ave. (bet. Logan & Penn Sts.), Denver, 303-832-6614

An incandescently hot restaurant and late-night haunt of the city's dazzling younger set, this Capitol Hill New American with Provençal influences (read: arugula with shaved foie gras) bleu . . . um, blew a bundle on Denver's slickest, East Coast–ish decor; a super wine list bolsters the menu.

Splendido [S] — 27 | 27 | 26 | $58

The Chateau at Beaver Creek Resort, 17 Chateau Ln. (Scott Hill Rd.), Avon, 970-845-8808

■ This "elegant" New American in an "awesome" setting high above Beaver Creek Valley offers "sublime" food and a "great wine list", delivered by a refreshingly "down-to-earth" staff that will nonetheless treat you "royally"; so while "expensive", the "fully satisfied" find it "worth it" – "save for a very special occasion."

Strings [S] — 26 | 23 | 24 | $34

1700 Humboldt St. (17th Ave.), Denver, 303-831-7310

◩ "As close to casual but elegant dining as can be had in Denver" claim buffs of this "bright, appealing" and affordable Uptown New American–Med "institution" that's *the* place for "power lunching"; however, there are grumbles about "uneven service."

Sushi Den 🖺   27 | 24 | 20 | $30
1487 S. Pearl St. (Florida Ave.), Denver, 303-777-0827
☑ This Washington Park high-end Japanese "home to the beautiful people" may be "painfully hip" and as "chichi as they come", but most concur it also "puts the fresh in sushi" and is "worth the wait you'll undoubtedly have"; wet blankets cite "arrogant" patrons and staff and insist "there's better sushi in Denver", but they're loudly overruled by enthusiasts who swear "nothing even compares."

Sweet Basil 🖺   28 | 23 | 24 | $40
193 E. Gore Creek Dr. (Bridge St.), Vail, 970-476-0125
■ Whether it's the "ultra-hip" cuisine, "well-done service", "great outdoor seating" or the "sound of the river below", the bottom line on this Vail New American is that it "reaches great heights without being unreasonably expensive"; not surprisingly, it's "always crowded", so "make reservations."

Tante Louise   27 | 26 | 26 | $42
4900 E. Colfax Ave. (Eudora St.), Denver, 303-355-4488
■ "A favorite after all these years", this East Denver French vet still delivers "romantic dining" and "unpretentious elegance" in a "lovely old home"; "gracious host" Corky Douglass "uncorks a great meal" and "oversees a great wine list", and if a few callow souls consider this "classic" a "fossil", its adoring clientele cherishes it as a "sanctuary for life before baseball caps and jeans."

240 Union 🖺   26 | 22 | 24 | $31
240 Union Blvd. (3 blocks south of 6th Ave. Frwy.), Lakewood, 303-989-3562
■ It's unanimous: this "underappreciated" New American "jewel" is "hands down the best restaurant" on the West Side of the Denver area, serving a "creative", "fabulous" menu in a "congenial setting"; it's for "that special night" made better by "superb service" – just beware "the noisy, yuppie lunch crowd."

Vesta Dipping Grill 🖺   22 | 24 | 21 | $29
1822 Blake St. (bet. 18th & 19th Sts.), Denver, 303-296-1970
☑ "Smart, sexy and tasty" sum up this LoDo Eclectic, well regarded for its "inventive, hip and urban" decor and "awesome", "unique" menu that's "the freshest idea to hit Denver this decade" (the specialty is skewers of grilled meat or seafood served with dipping sauces); those out of the loop whine that it's "noisy" and "too trendy by half", but most give a thumbs-up to this "fun place to dip."

Watercourse Foods 🖺   22 | 13 | 19 | $12
206 E. 13th Ave. (bet. Grant & Sherman Sts.), Denver, 303-832-7313
■ This "New Age–style", "very affordable" and "friendly" Capitol Hill Vegetarian sports a "thinking" chef who's earning big kudos (and a "place in Denver's eating scene") for his "incredible", "creative" and "satisfying" eats; it's "people-watching" central, and now serves dinner as well as breakfast ("the best") and lunch.

Wildflower 🖺   27 | 27 | 25 | $46
The Lodge at Vail, 174 E. Gore Creek Dr. (base of Vail Mountain), Vail, 970-476-5011
■ Superlatives abound for this "beautiful", "fabulous" and "expensive" Vail New American, with diners throwing bouquets for the "world-class", "super-elegant" food, "wonderful service" and "gorgeous" decor with "flowers everywhere"; those in the know say it's "lovely to eat outside [on the patio] in the summer."

Fort Lauderdale

TOP 10 FOOD RANKING

	Restaurant	Cuisine Type
28	Eduardo de San Angel	Mexican
	Darrel & Oliver's Cafe Maxx	New World
26	Armadillo Cafe	Southwestern
	Mark's Las Olas	New American
	Black Orchid Cafe	Continental
	Primavera	N/S Italian
25	Ruth's Chris	Steakhouse
	Brooks	Continental
	Sunfish Grill	Seafood
	Hobo's Fish Joint	Seafood

ADDITIONAL NOTEWORTHY PLACES

Bistro Mezzaluna	New American
Burt & Jack's	Steakhouse/Seafood
Cafe Martorano	N/S Italian
Casa D'Angelo	N/S Italian
Himmarshee Bar & Grill	New American
Hot Chocolates	Eclectic
Left Bank	French Bistro
Nevis	New American
Samba Room	Latin American/Fusion
Victoria Park	Eclectic

	F	D	S	C
Armadillo Cafe [S]	26	19	23	$40

4630 SW 64th Ave. (Griffin Rd.), Davie, 954-791-5104

■ "Worth a trip" to "out-of-the-way" Davie, this culinary pioneer "brought Southwestern cooking to South Florida" and continues to produce "outstanding", "innovative" cuisine out of a recently expanded, but still "unlikely", strip mall storefront; expect a "quiet" atmosphere, "friendly" service and such signature dishes as porcini-dusted sea bass (a "must try") and lobster quesadilla; N.B. a move to South University Drive was in the works at press time.

	F	D	S	C
Bistro Mezzaluna	23	20	21	$37

741 SE 17th St. (S. Federal Hwy.), 954-522-6620

■ A Central Broward "place to be seen" for "trendy yuppies", especially at its "upbeat bar", this Italian-accented New American also delivers "wonderful" food in an "elegant setting"; while spoilers warn about a "loud" decibel level, a visit is usually "a treat."

F | D | S | C

Black Orchid Cafe [S] 26 | 23 | 22 | $43
2985 N. Ocean Blvd. (south of E. Oakland Park Blvd.), 954-561-9398
■ This "very romantic" Central Broward Continental lives up to its film-noir name with live music, a "classy", orchid-filled setting and a "fantastic selection of exotic food", including African game pheasant and ostrich matched with "great wines"; it doesn't come cheap, but daring diners confirm that "everything is wonderful."

Brooks [S] 25 | 23 | 24 | $38
500 S. Federal Hwy. (¼ mi. south of Hillsboro Blvd.), Deerfield Beach, 954-427-9302
■ An ideal "opportunity to dress up" in casual Deerfield Beach, this "classy" Continental attracts "older" "groups" who like to mark "special occasions" in its "intimate", formal rooms, which are furnished with comfortable Queen Anne chairs; whippersnappers find the atmosphere a little "stiff" and "not very exciting", but appreciate the "quality" food and conscientious service.

Burt & Jack's [S] 22 | 25 | 22 | $45
Berth 23 (South Terminal), Port Everglades, 954-522-5225
◪ "A fabulous view of cruise ships plying Port Everglades" is the star attraction at this "upscale" surf 'n' turfer, co-owned by Burt Reynolds and recommended for "romantic" "special occasions" ("we got married here"); critics dis it as an "overpriced", "expense-account venue" with an "outdated" jacket-required policy.

Cafe Martorano 25 | 17 | 19 | $50
3343 E. Oakland Park Blvd. (A1A), 954-561-2554
◪ While it attracts a "superstar" clientele and serves undeniably "excellent" Philadelphia-accented Italian food, this "very small", "trendy" Central Broward venue otherwise plays to mixed reviews, with dissenters reporting "very expensive" prices, service issues ("snooty") and a high decibel level fueled by loud music.

Casa D'Angelo [S] 24 | 22 | 24 | $38
Sunrise Sq. Plaza, 1201 N. Federal Hwy. (bet. E. Sunrise Blvd. & NE 13th Ave.), Ft. Lauderdale, 954-564-1234
■ One of the "best" "upscale" Italians in Central Broward, this handsome Tuscan eatery has a wood-burning brick oven that produces fine roasted meat and fowl; the few who find the edibles "inconsistent" are easily assuaged when chef Angelo Elia's mom gets behind the stove to concoct her "incredible" fusilli.

Darrel & Oliver's Cafe Maxx [S] 28 | 21 | 26 | $48
2601 E. Atlantic Blvd. (east of N. Federal Hwy.), Pompano Beach, 954-782-0606
■ Chef Oliver Saucy ("a local treasure") continues to "set the standard" at this celebrated Pompano Beach foodie shrine, with a daily-changing menu of "dependably excellent" New World cuisine, an "excellent wine selection", "fine service" and a casual, upscale interior marked by warm earth tones and an open kitchen.

Eduardo de San Angel 28 | 23 | 26 | $43
2822 E. Commercial Blvd. (bet. Bayview Dr. & 28th Ave.), 954-772-4731
■ With the departure of his brother Luis, gifted chef Eduardo Pria is manning the stoves solo at this "romantic" North Lauderdale source for "serious" "gourmet Mexican" (read: "no chips and salsa", but 50 wines by the glass); with the No. 1 Food rating in the Fort Lauderdale *Survey*, it will "change your idea" of this cuisine.

Himmarshee Bar & Grille S   25 | 19 | 21 | $37

210 SW Second St. (NW 2nd Ave.), 954-524-1818
■ "Conveniently" located near the Broward Center for the
Performing Arts, this South Lauderdale New American is called
a "great" pre- and post-performance choice because of its
"innovative" menu, "attentive" service and "people-watching"
from the mezzanine bar and outdoor tables; it can get "noisy",
but that's par for any "cool scene."

Hobo's Fish Joint S   25 | 19 | 20 | $39

Palm Spring Plaza, 10317 Royal Palm Blvd. (Coral Springs Dr.),
Coral Springs, 954-346-5484
■ "Perhaps the best seafood restaurant in Broward County", this
Coral Springs favorite offers "huge portions" of fresh fish prepared
16 different ways; the masculine, steakhouse-style setting includes
wood floors and white tablecloths, which along with the menu's
meat offerings make carnivores feel at home.

Hot Chocolates S   24 | 23 | 22 | $40

3101 N. Federal Hwy. (Oakland Park Blvd.), 954-564-5552
■ A "stunning" marble-and-flower-filled, Erté-meets-the-
Flintstones interior, Eclectic cuisine "on a par with the setting"
and a "hot" after-dinner nightclub with live music and dancing
("couples all over each other") are why this late-night North
Lauderdale spot "is fun from beginning to end" and "one of the
best" in the area.

Left Bank S   24 | 21 | 23 | $44

214 SE Sixth Ave. (north of Las Olas Blvd.), 954-462-5376
■ Chef-owner Jean-Pierre Brehier's TV show is now in syndication,
giving him more time to focus on this "long-established" Central
Broward French bistro that continues to serve "excellent" Provençal
cuisine complemented by a large wine list; the "charming" room
features dark woods and an Impressionist-style mural.

Mark's Las Olas S   26 | 24 | 24 | $49

1032 E. Las Olas Blvd. (bet. 10th & 11th Sts.), 954-463-1000
▨ An "attractive", "see-and-be-seen" crowd knows to "make
reservations" before dining at chef-owner Mark Militello's
globally accented New American, the Most Popular restaurant in
the Fort Lauderdale *Survey,* which "does not disappoint" thanks
to a "stylish" interior and "imaginative" dishes using "quality
ingredients"; critics find it "noisy" and "overpriced", with a clientele
that looks "too thin" to appreciate the "excellent food."

Nevis S   – | – | – | E

3051 NE 32nd Ave. (bet. Intracoastal & Oakland Park Blvd.),
954-566-9314
This yacht-elegant New American newcomer seems to have it
all, with an outdoor, canopied setting with cushy banquettes on
Ft. Lauderdale's Intracoastal waterfront and a winning menu
featuring chef Twain Schrieber's masterful grill fare, backed up
by top-notch housemade desserts; the romantic, copper-topped
bar and lounge offer more reasons to stop by, with DJs spinning
until the wee hours on weekends.

Primavera S

| 26 | 22 | 23 | $43 |

Primavera Plaza, 830 E. Oakland Park Blvd. (west of N. Dixie Hwy.),
954-564-6363

■ "Our restaurant for celebrations", this long-standing Italian
remains "a classic" with "consistently excellent" cuisine –
including a tempting antipasti table, homemade pasta and "great"
desserts – plus "very good", "formal" service and a "quiet",
flower-filled setting; the tab can be "expensive", but the off-
season prix fixe meal for two is a bargain.

Ruth's Chris Steak House S

| 25 | 21 | 23 | $45 |

2525 N. Federal Hwy. (bet. Oakland Park & Sunrise Blvds.),
954-565-2338

■ Despite heavy competition, this "dependable" New Orleans–
based steakhouse chain is considered by many carnivores to
serve South Florida's "finest combination of steaks and sides";
though a few find it "too stuffy", most laud its "serious approach
to food and professional service"; P.S. "all items are à la carte",
so expect the tab to build up.

Samba Room S

| – | – | – | E |

350 E. Las Olas Blvd. (SE 3rd Ave.), 954-468-2000

Downtown Ft. Lauderdale's latest hot spot draws a well-heeled
crowd with its elegant digs and artfully prepared and presented
Caribbean, Spanish and Portuguese fusion fare; hip yuppies and
singles samba in for both the bar scene and distinctly flavorful
dishes along the lines of ceviches, paella and sauteed shrimp
and chicken in coconut broth.

Sunfish Grill

| 25 | 15 | 20 | $39 |

2771 E. Atlantic Blvd. (Intracoastal Waterway), Pompano Beach,
954-788-2434

■ Visitors to this "tiny", funky Pompano Beach grill say chef-
owner Tony Sindaco "really understands seafood", producing
"excellent", "flavorful" dishes complemented by a midpriced
wine list; while fish is his forte, there's also steak, chicken and
fine homemade breads and desserts, which help make this a
"real find" ("would hate for it to be discovered").

Victoria Park S

| – | – | – | M |

900 NE 20th Ave. (Sunrise Blvd.), 954-764-6868

A cozy, color-splashed Ft. Lauderdale Eclectic that's making its
mark with an assortment of fresh, tasty creative fare drawing
inspiration from many cuisines (i.e. the menu ranges from smoked
salmon to Jamaican pork to apple tart and other uniformly delicious
desserts); modest prices and helpful, attentive servers should
add up to staying power for this Victoria Park yearling.

Fort Worth

TOP 10 FOOD RANKING

	Restaurant	Cuisine Type
28	Cacharel	New French
	Del Frisco's	Steakhouse
27	Saint-Emilion	Country French
26	Bistro Louise	Mediterranean
25	Railhead Smokehouse	Barbecue
	Angeluna	New American
	Kincaid's	Hamburgers
	La Piazza	N/S Italian
24	Angelo's Barbecue	Barbecue
23	Cafe Aspen	New American

ADDITIONAL NOTEWORTHY PLACES

Buffet at the Kimbell	New American
Cafe on the Green	New American
Classic Cafe	Eclectic
Esperanza's	Mexican
Grape Escape	Eclectic
Joe T. Garcia's	Mexican
Michaels	Southwestern
Michel's at the Balcony	Continental
Randall's	Eclectic
Reata	Southwestern

	F	D	S	C
Angelo's Barbecue 🚫	24	15	17	$11

2533 White Settlement Rd. (University Dr.), 817-332-0357

■ The granddaddy of Fort Worth smoked meats is "a museum of BBQ" to fans who say this "dark and smoky" "golden oldie" dishes up "the best damn 'cue in the state", or maybe "the universe", along with the "coldest beer"; if a few doubters say "good but no longer the best", more consider this "the real deal."

	F	D	S	C
Angeluna [S]	25	23	22	$29

215 E. Fourth St. (bet. Calhoun & Commerce Sts.), 817-334-0080

◪ Some of "Fort Worth's most original food" can be found at this "trendy" Downtowner praised for its "nouveau" American fare and "light, airy" setting with a cloud-motif ceiling; though it also draws some complaints ("loud", "uneven", "all show"), it's a definite "hot spot" and a "great location for Bass Hall" concertgoers.

	F	D	S	C
Bistro Louise	26	25	22	$27

Stonegate Commons, 2900 S. Hulen St. (Oak Park Ln.), 817-922-9244

■ With "lovely" decor that hints of Provence and the Riviera, Fort Worth's Most Popular restaurant is an "elegant, comfortable" retreat offering "fresh, innovative" Mediterranean fare that makes "excellent use of spices"; it's "perfect for a ladies' lunch" and enough of a "treat" to "drive from Dallas to eat here."

F	D	S	C

Buffet at the Kimbell, The [S] 19 | 23 | 16 | $12

Kimbell Art Museum, 3333 Camp Bowie Blvd. (University Dr.), 817-332-8451

■ This lunch favorite in the acclaimed Kimbell Art Museum boasts (no surprise) "beautiful surroundings" plus "interesting" New American food that's "outstanding for a museum" – in fact, some go for "lunch first, then art"; regulars are especially happy now that chef "Shelby's back"; N.B. dinner served Fridays only.

Cacharel 28 | 25 | 26 | $40

2221 E. Lamar Blvd. (bet. Ballpark Way & Hwy. 360), Arlington, 817-640-9981

■ Rated No. 1 for Food in FW, this "exceptional", "elegant" Arlington New French is considered "the place for any important occasion"; offering "very consistent" food (including "soufflés to die for"), a "quiet" setting and "attentive service", it's "expensive" but could show other restaurants "how it's done."

Cafe Aspen 23 | 20 | 22 | $26

Frost Bank Shopping Plaza, 6103 Camp Bowie Blvd. (Bryant Irvin Rd.), 817-738-0838

◪ A Fort Worth pioneer in New American cuisine that's still a "favorite" for "wonderful seasonal fare" served in a cozy, romantic setting by a "courteous" staff led by an owner "who's always there and concerned"; despite scattered reports of "disappointing" meals, the fact that it has a "steady loyal following" says a lot.

Cafe on the Green [S] ▽ 25 | 25 | 24 | $32

Four Seasons Resort, 4150 N. MacArthur Blvd. (Northgate Dr.), Irving, 972-717-0700

■ "Beautiful, fresh and healthy fare" is the essence of this "informal yet elegant" Irving New American that's dominated by a dramatic skylight; fans recommend this "peaceful place" for its "impeccable service", spa menu and "inviting buffet."

Classic Cafe ▽ 26 | 18 | 23 | $28

504 N. Oak St. (Denton St.), Roanoke, 817-430-8185

621 E. Southlake Blvd. (Byron Nelson Pkwy.), Southlake, 817-410-9001

■ It might be "a long way from home", but this "casual cafe in sleepy Roanoke" is "worth the drive" for "excellent" Eclectic eating, making this "great find" "one of the best-kept secrets around; N.B. the Southlake branch opened post-*Survey*.

Del Frisco's Double Eagle Steak House 28 | 26 | 26 | $47

812 Main St. (8th St.), 817-877-3999

◪ The "classiest joint to get a steak and still wear your boots" describes this dark, clubby "meat-lover's paradise" with beef "to die for" (rated No. 2 for Food in Fort Worth); "superb service" is a plus, and though some find "cigar smoke a turnoff" and call it "too noisy" and "expensive", most consider it "well worth" the tab.

Esperanza's [S]≠ ▽ 23 | 19 | 22 | $13

(fka Joe T. Garcia's Bakery)

2122 N. Main St. (Commerce St.), 817-626-5770

1109 Hemphill St. (Rosedale St.), 817-332-3848

■ These "casual", "authentic Mexican" cafes are often dubbed Joe T.'s Bakeries, due to the "family fame" of the parent restaurant; lines form every morning for the "great breakfasts" (love those "can't-be-beat *migas*") served in a "festive atmosphere"; N.B. the lunch specials are a bargain, as are the combo dinners.

Grape Escape [S] 21 | 21 | 22 | $22

500 Commerce St. (4th St.), 817-336-9463

◪ The city's first wine bar, in an ideal location facing Bass Performance Hall, is "a small, fun place" serving "surprisingly good" Eclectic nibbles in a stylish, "relaxed atmosphere"; though grumblers say it's hard to make "a full meal" out of the small plates and call it "pricey for what you get", most are happy to focus on the "great wine flights" served by an "extremely knowledgeable" staff.

Joe T. Garcia's [S]⊄ 21 | 21 | 20 | $16

2201 N. Commerce St. (bet. N. Main & 22nd Sts.), 817-626-4356

◪ A Fort Worth "landmark" for over 60 years and "still going strong", thanks to some of "the best margaritas and Mexican food" around, plus a "fantastic" patio ("sit by the pool") that makes "you feel you're really in Mexico"; not everyone agrees ("tourist-oriented", "bland food"), but to its "cult following" it's "unbeatable."

Kincaid's Hamburgers ⊄ 25 | 14 | 18 | $8

4901 Camp Bowie Blvd. (Eldridge St.), 817-732-2881

■ "No decor, no service, who cares? – best burger ever" sums up this ancient grocery store beloved for its "good, old-fashioned, greasy burgers" made from "high-quality meat"; sit at a picnic table or follow the lead of regulars and eat standing at the counters.

La Piazza [S] 25 | 25 | 22 | $33

University Park Village, 1600 S. University Dr. (I-30), 817-334-0000

◪ Surveyors say this is easily the most elegant Italian nook in town ("great for a date"), with a "loyal following" for its "consistently first-rate food", but the experience doesn't come cheap and may be served with a side of "attitude."

Michaels ◐ ▽ 24 | 21 | 20 | $22

3413 W. Seventh St. (bet. Montgomery Ave. & University Dr.), 817-877-3413

■ Chef Michael Thomson mans the kitchen of this "hip and trendy" Southwestern in the Cultural District: the "citified", "fresh, seasonal fare" is "designed for the urban cowboy", including "appetizer pizzas" that simply "are a wonder."

Michel's at the Balcony 23 | 19 | 21 | $26

Ridglea Village, 6100 Camp Bowie Blvd. (bet. Westridge & Winthrop Aves.), 817-731-3719

■ "Romantic" and "elegant", the "tasty time warp" in Ridglea Village that used to be The Balcony of Ridglea now benefits from an infusion of energy courtesy of new owner Michel Baudouin (Grape Escape); the menu of Continental faves is spiked with just the right amount of savoir fare, and most agree it's a "good place for an anniversary", thanks to candlelit dining rooms and "nice piano bar music."

Railhead Smokehouse 25 | 18 | 19 | $12

2900 Montgomery St. (I-30), 817-738-9808

5220 Hwy. 121 (Hall Johnson Rd.), Colleyville, 817-571-2525

■ Rave reviews go to the "best all-around BBQ in FW", serving up "huge platters" of "superior" beef, ribs and chicken that are "worth the pounds" gained; a "clean, safe location" can mean long lines and noise, which make for "interesting customers" and a "great patio scene"; N.B. the Colleyville branch opened post-*Survey.*

Randall's Gourmet Cheesecake Co.

▽ 25 | 25 | 22 | $24

907 Houston St. (bet. 8th & 9th Sts.), 817-336-2253

■ "Don't let the name fool you" – this "quiet, intimate" Downtown Eclectic hideout offers a "great overall dining experience"; the menu is "limited" but "delicious", enhanced by a "good wine list" and ambiance that makes you "feel you're in NYC"; in sum, a "little jewel" – and yes, "save room" for the cheesecake.

Reata 🅂

23 | 26 | 22 | $30

Bank One Bldg., 500 Throckmorton St., 35th fl. (bet. 4th & 5th Sts.), 817-336-1009

🗹 Perched high atop a bank building, this nouveau Southwestern named for the ranch in *Giant* offers "cowboy cuisine with an upscale twist that works" in a matching setting that's rated No. 1 for Decor in Fort Worth; though some call it "overpriced" and wish the "food matched" the "beautiful view", most like its "unique" style and call it the ideal place to impress "a Yankee."

Saint-Emilion

27 | 24 | 25 | $36

3617 W. Seventh St. (Montgomery Rd.), 817-737-2781

■ A favorite for elegant Country French cuisine, this intimate winner is lovely for "an anniversary or special celebration", thanks to "superb duck" and other "authentic", "high-quality" bistro fare enhanced by a "very good wine list", attentive service and "romantic" ambiance; a caring owner is another reason why it's considered "one of the best."

TOP 10 FOOD RANKING

Restaurant	Cuisine Type
27 Alan Wong's	Pacific Regional
26 La Mer	Classic French
Roy's	Eurasian
Hoku's	International
Ruth's Chris	Steakhouse
25 Yohei Sushi	Japanese
Orchids	International/Seafood
Kyo-Ya	Japanese
3660 on the Rise	Pacific Rim
Hy's Steak House	Steakhouse

ADDITIONAL NOTEWORTHY PLACES

A Pacific Cafe	Pacific Rim
Bali-By-The-Sea	Eurasian
Chef Mavro's	French/Hawaiian
Golden Dragon	Chinese
Indigo	Eurasian
OnJin's Cafe	Asian/French Bistro
Padovani's Bistro	Hawaiian
Palomino Euro Bistro	American/Mediterranean
Pineapple Room	Hawaiian
Prince Court	Trad. American/Japanese

F	D	S	C

Alan Wong's S

27	20	25	$48

McCully Ct., 1857 S. King St. (bet. Hauoli & Pumehana Sts.),
808-949-2526
■ Voted Oahu's Most Popular restaurant as well as No. 1 for Food, this Pacific Regional boasts the "most creative chef in Hawaii", Alan Wong, who is simply "da man" of "innovative", "creative" cooking; despite a "crowded", "uninspired" room, the "exceptionally exceptional" (albeit "pricey") food and "imaginative presentations" make this an "event" for locals and a "must-go for out-of-towners."

A Pacific Cafe S

22	21	20	$37

Ward Ctr., 1200 Ala Moana Blvd. (bet. Piikoi St. & Ward Ave.),
808-593-0035
☑ Chef Jean-Marie Josselin's Ward Centre spot delivers some "creative" (and "pricey") Pacific Rim delicacies that "appeal to both the stomach and the soul"; but while ratings suggest it's "better than most", "disappointed" dissenters insist it "doesn't meet the hype" and find both food and service "hit or miss"; the "funky" art deco decor similarly has its friends and foes.

Bali-By-The-Sea
23 | 25 | 24 | $47

Hilton Hawaiian Village, 2005 Kalia Rd. (Ala Moana Blvd.), 808-941-2254
■ One of the islands' top "impress-your-date" restaurants, this "elegant yet comfortable" dining room in a "romantic" Waikiki Beach locale specializes in "excellent" Eurasian cuisine with a Hawaiian accent courtesy of chef Jean Luc Voegele; despite a few doubters ("a lot of hype"), most agree that the "super wine list and steward", "classy decor" and "great service" add up to an experience that's simply "the best for special occasions."

Chef Mavro's S
23 | 23 | 24 | $62

1969 S. King St. (McCully St.), 808-944-4714
☑ "Serious food for serious diners" comes courtesy of chef George Mavrothalassitis (ex La Mer) at this "superior" McCully French–Hawaiian, where the "fabulous food and wine pairings" draw huzzahs; sure, it's "expensive with a capital E" and hearty eaters groan that the servings are "microscopic", but to its many fans, this "must-try" spot is simply "ahead of its time."

Golden Dragon S
24 | 23 | 22 | $35

Hilton Hawaiian Village, 2005 Kalia Rd. (Ala Moana Blvd.), 808-946-5336
■ For Oahu's "consummate Chinese restaurant", look no further than this "superb", "top-of-the-line" spot where "exquisite" dishes like the "to-die-for" lobster curry arrive in a "beautiful" setting within a prestigious Waikiki hotel; it's "expensive", but for "truly gourmet" cooking, this "class act" is worth it.

Hoku's S
26 | 26 | 25 | $48

Kahala Mandarin Oriental Hotel, 5000 Kahala Ave., 808-739-8779
■ The name means 'star' in Hawaiian, and surveyors say this "classy" yet "informal" International set in a top-drawer hotel is celestial in every way; "breathtaking views", "delicate, nonrushed" service and "amazing food" come together for a "first-class" "fine dining" experience; the only quibbles: "costly" tabs and "a little too much noise"; N.B. new chef Wayne Hirabayashi is expected to maintain the same high standards.

Hy's Steak House S
25 | 23 | 23 | $42

Waikiki Park Heights Hotel, 2440 Kuhio Ave. (Uluniu Ave.), 808-922-5555
☑ "Top-of-the-line", dinner-only American steakhouse in Waikiki done up like an "old boys' club", with "dark wood and a fireplace" that complement its "great steaks and chops"; though prices are on the "expensive" side, fans call it "a solid value."

Indigo
23 | 22 | 21 | $30

1121 Nuuanu Ave. (Hotel St.), 808-521-2900
■ "Always an adventure", this Eurasian "culinary treasure" in Chinatown offers a "unique" mix of "interesting" cuisines – everything from potstickers to pizza – in a "Polynesian atmosphere" complete with an "enchanting garden patio"; though many describe the food as "shockingly good", a very vocal minority derides its "small portions, high cost" formula.

Kyo-Ya S
25 | 25 | 23 | $38

2057 Kalakaua Ave., 808-947-3911
■ For an "excellent visual" experience, sample this "consummate" Japanese with "great decor" and "superb, beautifully served" fare; it's "pricey", but for "authentic" dining that's among the "classiest on Waikiki", admirers suggest you "splurge on a leisurely lunch."

La Mer S
26 27 26 $63

Halekulani Hotel, 2199 Kalia Rd. (Lewers St.), 808-923-2311

■ "Tops in all categories", this "legendary" Classic French is the "crème de la crème" of Waikiki, with a "fabulous" menu courtesy of chef Yves Garnier, "outstanding service" and a "*très* elegant" setting in the Halekulani resort; but "bring lots of money" – it just might be "the most expensive restaurant" around – and don't forget to "wear a sport coat" or long-sleeved shirt, required for entry.

OnJin's Cafe S
– – – M

401 Kamakee St. (Kapiolani Blvd.), 808-589-1666

OnJin Kim whips up creative, upscale dishes on the site of the former Meeting Place Cafe near Ala Moana; look for Asian plate lunches by day and French bistro–style preparations at night.

Orchids S
25 27 24 $43

Halekulani Hotel, 2199 Kalia Rd. (Lewers St.), 808-923-2311

■ Located in a "beautiful", "romantic" Waikiki oceanfront setting, this International seafooder is an "oasis" where "five-star" dishes are served by an "impeccable" staff; whether you go for a "delightful" lunch, "lovely" sunset dinner or the "superior" Sunday brunch, diners agree this exercise in "classic hedonism" might be "pricey" but is still a "wonderful splurge"; N.B. fin fans will appreciate the new seafood appetizer bar.

Padovani's Bistro & Wine Bar S
25 24 23 $55

Doubletree Alana Hotel, 1956 Ala Moana Blvd. (Kalakaua Ave.), 808-946-3456

◪ "First-class" chef Philippe Padovani (ex La Mer) has created a "bright star" in Waikiki – a wine bar offering a selection of 48 vintages by the glass abetted by a "superb" Hawaiian bistro menu; "impressive" decor (though there's "no view") adds to the "quality" experience, and most say the "expensive" prices are "worth every penny"; N.B. a mandatory tipping policy has been scratched.

Palomino Euro Bistro S
22 25 21 $30

Harbor Sq., 66 Queen St. (bet. Bethel & Nimitz Sts.), 808-528-2400

■ "Stunning" decor and a "happening", "lively" atmosphere draw "scenesters" to this "trendy" Downtown American-Mediterranean where the "creative" cooking comes at "reasonable" prices; the only drawback at this "oh so cosmopolitan" spot seems to be the service, which some say "depends on who you are or appear to be."

Pineapple Room S
– – – E

Liberty House, Ala Moana Shopping Ctr., 1450 Ala Moana Blvd. (Atkinson Dr.), 808-945-8881

The remarkable Hawaiian cuisine of chef Alan Wong is available for breakfast, lunch and dinner in an airy, tropical room complete with an exhibition kitchen on the third floor of a department store at Ala Moana Shopping Center; nothing here is traditional, from the braised roast duck for breakfast to the ahi meat loaf for lunch.

Prince Court Restaurant S
23 22 22 $36

Hawaii Prince Hotel Waikiki, 100 Holomoana St. (Ala Moana Blvd.), 808-944-4494

■ This Traditional American-Japanese overlooking Ala Wai Yacht Harbor remains a "favorite" (particularly for special occasions or "expense- account" meals), even after the departure of popular chef Gary Strehl; credit "impressive" buffets and "delicious" Sunday brunches for making this a "great dining experience."

Roy's S

26 | 20 | 23 | $42

6600 Kalanianaole Hwy. (Keahole St.), 808-396-7697
■ The "original" Hawaii Kai flagship of the global Eurasian chain founded by award-winning chef-owner Roy Yamaguchi is "still the best", thanks to always "innovative" cuisine from the "wonderful" open kitchen, a "friendly" staff and the "best" sunset views around; but the "packed-in tables" and "intolerable noise level" in the main dining room make eating in the lounge an option to consider, short of bringing "earplugs."

Ruth's Chris Steak House S

26 | 20 | 23 | $42

Restaurant Row, 500 Ala Moana Blvd. (bet. Punchbowl & South Sts.), 808-599-3860
■ Carnivores crow that "you'll leave happy and full" after dining at this "high-energy" Restaurant Row branch of a chain chop shop where the "à la carte everything" includes "oh so tender" steaks that are "consistent 100 percent of the time"; a "great wine list" ("three different Turley's – rare for Hawaii") rounds out this impressive, if "pricey", experience.

3660 on the Rise S

25 | 20 | 22 | $39

3660 Waialae Ave. (Wilhelmina Rise), 808-737-1177
■ "Nouvelle Pacific Rim cuisine at its best" wins raves for this "cutting-edge" Kaimuki entry led by "innovative", "outstanding" chef Russell Siu; after a redo there are fewer tables and "a more relaxed", "personable" ambiance, and partisans predict this "consistent" "favorite" could "reach the top."

Yohei Sushi

25 | 16 | 19 | $31

Kokea Business Complex, 1111 Dillingham Blvd. (Kokea St.), 808-841-3773
☑ Despite an "out-of-the-way" location on the edge of Kalihi, reservations are strongly recommended for this "always crowded" Japanese seafooder with "one of the best sushi bars in town"; signature dishes include soba and the Yohei bento box at lunch and tempura and broiled salmon at dinner.

Houston

TOP 20 FOOD RANKING

Restaurant	Cuisine Type
28 DeVille	New French
27 Rotisserie/Beef & Bird	Traditional American
Chez Nous	French Bistro
Cafe Annie	Reg. American/SW
La Réserve	Continental
Mark's	New American
Brennan's	Creole
26 Ruggles Grill	Southwestern
Riviera Grill	Mediterranean
Damian's	N/S Italian
Anthony's	Continental
Brenner's	Steakhouse
Patisserie Descours	Desserts/Sandwich Shop
Tony's	Continental
Lynn's Steakhouse	Steakhouse
25 C & H Steak Company	Steakhouse
Pappas Bros. Steakhouse	Steakhouse
La Mora Cucina	Northern Italian
Churrascos	South American/Steakhse.
Nino's	N/S Italian

ADDITIONAL NOTEWORTHY PLACES

Américas	S. American/New World
Benjy's	Asian/Californian
Bistro Provence	French Provençal
Cafe Perrier	French Provençal
Daily Review Cafe	New American
Da Marco	Northern Italian
Empress	Chinese/French
Goode Co. Barbecue	Barbecue
La Colombe d'Or	Classic French
La Vista	Italian/Southwestern
Ouisie's Table	Southern
Rainbow Lodge	Regional American
River Cafe	Southwestern
Sake Lounge	Japanese/New American
Scott Chen's	Asian
Sierra Grill	Southwestern/New Amer.
Simposio	Northern Italian
Tasca	New American/Spanish
Tony Ruppe's	New American
Urbana	New American

Américas 24 | 26 | 22 | $31

Pavilion on Post Oak, 1800 Post Oak Blvd. (bet. San Felipe & Westheimer), 713-961-1492

■ "Holy Columbus – what a discovery!"; gifted chef Michael Cordúa's "original", "exquisite" South American menu is "out of this world", spinning "imaginative" twists on New World ingredients with "flair"; equal to the "exciting" cuisine is the "must-see", "knockout decor" that "looks like it was done by Picasso on drugs"; with its "superb" staff and "festive atmosphere", the only drawback to this "winner" near The Galleria is its pandemonium decibel level.

Anthony's 26 | 25 | 24 | $42

Highland Village, 4007 Westheimer (Drexel), 713-961-0552

■ "One of Houston's premier tables", this "sleek, sexy and tantalizing" Continental in Highland Village with "fabulous decor and service to match" is "much more relaxed" than Tony's, its older sibling; "the place to be seen", it offers "serious power meals" "prepared with care and flair" and a "top-notch wine list"; while a few deem it "a bit pretentious", most revel in a "special dining experience" that "delivers luxurious excess with style."

Benjy's Restaurant [S] 23 | 21 | 21 | $26

Rice Village, 2424 Dunstan (bet. Rice & Sunset), 713-522-7602

■ "Hip and trendy", this Rice Villager is "constantly morphing into something new", but it always turns out "exciting" Asian-Cal "fusion fare that actually fuses" with a "beautiful blending of flavors"; the "laid-back" staff works the "elegantly stark", "lofty space" with full "attention" too, but still a few "underwhelmed" detractors quip "cutting edge?" – more like "over the edge."

Bistro Provence – | – | – | M

11920 J Westheimer (Kirkwood), 281-497-1122

13616 Memorial Dr. (bet. Wycliffe & Yorkchester Drs.), 713-827-8008

This twosome presents area Francophiles with a chance to sample the intensely flavorful Provençal cooking of chef Georges Guy in casual, affordable style; the Westheimer location offers a bistro menu and down-to-earth dining, while the cozy Memorial venue has all the charm of a cottage in the French countryside.

Brennan's of Houston [S] 27 | 27 | 26 | $39

3300 Smith (Stuart), 713-522-9711

■ For 34 years, this "impressive" Downtown "Texanized" sibling of the renowned Commander's Palace in New Orleans has been ordained Houston's "Creole heaven", with a romantic courtyard and an "elegant" room; Carl Walker serves up "turtle soup that will cure whatever ails you", "creative fish dishes and divine bananas Foster", and dinner at his private table in the kitchen is "a classy treat"; all in all, this is "a superior restaurant in every respect."

Brenner's Steak House [S] 26 | 17 | 22 | $38

10911 Katy Frwy./I-10 W. (near Wilcrest), 713-465-2901

■ Cut into the best steak in Houston at this modest-looking Katy Freeway "old reliable", which has remained "virtually unchanged" for decades; most folks evidently like its retro ways, touting the "old-fashioned atmosphere" and "waitresses in white" who still recite the menu; you can't go wrong with the "mouthwatering steaks" and "excellent" German-style fried potatoes.

Cafe Annie   27 26 26 $48
1728 Post Oak Blvd. (San Felipe), 713-840-1111
■ "How many more awards can they win?" ask devotees who
award this Tanglewood Regional American with a Southwestern
bent yet another citation: Houston's Most Popular restaurant;
chef Robert Del Grande presents cuisine that's "world-class on all
counts" in richly paneled rooms reminiscent of "dining on a fine
luxury liner"; though "small portions at huge prices" give pause to a
few, the clear verdict is "drop-dead gorgeous in every respect."

Cafe Perrier   _ _ _ E
4304 Westheimer (Mid Ln.), 713-355-4455
With its bare-wood floors and undraped windows, Frederic Perrier's
popular French near the Galleria is somewhat spartan-looking,
but the Provençal food and fine service lend it the feel of luxury
dining; habitués indulge in dishes like rack of lamb or gratin of
lobster, topped with elaborate dessert concoctions like the
'pyramid of chocolate.'

C & H Steak Company 🖪   25 25 23 $33
(fka C & H Steakhouse)
*12000 Southwest Frwy. (bet. W. Airport & Wilcrest), Stafford,
281-277-9292*
■ The "excellent beef" "meets all expectations" at this "fine"
chophouse courtesy of über-restaurateurs Chris and Harris Pappas;
though the "pricey" menu is strictly à la carte, the "beautiful
interior" and "quiet atmosphere" pay off at this "good place to take
clients when you're in the [Southwest] suburbs"; P.S. cognoscenti
rate "the rib eye better than the filet."

Chez Nous   27 23 26 $44
217 S. Ave. G (Staitti), Humble, 281-446-6717
■ Francophiles cheerfully trek the "zillion miles" to this "remote"
French bistro in Humble to indulge in an "authentic European"
experience; enthusiasts rate the food "close to perfection", singling
out the "sublime" duck, fresh crab and "incredibly good" pâté; in
addition, the staff is so "warm and friendly" that it's voted No. 1
for Service in the *Houston Survey*.

Churrascos   25 21 22 $28
9705 Westheimer (Gessner), 713-952-1988
Shepherd Sq., 2055 Westheimer (S. Shepherd), 713-527-8300
*1320 W. Bay Area Blvd. (bet. Baybrook Mall & Gulf Frwy.),
Friendswood, 281-461-4100*
■ With its signature "melt-in-your-mouth" tenderloin, the Cordúa
brothers' South American steakhouse trio is winning carnivorous
converts far and wide; besides the "unbeatable beef", the menu
includes "great vegetarian platters", plantain chips ("a hit")
and a "*tres leches* dessert" to "dream about", presented by a
"well-trained staff"; true believers tout it as "a must-visit."

Daily Review Cafe 🖪   23 16 19 $21
3412 W. Lamar (Dunlavy), 713-520-9217
■ Set in a cinder-block edifice off Allen Parkway, Claire Smith's
New American impresses with an "imaginative" menu; it attends
to details with herbs cut from its "backyard garden", "nicely
priced" wines and "great service", and if the seating is "close"
that's to enhance the "picnic" feel.

Da Marco

– | – | – | E |

1520 Westheimer (bet. Ridgewood & Windsor), 713-807-8857
Small, serene and sunny, this Montrose bungalow makes its mark
with Tuscan and other Northern Italian tastes courtesy of chef-
owner Marco Wiles; artfully arranged appetizers precede primo
pastas or meatier dishes like the inch-thick grilled lamb chops,
matched with a nicely priced list of regional Italian vintages.

Damian's Cucina Italiana

26 | 23 | 23 | $34 |

3011 Smith (Rosalie), 713-522-0439
■ The "grande dame" of Downtown's southern edge, this Italian
has earned "top-notch" status with its "superb food", "romantic"
room and "professional service"; preserving a "Euro-feel with a
touch of class", it's "still firing on all cylinders" in spite of chef
Luigi Ferre's departure, and partisans pardon its "stuffy" side
because "they spoil me."

DeVille

28 | 27 | 26 | $43 |

Four Seasons Hotel, 1300 Lamar (Austin), 713-652-6250
■ "The classiest place Downtown" is also the *Houston Survey*'s
No. 1 for Food and Decor; chef Tim Keating has "restored this
Cadillac to a shine" with his "creative, delicious" New French
menu; neophytes may find the richly appointed Four Seasons dining
room "a little stiff", but the cuisine's "embarrassment of riches"
and the staff's "attentive" treatment define "elegant" dining.

Empress

25 | 20 | 22 | $28 |

*Champions Village, 5419 A FM 1960 W. (bet. Champions Forest &
Glen Erica Drs.), 281-583-8021*
☑ Stirring up "Chinese with a French flair", chef-owner Scott
Chen's Pacific powerhouse in Champions Village wins respect for
the "best fusion in town"; the "exquisite" fare is matched with an
"outstanding wine list" and an "elegant" setting, and if the experience
strikes some as "overrated", they are badly outnumbered.

Goode Co. Barbecue 🅢

24 | 17 | 18 | $12 |

8911 Katy Frwy./I-10 W. (Campbell Rd.), 713-464-1901
5109 Kirby Dr. (bet. Bissonnet & Westpark), 713-522-2530
■ Perfuming the air of Kirby and the Katy Freeway, this duo's "great
and authentic Texas BBQ" inspires "rabid loyalty"; 'cue connoisseurs
rate it "best of breed" and advise "don't skip the pecan pie."

La Colombe d'Or 🅢

23 | 25 | 22 | $43 |

La Colombe d'Or Hotel, 3410 Montrose (Harold), 713-524-7999
☑ "Lots of great calories" lie in wait at this "elegant, incredibly
romantic" Classic French housed in a Montrose luxury hotel that
affords the "best atmosphere" in Houston; mixed reactions – it
"can be excellent or mediocre" – seem due to a "revolving-door
chefs" problem, yet ratings suggest that this can be a "wonderful
special-occasion spot – if you get the right waiter."

La Mora Cucina Toscana

25 | 22 | 23 | $28 |

912 Lovett Blvd. (bet. Hawthorne & Westheimer), 713-522-7412
■ Taking "[Northern] Italian food to a higher level", this "top-
notch" "hideaway" in an "unusual place" off Montrose seduces
with "great Tuscan cuisine"; Florence-bred chef-owner Lynette
Hawkins Mandola "learned well and is always there to keep things
humming", though enough call this "lovely" spot a "well-kept
secret" to suggest that it might "need more advertising."

La Réserve　　　　　　　27 │ 27 │ 25 │ $49

Omni Hotel, 4 Riverway (S. Post Oak Ln. & Woodway), 713-871-8181

■ Lauded by most as "perfect in every way", this Omni Hotel Continental has had three chefs in recent years, leaving well-wishers with their "fingers crossed" for the latest arrival, toque Mercer Mohr; the many kudos for "fine, civilized dining", "impeccable preparation" and a "wonderful atmosphere", however, are slightly offset by brickbats for "outdated", "overpriced" fare.

La Vista S　　　　　▽ 27 │ 13 │ 22 │ $15

1936 Fountain View (bet. San Felipe & Westheimer), 713-787-9899

■ This "small", BYO "gem" in a Tanglewood strip mall serves "very solid" "Italian food with a Southwestern accent" that "costs half of what it's worth"; the smitten "hope that word doesn't get around too fast."

Lynn's Steakhouse　　　　26 │ 21 │ 24 │ $40

955 Dairy-Ashford (bet. Katy Frwy./I-10 W. & Memorial Dr.), 281-870-0807

■ Lynn Foreman's "small" steakhouse on the West Side specializes in "melt-in-your-mouth" beef presented with extras like "superb gumbo and creamed spinach" and "endless freshly baked bread"; the "peaceful atmosphere" and "attentive" service also appeal, making this "best-kept secret in town" "perfect for a rendezvous."

Mark's American Cuisine S　　27 │ 24 │ 23 │ $37

1658 Westheimer (bet. Dunlavy & Ralph), 713-523-3800

■ Chef-owner Mark Cox brings a "serious pedigree" from his tenure at Tony's to his Montrose New American, set in a "beautiful old church"; he creates dishes so "excellent" that his establishment garnered Houston's sixth highest food rating, so despite some gripes about "tables too close" together, the consensus is "Cafe Annie better watch out."

Nino's　　　　　　　　25 │ 21 │ 22 │ $26

2817 W. Dallas (bet. Montrose & Waugh Dr.), 713-522-5120

■ For 22 years, this "fun" Montrose Italian has been the Mandolas' most popular venue, a "spontaneous", "innovative", "authentic table" with "family recipes from Mama M." and "excellent" pasta, veal and chicken dishes; the "gracious, professional" service, "dark", "cozy" atmosphere and "reasonable" prices further explain why it remains an "enchanting treasure."

Ouisie's Table　　　　　21 │ 21 │ 19 │ $25

3939 San Felipe (bet. Drexel & Willowick), 713-528-2264

☑ Elouise Cooper's River Oaks Southern eatery pleases with "delicious", "classy" "comfort" fare such as "to-die-for" crab cakes and "chocolate cake that's a 10"; a flexible setting – "one room is lofty and urbane, the other down-home" – has its fans too.

Pappas Bros. Steakhouse　　25 │ 25 │ 23 │ $44

5839 Westheimer (Bering), 713-780-7352

☑ It's those Pappas boys again, this time with a steakhouse in a "beautiful building" near The Galleria; supporters marvel over "fantastic, classic steaks", winning sides ("the [roasted] mushroom is unbelievable") and the "best cigar room in town"; dissenters say "hang onto your wallet" and prepare for an "unbearably noisy", "smoky" environment that exemplifies the "type of excess that leads to revolutions."

Patisserie Descours | 26 | 14 | 18 | $11

1330 D Wirt Rd. (Westview), 713-681-8894

■ Patrons swoon over the "fantastic sandwiches" and sweet "works of art" created at Marilyn Descours' Spring Branch pâtisserie/cafe, the *Houston Survey's* No. 1 Dessert stop and the source for the city's "best wedding cakes"; since tables are at a premium, it's best to "go early"; N.B. dinner Tuesday–Saturday.

Rainbow Lodge [S] | 22 | 26 | 21 | $35

1 Birdsall (Memorial Dr.), 713-861-8666

■ "Who wouldn't want to eat" at this "romantic and rustic", antiques-filled lodge with a "knock-your-socks-off" view of Buffalo Bayou and a Regional American menu featuring wild game and Gulf Coast seafood?; while "brunch is great too" and the service capable, voters can't help but focus on the "most interesting decor and grounds in Houston."

River Cafe [S] | 20 | 18 | 19 | $23

3615 Montrose (Westheimer), 713-529-0088

■ "Sit outside [on the patio], sip wine and enjoy the evening" is the advice that arty types give on this longtime Southwestern haven, a "people-watching" place whose food is called "dependable" and "creative" by fans; "overhyped" say foes.

Riviera Grill | 26 | 15 | 21 | $32

Radisson Suites, 10655 Katy Frwy./I-10 W. (Beltway 8), 713-974-4445

■ "It's hard to imagine a better fish dish than the Chilean sea bass" prepared by chef-owner John Sheely at this "exquisite" Mediterranean in a "weird location" next to the Town & Country Mall; while the interior is "not much to look at", it hardly matters because the "innovative and flavorful" food "outshines" any drawbacks and "gives hotel dining a good name."

Rotisserie for Beef & Bird | 27 | 24 | 26 | $40

2200 Wilcrest (north of Westheimer), 713-977-9524

■ "Personable" chef-owner Joe Mannke and his staff always "make you feel welcome" at this Far West Traditional American, beloved by Houstonians for "an anniversary dinner or a romantic night out"; expect "fantastic" game dishes, an "extensive wine list" and historic American oil paintings that are an "education too"; the bottom line: "a class act that does everything well."

Ruggles Grill [S] | 26 | 18 | 18 | $29

903 Westheimer (Montrose), 713-524-3839

◪ There's no question that chef-owners Bruce and Susan Molzan "pile on" "always" "outstanding food" at this trendy Southwestern on Westheimer known for its "famous" grilled veggies and "out-of-this-world desserts"; however, hordes of surveyors howl at the "deafening" noise level, "way-too-crowded seating" and a "worthless" reservations policy, which results in hour-long waits.

Sake Lounge [S] | 22 | 21 | 18 | $23

Bayou Place, 550 Texas Ave. (Smith), 713-228-7253

■ This "cool" Japanese-New American fusion spot in Bayou Place has a magnificent Downtown view, "helpful" waiters and top-notch, "creative" sushi; but diners say "don't overlook the other menu items" such as "very fresh sashimi", "excellent" *udon* noodles and sublime seaweed salad; the perennially jaded say "only in Texas – sushi with fried crawfish."

Scott Chen's
— — — VE
6540 San Felipe (S. Voss), 713-785-8889
The eponymous Mr. Chen (of Empress renown) presides over a Far Memorial venue where the ambition of the menu is matched only by the grandeur of the 15,000-bottle wine cellar; expect culinary pyrotechnics with a Nouvelle Asian accent, impeccable service, tables set with Christofle silver and Riedel crystal, and (of course) premium prices.

Sierra Grill 🅂
23 19 20 $29
4704 Montrose (south of Southwest Frwy./59 S.), 713-942-7757
■ Daring diners say "charming" chef-owner Charlie Watkins' Museum District Southwestern–New American showcases "the most creative menu in Houston", including "indescribably delicious" sesame-crusted tuna and "enchanting aged buffalo"; P.S. since it's now open only for dinner, "a lunch favorite is gone."

Simposio 🅂
22 17 19 $29
5591 Richmond Ave. (Chimney Rock), 713-532-0550
■ "This one's a sophisticated keeper" declare fans of this Northern Italian that's ensconced on a corner of an otherwise featureless strip center; expect a "*simpatico*" staff, an owner who "shows an interest in diners" and "excellent" food, especially the "heavenly" risotto; the only question – "why isn't this restaurant better known?"

Tasca
23 24 22 $28
908 Congress (Travis), 713-225-9100
■ Handsome New American–Spanish Downtowner that earns raves for its "far-out tapas menu", "beautiful atmosphere" and weekend jazz; its roomy bar and wide selection of wines by the glass make it popular before or after a show, but some note that the "lines won't last if they don't start honoring reservations."

Tony Ruppe's
— — — E
3939 Montrose (bet. Alabama & Richmond), 713-852-0852
Tony Ruppe, the longtime chef at swanky DeVille, is now on his own at this eponymous New American in the Montrose/Museum District; the menu manifests influences from Asia to Arizona in dishes like the hoisin beef summer roll and citrus-grilled salmon, served in a soaring, modern space.

Tony's
26 26 25 $53
1801 Post Oak Blvd. (south of San Felipe), 713-622-6778
■ "Still the place to see and be seen", Tony Vallone's firstborn eatery in The Galleria area has come back "better than ever after a slump" say many advocates who caution that its Continental cuisine is "wonderful, but priced like jewelry"; even the few critics who complain that eating here is "an over-produced epic" admit it's "fun to go and watch the ultra-rich in action."

Urbana 🅂
23 19 20 $26
Hawthorne Sq., 3407 Montrose Blvd. (Hawthorne St.), 713-521-1086
■ "Spiffy", "sophisticated and urbane" Montrose New American that charms its "hip" clientele with an "inventive kitchen" and "beautiful presentations"; the "stuff of ecstasy" includes "tasty appetizers", "wonderful tuna steak with guacamole" and "awesome crème brûlée"; the hard-edged concrete interior can be "noisy", so move out to the "great patio", which is one of the prettiest in town.

Kansas City

TOP 10 FOOD RANKING

Restaurant	Cuisine Type
28 Cafe Allegro	New American
27 American Restaurant	New American
Tatsu's	Classic French
Ruth's Chris	Steakhouse
26 Metropolis	New American
Lidia's	N/S Italian
Stolen Grill	New American
Cafe Sebastienne	New American
Stroud's	Traditional American
Starker's Reserve	New American

ADDITIONAL NOTEWORTHY PLACES

Bristol Bar & Grill	Seafood
Fiorella's Jack Stack	Barbecue
Garozzo's	N/S Italian
Grand St. Cafe	Eclectic
Grille on Broadway	New American
JJ's	Steakhouse/Seafood
McCormick & Schmick's	Seafood
Pierpont's	Steakhouse/Seafood
Plaza III	Steakhouse
Zin	New American

F	D	S	C

American Restaurant
27	28	28	$45

Crown Ctr., 250 Grand Ave. (Main St.), 816-426-1133

■ "KC's showplace", this Downtown New American "continues to get better and better", thanks to "outstanding", "innovative" dishes from husband-and-wife chefs Michael Smith and Debbie Gold and a highly "knowledgeable" staff that's ranked No. 1 for Service in the *Kansas City Survey;* factor in a "breathtaking" setting with two-story-high windows offering "great views" of the city, and it's clear why "everything is astounding – including the tab."

Bristol Bar & Grill **S**
25	24	23	$25

5400 W. 119th St. (Nall Ave.), Leawood, KS, 913-663-5777

■ While many are "sorry it left" its Plaza digs for Johnson County, this finny "fave" still retains a staff that "makes you feel special", a "classy" if "noisy" setting and the "best seafood in KC"; the hooked insist that no visit is complete without a taste of the "to-die-for" sweet biscuits.

Cafe Allegro
28	24	27	$40

1815 W. 39th St. (State Line Rd.), 816-561-3663

■ Retaining its No. 1 ratings for Food and Popularity in KC, this "high-style" Westport New American proffers "beautifully presented" dishes prepared from seasonal ingredients; add an impressive wine list, "wonderful" service and an "elegant" setting and the result is a "special-occasion place that makes the occasion."

Cafe Sebastienne S
26 | 26 | 22 | $17

Kemper Museum, 4420 Warwick Blvd. (45th St.), 816-561-7740

■ Reverent reviewers remark that chef Jennifer Maloney's "artistically presented" New American cooking is nicely complemented by a "colorful" setting in the Kemper Museum; although dinner is now being served on Friday and Saturday, many "wish it were open" the rest of the week, thanks to a "magnificent job" on everything.

Fiorella's Jack Stack
25 | 21 | 21 | $16

13441 Holmes Rd. (135th St.), 816-942-9141
9520 Metcalf Ave. (95th St.), Overland Park, KS, 913-385-7427 S

■ This "upscale" BBQ landmark on the South Side now has a Johnson County sib, and both offer "big menus" that "go beyond" one's expectations to include "luscious lamb ribs"; "fabulous sides" ("excellent onion rings") further fuel their rep as "perfect" places to "take out-of-town guests."

Garozzo's Ristorante
24 | 17 | 21 | $18

526 Harrison St. (5th St.), 816-221-2455
Garozzo's Ristorante Due S
12801 E. 40 Hwy. (east of Blue Ridge Mall), Independence, 816-737-2400
Cafe Garozzo S
9950 College Blvd. (Mastin St.), Overland Park, KS, 913-491-8300

■ Italian trio that supplies "food so good you will taste it in your dreams" in a "Sinatra's kind of hangout" setting; the draws include "frighteningly huge portions" and a signature chicken spiedini that's "among the best dishes in town"; converts cry "mama mia!", it's "well worth the wait – and there usually is one."

Grand St. Cafe S
25 | 24 | 24 | $22

Country Club Plaza, 4740 Grand Ave. (bet. 47th & Main Sts.), 816-561-8000

■ "Grand in all ways", this "upscale" Plaza-area Eclectic is a bastion of "continued culinary innovation", home to the "best and biggest pork chop around" and specials that "make your mouth water", all delivered by "friendly" servers; "eating outside in the summer" is sublime, but indoorsy types can "sit at the counter and watch the cooking."

Grille on Broadway, The
26 | 19 | 25 | $28

3605 Broadway (Valentine Rd.), 816-531-0700

■ The "food, wine, owner and intimacy" are all pluses at this "tiny" Midtown New American, "a real gem" where the "superb" "fresh fish" stands out on the "imaginative menu"; owner "Sean Cummings is a wonderful, witty host" whose charming "blarney" suggests "being served in someone's dining room" – but "don't go if you're claustrophobic."

JJ's S
25 | 23 | 24 | $28

910 W. 48th St. (Belleview St.), 816-561-7136

■ "Always hopping with a trendy crowd", this "bright, airy" steakhouse-seafooder "on the edge of the Plaza" pairs a "stunning", award-winning wine list with a "superb" menu; fans add they "can't think of a better place for someone to buy me lunch."

Lidia's 🖪

26 | 29 | 23 | $26

101 W. 22nd St. (Baltimore Ave.), 816-221-3722

■ Owned by Lidia Bastianich, this Downtown Italian just might be KC's "best restaurant in years"; it debuts with the No. 1 Decor score in the *Kansas City Survey*, thanks to David Rockwell's "spectacular" design, complete with a 30-foot fireplace; factor in a "creative menu" and an "affordable wine list" and this is the "hottest ticket in town."

McCormick & Schmick's 🖪

– | – | – | E

Valencia Place, 448 W. 47th St. (Pennsylvania St.), 816-531-6800

Freshness rules at this Plaza seafood specialist, a link in an upscale national chain where the menus are printed daily and an array of oysters is flown in from both coasts; the whale of a room features an attention-grabbing stained-glass dome, but it's the flavorful fish and specialties like crab cakes that steal the show.

Metropolis American Grill

26 | 22 | 24 | $29

303 Westport Rd. (Central St.), 816-753-1550

■ Some of the "most artistic", "beautifully presented" cooking in town can be found at this "innovative" Westport New American where "excellent" tandoori sea bass is the signature dish; a "cozy", "cosmopolitan" setting that oozes style, combined with the "personal charm" of the staff, makes this "one of KC's finest"; P.S. "out-of-this-world catering" is available too.

Pierpont's 🖪

– | – | – | E

Union Station, 30 W. Pershing Rd. (Main St.), 816-221-5111

Named for famed railroad-era financier J. Pierpont Morgan, this Downtown steak-and-seafood specialist is set within the turn-of-the-century Union Station, recently restored to its original grandeur; the high ceilings, ornate trim and plush appointments make for a first-class complement to a sizzling Kansas City strip.

Plaza III The Steakhouse 🖪

26 | 24 | 24 | $32

Country Club Plaza, 4749 Pennsylvania (Ward Pkwy.), 816-753-0000

■ "One of America's top" beef palaces, this Plaza favorite offers "excellent" steaks and an award-winning wine list; while some feel the "old-style" decor "could be updated" and find the "pricey" tabs too up-to-date, the majority calls it *the* KC "destination" for "power" dining.

Ruth's Chris Steak House 🖪

27 | 24 | 25 | $38

700 W. 47th St. (Jefferson St.), 816-531-4800

■ Native sons say it's "hard to admit a nonlocal can do the best" porterhouse or filet mignon, but this Plaza outpost of a high-end national chain "knows its business" well and wins over many with "luscious steaks" "drenched in butter", accompanied by "wonderful sides"; the "very elegant" dining room (reminiscent of a "men's club") is perfect for expense-accounters, but everyone else should "take out a loan."

Starker's Reserve

26 | 25 | 25 | $36

Country Club Plaza, 201 W. 47th St. (Wyandotte St.), 816-753-3565

■ While widely renowned as "the best spot for hosting a private party" in Kansas City, this Country Club Plaza New American is also open to the public for dinner Tuesday–Saturday; "A+ food", a 1,600-label, award-winning wine list and one of "the most romantic views in town" most assuredly add up to "a perfect meal" for many.

Stolen Grill, The 26 | 18 | 22 | $34

904 Westport Rd. (Southwest Tfwy.), 816-960-1450

■ Inspired surveyors "steal away" to this "wonderful addition to Kansas City's dining scene", a "hip" Westport New American that dazzles with "innovative" cuisine; though a few quibblers call it "pricey", "crowded" and "too noisy even for an extrovert", many others wonder "why aren't there more like this in town?"

Stroud's [S] 26 | 16 | 21 | $16

1015 E. 85th Ave. (Troost Ave.), 816-333-2132
5410 NE Oak Ridge Dr. (bet. I-35 & Vivion Rd.), 816-454-9600

■ "Drop your sophisticated veneer" and head for this South Side Traditional American or its Northland cousin, where "large portions" of the "best fried chicken on the planet" (and other "vehicles to get more gravy") are dished up; sure, this might be "the reason Kansas City is the fourth fattest city in the USA", but once you've "stuffed" yourself and found someone to "roll you out to the car", you'll agree it was "worth it" – even if the waits are "inhumane."

Tatsu's 27 | 21 | 24 | $29

4603 W. 90th St. (½ block east of Roe Ave.), Prairie Village, KS, 913-383-9801

■ "Don't judge a restaurant by its exterior" say supporters of this "quietly charming" "jewel" in a Johnson County strip mall, where a Japanese-trained chef turns out Classic French cuisine "like Julia Child used to cook", including "outstanding carrot soup" and the "best salmon encroûte"; while critics note that the "limited", "old-fashioned" "menu doesn't change much, regulars never complain."

Zin – | – | – | VE

1900 Main St. (19th St.), 816-527-0120

Sleek contemporary decor sets the stage for chef Shelly Pierre Rash's spectacular New American creations at Downtown's most exciting newcomer, sited in the burgeoning Crossroads arts and entertainment district; dinner-only crowds flock to the restored 90-year-old storefront to savor specialties such as seared foie gras or wild mushroom ragout.

Las Vegas

TOP 20 FOOD RANKING

Restaurant	Cuisine Type
27 Andre's	Classic French
Michael's	Traditional American
26 Steak House	Steakhouse
Emeril's New Orleans	Cajun/Creole
Drai's	French Provençal
Suzette's	Classic French
Second Street Grill	Asian/Pacific Rim
Spago	New American
Neros	Steakhouse/Seafood
25 Buzio's	Seafood
Mayflower Cuisinier	New Chinese
Morton's of Chicago	Steakhouse
Fiore Rotisserie	Continental
Isis	Continental/Classic French
Piero's	Northern Italian
Napa	New French
Palm	Steakhouse
Hugo's Cellar	Continental/Steakhouse
Empress Court	Chinese
Chinois	Californian/Asian

ADDITIONAL NOTEWORTHY PLACES

Aqua	Seafood
Aureole	New American
Border Grill	Contemporary Mexican
Charlie Palmer Steak	Steakhouse
Delmonico	Steakhouse
Eiffel Tower	New French
Japengo	Pacific Rim
Le Cirque	Classic French
Lupo, Trattoria del	N/S Italian
Nobu	Japanese
Olives	Mediterranean
P.F. Chang's	Chinese
Picasso	New French/Spanish
Pinot Brasserie	Californian/French Bistro
Postrio	Californian/New American
Prime	Steakhouse
Renoir	New French
Royal Star	Chinese/Seafood
Star Canyon	Southwestern/Tex-Mex
Valentino	Northern Italian

Andre's
27 | 25 | 26 | $52

401 S. Sixth St. (bet. Bridger Ave. & Las Vegas Blvd.), 702-385-5016
Monte Carlo Resort, 3770 Las Vegas Blvd. S. (Tropicana Ave.),
702-798-7151 **S**

■ "Drippingly romantic", this "exquisite" Downtown Classic French and its newer sibling in the Monte Carlo have been voted Most Popular and No. 1 for Food in Las Vegas, thanks to their "*magnifique*" fare, "top-of-the-line wine cellar" and "unmatched atmosphere"; granted, the original location might be "remote" and some say their "most outstanding feature is the price", but for "serious gourmets", they are "unquestionably the finest in LV."

Aqua **S**
— | — | — | E

Bellagio Hotel, 3600 Las Vegas Blvd. S. (Flamingo Rd.), 702-693-7223
Next to the Bellagio's Botanical Gardens, this transplanted SF seafooder, founded by Michael Mina and Charles Condy, features Mark Lo Russo (former sous chef at the California locale) at its helm, who offers extravagant tasting menus and wine pairings in addition to à la carte offerings; the dynamite environment is all rare woods and sumptuous fabrics, and it offers a fine view of the pool.

Aureole **S**
— | — | — | E

Mandalay Bay Hotel, 3950 Las Vegas Blvd. S. (Hacienda Ave.), 702-632-7401
Charlie Palmer's Mandalay Bay version of his celebrated NYC eatery boasts live swans, a view of a waterfall and a four-story wine tower accessed by sleek young women hoisted in harnesses to retrieve bottles (there are some 9,000); still, the New American fare (courtesy of husband-and-wife chefs Megan and Joe Romano) is as memorable as the decor; N.B. prix fixe only.

Border Grill **S**
— | — | — | M

Mandalay Bay Hotel, 3950 Las Vegas Blvd. S. (Hacienda Ave.),
702-632-7403
Those energetic Food Network stars Susan Feniger and Mary Sue Milliken (aka the *Too Hot Tamales*) have made their first foray out of Southern California with this bi-level Contemporary Mexican that's parked near Mandalay Bay's Conference Center; look for zesty takes on the Latin street foods they love so well at this hopping, well-priced scene.

Buzio's **S**
25 | 23 | 22 | $30

Rio Suite Hotel, 3700 W. Flamingo Rd. (I-15), 702-252-7697
■ For "seafood in the desert that one would expect by the sea", try this "standout" fish palace in the Rio that beats its rivals "by a mile"; a "great raw bar", some of "the best Manhattan clam chowder outside of NYC" and irresistible artisanal breads baked on-site equal a "solid", "high-class" experience, although – no surprise – "you pay for it."

Charlie Palmer Steak **S**
— | — | — | E

Four Seasons Hotel, 3960 Las Vegas Blvd. S. (Hacienda Ave.),
702-632-5123
On the heels of his smash success, Aureole, celeb chef Charlie Palmer presents his second Las Vegas venture, a serene steakhouse in the Four Seasons Hotel that specializes in luscious chops and sensational side dishes that are sized to be shared; carnivores concur the bone-in NY strip and truffled baked potato is a match made in heaven.

Chinois S | 25 | 25 | 24 | $36 |
Forum Shops at Caesars, 3500 Las Vegas Blvd. S. (Flamingo Rd.),
702-737-9700

☑ From über-chef Wolfgang Puck comes this "delightful" recreation of his boffo Cal-Asian in Santa Monica, deftly transplanted to the Forum Shops at Caesars; the "creative", "pricey" cuisine spotlights sushi and splendid Shanghai lobster, presented both à la carte and family-style; though "service is sometimes slow", the smitten still sigh "it's everything you could ask for and more."

Delmonico S | – | – | – | VE |
Venetian Hotel, 3355 Las Vegas Blvd. S. (bet. Flamingo &
Spring Mountain Rds.), 702-414-3737

Emeril Lagasse's ode to beefdom in the Venetian is a very hot ticket, so book your table well in advance, though you might have a wait even with a reservation; if so, slip into the elegant bar/cigar lounge where the homemade potato chips with Parmesan cheese and a drizzle of truffle oil are the perfect nibble as you giddily anticipate the thick steaks and superb seafood that lie ahead.

Drai's S | 26 | 27 | 24 | $49 |
Barbary Coast Hotel, 3595 Las Vegas Blvd. S. (Flamingo Rd.), 702-737-0555

■ Despite a "strange location" in the Barbary Coast, this "very chichi" "hidden jewel" transcends its surroundings with a "sexy", "romantic setting" that's No. 1 for Decor in Las Vegas; look for an "innovative" French Provençal menu that's "worthy of special note"; P.S. there's "exceptional jazz" on weekends in the library lounge.

Eiffel Tower Restaurant S | – | – | – | VE |
Paris Hotel, 3655 Las Vegas Blvd. S. (bet. Flamingo & Tropicana Rds.),
702-948-6937

Chic and *magnifique,* this New French aerie in the Paris Hotel soars 11 stories above the Strip, offering a jaw-dropping view of the around-the-world-in-a-glance Vegas landscape; chef Jean Joho (of Chicago's equally stratospheric Everest) takes the kitchen to impressive heights, turning out sumptuous, innovative cuisine that might be *très cher,* but is more than worth every franc.

Emeril's New Orleans Fish House S | 26 | 24 | 24 | $46 |
MGM Grand Hotel, 3799 Las Vegas Blvd. S. (Tropicana Ave.),
702-891-7374

■ It's "difficult to get reservations" at this "expensive" Cajun-Creole in the MGM Grand that's the brainchild of famed New Orleans chef Emeril Lagasse, and with good reason: enthusiasts exclaim the "extraordinary, beautifully presented food" is "perhaps the best in Vegas"; despite "parking that can be a chore" (think sensible shoes for the "long walk" to get there), dining at this Delta transplant is "always a treat."

Empress Court S | 25 | 24 | 27 | $52 |
Caesars Palace Hotel, 3570 Las Vegas Blvd. S. (Flamingo Rd.),
702-731-7888

■ Caesars Palace Tower is home to this relocated Chinese boasting a "killer" view and even more "opulent" decor that help make the "impeccable" cuisine taste even better (grumps say it "should for the price"); though a few say there's "too long a wait for the food", most "love it" here and say "Caesars has done it again."

Fiore Rotisserie & Grille [S] | 25 | 25 | 25 | $46 |

Rio Suite Hotel, 3700 W. Flamingo Rd. (I-15), 702-252-7702

■ Ladies "love the handbag stools" at this "romantic" West Side Continental in the Rio, where everything is "superb in all respects", from the "fabulous food" and "excellent wine list" to the "pampering service" and "beautiful setting"; admittedly, it's "pricey", but besotted fans whisper it "quietly ranks among the best in the city" and find it "hard to believe it's in a casino."

Hugo's Cellar [S] | 25 | 23 | 25 | $39 |

Four Queens Hotel, 202 Fremont St. (N. Casino Ctr. Blvd.), 702-385-4011

■ Long-stemmed "roses for the ladies" are a "nice touch" at this "romantic" Downtown Continental steakhouse where an "unbelievable salad cart" and chocolate-covered strawberries earn honorable mentions; foes fret that this dinner-only "relic" is "past its prime" and should "retire", but they're drowned out by adherents who simply say "how can you go wrong?"

Isis [S] | 25 | 25 | 24 | $53 |

Luxor Hotel, 3900 Las Vegas Blvd. S. (Tropicana Ave.), 702-262-4773

■ A serene ode to the Egyptian fertility goddess Isis, this "quiet, romantic" Continental-French in the Luxor reflects her splendor in perhaps the "most beautiful dining room in Vegas", with food to match; expect "fabulous" fare and "marvelous service", though it might be "hard to get reservations" unless you're a hotel guest.

Japengo [S] | – | – | – | E |

Hyatt Regency at Lake Las Vegas Resort, 101 Montelago Blvd. (Boulder Hwy.), Henderson, 702-567-1234

Cloned from San Diego's popular Cafe Japengo, this Pacific Rimmer in the Moroccan-themed Hyatt Regency is equally stylish, albeit somewhat off the beaten track (the resort is 14 miles east of the Strip); still, travelers tout the first-rate food and stunning mountain and lake vistas from its floor-to-ceiling windows; N.B. dinner only, plus an exotic Sunday brunch.

Le Cirque [S] | – | – | – | VE |

Bellagio Hotel, 3600 Las Vegas Blvd. S. (Flamingo Rd.), 702-693-8100

Manhattan's legendary Classic French, created by Sirio Maccioni, is a smashing success at this transplant in the Bellagio, where a festive, circus-inspired setting provides the backdrop for some culinary derring-do by executive toque Marc Poidevin (ex chef de cuisine at NYC's Le Cirque); reserve well in advance unless you're staying in the hotel, and remember that jackets and ties are required.

Lupo, Trattoria del ◐ [S] | – | – | – | M |

Mandalay Bay Hotel, 3950 Las Vegas Blvd. S. (Hacienda Ave.), 702-632-7410

Wolfgang Puck's family-style Italian at Mandalay Bay is a product of his travels abroad with Lupo chef Mark Ferguson (ex Spago), where the two gathered recipes and accessories for this inviting villa; the menu is a mix of dishes from many regions of Italy.

Mayflower Cuisinier | 25 | 20 | 23 | $29 |

Sahara Pavilion, 4750 W. Sahara Ave. (Decatur Blvd.), 702-870-8432

■ "They get it all right" at this "extraordinary" New Chinese in the West Side Sahara Pavilion, where "marvelous chef" Ming See Woo ("who really cares") turns out "ingenious", "always divine" dishes; though a few tightwads call it "pricey" ("too much for too little"), most concur "everything is wonderful" at this "gem."

Michael's [S] | 27 | 23 | 27 | $63

Barbary Coast Hotel, 3595 Las Vegas Blvd. S. (Flamingo Rd.), 702-737-7111

■ "They make you feel like royalty" at this "fabulous" Traditional American in the Barbary Coast that presents some of the "best Dover sole, stone crabs and coquilles St. Jacques" around; reservations can be tough – or all but "unavailable to mere mortals" – but it does help if you're a hotel guest or a high roller; and yes, it's "ridiculously expensive", though devotees declare it's "worth every penny."

Morton's of Chicago [S] | 25 | 22 | 23 | $47

400 E. Flamingo Rd. (Paradise Rd.), 702-893-0703

◪ "If meat's your thing", this "steak-eater's dream" turns out "huge portions" of "great beef" in a "sophisticated" setting; though a chorus of killjoys wishes they would do something about the "nasty cigar smoking", the "loud" noise level and the "great big prices", in the end the ayes have it: this "carnivore heaven" is nothing less than "sensational"; a move to expanded digs on the East Side is not reflected in the decor score.

Napa [S] | 25 | 26 | 25 | $59

Rio Suite Hotel, 3700 W. Flamingo Rd. (I-15), 702-247-7961

■ For a taste of "New York in Las Vegas", sample this Contemporary French in the Rio that delivers an "adventurous", "world-class" menu (courtesy of its "famous" executive chef, Jean-Louis Palladin), along with a "great wine list" that offers over 300 selections by the glass; scattered grouches grumble it's "overpromoted" and "overpriced", but the clear majority finds it "outstanding", simply "one of the best in the country."

Neros [S] | 26 | 22 | 26 | $48

Caesars Palace Hotel, 3570 Las Vegas Blvd. S. (Flamingo Rd.), 702-731-7731

■ This "terrific" steak-and-seafood house in Caesars Palace features an "imaginative menu" created by a talented young chef; fans "love the crab cakes" and daily specials that arrive looking like pieces of art, and the "excellent, upscale" mood is maintained by a "great host."

Nobu ◐ [S] | – | – | – | E

Hard Rock Hotel, 4455 Paradise Rd. (Harmon Ave.), 702-693-5090

Forget serene, forget tranquil: this Nouvelle Japanese in the Hard Rock Hotel is crackling with exotic Asian flavors jazzed up by a touch of Peru, thanks to the intuitive genius of executive chef/co-owner Nobu Matsuhisa, a famed name on both coasts (NY's Nobu, LA's Matsuhisa); hip picks include a silky signature black cod with miso and a splendid tasting menu, but desserts are the real surprise here – Japanese, no; delectable, yes.

Olives [S] | – | – | – | M

Bellagio Hotel, 3600 Las Vegas Blvd. S. (Flamingo Rd.), 702-693-7223

A spin-off of the celebrated Boston eatery created by Todd English, this Mediterranean delight in the Bellagio is always bustling, with a particularly high demand for seating on its glorious patio with a lakeside view; chef Victor LaPlaca (from the original Olives) replicates many of the Beantown favorites and more, all utterly delicious.

Palm Restaurant 🅂   25 21 23 $42
Forum Shops at Caesars, 3500 Las Vegas Blvd. S. (Flamingo Rd.),
702-732-7256
■ "Huge lobsters" and perhaps "the best porterhouse ever"
keep this "always superb" steakhouse in the Forum Shops at
Caesars packed with the "power elite"; true, it's "expensive" and
can be "loud", but its uptrodden clientele can't get enough of its
"tasty beef", crying "damn the cholesterol, full speed ahead."

P.F. Chang's China Bistro 🅂   23 23 21 $23
4165 S. Paradise Rd. (Flamingo Rd.), 702-792-2207
☑ "If you're looking for action", try this "trendy" "American idea
of a Chinese restaurant", just East of the Strip, where the "upscale
yuppie" crowd goes "to be seen", "but not heard" – it's "too noisy";
though diehards "can't get enough of those lettuce wraps" and
are happily "willing to wait" for them, faultfinders dismiss the
"franchise-style" fare and only show up "for the bar scene."

Picasso 🅂   – – – VE
Bellagio Hotel, 3600 Las Vegas Blvd. S. (Flamingo Rd.), 702-693-7223
An exquisite tribute to the artist in the Bellagio, where the master's
paintings and ceramics adorn the dining room and acclaimed SF
chef Julian Serrano (ex Masa's) creates another kind of art – a
melding of New French and Spanish dishes – in the kitchen; visitors
say this flower-filled room with a lake view is as romantic as it gets.

Piero's 🅂   25 22 24 $48
355 Convention Ctr. Dr. (Paradise Rd.), 702-369-2305
■ "Osso buco par excellence" is the stellar signature dish at this
"sophisticated" Italian near the Convention Center, an "old-guard
clubhouse" where the "movers and shakers" include sports figures
and entertainers; though service draws a mixed response ("rude"
vs. "impeccable"), there's no debate about the "opulent setting"
and "appealing entrees" at this "perennial favorite."

Pinot Brasserie ●🅂   – – – E
Venetian Hotel, 3355 Las Vegas Blvd. S. (bet. Flamingo &
Spring Mountain Rds.), 702-414-8888
An authentic brasserie in the Venetian Hotel via über-chef Joachim
Splichal (LA's Patina) that's casually elegant, with Parisian flea-
market antiques in a brass-and-burnished-wood interior; its Cal-
French menu draws from a rotisserie and oyster bar for inspiration.

Postrio 🅂   – – – E
Venetian Hotel, 3355 Las Vegas Blvd. S. (bet. Flamingo &
Spring Mountain Rds.), 702-796-1110
Set in the Venetian, Wolfgang Puck's new LV entry is a reinterpretation
of his SF smash; chef John Lagrone's daily-changing Cal-American
menu takes some geographic detours (e.g. sublime Hudson Valley
foie gras), but ultimately it's pure Puck – reliably delectable.

Prime 🅂   – – – E
Bellagio Hotel, 3600 Las Vegas Blvd. S. (Flamingo Rd.), 702-693-7223
Style comes to the steakhouse at this stunning spot in the Bellagio
conceived by award-winning chef and restaurateur Jean-Georges
Vongerichten (NYC's Jean Georges); the highest-quality meats,
seafood and chops, overseen by executive chef Kerry Simon, are
accompanied by a choice wine list and served in an ethereal space
done in shades of chocolate-brown and powder-blue; pounce!

Renoir S

| – | – | – | VE |

Mirage Hotel, 3400 Las Vegas Blvd. S. (Spring Mountain Rd.),
702-791-7111

Wooed from his post at a posh Phoenix hotel, award-winning
chef Alessandro Stratta has brought acclaim to this class act at
the Mirage; it's an exciting, albeit expensive, dining experience
featuring creative New French cuisine that emphasizes seasonal
ingredients; N.B. jacket suggested.

Royal Star S

| – | – | – | E |

Venetian Hotel, 3355 Las Vegas Blvd. S. (bet. Flamingo &
Spring Mountain Rds.), 702-414-1888

Mammoth tanks of live fin fare are hidden in the kitchen of this
Chinese seafooder in the Venetian courtesy of chef-owner Kevin
Wu, who has transplanted it from its successful roots in LA and
Santa Monica; exceptional dim sum, authentic Hong Kong specialties
and a lavish tasting menu make it a strong contender for the title
of the Strip's top Asian.

Second Street Grill S

| 26 | 23 | 24 | $29 |

Fremont Hotel, 200 E. Fremont St. (Casino Ctr. Blvd.), 702-385-6277

■ It might be "the best reason to come Downtown" say fans of
this "innovative" Asian in the Fremont Hotel that specializes in
Pacific Rim dishes expertly prepared by one of the few female
chefs in LV; "reasonable prices" and "excellent specials"
make it sometimes "hard to get in."

Spago S

| 26 | 24 | 24 | $37 |

Forum Shops at Caesars, 3500 Las Vegas Blvd. S. (Flamingo Rd.),
702-369-6300

■ "Beautiful people" populate this "loud, hip and trendy" New
American in the Forum Shops at Caesars that's the brainchild of
Wolfgang Puck, the man who "generated the restaurant renaissance
in Las Vegas"; whether you "eat in the little cafe in the front"
that's "less expensive" or in the more formal, pricier dining
room, expect some of "the best people-watching" around at
this "phenomenal" experience that's a "must-do when in town."

Star Canyon S

| – | – | – | E |

Venetian Hotel, 3355 Las Vegas Blvd. S. (bet. Flamingo & Spring
Mountain Rds.), 702-414-3772

Buckaroos and buckarettes are galloping over to the Venetian to
dig into some mighty tasty Southwestern–Tex-Mex vittles courtesy
of star chef Stephan Pyles at this clone of his famed Dallas eatery;
droll, Lone Star State decor (a branded ceiling, plenty of cowboy
boots, decorative barbed wire) sets an amiable tone for the dandy
dishes that emerge from the kitchen's wood-burning oven.

Steak House, The S

| 26 | 23 | 24 | $34 |

Circus Circus Hotel, 2880 Las Vegas Blvd. S. (Sahara Ave.),
702-794-3767

■ "Too bad you have to walk through Circus Circus" to get to this
"consistently good" chophouse, a "big surprise" that still draws
diehards "despite its location"; carnivores say you'll find "Ruth's
Chris quality for much less" money here, which is why reservations
are so tough to get, so plan ahead – way ahead.

Suzette's

26 | 25 | 26 | $46

Santa Fe Hotel, 4949 N. Rancho Dr. (Hwy. 95 N.), 702-658-4900
■ "A little-known hideaway" in the Santa Fe Hotel on the Northwest
Side, this "tiny" Classic French "gem" has just 40 seats, and they're
usually filled with locals; sybarites say "you'll never feel so
pampered", adding "they need to advertise" more – but selfish
types hope it remains undiscovered.

Valentino ●S

– | – | – | E

Venetian Hotel, 3355 Las Vegas Blvd. S. (bet. Flamingo &
Spring Mountain Rds.), 702-414-3000
Bask in the best of Italy à la veteran restaurateur Piero Selvaggio
at this Venetian Hotel Northern Italian transplanted from Santa
Monica and helmed by chef Luciano Pellegrini; with camera-ready
fare backed by a legendary wine collection – over 24,000 bottles –
that's displayed throughout the handsome space, this is just plain
don't-miss dining; N.B. the Italian Grill, nestled in the entryway,
offers a lower-priced, pared-down menu.

Long Island

TOP 20 FOOD RANKING

Restaurant	Cuisine Type
27 Mill River Inn	New American
Mirabelle	New French
Peter Luger	Steakhouse
Kotobuki	Japanese
La Piccola Liguria	Northern Italian
26 La Plage	Eclectic
Piccolo	Northern Italian
Mirepoix	Eclectic
Siam Lotus	Thai
Panama Hatties	New American/Eclectic
Mirko's	Continental/Eclectic
Tuscany	Northern Italian/Eclectic
Starr Boggs	New American
Bravo! Nader	N/S Italian
Stone Creek Inn	New French/Med.
La Pace	Northern Italian
Enoteca il Castello	Northern Italian
Louis XVI	New French
25 Sempre Vivolo	N/S Italian
Da Ugo	N/S Italian

ADDITIONAL NOTEWORTHY PLACES

American Hotel	Classic French
Barney's	New American/New French
Bryant & Cooper	Steakhouse
Dario	N/S Italian
Focaccia Grill	New American
La Marmite	Classic French
L'Endroit	Classic French/N. Italian
Le Soir	French Bistro
Maidstone Arms	Traditional American
Mazzi	Continental
Navona	N/S Italian
Pacific East	Asian
Palm	Steakhouse
Palm Court/Carltun	Continental
Plaza Cafe	New American/Seafood
Polo Grill	New American
Stresa	N/S Italian
Tierra Mar	New American
Trattoria Diane	Northern Italian
Tupelo Honey	Caribbean/Eclectic

American Hotel [S]

24 | 25 | 22 | $49

The American Hotel, 25 Main St. (Washington St.), Sag Harbor, 631-725-3535

■ Scott and Zelda would certainly feel right at home with the "Gatsby-esque interior" of this "intimate and classy" "old-world" Sag Harbor stalwart; the "inventive" Classic French cuisine, "great wine list" and "romantic" ambiance are just this side of paradise, though "stuffy service" rates a mention too; count on "Hamptons celebs" to make the scene, and don't miss Hunky Page at the piano on Saturdays.

Barney's [S]

24 | 22 | 22 | $46

315 Buckram Rd. (Bayville Rd.), Locust Valley, 516-671-6300

■ "Utterly romantic", this "quaint country inn" in Locust Valley with a "New England ambiance" is renowned for its "awesome" New French–New American cuisine; savor the experience in the inviting fireplace room, on the intimate enclosed porch or in the lounge; even those who feel it's "a bit pricey" concede that "it's worth it."

Bravo! Nader [S]

26 | 15 | 23 | $44

9 Union Pl. (bet. New York Ave. & Wall St.), Huntington, 631-351-1200

■ The heartiest bravos at this Huntington "shoe box" go to modest chef-owner Nader Gebrin's "fabulous" peasant-style Italian cooking, some of "the best on LI"; it's complemented by "friendly", "gracious" service, but some call the "cramped", "noisy" space "uncomfortable"; insiders advise "go during the week."

Bryant & Cooper Steakhouse [S]

25 | 19 | 20 | $45

2 Middle Neck Rd. (Northern Blvd.), Roslyn, 516-627-7270

■ Among the top steakhouses on LI, this "stately place" in Roslyn serves "superb" cuts of "aged meats" "cooked to perfection" and also satisfies "non–steak lovers with dishes like sesame tuna"; but "avoid the weekend" hordes, especially since they "don't always honor reservations."

Dario

25 | 19 | 23 | $44

13 N. Village Ave. (bet. Merrick Rd. & Sunrise Hwy.), Rockville Centre, 516-255-0535

◪ "An elegant find", this "formal little" Rockville Centre Italian is praised for its "phenomenal" food (especially the "superlative veal and fish dishes") and "attentive service", energized by the "watchful eyes" and "family pride" of Dario Viscovich and his sons; a few find it "pretentious" and "overpriced", but most say it's "a winner."

Da Ugo

25 | 20 | 24 | $39

509 Merrick Rd. (Long Beach Rd.), Rockville Centre, 516-764-1900

■ "Manhattan dining comes to LI" at this "cosmopolitan" Italian in Rockville Centre, which covers all bases with "top-notch" food ("incredible stuffed veal chop"), an "intimate atmosphere" and "attentive", "professional" service; P.S. it's "hard to get a reservation" given the "very small" room, but it's "worth the wait."

Enoteca il Castello
26 | 26 | 22 | $53

*146 Birch Hill Rd. (Soundview Ave.), Locust Valley,
516-671-9486*

☑ "Everything a restaurant should be" is how admirers view this "wonderful addition" to Locust Valley; while a new chef and a Northern Italian menu were installed post-*Survey* (thus outdating the food rating), it retains its "gorgeous, spacious" setting and "classy service" (even though a few report "snobby staff"); regulars only hope it remains a "refined" destination "worthy of a special occasion."

Focaccia Grill S
25 | 18 | 21 | $35

*2010 Wantagh Ave. (Woodward Ave.), Wantagh,
516-785-7675*

■ Brian Arbesfeld, the "fantastic chef"-owner of this Wantagh New American "gem", creates "exciting" "dishes that make your taste buds dance"; his "masterpieces" are complemented by a "fine wine" selection and are served by a "courteous" staff in an "understated" space; epicures only "wish it were quieter", but the "unbelievable" cuisine makes a visit "a night to remember."

Kotobuki S
27 | 16 | 20 | $28

*86 Deer Park Ave. (Main St.), Babylon, 631-321-8387
377 Nesconset Hwy. (Rte. 111), Hauppauge, 631-360-3969*

■ Voted once again the No. 1 Japanese on LI, this pair of siblings in Babylon and Hauppauge is a "sushi heaven" that features "exquisite plates" of "inventive", "fabulous" creations (the "deluxe" platter "for two is a gargantuan bargain"); though there's "not much atmosphere" in the "cramped" quarters and there's usually a "long wait" for a "too-small table", disciples swear it's "worth the tumult."

La Marmite S
24 | 22 | 24 | $44

*234 Hillside Ave. (Mineola Blvd.), Williston Park,
516-746-1243*

■ "*Mais oui*" rhapsodize devotees of "*la grande dame*" of Williston Park, a "charmer" that's "guaranteed to impress"; proffering "fine dining in relaxed luxury", a "superior" staff presents "exceptional" Classic French and Northern Italian fare; though a few frown about the "stuffy" ambiance, most say "how nice to get dressed up" for "a special night at a special place."

La Pace S
26 | 24 | 24 | $44

51 Cedar Swamp Rd. (2nd St.), Glen Cove, 516-671-2970

■ The "epitome of gracious dining" for more than two decades, this "unique" "LI classic" in Glen Cove remains "memorable" for its "absolutely delicious" Northern Italian cuisine served in a "romantic" room and its "professional" staff; though "a bit pricey", this "special-occasion" "treat" is "outstanding across the board."

La Piccola Liguria S
27 | 20 | 25 | $42

47 Shore Rd. (Main St.), Port Washington, 516-767-6490

■ Voted the No. 1 Northern Italian on LI, this Port Washington charmer promises "a transporting culinary experience" with "marvelous" cuisine marked by "a variety of tastes"; the service is nearly as "incredible" as the "imaginative kitchen", so despite "tight" seating, a meal here will be one "to remember."

La Plage [S]
26 | 20 | 24 | $40

131 Creek Rd. (Sound Rd.), Wading River, 631-744-9200

■ Discover the "best-kept secret on Eastern LI" at this "romantic" "oasis" "off the beaten path" in Wading River in an "unsurpassable setting" "by the beach"; it may look like a "tiny shack", but it's a "fantastic find" for "unbelievable", "inventive" cuisine, a "fine wine list" and a "friendly yet sophisticated" staff.

L'Endroit
25 | 24 | 23 | $47

290 Glen Cove Rd. (Park Dr.), East Hills, 516-621-6630

■ "One of the very best restaurants on LI", this "fancy" East Hills landmark is "romantic, beautiful" and "elegant" in an "old-world" way; specializing in a Classic French and Northern Italian menu, the fare is "stellar", if "fusty"; likewise, the decor is "dated", though the "Ruben-esque" artwork is certainly "interesting"; factor in "classy" service and most feel this "special-occasion place doesn't disappoint", although it's even "better during the week."

Le Soir [S]
25 | 20 | 23 | $39

825 Montauk Hwy. (Bayport Ave.), Bayport, 631-472-9090

■ "You feel as if you're in the French countryside rather than on Montauk Highway" at this "joy of a restaurant" in Bayport, an "intimate", "charming bistro" that turns out "fabulous", "true" Gallic fare; a "professional" staff "with no pretensions" ensures "a terrific dining experience" at this "little gem."

Louis XVI [S]
26 | 28 | 25 | $57

600 S. Ocean Ave. (Great South Bay), Patchogue, 631-654-8970

■ Voted No. 1 for Decor in the *LI Survey* – devotees swear it could rival "the Palace of Versailles" – this "extravagant", "elegant" and "exquisite" "crown jewel" boasts "gorgeous views" of Great South Bay from its "beautiful setting on the water" in Patchogue; indulge in "extraordinary", "imaginative" New French cuisine "magnificently presented" by an "impeccable" staff; dip into the "kids' college fund" or "mortgage the house" if you must, but it's "worth every franc."

Maidstone Arms [S]
25 | 25 | 23 | $48

207 Main St. (Mill Hill Ln.), East Hampton, 631-324-5006

■ The "classic East Hampton experience" lives on at this "beautiful and charming" "historic inn" (circa 1840) where the "romantic" dining rooms provide "quiet and dignified" backdrops for the "sophisticated" Traditional American cuisine; "gracious and friendly service" adds a truly "civilized" air.

Mazzi
25 | 22 | 23 | $44

493 E. Jericho Tpke. (Melville Rd.), Huntington Station, 631-421-3390

■ Admirers of this "small, elegant" jewel set in a "quaint old house" in Huntington Station "love it" for its "exceptional" Continental cuisine; the "beautiful interior is romantic and intimate", the ambiance "relaxing" and the service "helpful"; "superior in all categories", this is a "special place for that special dinner."

Mill River Inn 🅂   27 | 23 | 25 | $52

*160 Mill River Rd. (bet. Lexington Ave. & Rte. 25A), Oyster Bay,
516-922-7768*

■ "If you want perfection", look no further: this "fantastic" Oyster
Bay New American is voted No. 1 for Food and No. 2 for both
Popularity and Service in the *LI Survey*; since the "romantic"
atmosphere will "transport you to another world" that many say
is the "ultimate" "special treat", "reservations can be hard to
get", so plan ahead; N.B. a recent chef change may outdate the
above food score.

Mirabelle 🅂   27 | 23 | 25 | $53

*404 N. Country Rd. (Edgewood Ave.), St. James,
631-584-5999*

■ "Superlative in every way" rhapsodize sophisticates about this
"intimate", "classy" New French "gem" set in a "charming old
house" in St. James; it's such a "sublime experience" that if
you "close your eyes, you could be transported to France" by
"marvelous" chef-owner Guy Reuge's "phenomenal" cuisine
(even if it's doled out in "very small portions"); be pampered by
an "impeccable" staff that tends "without attitude" – it was voted
No. 1 for Service in the *LI Survey* yet again.

Mirepoix   26 | 20 | 25 | $49

70 Glen Head Rd. (Glen Cove Rd.), Glen Head, 516-671-2498

■ Admirers of this "tiny treasure" near the train station in Glen
Head say it serves "such good food that it should be in larger
quarters" ("if only they could stretch the walls"); along with
"creative" Eclectic fare, expect an "elegant ambiance", "caring
service" and "petite portions for a grand prix", though most concur
it's "worth it."

Mirko's 🅂   26 | 22 | 24 | $50

*Water Mill Sq., Montauk Hwy. (opp. Windmill), Water Mill,
631-726-4444*

■ Winning the top food rating on LI's South Fork, "hands-on
owners" Mirko and Eileen Zagar offer an "antidote to Hamptons
chic" at this Water Mill "class act"; it's a "hidden" outpost for
"romantic" "fine dining" on "spectacular" Continental-Eclectic
cuisine; despite "high prices", there's "never a misfire" here.

Navona   25 | 22 | 22 | $44

*218 Middle Neck Rd. (Clover Dr.), Great Neck,
516-487-5603*

■ "Great Neckers love" this "sensational" Italian, as "everything
about it spells class" – from the "delicious, elegant" fare to the
"beautiful" "pastel" room embellished with "flowers galore"; the
one hot button – "too much preferential treatment to regulars" –
makes a few moan it "pays to be recognized"; nonetheless, the
majority agrees this is an "outstanding gastronomical experience."

Pacific East 🅂   25 | 23 | 20 | $48

415 Main St. (Atlantic Ave.), Amagansett, 631-267-7770

■ Trendsetters tag this Amagansett Asian fusion house one of
the "most creative" venues around, an "exotic" "hot spot" that
offers "outstanding presentations" of "provocative dishes" with
a stress on seafood; despite "stratospheric prices", it's "worth a
day trip" anytime to indulge in "stylish", "see-and-be-seen" dining.

Palm [S]

F	D	S	C
25	20	21	$53

The Huntting Inn, 94 Main St. (Rte. 27), East Hampton, 631-324-0411

■ The parking lot "looks like a Mercedes" dealership at this branch of the masculine powerhouse chain, a "winner every time" in the eyes of East Hampton meat mavens; it's "*the* place for steaks" and "huge lobsters", with creamed spinach and "super" crispy onions on the side, all delivered by a "first-rate" staff – "just like in NYC but more charming."

Palm Court at Carltun on the Park [S]

F	D	S	C
24	28	23	$48

Eisenhower Park (Merrick Ave.), East Meadow, 516-542-0700

■ "When you want elegance", this "gorgeous" Eisenhower Park Continental is a "must for special occasions", with "unparalleled" cuisine, an "incredible wine cellar", a cigar room and live jazz Friday–Saturday; while the "pricey" tabs displease a few, the majority feels that this "breathtaking" place will definitely "put you in a romantic mood."

Panama Hatties [S]

F	D	S	C
26	24	24	$55

Post Plaza, 872 E. Jericho Tpke. (2 mi. east of Rte. 110), Huntington Station, 631-351-1727

■ "Wow!" – since sous chef Matthew Hisiger took over the range, this "extraordinary" Huntington Station "dream" is even better than before, preparing "exquisite" New American–Eclectic cuisine and "magnificently presenting" "each dish like a work of art"; "despite the strip mall location", the interior is "elegant" and "romantic" and the staff "knowledgeable" (if "pretentious"); "inventive" and "memorable", this is "one of the best restaurants on LI."

Peter Luger Steak House [S]≠

F	D	S	C
27	18	21	$49

255 Northern Blvd. (bet. Lakeville Rd. & Little Neck Pkwy.), Great Neck, 516-487-8800

■ The "king of steaks" and once again voted the Most Popular restaurant on LI, this Great Neck beef shrine projects patrons into "porterhouse heaven", where they also encounter "great" sides and desserts; sure, it may be a "tick below" its Brooklyn sibling, and there are scattered barbs about "curt" waiters and the "no-credit-card policy", but for "stupendous steaks", most say "this is the place."

Piccolo [S]

F	D	S	C
26	21	24	$44

Southdown Shopping Ctr., 215 Wall St. (Mill Ln.), Huntington, 631-424-5592

■ "Simply wonderful" rave the Huntington cognoscenti of this Northern Italian "gem" that proffers "all you could want from a great restaurant" – "exceptional" fare "perfectly presented" by a "polished" staff in an "elegant" room with a "warm, welcoming atmosphere"; it's "tough to get a reservation, but be persistent – you don't want to miss this" "treat."

Plaza Cafe [S]

F	D	S	C
25	20	21	$44

61 Hill St. (bet. First Neck & Pond Lns.), Southampton, 631-283-9323

■ Southampton sophisticates say this "superb" New American–seafooder sets "a new standard" with "inventive dishes" like its signature lobster-and-shrimp shepherd's pie ("a must"); "expertly run" by chef-owner Douglas Gulija and kin, it may be "pricey", but the performance is "a cut above the rest."

	F	D	S	C

Polo Grill [S]

25	25	24	$48

Garden City Hotel, 45 Seventh St. (Franklin Ave.), Garden City, 516-877-9353

■ A "class act all the way" is how connoisseurs sum up this "elegant" New American in Garden City, where the "superb" seasonal cuisine is "presented like a work of art" by "professional" servers; though "expensive", this "special-occasion" venue is clearly "not your average hotel restaurant"; P.S. the Sunday brunch is "outstanding."

Sempre Vivolo

25	23	24	$42

696 Motor Pkwy. (Old Willets Path), Hauppauge, 631-435-1737

■ A "sophisticated crowd" that doesn't seem to mind the "jacket-required" policy (on Saturdays) at this "throwback" in Hauppauge enjoys "a fine dining experience" here, with "well-prepared" Italian cuisine served by a "classy" staff in an "intimate setting"; though it's "expensive", most say it's "worth the money" for a "special" "dress-up occasion."

Siam Lotus [S]

26	16	25	$26

1664 Union Blvd. (opp. LIRR station), Bay Shore, 631-968-8196

■ Voted the No. 1 Thai on LI, this "divine" Bay Shore "find" is renowned for "fabulous, spicy food"; the quarters are "a little tight", but the room is made "comfortable" enough by a "gracious owner" and "polite" staff that's "on the ball"; the tabs are "affordable", leading regulars to beg "please don't tell anyone about this place."

Starr Boggs [S]

26	23	22	$49

Dune Deck Hotel, 379 Dune Rd. (east of Harbor Rd.), Westhampton Beach, 631-288-5250

■ Sure, this "cool, classy" "gem" boasts the "ultimate" "romantic" setting in Westhampton Beach's Dune Deck Hotel, but "the brightest star of all" is the "innovative" New American menu, showcasing "local seafood and vegetables" ("best crab cakes ever"); in season (May–Sept.), the "Hamptons wanna-be-seen" clientele competes for attention with the "wonderful ocean view."

Stone Creek Inn [S]

26	25	23	$48

405 Montauk Hwy. (Wedgewood Rd.), East Quogue, 631-653-6770

■ A "wonderful dining experience" in unhip East Quogue is what surveyors say about this New French–Med showstopper in a "beautiful country inn" with an "exquisite setting"; "excellent" cuisine and "no-nonsense" service only add to its charms.

Stresa [S]

25	23	22	$45

1524 Northern Blvd. (east of Shelter Rock Rd.), Manhasset, 516-365-6956

■ "European elegance fit for royalty" is the "classy" allure of this Manhasset Italian "gem", a "special place that seems insulated from the world"; while "beautiful people" "feast" on "outstanding" cuisine in "beautiful surroundings", a few complain that the "pretentious" staff "obviously favors regulars."

Tierra Mar S   25 | – | 22 | $48
Westhampton Bath & Tennis Club, 231 Dune Rd. (Jessup Ave. Bridge),
Westhampton Beach, 631-288-2700
■ Todd Jacobs, "one of the best" chef-owners on LI, has moved
his "classy" Westhampton standout to the fabulous oceanfront
site where he used to operate Atlantica; his "creative" New
American dishes are even more "alluring" when savored from
the beautiful deck overlooking the water; of course, the package
is "a bit pricey", but it is a "total dining experience" "done with
ingenuity and style."

Trattoria Diane S   25 | 21 | 22 | $41
23 Bryant Ave. (Northern Blvd.), Roslyn, 516-621-2591
■ The "jewel of Roslyn", this "sophisticated" Northern Italian
shines with "imaginative" Tuscan-inspired cuisine, "perfectly"
executed (definitely "save room" for the "divine desserts"); an
"attentive" staff and "softly understated" rooms also make a
meal here an "indulgent retreat"; N.B. sample the impressive
wine-tasting dinners.

Tupelo Honey S   25 | 24 | 21 | $41
39 Roslyn Ave. (Sea Cliff Ave.), Sea Cliff, 516-671-8300
■ South Beach meets Sea Cliff at this "fusion fantasy", which
features "avant-garde decor" (wild mosaic tiles on the tables and
walls) and "excellent" Caribbean-Eclectic cooking courtesy of chef/
co-owner Michael Meehan; "unbearable noise" is a drawback,
but otherwise this "cool" place is a "yuppie" standout with a
"tropical vacation" feel.

Tuscany S   26 | 21 | 23 | $43
187 N. Long Beach Rd. (bet. Greystone Rd. & Lakeview Ave.),
Rockville Centre, 516-763-9313
■ Joseph Bonacore, the chef-owner of this "outstanding" Tuscan
treasure in Rockville Centre, has passed the toque on to a new
chef-owner, John Mancuso, who puts his own stamp on a Northern
Italian–Eclectic menu with dishes like bourbon-marinated pork
tenderloin; N.B. the chef shuffle may outdate the above food score.

Los Angeles

TOP 20 FOOD RANKING

Restaurant	Cuisine Type
28 Matsuhisa	Japanese
Sushi Nozawa	Japanese
27 L'Orangerie	Classic French
Chinois on Main	Asian/New French
Belvedere, The	Californian/French/Asian
Patina	Californian/New French
Water Grill	Seafood
Valentino	N/S Italian
Spago Bev. Hills	Californian/Eclectic
Asanebo	Japanese
Shiro	Californian/Asian/Seafood
Joe's	Californian
Hotel Bel-Air	Californian/French
26 Campanile	Mediterranean
Mélisse	Californian/New French
Gardens	Mediterranean
La Cachette	French
Brent's Deli	Deli/Jewish
Frenchy's Bistro	French Bistro
Ruth's Chris	Steakhouse

ADDITIONAL NOTEWORTHY PLACES

Bistro 45	Californian/French Bistro
Cafe Bizou	French Bistro
Cafe Blanc	Californian/Asian
Chaya Brasserie	Asian/Eclectic
Chef Shafer's Depot	Californian/Eclectic
Chez Melange	Eclectic
Devon	Californian
Diaghilev	French/Russian
Grill, The	Traditional American
JiRaffe	Californian/New American
Jozu	Pacific Rim
Lawry's	Steakhouse
Locanda Veneta	Northern Italian
Michael's	New American
Mimosa	French Bistro
Palm, The	Steakhouse
Pinot Bistro	Californian/French Bistro
Saddle Peak Lodge	New American
Tung Lai Shun	Islamic Chinese
Yujean Kang's	Chinese

Asanebo [S] 27 | 15 | 22 | $46

11941 Ventura Blvd. (bet. Colfax Ave. & Laurel Canyon Blvd.), Studio City, 818-760-3348

■ One of the top destinations on Studio City's sushi row, this former sashimi-only shop now serves sushi and does it well enough to be dubbed "the middle-class version of Matsuhisa"; habitués hint you should "let the chef decide" by opting for the "set-dinner menu", and even though it's "worth the expense", come prepared to "max out your credit card."

Belvedere, The [S] 27 | 28 | 28 | $56

Peninsula Beverly Hills Hotel, 9882 Little Santa Monica Blvd. (Wilshire Blvd.), Beverly Hills, 310-788-2306

■ Voted No. 1 for Service in LA yet again, this "special night out" at the Peninsula has also regained its title as the best hotel dining room (edging out its archrival, the Bel-Air, by a well-coiffed hair); credit the "faultless" Cal/French/Asian menu (including what might be the "best Sunday brunch in town") and "unsurpassed ambiance" for its "welcomed formality in a casual city"; as a bonus, a "pampered" crowd comprised of the "rich, famous and beautiful" supplies "stargazing galore."

Bistro 45 [S] 25 | 23 | 24 | $44

45 S. Mentor Ave. (bet. Colorado Blvd. & Green St.), Pasadena, 626-795-2478

■ "Exceptional" Cal-French bistro in an art deco setting that's a "civilized oasis" with "a lot of heart" thanks to its "excellent host, Robert Simon", and "bend-over-backward" staff; locals call it their "saving grace", day-trippers deem it an "absolutely charming" stop "after a day at the Rose Bowl or Santa Anita" and the amorously inclined say it provides "Pasadena's most romantic dining."

Brent's Deli [S] 26 | 14 | 22 | $15

19565 Parthenia Ave. (bet. Corbin & Tampa Aves.), Northridge, 818-886-5679

■ Once again voted SoCal's top deli, this "first-rate experience" is "still the very best", so "superior in every way" that "no other comes close"; "delicious, reasonably priced" Jewish soul food that arrives in "large portions" is its secret, despite a "nothing location" in a "godforsaken Northridge" mall; "buxom waitresses who call you 'dearie'" lend color to the proceedings.

Cafe Bizou [S] 25 | 19 | 22 | $27

91 N. Raymond Ave. (Holly St.), Pasadena, 626-792-9923
14016 Ventura Blvd. (Hazeltine Ave.), Sherman Oaks, 818-788-3536

■ "How do they do it?" wonder fans of this pair of "spectacular deal" French bistros with "gourmet food at rock-bottom prices" and an "unbelievable $2 corkage" fee; delivering the "most bang for the franc", it's a "perennial favorite" and this year it was voted LA's Most Popular restaurant; P.S. needless to say, prepare for the "daunting crowds."

Cafe Blanc 25 | 16 | 22 | $42

9777 Little Santa Monica Blvd. (Wilshire Blvd.), Beverly Hills, 310-888-0108

■ One of the purest of the remaining Cal-Asians, this "tiny", "minimalist heaven" turns out "maximum taste" in an understated white box located at one of the busiest intersections in Beverly Hills; expect "exquisite food" prepared by a "most caring chef" operating at the "apex of creativity" at this "top-notch", "best-kept secret in town."

Campanile [S] | 26 | 24 | 23 | $44 |

624 S. La Brea Ave. (bet. 6th St. & Wilshire Blvd.), LA, 323-938-1447

■ Ranked as the top Med in LA, this "gloriously romantic" "special-occasion" destination set in a unique building built by Charlie Chaplin is a tribute to both the city's past and present; it's a "favorite" "treat" from beginning ("fabulous breads" from the adjacent La Brea Bakery and "awesome olive oil choices") to end (the signature apple puff pastry with zabaglione is "delicious").

Chaya Brasserie ◐[S] | 24 | 23 | 22 | $41 |

8741 Alden Dr. (bet. Beverly Blvd. & 3rd St.), LA, 310-859-8833

■ "Amazingly hip after all these years", this Asian-Eclectic "scene" still offers the "beautiful people" the "consummate LA dining experience" – a "beauty contest between the food" (a "visually pleasing", "delicious fusion of East and West"), decor (described as "John Muir goes to Thailand") and staff ("good looking" and "on target"); West Hollywood's "smart set" swears "you can't go wrong" here.

Chef Shafer's Depot | 24 | 22 | 23 | $34 |

(fka Depot)

1250 Cabrillo Ave. (Torrance Blvd.), Torrance, 310-787-7501

■ "Quirky chef" Michael Shafer "performs culinary miracles" at this Torrance Cal-Eclectic with an Asian emphasis that he recently purchased from his Chez Melange partners; housed in a "beautiful" "old train station", it "always surprises" with "inspired", "creative" "combinations of ingredients."

Chez Melange [S] | 25 | 18 | 24 | $33 |

Palos Verdes Inn, 1716 PCH (bet. Palos Verdes Blvd. & Prospect Ave.), Redondo Beach, 310-540-1222

■ Robert Bell and Michael Franks keep opening new places, but their Redondo Beach original remains a "consistent favorite", "still tops in the South Bay" for "innovative" Eclectic cuisine with an edge; it only "needs a face-lift" to match the "memorable" menu that always entices with "something new."

Chinois on Main [S] | 27 | 22 | 23 | $49 |

2709 Main St. (bet. Ocean Park Blvd. & Rose Ave.), Santa Monica, 310-392-9025

■ Spago may be more famous, but year after year, this "absolutely great" Santa Monica "innovator" is the highest-rated of Wolfgang Puck's many restaurants and among "LA's best" overall; "sit at the counter and watch culinary stars work their magic" on an "extraordinary" Asian-inspired New French menu; while the front of the house is admittedly too "crammed" and the "dreadful" noise could well "break the sound barrier", the kitchen transcends its earthly limits with "unusual combinations" that are "simply divine."

Devon [S] | 26 | 21 | 24 | $44 |

109 E. Lemon Ave. (Myrtle Ave.), Monrovia, 626-305-0013

■ The restaurant that "put Monrovia on the map", this "upscale" "storefront" Californian set in a "bucolic" hamlet at the foot of the San Gabriel Mountains just keeps getting "better and better"; it clearly "aspires to the first tier" with its "superb", "cutting-edge cuisine", "great wine list" and "excellent" service.

Diaghilev
26 | 27 | 27 | $60

Wyndham Bel Age Hotel, 1020 N. San Vicente Blvd. (Sunset Blvd.), W. Hollywood, 310-854-1111

■ "Stars eat like czars" at this West Hollywood "Franco-Russian" that's perhaps the most "elegant" restaurant in SoCal; winning nearly as much praise as the "dreamy" "vodka-and-caviar" menu is ingratiating "host Dmitri Dmitrov", who may be "LA's No. 1 maitre d'"; surveyors suggest "save your pennies" (it's "pricey") and "start with a great vodka – it just gets better from there."

Frenchy's Bistro S
26 | 16 | 23 | $33

4137 E. Anaheim St. (bet. Termino & Ximeno Aves.), Long Beach, 562-494-8787

■ "C'est magnifique!" rave devotees of Andre and Valerie Angles' "honest", "intimate" French bistro that's like a little slice of Provence relocated to a "culinary no-man's land" in Long Beach; the "authentic" fare is "sublime", the menu "ever changing" and the "personal" service downright "wonderful"; P.S. it features a new "wine bar" and a recently expanded dining room.

Gardens S
26 | 27 | 27 | $49

Four Seasons Hotel, 300 S. Doheny Dr. (Burton Way), LA, 310-273-2222

■ "Lovely in every way" sigh fans of this "purely luxurious" hotel Mediterranean in Beverly Hills that draws moguls and "stars galore" to its "beautiful, tranquil" "power rooms"; its "no-nonsense gourmet" cuisine and "delightful" service "sparkle" with "elegance", though steep prices make it "best on an expense account"; P.S. "learn firsthand what Morgan Freeman likes in his omelet" at the "Sunday brunches fit for Hollywood royalty."

Grill, The S
24 | 21 | 23 | $43

9560 Dayton Way (Wilshire Blvd.), Beverly Hills, 310-276-0615

■ Some still expect the likes of Humphrey Bogart to show up at this "old"-school Beverly Hills Traditional American "man's restaurant", a "chophouse of the stars" and "power brokers" that's "a sure bet" for "generous cocktails" and "steaks done the way they should be"; it "runs like clockwork", though the "pro" staff's a bit "pompous"; P.S. bring the "business credit card."

Hotel Bel-Air S
27 | 28 | 27 | $56

701 Stone Canyon Rd. (Sunset Blvd.), Bel Air, 310-472-1211

■ Once again ranked No. 1 for Decor in LA, this "peerless" Cal-French earns waves of raves as an adventure in "plush and lush", a "classic that never disappoints" with its "verdant" "Garden-of-Eden" setting; "absolutely amazing food" and "star-quality service" by "real waiters" make this "romantic dream getaway" simply the "best place to celebrate a special event"; "movers and shakers" tout "incredible Table One", the private dining room in the kitchen where guests are tended to like hothouse orchids.

JiRaffe S
25 | 22 | 23 | $41

502 Santa Monica Blvd. (5th St.), Santa Monica, 310-917-6671

■ Josiah Citrin left to open Mélisse, but his partner, the "talented" Raphael Lunetta, still "carries on the tradition" at this Cal–New American; it's the "epitome of Californian" "sophistication": "creative", "elegant" cuisine "that's never overwrought", a "great", "intimate" room and a staff that can "intuit what you want."

Joe's S
27 | 19 | 23 | $39

1023 Abbot Kinney Blvd. (bet. Main St. & Westminster Ave.), Venice, 310-399-5811

■ "If chef Joe Miller started a cult, I'd be there" vow disciples of this "friendly" Californian "gem among restaurants", the keystone of the burgeoning Abbot Kinney Boulevard dining scene; its "incredible", "always innovative" menu offers "some of the most on-the-mark food in town", so it's no surprise that the "crowded", "noisy" spot's "still a tight squeeze" even after a recent expansion.

Jozu S
25 | 23 | 23 | $45

8360 Melrose Ave. (La Cienega Blvd.), W. Hollywood, 323-655-5600

■ "Masterful restaurateur" Andy Nakano promises "wonderful memories" at this West Hollywood Pacific Rim "miracle on Melrose", a "spare, Zen-like" setting for a near-"spiritual" "dining experience"; "new chef Hisashi Yoshiara" creates some of the "best and most innovative dishes in LA", evoking ecstatic praise.

La Cachette S
26 | 25 | 24 | $48

10506 Little Santa Monica Blvd. (bet. Beverly Glen Blvd. & Overland Ave.), Century City, 310-470-4992

■ This aptly named "little hideaway is a real find", both for its "French food that could be eaten every day without guilt" ("how do they do it without butter or cream?") and for its "romantic, plush and special" ambiance ("one of the few restaurants that has real space between the tables"); though all this "elegance" is "expensive", "Century City's finest" is "that special place for event dining" – and for "sending others without worrying."

Lawry's the Prime Rib S
25 | 23 | 25 | $38

100 N. La Cienega Blvd. (Wilshire Blvd.), Beverly Hills, 310-652-2827

■ "Forget those new entrees" – "you shouldn't be caught not eating the prime rib" at this "delicious anachronism" in Beverly Hills, "a family tradition for every special event" because it "sets the standard" for steakhouses (the "spinning salad" and side dishes aren't bad either); though some find the old-timers and tourists a turnoff, most agree "there's never a bum steer" here.

Locanda Veneta
25 | 17 | 21 | $39

8638 W. Third St. (bet. Robertson & San Vicente Blvds.), LA, 310-274-1893

■ Consistently ranked as one of LA's top Italians, this "awesome" Third Street Venetian is "romance personified", with "unbelievable pastas" and "lobster specials"; despite the cramped quarters, the "extremely tight seating" does make it easier to gaze at the movie star or two who's always present ("I was totally distracted sitting next to Holly Hunter").

L'Orangerie S
27 | 28 | 26 | $66

903 N. La Cienega Blvd. (bet. Melrose Ave. & Santa Monica Blvd.), W. Hollywood, 310-652-9770

■ One of the last of the "serious dining" experiences in LA, this Classic French is "as close to perfection as it gets"; for the tie-and-jacket crowd, it's "the only event restaurant" – "beautiful, sophisticated and exceptional in every way", from the "exquisite service" to the "breathtaking flowers" to the "purely sinful food" ("like eating money" – which in a way you are); most say "if the choice is a down payment on a car or eating here, then eat here – at least once."

Matsuhisa [S]

F	D	S	C
28	18	24	$57

129 N. La Cienega Blvd. (Wilshire Blvd.), Beverly Hills, 310-659-9639

■ Chef-owner "Nobu is god", and his eponymous Beverly Hills establishment is again rated LA's No. 1 for Food; whether you go "for straight sushi or the more exotic prepared dishes", the Japanese master's seafood embellished with a global twist is "the best thing to happen to fish since gills" and really worth "the body blow to the wallet"; "now, if only something could be done with the decor."

Mélisse [S]

F	D	S	C
26	24	24	$60

1104 Wilshire Blvd. (11th St.), Santa Monica, 310-395-0881

■ Already one of LA's Most Popular restaurants, this "rising star in SM" has fast become a "favorite special-occasion" place; chef-owner Josiah Citrin (ex JiRaffe) not only "does wonders" with the "very sophisticated" Cal–New French menu, but "thinks of everything" – from a retractable ceiling to sterling-silver cutlery – for diners' comfort; though some feel it's "overpriced", given the erratic service, the majority dubs this yearling "a winner."

Michael's

F	D	S	C
25	26	24	$52

1147 Third St. (Wilshire Blvd.), Santa Monica, 310-451-0843

■ Even after two decades, this "California original" miraculously remains on the cutting edge of The Way We Eat Now, with a "beautiful garden setting" that "enhances the creative, luscious" New American preparations; "when he's in town, [owner] Michael McCarty goes out of his way to make your evening special"; "despite many changes in the kitchen over the years, you can always count on" this Santa Monica "landmark."

Mimosa ◐

F	D	S	C
22	19	20	$38

8009 Beverly Blvd. (Crescent Hts. Blvd.), LA, 323-655-8895

■ Offering a "quick trip to the Left Bank", this Beverly eatery is a "madhouse but worth it" for its variety of "simply delightful" dishes, along with monthly specials from different regions of France; it's arguably the most "authentic bistro" in SoCal, except for one thing: here, "the French are nice to you."

Palm, The [S]

F	D	S	C
25	20	21	$50

9001 Santa Monica Blvd. (bet. Doheny Dr. & Robertson Blvd.), W. Hollywood, 310-550-8811

■ "Bring an appetite", "bring earplugs" and "bring your wallet" to this "noisy and hustling" West Hollywood hot spot with power plays in the air and "outrageous portions" ("lobsters the size of helicopters") on the plates; yes, the servers move with "McDonald's speed" and the prices virtually resemble car payments, but "if you're into celebrity-watching, this is the place to be."

Patina [S]

F	D	S	C
27	24	25	$59

5955 Melrose Ave. (bet. Highland Ave. & Vine St.), LA, 323-467-1108

■ Even though it's no longer LA's Most Popular restaurant, this Hollywood "budget-be-damned" place still rates as "LA's flagship in fine dining"; we begin with Joachim Splichal's Cal–New French cooking that's "constantly ahead of the culinary curve" with its "potpourri of tastes and textures" and augment it with "tactful, polite service" and a starkly "elegant" blond-oak setting; in sum, it's a place "to die for" – after all, this is "what heaven's restaurant must be like."

Pinot Bistro 🗖
25 | 23 | 23 | $41

12969 Ventura Blvd. (Coldwater Canyon Ave.), Studio City, 818-990-0500
■ The first of Joachim Splichal's Pinot empire, this "casually elegant" Cal–New French bistro "consistently upholds its standard of excellence" and is regarded as the "best restaurant in the Valley"; "imaginative chef" Octavio Becerra creates "smashing" dishes (his signature roasted farm chicken with fries will "keep you going back"), brought to table by an "accommodating" staff in an "inviting room"; this is an "absolute winner."

Ruth's Chris Steak House 🗖
26 | 21 | 23 | $45

224 S. Beverly Dr. (bet. Olympic & Wilshire Blvds.), Beverly Hills, 310-859-8744
■ Once again the top-rated temple of meat in SoCal, this chain outlet with roots in N'Awlins plates up "absolutely the best steaks, hands down"; the "awesome" prime cuts are served sizzling in butter and team up perfectly with the "rich traditional sides"; even if it's "cholesterol city", it's a "real treat", so "take your appetite and your parents" to this "favorite" that "lives up to its rep."

Saddle Peak Lodge 🗖
26 | 28 | 25 | $49

419 Cold Canyon Rd. (Malibu Canyon Rd.), Calabasas, 818-222-3888
■ A "getaway" journey to this "idyllic" New American "spot in the hills" above Malibu will make you "feel like you're on vacation in an old hunting lodge"; a "man's restaurant" with lots of "animal heads on the walls", it's a true "peak experience" for "hearty", "exceptional" game dishes like the signature elk tenderloin Rossini; "beautiful" and "tranquil", it's blessed with the "perfect location to forget the stresses of the day" and "well worth the drive."

Shiro 🗖
27 | 18 | 23 | $41

1505 Mission St. (Fair Oaks Ave.), S. Pasadena, 626-799-4774
■ Many regulars don't seem to know there's more than one item on the menu at this Cal-Asian seafood house in South Pasadena because they're totally addicted to its signature dish, the "best-ever catfish with *ponzu* sauce"; they "can't help it" – they hear the "memorable" fish "sizzle" and they lose all control; P.S. it does serve other "light and flavorful dishes."

Spago Beverly Hills 🗖
27 | 26 | 24 | $55

176 N. Cañon Dr. (Wilshire Blvd.), Beverly Hills, 310-385-0880
■ Wolfgang Puck's flagship is easily the most famous restaurant in SoCal, a Cal–Eclectic "celebrity hangout" where diners – if they can get a reservation – are "treated" to an experience that's "wonderful from start to finish", from the "incredible" cooking to the "gorgeous" digs to the "professional" service; "in a town where restaurants come and go, you can always count on Spago" – "they know how to do it right" at this glimpse of "heaven."

Sushi Nozawa
28 | 9 | 16 | $39

11288 Ventura Blvd. (Vineland Ave.), Studio City, 818-508-7017
■ "Be humble, take what they give you and enjoy the best fish around" at this Studio City Japanese storefront run by a "sushi god" "who tells you what to eat . . . or else"; "only serious sushi eaters" are fit to face this "moody" "master chef" who's "difficult but worth" the challenge because if you "trust Nozawa", then "this is the bomb!"

Tung Lai Shun [S] ▽ 22 | 11 | 13 | $19

140 W. Valley Blvd. (Del Mar Ave.), San Gabriel, 626-288-6588

■ For a "terrific change of pace", take an "amazing" "adventure" at this Islamic Chinese eatery in San Gabriel; for a "blissful" "experience", start with the "wonderful" sesame-scallion bread, followed by a "delicious", "unusual" lamb dish; there's "no pork" and "no liquor", but it's an "outstanding value" "with a twist."

Valentino 27 | 24 | 26 | $58

3115 Pico Blvd. (bet. 31st & 32nd Sts.), Santa Monica, 310-829-4313

■ Once again ranked as the top Italian in SoCal, Piero Selvaggio's "ultimate dining experience" earns him "very high ratings in all departments" – "grand", "magical" cuisine (accompanied by a "stupendous", "mind-boggling wine list") proffered in a "world-class" dining room by a staff that's "professional in every sense"; of course it's "pricey", but it's very much a "special-occasion delight", especially if you "ask Piero to plan your meal."

Water Grill [S] 27 | 25 | 25 | $45

544 S. Grand Ave. (bet. 5th & 6th Sts.), Downtown LA, 213-891-0900

■ "If it swims and it's delicious, they've got it" at this "classy", "clubby", top-rated Downtown seafood house that's "A-1 in all respects", a "fabulous" restaurant that's LA's answer to NYC's Le Bernardin; "every dish is an elegant masterpiece" – from the "world-class clam chowder" to the "perfectly prepared" fish to the "desserts that'll send you to heaven"; enhancing the experience even more is the "intelligent staff that really cares about the food"; "this is why we go out to eat."

Yujean Kang's [S] 25 | 21 | 22 | $36

67 N. Raymond Ave. (bet. Colorado Blvd. & Walnut St.), Pasadena, 626-585-0855

8826 Melrose Ave. (Robertson Blvd.), W. Hollywood, 310-288-0806

■ "Mr. Kang is never boring" and he proves it time and time again at his "pretty" pair of "original" "East-meets-West" hybrids that spin "truly unique twists on Chinese dishes" "as far from chow mein as you can get"; "bring a crowd to share" the "excellent modern interpretations", delivered by an "attentive" staff; his admirers attest that he "deserves a spot with the Big Boys of LA's restaurant scene."

Miami

TOP 20 FOOD RANKING

	Restaurant	Cuisine Type
27	Norman's	New World
	Osteria del Teatro	Northern Italian
26	Chef Allen's	New World
	Tropical Chinese	Chinese
	Palm	Steakhouse
	Pacific Time	Pan-Asian
	Baleen	Seafood
	Toni's Sushi	Japanese
	Joe's Stone Crab	Seafood
	Caffé Abbracci	N/S Italian
25	Escopazzo	N/S Italian
	Ruth's Chris	Steakhouse
	Crystal Cafe	Continental
	Nemo	Eclectic
	Forge, The	Continental
	Tuscan Steak	N. Italian/Steakhouse
	Morton's of Chicago	Steakhouse
24	Astor Place	New American
	Miss Saigon	Vietnamese
	Siam Palace	Thai

ADDITIONAL NOTEWORTHY PLACES

Restaurant	Cuisine Type
Atlantic	New American
Bambú	Pan-Asian
Blue Door	New French
Carpaccio	Northern Italian
China Grill	Eclectic
Chrysanthemum	Chinese
Hy-Vong	Vietnamese
La Palme d'Or	New French
Maiko	Japanese
Mark's South Beach	New American
Max's Place	New American
Ortanique on the Mile	Caribbean
Pascal's on Ponce	New French
Porcao	Brazilian/Steakhouse
Red Fish Grill	Seafood
Tantra	Eclectic
Two Chefs	New American
Versailles	Cuban
Wish	New American
Wolfie Cohen's Rascal House	Deli

Astor Place S
24 | 24 | 21 | $45

*Hotel Astor, 956 Washington Ave. (10th St.), Miami Beach,
305-672-7217*

■ After a yearlong hiatus, the original Caribbean Cowboy, Johnny
Vinczencz, is back in the saddle again at this "airy" "art deco"
New American set in the trendy Hotel Astor; see-and-be-seen
scenesters are hoping he'll be able to re-stoke the fires at this
former South Beach "hot spot."

Atlantic S
– | – | – | E

*Beach House Bal Harbour, 9449 Collins Ave. (94th St.), Surfside,
305-695-7930*

With its blue-and-white cabana stripes, the look is more Nantucket
than Miami, but this utterly tasteful hotel eatery seems right at
home overlooking Bal Harbor; its New American menu, designed
by Sheila Lukins of Silver Palate fame, offers above-average fare
with interesting twists (e.g. mac 'n' cheese with truffles) plus a
bargain Sunday brunch; N.B. check out the Seahorse bar's
aquarium and other eye-catching attractions.

Baleen S
26 | 27 | 20 | $53

Grove Isle Hotel, 4 Grove Isle Dr., Coconut Grove, 305-858-8300

■ Chef "Robbin Haas continues to be a marvel" with his "superb"
seafood at this country-clubbish upstart at the Grove Isle Hotel;
the "totally romantic" experience comes with "beautiful decor"
(rated No. 1 in the *Miami Survey*) and "one of the best views in
town", though hedgers hint the "service could improve" given the
"shockingly expensive" tabs.

Bambú ●S
– | – | – | VE

1665 Meridian Ave. (16th St.), Miami Beach, 305-531-4800

Your chances of seeing co-owner Cameron Diaz at this sultry
Pan-Asian Lincoln Roader are about as likely as your being able
to pronounce all the obscure ingredients on the menu, but that
won't mar the pleasure of sampling the exotic (and pricey) fare
from up-and-coming celebrity chef Rob Boone; although it's
trendy for sure, with gorgeous model waitresses, the kitchen's
approach to seafood is serious.

Blue Door ●S
23 | 27 | 20 | $54

Delano Hotel, 1685 Collins Ave. (17th St.), Miami Beach, 305-674-6400

◪ "Wow!"; this "very chic" nouveau French in the Delano Hotel
presents chef Claude Troisgros' "amazing" cuisine against a
candlelit backdrop of "floor-to-ceiling curtains that make you feel
as if you're onstage"; it's "the place for the glitterati to dine", as
"the food is as beautiful as the people", though holdouts maintain
the "service needs help."

Caffé Abbracci ●S
26 | 22 | 23 | $39

*318 Aragon Ave. (bet. Le Jeune Rd. & Miracle Mile), Coral Gables,
305-441-0700*

■ Thanks to "superb host" Nino Pernetti, local players "can always
count on a wonderful meal" at this "elegant" Coral Gables Italian,
a "power" scene that pulls in a "great-looking", celeb-studded
clientele; for "delicious food" and "professional service", it's "one
of the best" in town and its rep keeps it "crowded and noisy."

Carpaccio 🖪

| 24 | 21 | 21 | $32 |

Shops of Bal Harbour, 9700 Collins Ave. (97th St.), Bal Harbour, 305-867-7777

■ Really darling, it's "the only place to eat in Bal Harbour" insist fans of this "attractive" Northern Italian with a *"Lifestyles"* atmosphere that lures in the Prada set for "excellent" handmade pastas, "fabulous profiteroles" and carpaccio in a dozen variations; "consistency" and a "well-trained staff" compensate for the sometimes long wait for a table.

Chef Allen's 🖪

| 26 | 23 | 25 | $52 |

19088 NE 29th Ave. (NE 191st St.), Aventura, 305-935-2900

☑ "One of the greatest culinary experiences in South Florida – a must!" swear devotees of this "classy" star in an Aventura strip mall, created by "chef's chef" Allen Susser, a member of the 'Mango Gang' that originated New World cuisine; the "pricey" "designer food" wins acclaim as "imaginative" and "superb"; though a few feel it "doesn't live up to its PR", most attest it's "always a pleasure."

China Grill ◐🖪

| 23 | 23 | 19 | $47 |

404 Washington Ave. (5th St.), Miami Beach, 305-534-2211

☑ A celebrity "mob scene" attracts those who want to "see and be seen" – but not those "who want to hear and be heard" – at this "loud" link in the national chain; it's a night spot for the "glitzy" SoBe crowd, but even fans of the "exceptional" Eclectic menu snipe at service "attitude."

Chrysanthemum 🖪

| 23 | – | 20 | $30 |

Mayfair, 2911 Grand Ave. (Virginia St.), Coconut Grove, 305-443-6789

■ This "fave", "upscale" Chinese may have moved to the Grove and pared down its menu, leaving the more commercial options, but it's still turning out excellent Asian cuisine 'a la Miami', including crispy spinach and chicken; but whether it remains the "best Chinese in the city" remains to be seen.

Crystal Cafe 🖪

| 25 | 20 | 25 | $34 |

726 41st St. (bet. Chase & Prairie Aves.), Miami Beach, 305-673-8266

■ Few establishments earn such consistently positive buzz as this "fabulous neighborhood" modern Continental run by "charming" chef-owner Klime Kovaceski and his wife; a Miami Beach standout, it racks up raves for osso buco "to die for", "wonderful" service and "outstanding value"; 'nuff said.

Escopazzo ◐🖪

| 25 | 20 | 23 | $39 |

1311 Washington Ave. (bet. 13th & 14th Sts.), Miami Beach, 305-674-9450

■ At this "perfect little gem", an expanded but still "tiny and terrific" South Beach Italian, owner Giuseppe 'Pino' Bodoni greets regulars as well as first-timers with "loving care" and feeds them "superb" hand-rolled pastas, authentic risottos and fresh seafood; the "romantic" mood is enhanced by "friendly service", so while it's "expensive", most agree the "prices are fair" for the quality.

Forge, The 🖪

| 25 | 26 | 23 | $53 |

432 Arthur Godfrey Rd. (Royal Palm Ave.), Miami Beach, 305-538-8533

☑ Ever a "memorable experience", this Miami Beach Continental is a "sentimental fave" that impresses with "excellent", "old-fashioned" cooking and a "great wine list", presented in an "over-the-top" room; it's "still one of the best", though critics cry "overhyped" and "pricey."

Hy-Vong S   24 8 11 $23
3458 SW Eighth St. (SW 34th Ave.), 305-446-3674
☑ The "slow service" "with an attitude" at this "hole-in-the-wall" near Little Havana could "try the patience of a saint", but many think the "long wait" is "worth it" for "the best Vietnamese in the city" at a "good price"; a few fussy detractors, however, "don't know what the appeal is."

Joe's Stone Crab S   26 20 22 $46
11 Washington Ave. (First St.), Miami Beach, 305-673-0365
■ "The season is too short" lament fans of this Miami Beach seafood "landmark" (open mid-October–mid-May) where tourists, celebrities and natives all make the "pilgrimage" to feast on "the best stone crabs ever", plus creamed spinach "you can easily OD on" and "awesome Key lime pie"; but everyone crabs about the "looong waits" and suggests ways around them: "tip heavily", "get there at 5 PM" or "order takeout" from the adjacent store.

La Palme d'Or S   ▽ 26 30 27 $52
Biltmore Hotel, 1200 Anastasia Ave. (Granada Blvd.), Coral Gables, 305-445-1926
■ "Life never felt so good" as at this "elegant" venue in the "historic" Biltmore Hotel, where visiting Michelin-starred chefs create "splendid menus" that change monthly but always feature "superb" New French fare; "a table overlooking the pool" is perfect for basking in Gallic refinement against a backdrop that preserves a touch of the Jazz Age.

Maiko ●S   ▽ 25 15 18 $23
1255 Washington Ave. (bet. 12th & 13th Sts.), Miami Beach, 305-531-6369
■ "Huge pieces" of fish – "fresh off the boat" and "prepared and presented creatively" – prompt young, hip patrons to "put up with" the "bad decor" at this SoBe Japanese; it's nothing fancy, but for the money it's "one of the best" sushi joints around.

Mark's South Beach S   – – – E
Nash Hotel, 1120 Collins Ave. (11th St.), Miami Beach, 305-604-9050
One of the original 'Mango Gang' chefs, Mark Militello returns to his Miami roots (he's got eponymous eateries in Ft. Lauderdale, Boca Raton and soon Palm Beach) with this impressive newcomer in the lobby of the chic Nash Hotel, where Gucci and Prada-clad hipsters show up to nibble on his globally accented New American cuisine.

Max's Place S   – – – E
Shops of Bal Harbour, 9700 Collins Ave. (96th St.), Bal Harbour, 305-861-6121
A mini-replica of the successful Boca Raton eatery owned by the indefatigable Dennis Max, this version offers the same casual, contemporary vibe and up-to-the-minute New American fare (e.g. Chinese barbecued chicken salad, crispy duck tacos) – only here it caters to the more international shop-till-you-drop set at the tony Shops of Bal Harbour.

Miss Saigon Bistro S   24 13 23 $25
146 Giralda Ave. (Ponce de Leon Blvd.), Coral Gables, 305-446-8006
■ For "fabulous" Vietnamese in a "friendly" setting, this "family-owned" Coral Gables entry is the new destination of choice; it may be "cramped", but the "knowledgeable" staff serves with "humor and pizazz", making everyone feel like a "guest in someone's home."

F | D | S | C

Morton's of Chicago [S] 25 | 23 | 22 | $50
1200 Brickell Ave. (Coral Way), 305-400-9990
17399 Biscayne Blvd. (NE 173rd St.), North Miami Beach, 305-945-3131
■ A surefire "carnivore's delight", these "classy" (and "pricey") outposts of the national chophouse chain offer a "private club" feel to enhance their "first-rate steak" and lobster, "exceptional wine list" and deadly Godiva chocolate cake; "comfortable" "standbys", they "never disappoint."

Nemo ◐[S] 25 | 23 | 22 | $42
100 Collins Ave. (1st St.), Miami Beach, 305-532-4550
■ Sited in a "funky" art deco space in trendy SoFi, this "lively" Eclectic is the "epitome of South Beach cool"; attractions include "wonderful flavors" courtesy of chef-owner Michael Schwartz (ex LA's Chinois), a "divine" Sunday brunch, desserts that "wow", "outstanding" service and, of course, "good scenery" featuring plenty of "models."

Norman's 27 | 25 | 26 | $55
21 Almeria Ave. (Douglas Rd.), Coral Gables, 305-446-6767
■ "Do believe the hype": No. 1 for Food and Popularity in the *Miami Survey,* this "striking" Gables "standard" setter is where "the chic meet" to indulge in "astonishingly good" "treats for the tongue" delivered by a "superb" staff; "chef Norman Van Aken is a master" of "exceptional", "inventive" New World cuisine, though the "superpremium prices" lead a few to cite "mucho dinero" for such "small portions."

Ortanique on the Mile [S] – | – | – | E
278 Miracle Mile (Le Jeune Rd.), Coral Gables, 305-446-7710
A spin-off of the defunct Norma's on the Beach, this colorful, upscale hot spot next door to the Miracle Theater lures in the smart set with its unique takes on Caribbean specialties.

Osteria del Teatro 27 | 18 | 24 | $44
1443 Washington Ave. (Española Way), Miami Beach, 305-538-7850
■ "Consistently the best Italian" in town, this "little jewel" of a South Beach "storefront" is "famous" for its "excellent" Northern-style specialties; it's "charming", "hospitable" and "very Italian", and regulars ensure the "intimate" room stays "crowded."

Pacific Time [S] 26 | 21 | 22 | $47
915 Lincoln Rd. (bet. Jefferson & Michigan Aves.), Miami Beach, 305-534-5979
■ A South Beach trendsetter, this "high-end" hot spot is home to chef-owner Jonathan Eismann's "fabulous", "complex" Pan-Asian fusion creations, served in a "casual" space that's "loud, loud, loud"; it's a showcase for "fresh, startling" fare, including some of the "best seafood anywhere" and a dynamite dessert list.

Palm [S] 26 | 20 | 24 | $52
9650 E. Bay Harbor Dr. (Kane Concourse), Bay Harbor Island, 305-868-7256
■ It's "like going back to the '30s" at this "NY–type" Bay Harbor Island chophouse where meat eaters can count on "big slabs" of "the best steak in Miami" as well as mammoth lobsters and all the classic sides, prepared "simply" and served by pros; it may be "plain" and "pricey", but hey, "everybody goes here."

Pascal's on Ponce 🅂

– | – | – | E

2611 Ponce de Leon Blvd. (bet. Almeria & Valencia Aves.), Coral Gables, 305-444-2024

With just 55 seats, this cozy (some might say cramped) New French in the former Thoa's is everything chef-owner Pascal Oudin ever wanted since his arrival in Miami more than a decade ago: a little place to call his own and to showcase his classical training and inventive style; his delicious cooking is enhanced by a friendly ambiance, courtesy of wife Ann-Louise (co-owner) and brother Jean-Marc (manager).

Porcao ●🅂

23 | 18 | 20 | $37

801 Brickell Bay Dr. (SE 8th St.), 305-373-2777

■ "Considering it's not Rio", the "outstanding Brazilian-cut meats" provide an "excellent" selection at this rodizio-style Downtown "beef-lover's paradise"; insiders advise "come hungry" because between the "great salad bar" and the parade of grilled goodies, everyone's in for a "pig out."

Red Fish Grill 🅂

21 | 25 | 20 | $35

9610 Old Cutler Rd. (N. Kendall Dr.), Coral Gables, 305-668-8788

☑ "If you can find" this "beautiful" bayside seafood grill tucked away in "tropical" Matheson Hammock park, you'll be thrilled by the "extremely romantic" setting; it's widely considered to have "the best view in town", though some are frustrated by the "limited menu" and "rushed" service.

Ruth's Chris Steak House 🅂

25 | 21 | 23 | $45

2320 Salzedo St. (bet. Aragon & Giralda Aves.), Coral Gables, 305-461-8360

■ Despite heavy competition, this "dependable" New Orleans–based steakhouse chain is considered by many carnivores to serve South Florida's "finest combination of steaks and sides"; though a few find it "too stuffy", most laud its "serious approach to food and professional service"; P.S. "all items are à la carte", so expect the tab to build up.

Siam Palace 🅂

24 | 20 | 22 | $24

9999 Sunset Dr. (SW 102nd Ave.), South Miami, 305-279-6906

■ "Like Bangkok (but much better)", Miami's "premier Thai" offers "excellent" flavors that "never fail to please" (the "complex curries" earn special admiration); the "pleasant atmosphere" and "quality" make it "a definite favorite."

Tantra ●🅂

21 | 25 | 18 | $54

1445 Pennsylvania Ave. (Española Way), Miami Beach, 305-672-4765

■ Sure the "decor is memorable" at this "totally cool" SoBe hottie (best described as a "chic" seraglio carpeted with live grass), but the "fab experience" would be incomplete without the "sensual" Eclectic specialties; "celebs" who arrive for a taste of the "sexy late-night" scene are less likely than the average diner to "throw a tantrum over the prices."

Toni's Sushi Bar ●🅂

26 | 22 | 21 | $28

1208 Washington Ave. (12th St.), Miami Beach, 305-673-9368

■ SoBe's longest-standing sushi bar is also the "best on the beach" in the eyes of enthusiasts who extol the "wonderful presentations" of "A-1" fish, "beautiful" traditional Japanese decor and "pleasant" service; true sushi-heads just belly up to the bar, but couples note the booths are super "for a date."

F	D	S	C

Tropical Chinese [S] 26 | 18 | 21 | $28

Tropical Park Plaza, 7991 SW 40th St. (79th Ave.), 305-262-7576

■ "Can't beat their dim sum" say supporters of this Cantonese-Mandarin powerhouse in Southwest Dade, where the steel carts roll daily; it's noted for its "superb" and "authentic" fare ("chicken feet shocked me"), and if the regular menu can be "pricey", it provides "Hong Kong quality" and the "long lines tell the story."

Tuscan Steak ◐[S] 25 | 22 | 22 | $48

433 Washington Ave. (5th St.), Miami Beach, 305-534-2233

■ Even South Beach's "beautiful people" "arrive hungry" at this "hip" Northern Italian meatery, favored for its "plentiful" portions of "mouthwatering" Tuscan fare dished up "family style"; the "intense flavors" complement a "brilliantly renovated deco" space, and the "trendy" results are "expensive" and ever "so noisy!"

Two Chefs 23 | 18 | 21 | $41

8287 S. Dixie Hwy. (Ludlam Rd.), South Miami, 305-663-2100

◪ While it lacks the "atmosphere of a fine restaurant", this New American "gem hidden in a strip mall" wins mostly praise for its "imaginative" and "rich" ("not for calorie counters") fare from an "ever-changing menu"; however, detractors dis "inconsistent food."

Versailles ◐[S] 19 | 14 | 17 | $19

3555 SW Eighth St. (SW 35th Ct.), 305-445-7614

■ Even Anglos "appreciate the authenticity" at this "buzzing" Cuban diner, a Little Havana "landmark" with a "courteous" staff; the "stick-to-your-ribs" fare is served in a room that's "tacky in a charming way", evoking the French palace with mirrors and chandeliers ("bring sunglasses!").

Wish [S] ▽ 25 | 26 | 21 | $50

The Hotel of South Beach, 801 Collins Ave. (8th St.), Miami Beach, 305-674-9474

■ With up-and-comer Andrea Curto at the stoves, this "whimsical" Todd Oldham–decorated New American (no longer a vegetarian haven) has gained national attention; South Beach cognoscenti laud its "lovely presentations", "fun atmosphere" and personal service – "who needs a fourth wish?"

Wolfie Cohen's Rascal House ◐[S] 22 | 11 | 18 | $18

17190 Collins Ave. (172nd St.), Sunny Isles, 305-947-4581

■ "Forever great", this 24/7 "gem" is "always packed" at peak hours, and the "wait is part of the scene" as "Miami Beach's Jewish population" sits down to "hearty servings" of "genuine NY deli" classics and "more desserts than you can shake a stick at"; it "lives up to its rep", though even advocates marvel that the "best deli in town" is "such a dump" – go figure.

Minneapolis/St. Paul

TOP 10 FOOD RANKING

Restaurant	Cuisine Type
28 Goodfellow's	New American
27 D'Amico Cucina	N/S Italian
Bayport Cookery	Eclectic
Manny's Steakhouse	Steakhouse
26 Lucia's	New American
Ristorante Luci	N/S Italian
La Belle Vie	Classic French/Med.
Origami	Japanese
Kincaid's	Steakhouse/Seafood
510 Restaurant	Classic French/New American

ADDITIONAL NOTEWORTHY PLACES

Aquavit	Scandinavian
Buca di Beppo	N/S Italian
Chino Latino	Pan-Equatorial
Dakota Bar & Grill	Midwestern
Loring Cafe	New American
Oceanaire	Seafood
Palomino Euro Bistro	Mediterranean
Restaurant Alma	New American
St. Paul Grill	Traditional American
Zelo	Northern Italian

F	D	S	C
–	–	–	E

Aquavit
IDS Ctr., 75 S. Seventh St. (Nicollet Mall), Minneapolis, 612-343-3333
Twin Cities foodies are ecstatic about this smart Scandinavian
with an Asian accent in Downtown's IDS Center, transplanted
from Manhattan under the aegis of NYC executive chef Marcus
Samuelsson and under the supervision of chef Roger Johnsson,
who oversees the daily operation; look forward to sleek, stylish
and pricey fusion fare in an airy Nordic atmosphere.

27	21	23	$37

Bayport Cookery 🄢
328 Fifth Ave. N. (Hwy. 95), Bayport, 651-430-1066
■ Though its many fans "wish it were closer", that doesn't keep
serious foodies from this "unforgettable experience" in Bayport,
where "impressive" Eclectic fare is served in a "fastidiously
prepared" five-course prix fixe extravaganza that changes weekly
(don't miss the "annual morel mushroom dinners" in May and
June); what's more, fans feel that a "leisurely" meal here "increases
the chance that the evening will end romantically."

Buca di Beppo 🅂
20 | 21 | 20 | $18

(fka Buca)
1204 Harmon Pl. (Hennepin Ave.), Minneapolis, 651-638-2225
2728 Gannon Rd. (Shepard Rd.), St. Paul, 651-772-4388
14300 Burnhaven Dr. (143th St.), Burnsville, 612-892-7272
7711 Mitchell Rd. (Hwy. 5), Eden Prairie, 612-724-7266
☑ "Go with folks you like 'cause you're gonna share everything" at this "festive" Italian chain where the fare is served "family-style", and "loosen your belt" when the "ridiculously large portions" arrive; pros praise the "best garlic mashed potatoes ever" and "fair prices", but faultfinders fume that the "wait forever" for "bland" "factory food" is "not worth it."

Chino Latino ●🅂
– | – | – | E

2910 Hennepin Ave. (Lake St.), Minneapolis, 612-824-7878
With an over-the-top design that features a communal table and sunset colors, as well as a hip, young multi-ethnic staff and a trendy Pan-Equatorial menu ('street foods from the hot zone'), it's no surprise that this newcomer is the hottest ticket in town; once inside, trendy customers flood the satay bar, retro cocktails in hand, and toast their good fortune.

Dakota Bar & Grill 🅂
23 | 22 | 21 | $26

Bandana Sq., 1021 E. Bandana Blvd. (Lexington Ave.), St. Paul, 651-642-1442
■ "Hot food and hot jazz" are the hallmarks of this "class act" Midwesterner in St. Paul, overseen by Ken Goff, "one of the Twin Cities' best chefs"; foodies flock for his "amazing" seasonal recipes (like the signature Brie-and-apple soup), while hipsters pronounce it their "fave" for "sophisticated" jive; in sum, "eat and enjoy."

D'Amico Cucina 🅂
27 | 26 | 25 | $43

Butler Sq., 100 N. Sixth St. (bet. 1st & 2nd Aves.), Minneapolis, 612-338-2401
■ Ranked No. 2 for Food and Popularity in Minneapolis/St. Paul, this Warehouse District contemporary Italian proffers a "gorgeous, glorious" menu that's "the standard" by which "all others are judged" (it "doesn't get much better than this" rave admirers); "phenomenal service", an "excellent wine list" and a "beautiful space" make this the quintessential "place to celebrate something special, or nothing at all" – but "save up" before you reserve.

510 Restaurant
26 | 23 | 25 | $38

510 Groveland Ave. (Lyndale Ave.), Minneapolis, 612-874-6440
■ "An old-time classic" near Loring Park, this French-New American "institution for gourmets" is undergoing "an apparently successful transition" now that the next generation of owners has stepped in; while it still "reeks of old money", matching "first-class" dishes with a "very romantic" setting and "formal service" that "treats you like royalty", the younger crowd claims it's "a bit stuffy."

Goodfellow's
28 | 26 | 27 | $43

City Ctr., 40 S. Seventh St. (bet. Hennepin & Nicollet Aves.), Minneapolis, 612-332-4800
■ "Delectable combinations" of "edible art" on every plate, plus a "gorgeous" deco room and an "awesome wine list", make chef Kevin Cullen's New American "hands down the best in town", ranking No. 1 for Popularity, Food and Service in the *Minneapolis/ St. Paul Survey*; predictably, the "spectacular" package is priced up in "expense-account" territory.

Kincaid's §

| 26 | 24 | 25 | $32 |

8400 Normandale Lake Blvd. (84th St.), Bloomington, 612-921-2255
380 St. Peter St. (6th St.), St. Paul, 651-602-9000

◪ The "suburban business" crowd favors this surf 'n' turfer in a Bloomington "office tower" for "excellent all-around" meals, declaring that it defines yupscale dining and "oozes power at lunch"; skeptics say it's "cruising on reputation alone", citing "expensive cookie-cutter food" and a menu that "never changes except for the prices"; both camps concede that it's "hard to get in"; N.B. a new sib has opened in St. Paul.

La Belle Vie §

| 26 | 25 | 23 | $43 |

312 S. Main St. (Nelson St.), Stillwater, 651-430-3545

■ "Supercreative" Classic French–Med cuisine courtesy of two former D'Amico Cucina chefs earns this "charming" Stillwater entry enthusiastic foodie support, and the "historic" setting is an eye-pleaser; while some speak only of "great promise" and opine it "could be outstanding", converts are convinced it's already a "very special" "escape" that's well "worth the drive."

Loring Cafe §

| 22 | 25 | 17 | $28 |

1624 Harmon Pl. (16th St.), Minneapolis, 612-332-1617

◪ The "high-funk factor" at this "very urban", "artsy" hangout tends to overshadow a "creative" New American menu that some find "surprisingly uneven"; nonetheless, with "bohemian" decor and a staff to match, it's "unlike anything else in town."

Lucia's §

| 26 | 22 | 24 | $27 |

1432 W. 31st St. (Hennepin Ave.), Minneapolis, 612-825-1572

■ Tucked into an Uptown storefront, this "beautiful spot" features a menu devoted to "imaginative" New American dishes created from the "best seasonal ingredients"; the "sensitive treatment of food and guests" and "excellent wine list" make it a "special-occasion place" – maybe even the "Minnesota Chez Panisse."

Manny's Steakhouse §

| 27 | 23 | 26 | $43 |

Hyatt Regency, 1300 Nicollet Mall (Grant St.), Minneapolis, 612-339-9900

■ "Everything a beef lover wants" arrives in abundance at this "steakhouse *Satyricon*", a "macho" Downtown "powerhouse" where "fantastic" meat is delivered in "insanely huge portions", backed by "perfect service"; it's "expensive", but porterhouse partisans proclaim that "nobody does it better."

Oceanaire §

| – | – | – | E |

Hyatt Regency, 1300 Nicollet Mall (Grant St.), Minneapolis, 612-333-2277

Swanky '30s-style Downtown supper club where servers in white coats supply fresh and sassy seafood satisfying a sea of see-and-be-seeners at this latest spot to make a splash; N.B. dinner only.

Origami

| 26 | 21 | 21 | $26 |

30 N. First St. (1st Ave.), Minneapolis, 612-333-8430

■ It "feels like NY" at this "pristine" Warehouse District Japanese that proffers the "best sushi in town" (or at least the "best that can be expected in the middle of a continent"); though penny-pinchers say portions are "skimpy" for the price, sushiphiles feel that "every precious morsel" is "worth the splurge"; P.S. insiders suggest you "sit at the bar" – "the chefs are a blast."

Palomino Euro Bistro S
25 | 26 | 24 | $28

825 Hennepin Ave. (9th St.), Minneapolis, 612-339-3800

◪ "If you picked this horse, you've got a winner" say fans of this "upbeat" Downtown Mediterranean that's generating a "great buzz" thanks to an "artsy", "stylish" crowd that keeps coming back for some of the "best people-watching" around; wanna-bes sniff it's "full of itself", yet the beautiful ones rate it a "perfect night out."

Restaurant Alma S
– | – | – | E

528 University Ave. SE (5th St. E), Minneapolis, 612-379-4909

This city storefront near campus has been transformed into a cozy destination dining room done up in exposed brick, a stand of birches and other nods to nature; the short, daily-changing organic menu marries New American comfort food with classy touches and is parlayed by dedicated servers who also know their way through the list of unusual wines.

Ristorante Luci S
26 | 17 | 23 | $27

470 S. Cleveland Ave. (Randolph Ave.), St. Paul, 651-699-8258

◪ "Call way ahead" because it's "tough to get reservations" at this tiny Highland Park *"trattorissimo"* that presents "outstanding" Italian fare complemented by a "brilliant" wine list; though the "cramped" "sardine-like" seating means your evening "won't be romantic", fans say "the lack of atmosphere *is* the atmosphere" and insist that this "fabulous" place should "never change a thing."

St. Paul Grill S
25 | 26 | 24 | $33

Saint Paul Hotel, 350 Market St. (5th St.), St. Paul, 651-224-7455

◪ One of St. Paul's most "popular" spots, this "upscale" hotel grill has a "clubby feeling and historic setting" that alone "make it worthwhile" (ask for a "window seat for a wonderful view of Rice Park"); appointed with "beautiful wood paneling" and "cozy booths", it's "elegant in an F. Scott Fitzgerald-ish way" and staffed by a "gracious" team; though "everything" on the Traditional American menu is "excellent", skeptics nitpick that the "old- school" cuisine "needs updating."

Zelo S
– | – | – | E

Nicollet Mall, 831 Nicollet Mall (9th St.), Minneapolis, 612-333-7000

Urbane Tuscan grotto with a Northern Italian menu emphasizing things aquatic; generating almost as much buzz as the cooking is its breathtaking setting in the 1929 Medical Arts Building in Downtown's Nicollet Mall, which has been transformed into an avant-garde yet cozy hideaway, with abstract chandeliers, high ceilings and low lighting.

TOP 20 FOOD RANKING

Restaurant	Cuisine Type
28 Jeffrey's	New American
Saddle River Inn	New American/Classic French
27 Sagami	Japanese
Scalini Fedeli	Northern Italian
Ryland Inn	New French
Washington Inn	New American
Rosemary & Sage	New American
Cafe Panache	New French
410 Bank Street	Cajun/Caribbean
26 Fromagerie	Classic French
Cafe Matisse	Eclectic
Ebbitt Room	New American
Waters Edge	New American
Doris & Ed's	Seafood
Dining Room	New American
Frog & The Peach	New American
River Palm Terrace	Steakhouse
Acacia	New American
Joe & Maggie's	New American
Stage House Inn	New French

ADDITIONAL NOTEWORTHY PLACES

Bernards Inn	New American
Caspita! Cafe	International
Chez Catherine	Classic French
Daniel's on Broadway	New American
Esty Street	New American
Frenchtown Inn	New French
Giumarello's	N/S Italian
Harvest Moon Inn	New American
Karen & Rei's	New American
La Campagne	Classic French
LaTour	New French
Lilac	New French
Matisse	International
Meritage	New American
Mitchell's	New American
Moonstruck	Mediterranean
Rat's	New French
Serenäde Restaurant	New French
28 Oak Street	New American
Wild Ginger	Japanese

Acacia [S]
26 | 22 | 22 | $40

2637 Main St. (bet. Craven Ln. & Phillips Ave.), Lawrenceville, 609-895-9885

■ Chef-owner Bryan Brodowski "dares to be creative" at this Lawrenceville New American with "outstanding seasonal menus" offering "delicious", "artistically presented" food; it's a "find" that many call "the best in the area", and although the "ambiance can be noisy", most maintain that the atmosphere is "intoxicating – without drinks" (it's BYO, so you'll "save some dollars" as well).

Bernards Inn, The
25 | 27 | 24 | $48

The Bernards Inn, 27 Mine Brook Rd. (Quimbey St.), Bernardsville, 908-766-0002

■ Plaudits pour in for this "perfect hideaway for a romantic interlude" in Bernardsville, an "elegant country inn" with a "hunt club" setting fit for "aristocracy"; the "excellent and original" New American menu developed by celebrated chef Edward Stone is "masterfully" prepared and presented by a "gracious staff"; in sum, it's "one of the best."

Cafe Matisse [S]
26 | 20 | 23 | $44

167 Park Ave. (bet. E. Park Pl. & Highland Cross), Rutherford, 201-935-2995

■ While Matisse reproductions decorate the walls of this Bergen County Eclectic, inspired reviewers say the "real artist" is in the kitchen, turning out an "exciting" menu that includes some "spectacular seafood dishes"; though this BYO is set in a "cozy", late 19th-century firehouse with a "pleasant summertime garden", fans think it's so good that it "deserves an NYC address."

Cafe Panache
27 | 20 | 23 | $43

130 E. Main St. (Rte. 17), Ramsey, 201-934-0030

◪ The "Aureole of NJ" enthuse admirers of chef-owner Kevin Kohler's New French "gem" in Ramsey, a BYO with a "beautifully presented" seasonal menu that "far exceeds" its "tight" former setting; "discreet" service rounds out the picture of one of the Most Popular spots in the *NJ Survey*.

Caspita! Cafe [S]
– | – | – | E

Plaza 34, 1070 Rte. 34 (Lloyd Rd.), Matawan, 732-583-6000

Chef Terrence Tice crossed the state to bring an International menu to this nondescript Matawan storefront where dishes like porcini-crusted sea bass are bringing pizazz to an otherwise stark dining scene; the BYO policy makes diners all the more devoted.

Chez Catherine
25 | 21 | 22 | $48

Westfield Inn, 431 North Ave. (bet. Broad & Prospect Sts.), Westfield, 908-654-4011

■ "Hooray!" "she's back in Westfield" cheer fans of Catherine Alexandrou, who, along with her husband, celebrated NY chef Michel Bordeaux, has reclaimed this motel annex; "great" Classic French food and "lovely service" make this a "special-occasion" place once again.

Daniel's on Broadway [S]
– | – | – | E

416 S. Broadway (Congress St.), West Cape May, 609-898-8770

Set in a restored Victorian in West Cape May, this family-run New American BYO is a stunning mix of elegant dining rooms, flawless service and exquisitely prepared Asian-accented fare via chef Harry Gleason; it's easily one of the best finds in Cape May County, if not the entire region.

Dining Room, The   26 | 27 | 26 | $58

Hilton at Short Hills, 41 JFK Pkwy. (Rte. 24), Short Hills, 973-379-0100

■ "Luxury, style and grace" set the mood at this "extremely expensive" "special-occasion place" in the "posh" Short Hills Hilton, with "extraordinary" NYC–style New American dishes presented like "works of art", "indulgent", "personalized service" and an "elegant", flower-filled room complete with harpist; overall, it "makes you give up all preconceptions of hotel dining rooms."

Doris & Ed's 🖪   26 | 20 | 23 | $41

348 Shore Dr. (Waterwich Ave.), Highlands, 732-872-1565

■ Patrons of this "unequaled" James Beard Award winner feel like they've "died and gone to seafood heaven", especially those who indulge in the "chef's elegant signature dishes" paired with a selection from the "excellent wine list"; the tony types who frequent this "redecorated" Highlands destination don't mind the "eyebrow-raising prices", but could do without the "big waits."

Ebbitt Room, The 🖪   26 | 25 | 24 | $42

Virginia Hotel, 25 Jackson St. (bet. Beach Dr. & Carpenter's Ln.), Cape May, 609-884-5700

■ "An absolute delight", this "civilized", "classy" Cape May New American "delivers on expectations" with "inspired" seasonal cuisine and "wonderful service" amidst "Victorian elegance"; factor in Steve LaManna on piano and an after-dinner respite on the porch for a "very complete evening."

Esty Street   25 | 20 | 22 | $43

86 Spring Valley Rd. (Fremont Ave.), Park Ridge, 201-307-1515

■ "Is this heaven?" asks the "well-heeled" crowd that frequents this New American in Park Ridge, a showcase for "creative" dishes infused with "flavor"; "polished" service and an "excellent" wine list are pluses too, so reviewers "wish it weren't so far away."

410 Bank Street 🖪   27 | 22 | 23 | $41

410 Bank St. (bet. Broad & Lafayette Sts.), Cape May, 609-884-2127

■ "Every trip" to Cape May should include dinner at this "amazing" Cajun-Caribbean where chef Henry Sing Cheng is "a magician", blending "exotic seasonings with quixotic presentations" that make "everything on the menu wonderful"; despite "long waits" and "cramped seating", this "gussied-up Victorian house" is always a "hopping scene" – so reserve well in advance.

Frenchtown Inn, The 🖪   25 | 24 | 23 | $44

7 Bridge St. (Rte. 29), Frenchtown, 908-996-3300

■ This "beautiful country inn on the scenic Delaware" in "quaint" Frenchtown is worth a detour for its "inspiring menu" of New French cuisine with Asian accents and "rustic", "romantic" setting; while a few murmur it's "slipped a bit" and is "inconsistent", most maintain that it's a "classy operation" that "stands the test of time."

Frog and The Peach, The 🖪   26 | 23 | 23 | $47

29 Dennis St. (Hiram Sq.), New Brunswick, 732-846-3216

■ "Don't miss the culinary adventure" at New Brunswick's "pricey" granddaddy of New American fine dining, still the premier restaurant in town after 17 years; it's stayed that way because owners Elizabeth Alger and James Black keep it "civilized and friendly", making it the "place for first dates, first anniversaries and first impressions."

Fromagerie ☒
26 25 25 $49
26 Ridge Rd. (Ave. of Two Rivers), Rumson, 732-842-8088
■ "Rumson's pride and joy", this "exquisite" Classic French landmark is an "old-line" "romantic favorite" that offers "perfection without pretense": "memorable" meals, a "great vintage wine list", a "caring staff" and a "charming" locale; but "bring the Brinks truck – you'll need it."

Giumarello's
26 18 21 $30
329 Haddon Ave. (Crystal Lake Ave.), Westmont, 856-858-9400
■ "Robust, luscious Italian" cooking at "reasonable" prices makes this "quaint" Westmont spot an "all-time favorite" of fans who wonder "what more could you want?"; the "absolutely delicious, diverse menu" provokes fans to cry *mangia!* – but remember that "reservations are a must", though since the expansion into larger quarters it may now be easier to find a seat.

Harvest Moon Inn ☒
25 23 21 $44
1039 Old York Rd. (Rte. 202), Ringoes, 908-806-6020
■ Set in an 1811 Historic Register building, this "out-of-the-way" Ringoes New American with "fabulous food" offers "a multisensory experience" and the kind of "quiet luxury" diners desire for "special occasions"; "one of the best all-around in NJ", it's two restaurants in one – a "formal dining room" plus a family-style tavern with a "great bar menu" and a "good piano player" on weekends.

Jeffrey's
28 21 25 $37
73 Main St. (Washington St.), Toms River, 732-914-9544
■ Garnering the No. 1 rating for Food in the *NJ Survey*, chef-owner Jeffrey Schneekloth's New American BYO in Toms River is an "impeccable" "oasis in Ocean County's restaurant desert", a place that exudes "pride in everything served"; fans of this "unforgettable dining experience" admit it's "pricey, but worth every penny", and add "don't wait till the last minute for reservations."

Joe & Maggie's Bistro ☒
26 21 23 $37
591 Broadway (bet. Bath & Norwood Aves.), Long Branch, 732-571-8848
■ "Everything works" at this New American "haven in a dead part" of Long Branch that proffers a "versatile menu" of "innovative takes on old favorites"; fans of "stylish, cosmopolitan" dining rave "we often detour to eat here" since "other top places are dull by comparison."

Karen & Rei's ☒⇗
– – – M
2516 Dune Dr. (25th St.), Avalon, 609-967-4488
Already "so popular" that it's "difficult to get a reservation", this New American in Avalon delights fans with a "daring" menu accented with Southeast Asian touches; "everything is homemade and fresh", including the "incredible desserts", at this cash-only, seasonal BYO.

La Campagne ☒
25 24 23 $43
312 Kresson Rd. (bet. Brace & Marlkress Rds.), Cherry Hill, 856-429-7647
■ "Setting the standard for Camden County" is this "top-drawer" Classic French in Cherry Hill, a "superb oasis" offering "innovative" fare in a "delightful" "country-house setting"; "alfresco dining is a plus", and with chef Eric Hall on board, this BYO "makes dining special again" and is "worth any drive."

LaTour Ⓢ

| 25 | 19 | 20 | $38 |

6 E. Ridgewood Ave. (Broad St.), Ridgewood, 201-445-5056

■ Scores of fans are rooting for a long, happy life for this "up-and-coming" BYO "gem" in Ridgewood, with "excellent" New French fare and "awesome desserts" from a "personable chef"; while fans gush over dishes like duck with apple-and-onion choucroute, a few gently note that the "intimate" quarters are a tad "tight."

Lilac Ⓢ

| – | – | – | E |

194-196 Essex St. (Main St.), Millburn, 973-564-9600

Romance is in the air at this Millburn New French where a vast trompe l'oeil mural depicting a dish-decked cabinet supplies a homey touch; the sophisticated fare includes butter-braised lobster and various takes on venison courtesy of chef Adrien Gresnigt; N.B. a bottle of French *vin de pays* is de rigueur.

Matisse Ⓢ

| – | – | – | E |

1400 Ocean Ave. (14th St.), Belmar, 732-681-7680

Bold strokes of flavor make this International BYO in Belmar a true homage to the painter it's named after, and chef Anthony Wall's menu follows suit with artful dishes like mussels infused with ginger and chilies; despite the high-toned cooking, the dress code is come-as-you-are casual at this warm, wood-lined place.

Meritage Ⓢ

| – | – | – | VE |

1969 Rte. 34 (west of Allaire Circle), Wall, 732-974-5566

Luxurious, multilevel space off the beaten path in Wall that's home to a gracious New American overseen by chef-proprietors Richard Dowd and Robert Candiotti; while there are occasional organizational kinks, caring staffers know how to deal and heal, and there are no complaints about the globally accented cuisine.

Mitchell's: An American Bistro

| – | – | – | E |

Central Sq. Shopping Ctr., 72 Central Sq., Rte. 9 (Shore Rd.), Linwood, 609-927-8300

Few in South Jersey do it better than chef Keith Mitchell and his wife-partner Marla, who opened this eponymous New American BYO to rave reviews and still are luring crowds to Linwood with the likes of pistachio-crusted goat cheese with roasted pears and can't-resist-'em desserts; it may be set in a shopping center, but don't tarry in Talbots with food this terrific so close by.

Moonstruck Ⓢ

| 25 | 20 | 22 | $32 |

57 Main Ave. (Pilgrim Pathway), Ocean Grove, 732-988-0123

■ "Greenwich Village in the middle of Ocean Grove", this Med BYO "sparkles" in a "charming" "jewel" of a setting that's perfect for lovebirds "seeking a romantic interlude"; "fresh, innovative" cooking and "genuine, caring service" are additional pluses, while the only downside is the much-bemoaned "no-reservations policy."

Rat's Ⓢ

| – | – | – | VE |

16 Fairgrounds Rd. (Ward Ave.), Hamilton, 609-584-7800

Don't mind the name (an homage to a character in *The Wind in the Willows*): this New French just off the Grounds for Sculpture Museum in Hamilton is destined for national fame; in addition to the très haute cuisine of chef Eric Martin (ex NYC's Le Cirque), look for a 550-bottle wine list, a piano lounge and terrace dining beside a lily pond; N.B. jet-setter alert: there's a convenient helipad on the museum grounds.

River Palm Terrace [S] 26 | 18 | 21 | $44

1416 River Rd. (Palisade Terrace), Edgewater, 201-224-2013
41-11 Rte. 4W (bet. Paramus & Saddle River Rds.), Fair Lawn, 201-703-3500
209 Ramapo Valley Rd. (Rte. 17), Mahwah, 201-529-1111

■ Beef connoisseurs revere these "great NY–style steakhouses" where the "noisy", "suburban crowd" "likes to be seen" and "long waits" are the norm; "top-notch" sides take their rightful place beside "plentiful portions" of princely porterhouses, though indulgers caution that a visit is most satisfying "on someone else's nickel" since the tabs are right up there "with Peter Luger and The Palm."

Rosemary and Sage [S] 27 | 19 | 25 | $41

26 Hamburg Tpke. (I-287, exit 53), Riverdale, 973-616-0606

■ "Like wild herbs, it sprang up where least expected" and has grown into a "fabulous" New American serving "serious food in an unserious area" of Morris County; "knowledgeable servers" present a "creative", "changing menu" and "fine selection of wine" in "simple" but "soothing" surroundings.

Ryland Inn, The [S] 27 | 27 | 26 | $62

Rte. 22W (8 mi. west of Bridgewater Commons), Whitehouse, 908-534-4011

■ Some claim there are "not enough superlatives to describe how great this place is", but others go to town describing Craig Shelton's "marvelous" New French in Hunterdon County, voted the *NJ Survey's* Most Popular restaurant; the "transcendent kitchen" is enhanced by an "extensive wine list", a "knowledgeable staff" and "exquisite surroundings", though a minority maintains that the experience is "not worth" the "week's-salary" prices.

Saddle River Inn 28 | 26 | 26 | $49

2 Barnstable Ct. (bet. E. Allendale Ave. & W. Saddle River Rd.), Saddle River, 201-825-4016

■ A "world-class restaurant" that "puts special back in front of occasion", this New American–Classic French in Saddle River "never fails to impress", thanks to its "country-elegant" setting and chef-owner Hans Egg's "impressive" menu; "it all comes together" here at "the best BYO" around that's "worth the tremendous effort" to get a reservation; P.S. "try the balcony for privacy."

Sagami [S] 27 | 17 | 21 | $29

37 Crescent Blvd. (bet. Collingswood Circle & Haddon Ave.), Collingswood, 856-854-9773

■ "Don't go anywhere else" if you want "the best sushi in Jersey": this top-rated Japanese BYO in Collingswood is the equivalent of "Disney World for adult dining", thanks to chef-owner Shigeru Fukuyoshi's "meticulously prepared" fare that's so fresh the "sashimi is practically wiggling"; despite "cramped" conditions (a "tight room", "low ceilings" and "small tables"), this "champion" is "worth a weekly trip" – if you can get in.

Scalini Fedeli 27 | 26 | 25 | $55

63 Main St. (Parrot Mill Rd.), Chatham, 973-701-9200

■ "Reservations are scarcer than hen's teeth" at this "romantic" Chatham Northern Italian BYO, a "gourmet's dream" where "everything's an A-plus" – from chef-owner Michael Cetrulo's "superb food" to the "beautiful country-house setting" to the "attentive" servers who treat you like "kings and queens."

Serenäde Restaurant 25 26 25 $52

6 Roosevelt Ave. (Main St.), Chatham, 973-701-0303

■ "A star is born" in the form of husband-and-wife team James and Nancy Laird, who oversee this "outstanding" Chatham New French with an "attention to detail and obsession with freshness" that result in "truly luxurious eating"; it's a "place for elegant celebration", complete with an award-winning wine list.

Stage House Inn [S] 26 24 23 $46

366 Park Ave. (Front St.), Scotch Plains, 908-322-4224

■ "You'll forget you're in the suburbs" once seated in the "elegant rooms with fireplaces" of this "beautiful, romantic" 1737 structure in Scotch Plains, the home of a New French dining destination that can "hold its own against" NYC's finer restaurants; "hats off to chef-owner David Drake" for this "NJ gem."

28 Oak Street [S] – – – VE

28 Oak St. (bet. Franklin & Ridgewood Aves.), Ridgewood, 201-689-7313

Chef-owner Lee Ganbarg (ex Park Ridge's Esty Street) has devised one of North Jersey's most creative New American menus for this very personal venture, a pretty BYO in Ridgewood where braised duck quesadillas, pecan-crusted chicken with mustard sauce and decadent homemade pastries are making for some excellent word of mouth.

Washington Inn, The [S] 27 27 26 $42

801 Washington St. (Jefferson St.), Cape May, 609-884-5697

■ "Frasier and Niles" would hang out at this "historic, classy" Cape May New American if they lived on the Right Coast; "as-good-as-it-gets" food and an "extensive wine list" are served in a "top-notch Victorian" setting; P.S. "have dinner in the super-romantic cellar."

Waters Edge [S] 26 23 24 $43

Beach Dr. (Pittsburgh Ave.), Cape May, 609-884-1717

■ Chef-owner Neil Elsohn's "spectacular" New American cuisine impresses voters at this "hippest dining spot on Cape May", a "sophisticated yet casual" restaurant with oceanfront dining, "contemporary" decor and a black marble bar that's a "great meeting" place; even better, the location is "mercifully removed from the tourist crush."

Wild Ginger [S] – – – E

6 E. Palisades Ave. (Dean St.), Englewood, 201-567-2660

Englewood natives are going wild over this high-style Japanese BYO set in a "beautiful", contemporary space that ideally shows off the "creative" fare of chef Yoshiharu Suzuki; don't miss his signature *toro* steak or black cod, pristine fish dishes infused with seductive seasonings.

New Orleans

TOP 20 FOOD RANKING

Restaurant	Cuisine Type
27 Bayona	New American
Brigtsen's	Cajun
Gabrielle	Contemporary Louisiana
Grill Room	New American
Artesia	New French
Ruth's Chris	Steakhouse
Commander's Palace	Creole
26 Galatoire's	Creole
Crozier's	French Bistro
Sal & Judy's	Creole/Italian
Clancy's	Creole
Upperline	Creole/Eclectic
Emeril's	Creole/New American
25 Irene's Cuisine	Italian
Gautreau's	Creole
Louis XVI	Classic French
Mosca's	Italian
Kim Son	Vietnamese
La Provence	Classic French
Pelican Club	Contemporary Louisiana

ADDITIONAL NOTEWORTHY PLACES

Antoine's	Creole/Classic French
Arnaud's	Creole
Basil Leaf	Thai
Bistro at Maison de Ville	French Bistro
Brennan's	Creole
Cafe Giovanni	Italian
Christian's	Creole/Classic French
Dakota	Contemporary Louisiana
Emeril's Delmonico	Creole/New American
Gamay	Contemporary Louisiana
Gerard's Downtown	New French
La Crêpe Nanou	French Bistro
La Riviera	Northern Italian
Lemon Grass Rest.	Vietnamese
Le Parvenu	Creole
Mr. B's Bistro	Creole
Nine Roses	Vietnamese
Nola	Contemporary Louisiana
Peristyle	Louisiana/French
Rib Room	Continental/Steakhouse

Antoine's
22 | 24 | 23 | $48

713 St. Louis St. (bet. Bourbon & Royal Sts.), 504-581-4422
☑ Exuding "great old-world charm", this "venerable NO institution" is an arena-size Creole–Classic French in the Quarter that has remained a "grand tradition" since 1840; despite its "reputation", however, even veterans concede that for a "fine" meal here you must land "the right waiter and order the right food": "any oyster dish – Rockefeller, Bienville, Foch" – and for the entree, "stick to the filet."

Arnaud's 🔲
22 | 24 | 24 | $45

813 Bienville St. (bet. Bourbon & Dauphine Sts.), 504-523-5433
☑ "Romantic and festive", this French Quarter Creole "landmark" is regarded by its followers as the "best of the old guard", with a "superb" staff proffering "perpetual favorites" like "sensational" shrimp rémoulade in "elegant" surroundings (insiders recommend the "brilliant main room"); some are "disappointed" that it's "not what it used to be", but many feel it's still a "wonderful special-occasion treat", despite "too many tourists."

Artesia 🔲
27 | 25 | 24 | $40

21516 Hwy. 36 (Hwy. 59), Abita Springs, 504-892-1662
■ "Heaven in the country" is promised at this "first-class" Abita Springs New French housed in a "beautifully" restored Victorian-era mansion where "marvelous" chef John Besh prepares "tasty and appealing food"; it's "hard to find", but it's "well worth the drive" to the North Shore for a "memorable" experience.

Basil Leaf
24 | – | 21 | $26

1438 S. Carrollton Ave. (bet. Jeannette & Willow Sts.), 504-862-9001
■ A recent move from Metairie brings this "upscale", "clean and original" Nouvelle Thai to adoring Carrollton admirers; "wonderful presentations" of "fabulous fresh food", along with "great service", make this "healthy gourmet" spot one where diners are "treated like a friend of the family."

Bayona
27 | 26 | 25 | $45

430 Dauphine St. (bet. Conti & St. Louis Sts.), 504-525-4455
■ Hundreds of reviewers love the "consistently sublime" cuisine (voted No. 1 for Food in the *New Orleans Survey*) at this French Quarter New American, whose "chef Susan Spicer just gets better"; the "romantic", "lush" and "sophisticated" setting (including "beautiful patio dining in nice weather") and "attentive service" round out an "always exceptional experience."

Bistro at Maison de Ville 🔲
25 | 24 | 23 | $44

Maison de Ville, 727 Toulouse St. (bet. Bourbon & Royal Sts.), 504-528-9206
■ This "authentic" French bistro is not only "small and chic", it's also "wonderfully charming and romantic", making it a "tried-and-true" French Quarter "fave"; it may be a "little pricey", but admirers opine that, with "delicious food" and a maitre d' (Patrick) that's a "gracious host", it's "one of the best of its kind in the country."

Brennan's S

23 | 26 | 24 | $47

417 Royal St. (bet. Conti & St. Louis Sts.), 504-525-9711

☑ Fans feel that this French Quarter "high Creole" "classic" with a "great atmosphere", "beautiful patio" and an "excellent wine list" is a "must-visit landmark" that's a "fave for special occasions", "expense-account diners" and "wonderful breakfasts"; but critics contend that it's "pricey", with "too many tourists."

Brigtsen's

27 | 21 | 25 | $40

723 Dante St. (bet. Maple St. & River Rd.), 504-861-7610

■ It may be a bit "crowded and noisy", but its many devotees dismiss the decibels here because chef Frank Brigtsen is a "culinary genius" who cooks some of the "best Cajun-inspired food anywhere"; "wonderful caring service" and a "cozy", "quaint setting" also add to the appeal of this "hidden gem" in the lower-Carrollton area – "thank goodness, it's still not on the tourist map."

Cafe Giovanni S

24 | 23 | 23 | $37

117 Decatur St. (bet. Canal & Iberville Sts.), 504-529-2154

☑ Supporters say that this "excellent", "imaginative" French Quarter Italian is a "cut above most", but the less enthused shrug that the food is "solid but unremarkable"; still, the pleasant space makes a comfortable venue for Wednesday "opera night" and its "engaging singers."

Christian's

24 | 25 | 23 | $38

3835 Iberville St. (N. Scott St.), 504-482-4924

■ It's a "religious experience" and a "place to worship great food" declare devotees of this charming Mid-City Creole-French set in a "beautiful" "old converted church" and featuring fare that's a "delight to the taste and eyes"; since it's already "crowded and noisy", no wonder locals lament: "please don't tell the tourists!"

Clancy's

26 | 20 | 23 | $38

6100 Annunciation St. (Webster St.), 504-895-1111

■ A "comfortable" and "familiar" "insiders'" "hangout" Uptown with "consistently excellent" Creole-inspired dishes like oysters with brie and "the best soft shells and sweetbreads in town"; people-watching is part of the pleasure at this very N'Awlins "social scene" that's a "favorite of many locals."

Commander's Palace S

27 | 28 | 27 | $47

1403 Washington Ave. (Coliseum St.), 504-899-8221

■ "Feel the magic" say over 1,000 reviewers about the *New Orleans Survey*'s Most Popular restaurant, which is also voted No. 1 for Service; "first class in every way", this Garden District Haute Creole "shining star" is "always fabulous, festive and delicious" and that's because chef "Jamie Shannon and the Brennans know what true dining is", making it "perfect for a special occasion", as well as the "best for [weekend] jazz brunch."

Crozier's

26 | 21 | 24 | $39

Petite Esplanade, 3216 W. Esplanade Ave. N. (bet. N. Causeway Blvd. & Severn Ave.), Metairie, 504-833-8108

■ "Don't let the strip mall fool you" – you'll find "superb" French cooking at this "fine" Metairie bistro that's also prized for its "friendly", "relaxing" atmosphere, "amazingly fair wine prices" and owners who are "always there"; a "real gem", it suffers only from a "limited" menu that some feel stays too much the same.

Dakota, The　　　　25 | 22 | 23 | $36

629 N. Hwy. 190 (¼ mi. off I-12), Covington, 504-892-3712

■ A "consistently good" North Shore "asset", this "innovative" Contemporary Louisiana spot boasts a "crab meat and brie soup alone that's worth the drive"; the "first-class staff" and charming surroundings are more reasons it's "worth the trip", even if it is "a bit expensive."

Emeril's　　　　26 | 21 | 24 | $51

800 Tchoupitoulas St. (Julia St.), 504-528-9393

■ "Creative, innovative and oh-so-noisy" is the consensus on this Creole-based New American "jewel of the Warehouse District", the flagship of celeb chef Emeril Lagasse, that draws the "hip, young and cool" (plus plenty of tourists) with its "amazing food" and "energy level"; but even some admirers complain that stardom has led to sometimes "haughty service" and that the kitchen "suffers" when the "bam man" is out of town – "Emeril, please phone home."

Emeril's Delmonico 🅂　　　　23 | 27 | 24 | $57

1300 St. Charles Ave. (Erato St.), 504-525-4937

🗹 Though everyone raves over the decor at this "luxurious" Lower Garden District star in chef Emeril Lagasse's crown and some even hail it as the "most wonderful, elegant restaurant ever", the majority is less enthused about the Creole-influenced American food that's "good" but "doesn't meet expectations" ("too rich", "overblown") in light of the "outrageously expensive" prices; locals still "go for that special night", but warn "take a loan out" first.

Gabrielle　　　　27 | 20 | 24 | $43

3201 Esplanade Ave. (bet. Maurepas & Mystery Sts.),
504-948-6233

■ Although nearly everyone agrees this "great little jewel" near the New Orleans Museum of Art is "cozy and cramped", its very size reminds devotees of "a French country restaurant", as does its "superior and creative" Contemporary Louisiana and Haute Creole cooking; "hooray for Greg and Mary Sonnier" say the enchanted about "one of the city's most talented culinary couples."

Galatoire's 🅂　　　　26 | 24 | 26 | $42

209 Bourbon St. (Iberville St.), 504-525-2021

■ "A New Orleans original" (and No. 2 for Popularity in the *New Orleans Survey*), this French Quarter "institution" still boasts "great old ambiance", plus a newly renovated second floor; locals like things to stay the same, however, so they're pleased that "despite the changes, it remains constant", turning out "delicious" Haute Creole dishes that are "never a disappointment" and served by experienced waiters who know not only your name, but also your drink – it's "worth any wait."

Gamay　　　　25 | 24 | 23 | $42

Bienville House Hotel, 320 Decatur St. (additional entrance at 321 N. Peters St.), 504-299-8800

■ "A new star is born" and it's "off to a great start" say admirers of this second venue in the French Quarter for top restaurateurs Mary and Greg Sonnier; a "worthy sister to Gabrielle", it boasts a "busy, fashionable atmosphere", not to mention "very good" Contemporary Louisiana cooking with a Creole accent.

F	D	S	C

Gautreau's 25 | 22 | 24 | $42

1728 Soniat St. (Danneel St.), 504-899-7397

■ "Fabulous, innovative Creole food" and "wonderful service in charming surroundings" add up to a "true classic hidden in Uptown New Orleans"; despite efforts to lower the decibels (carpeting, table padding, sound baffles), many say it's "still too noisy", but that doesn't stop anyone from enjoying the "fine dining" in this beautifully remodeled "old pharmacy with a pressed tin ceiling"; it's unanimous: an "extraordinary" "local gem."

Gerard's Downtown 24 | 22 | 22 | $38

Parc St. Charles, 500 St. Charles Ave. (Poydras St.), 504-592-0200

■ "Impressive" say reviewers of chef Gerard Marais' return to New Orleans with this "elegant" New French cafe, one of the "best upscale" spots in the CBD; his "great attention to detail" translates into "well-prepared" "new and classic" dishes, "good service", a "comfortable setting" and valet parking that is much appreciated – in sum, a "real comer" so "get in while you can."

Grill Room, The [S] 27 | 29 | 27 | $58

Windsor Court Hotel, 300 Gravier St. (bet. S. Peters & Tchoupitoulas Sts.), 504-522-1992

■ "Beautiful", "classy", "elegant" (and No. 1 for Decor in the *New Orleans Survey*) are just a few of the accolades showered upon this dining room in the world-class Windsor Court Hotel, where the "outstanding" New American cuisine with French flair and "impeccable service" make it "a wonderful place to celebrate"; a few gripe that it's "too formal" and "not a happening place", but for the majority it's "well worth" any expense, so "mortgage the farm and eat here."

Irene's Cuisine [S] 25 | 22 | 22 | $33

539 St. Philip St. (Chartres St.), 504-529-8811

■ "Please don't tell the tourists" beg locals about this "great hidden restaurant" at the far end of the Quarter, a "cozy" Italian with a rep for "tasty, robust" cooking; though the "lusty" fare and "eclectic decor", combined with a "ridiculous no-reservations policy", result in "long waits", admirers agree the "challenge to get in is worth the try."

Kim Son 25 | 13 | 18 | $18

349 Whitney Ave. (Westbank Expy.), Gretna, 504-366-2489

■ Devotees of Vietnamese "dream about" the "incredibly tasty food" ("love that salt-baked stuff!") at this West Bank venue where the fare's "astonishing quality and complexity" comes at a "very reasonable price"; in spite of swipes at the service, it's still "worth crossing the river" for this town's "best Viet."

La Crêpe Nanou [S] 24 | 22 | 20 | $26

1410 Robert St. (Prytania St.), 504-899-2670

■ To its *amis,* "a trip to France is all that beats this bistro"; "a little loud" and always "crowded", it's an "Uptown favorite" for "delicious", "simple Gallic fare" ("best steamed mussels around") enhanced by a "romantic", "very European atmosphere"; P.S. there's no reserving, so "expect to wait" – "it's worth it."

La Provence [S] 25 | 25 | 24 | $45
25020 Hwy. 190 E. (bet. Lacombe & Mandeville), Lacombe, 504-626-7662
◪ "Inviting and welcoming", this "lovely country" inn in Lacombe matches a "beautiful setting" with "fantastic" Classic French cooking for some of the "best fine dining on the North Shore"; romantics from both sides of the lake are drawn to the "Provençal atmosphere", and if a few worry it's "overrated", by consensus it's "still worth the trip."

La Riviera 24 | 19 | 23 | $34
4506 Shores Dr. (bet. N. Clearview Pkwy. & W. Esplanade Ave.), Metairie, 504-888-6238
■ "Unforgettable crabmeat ravioli" is a menu star at this "long-standing Metairie Northern Italian"; the room's on the "noisy" side, but "delicious food" and "attentive" service qualify it as a "consistent" "classic" that "still holds its own after all these years."

Lemon Grass Restaurant [S] 24 | 18 | 21 | $30
International House Hotel, 217 Camp St. (bet. Common & Gravier Sts.), 504-523-1200
■ For "gourmet Vietnamese", surveyors select this "creative", "nouveau Asian" whose kitchen relies on "fresh organic" produce to produce "excellent cuisine" and "gorgeous presentations"; the International House Hotel setting is "upscale" and "*très* chic."

Le Parvenu [S] 25 | 22 | 21 | $33
509 Williams Blvd. (bet. Kenner Ave. & Short St.), Kenner, 504-471-0534
■ Cognoscenti consider this "quiet, charming" cottage a "best bet in Kenner" due to Dennis Hutley's "delicious" Creole-accented dishes; "lovely decor" and "attentive service" also ensure this "standout" stays "on top."

Louis XVI [S] 25 | 26 | 25 | $52
St. Louis Hotel, 730 Bienville St. (bet. Bourbon & Royal Sts.), 504-581-7000
■ An "old favorite that's still going strong", this "elegant special-occasion" stalwart in the heart of the French Quarter sets a "romantic" tone with a "*magnifique*", "old-style French" setting and "fantastic" food; it's one of the certified "classics", though a few Jacobins warn it's "dated" and ever so "stuffy."

Mosca's 🚫 25 | 12 | 18 | $33
4137 US Hwy. 90W (bet. Butler St. & Live Oak Rd.), Avondale, 504-436-9942
■ "Great", "old-fashioned New Orleans Italian" "mecca for garlic and olive oil" that still offers the "best oyster dish in the world", "unmatched BBQ shrimp" and "definitive garlic baked chicken"; it may be "cholesterol central" and "cash only", but it's a "one-of-a-kind roadside inn" located 40 minutes from Downtown that's a "favorite" for a "food frenzy."

Mr. B's Bistro [S] 25 | 24 | 24 | $34
201 Royal St. (bet. Bienville & Iberville Sts.), 504-523-2078
■ "Everyone loves" this "day-in and day-out consistent" and "clubby" French Quarter Haute Creole bistro serving "gumbo ya-ya to die for" and "ethereal BBQ shrimp"; a few feel it's "too noisy and crowded", but most maintain that it's "still the best of the more casual Brennan-owned restaurants."

Nine Roses 23 | 15 | 19 | $15

1100 Stephen St. (Westbank Expy.), Gretna, 504-366-7665 S
1116 Tulane Ave. (Loyola Ave.), 504-566-0950

■ Asian-food aficionados enthuse that this renovated "really good Vietnamese" with a "large selection" of "addictive", "fresh" and "light" dishes ("try the quail" and superb spring rolls) at "great prices" is "the best reason to go to the West Bank"; P.S. the simple CBD "express location is quick, easy, cheap and delicious."

NOLA S 24 | 22 | 23 | $37

534 St. Louis St. (bet. Chartres & Decatur Sts.), 504-522-6652

◪ "Bam"! – star chef Emeril Lagasse's other "hit" is "more casual and lighthearted" than his namesake spot, with "eclectic, tasty" Contemporary Louisiana cuisine served in an "electric", "jumpin'" French Quarter hot spot; but the "noisy", "cramped" ("tables so close you might be dining *en famille*") and "touristy" establishment irks others who complain about "inconsistent", "showy" food and "intrusive service."

Pelican Club S 25 | 24 | 23 | $40

312 Exchange Alley (bet. Bienville & Chartres Sts.), 504-523-1504

■ If you're looking for a "sophisticated" spot in the French Quarter in order to "impress a date", this is it; fans of fusion food favor the "innovative" Contemporary Louisiana menu that merges Asian and International cuisines, while wallet-watchers opt for the "early-bird prix fixe"; in fact, "noise is the only knock in an otherwise fabulous evening."

Peristyle – | – | – | E

1041 Dumaine St. (N. Rampart St.), 504-593-9535

"Brilliant", "delicious" Louisiana-French cuisine that's as "good as it gets" is what surveyors say about chef-owner Anne Kearney's French Quarter "classic bistro"; in fact, had not a fire partially destroyed its interior, temporarily closing the restaurant, it would have won the *New Orleans Survey's* No. 1 spot for Food; the good news is it's undergone a spiffy renovation and reopened on the same site.

Rib Room S 24 | 24 | 23 | $41

Omni Royal Orleans Hotel, 621 St. Louis St. (bet. Chartres & Royal Sts.), 504-529-7046

■ This "fashionable" Continental-steakhouse is a "French Quarter stalwart" that's "classy in every way", whether for a "two-martini" "power lunch" or a "very elegant" supper (though penny-pinchers protest it's "much too expensive at dinner"); habitués hint it's "best for prime rib" and recommend a "table by the window" for some dandy people-watching.

Ruth's Chris Steak House S 27 | 21 | 25 | $44

711 N. Broad St. (Orleans Ave.), 504-486-0810
3633 Veterans Memorial Blvd. (N. Causeway Blvd.), Metairie, 504-888-3600

■ "If you must have steak", look no further than these "reigning champions", links of the national chain that was hatched in NO; fans rave there's "nobody better" (despite the "pricey" tabs) and tout the original North Broad Street outpost for "power lunching" amidst "movers and shakers"; P.S. new ownership pledges to keep these "venerable institutions" just that.

Sal & Judy's [S] | 26 | 16 | 21 | $28

Hwy. 190 (14th St.), Lacombe, 504-882-7167

■ "Gargantuan portions" of "delectable" Creole-Italian cooking, "bargain" pricing and "can't-be-beat" quality make this "North Shore favorite" a "don't-miss" destination; regulars report "rezzies are a must" (and even then, there's "always a wait"), but it's "worth the drive" for one of "the best" dining experiences around.

Upperline [S] | 26 | 23 | 24 | $38

1413 Upperline St. (bet. Prytania St. & St. Charles Ave.), 504-891-9822

■ "Always a treat" sigh supporters of this Haute Creole–Eclectic where the "excellent" eating is complemented by "classy" fine art and "personal" attention courtesy of owner and "gracious hostess" JoAnn Clevenger; "comfortable and innovative", it's "a true original" that Uptowners insist is "much more pleasant" than its French Quarter competitors; N.B. dinner only, Wednesday–Sunday.

New York City

TOP 20 FOOD RANKING

Restaurant	Cuisine Type
28 Le Bernardin	New French/Seafood
Chanterelle	New French
Nobu	Japanese/Peruvian
Sugiyama	Japanese
Peter Luger	Steakhouse
Jean Georges	New French
Daniel	Classic French
27 Lespinasse	Classic French
Aureole	New American
La Grenouille	Classic French
Gramercy Tavern	New American
Union Square Cafe	New American
Bouley Bakery	New French
Il Mulino	Northern Italian
Gotham Bar & Grill	New American
Oceana	Seafood
Four Seasons	Continental
Café Boulud	Classic French/Eclectic
La Caravelle	Classic French
La Côte Basque	Classic French

ADDITIONAL NOTEWORTHY PLACES

Alain Ducasse	French
Aquavit	Scandinavian
Babbo	N/S Italian
Café des Artistes	Classic French
Carnegie Deli	Deli
Cello	Classic French/Seafood
Danube	Austrian
Eleven Madison Park	New American
Le Cirque 2000	Classic French
Lutèce	Classic French
Manhattan Ocean Club	Seafood
March	New American
Mercer Kitchen	New American
Milos, Estiatorio	Greek
Montrachet	French Bistro
Oyster Bar (Grand Central)	Seafood
Palm	Steakhouse
Park Avenue Cafe	New American
Picholine	Mediterranean
River Cafe	New American
Russian Tea Room	Russian
71 Clinton Fresh Food	New American
Shun Lee Palace	Chinese
Smith & Wollensky	Steakhouse
Sushisay	Japanese
Sylvia's	Southern/Soul
Tabla	New American/Indian
Tavern on the Green	New American
'21' Club	Traditional American
Union Pacific	New American
Veritas	New American
Windows on the World	New American

Alain Ducasse
−   −   −   VE

Essex House, 155 W. 58th St. (bet. 6th & 7th Aves.),
212-265-7300
Franc-ly NY's most expensive restaurant (with a $160 prix fixe), but for superdeluxe dining and decor plus silky smooth service you won't find better than this renowned haute French import that offers just one seating – i.e. no rushing to arrive or leave – per night (Monday–Friday) and at lunch (Wednesday–Thursday); is it worth it? – well, were the seats at the play-offs, the championship fight, or the Streisand concert worth it?

Aquavit S
25   26   24 $59

13 W. 54th St. (bet. 5th & 6th Aves.), 212-307-7311
■ "Fresh and cleansing", this Midtown Scandinavian sophisticate still "soars in every category", from its "serene" atrium complete with waterfall to Marcus Samuelsson's salmon-studded menu and "superb service"; if portions are "minimalist", prices are not, but the upstairs cafe is "a bargain" and the aquavits "ease all pain."

Aureole
27   26   26 $71

34 E. 61st St. (bet. Madison & Park Aves.), 212-319-1660
■ "Keeps shining brightly" say the myriad admirers of Charlie Palmer's flower-filled East Side duplex townhouse, revered for its No. 1–rated New American fare and desserts to "capture on canvas", as well as its "elegant" decor and "caring" staff; despite quibbles ("tight" tables, "a little stuffy"), most surveyors think it's "one of NY's best", "no matter what Grimes says"; dinner is $69 prix fixe only.

Babbo ●S
26   23   24 $60

110 Waverly Pl. (bet. MacDougal St. & 6th Ave.),
212-777-0303
■ Mario Batali "makes Italian taste brand-new" with his "inspired", "earthy" menu at this Village "instant classic" co-owned with Joe Bastianich; the "warm" duplex setting and "intriguing" wines add pleasure, and even if the "clairvoyant" staff is "rushed" and booking is a "pain", the last word is "bravo Babbo."

Bouley Bakery ●S
27   23   24 $63

120 W. Broadway (Duane St.), 212-964-2525
■ Though "usually fully committed", it's worth waiting for a seat at David Bouley's "stellar" TriBeCa bakery/dining room since you'll get "heavenly" New French fare in an "elegant but not stuffy" setting; perhaps "not as divine" as its predecessor, it's "looking better all the time" and though it's not cheap, the prix fixe lunch (five courses, $35) is an "unparalleled" bargain.

Café Boulud S
27   24   25 $68

Surrey Hotel, 20 E. 76th St. (bet. 5th & Madison Aves.),
212-772-2600
■ "All the wow without the formal attitude" is found at Daniel Boulud's more "casual" but still "elegant" East Side counterpart to his eponymous restaurant; given an "ingenious" French-Eclectic menu and "superior service", most forgive the "tight" space and even consider the tab "relatively reasonable."

Café des Artistes ◐ [S] | 24 | 27 | 24 | $59 |

1 W. 67th St. (bet. Columbus Ave. & CPW), 212-877-3500

■ "Fall in love again" at George and Jenifer Lang's "seminal" French "treasure" near Lincoln Center, a "sybaritic delight" that "never goes out of fashion" thanks to a "classic", "refined" menu served amidst "delightfully over-the-top" murals of "naked nymphs"; it may be the "most romantic room in NY" if you're yearning for "a quiet fling" "out of a novel"; if pricey at night, it's cheaper for a prix fixe lunch.

Carnegie Deli ◐ [S] ≠ | 21 | 9 | 12 | $23 |

854 Seventh Ave. (55th St.), 212-757-2245

◪ For many, this Midtown "fixture" (look for the lines out front) defines deli in NY, with a "staff as sour as the pickles" serving "can't-get-your-mouth-around-'em" sandwiches and other Jewish "classics" to elbow-to-elbow diners amid classically "bad" decor, i.e. rows of crowded tables; though tourists "love it", you're just as likely to meet Woody Allen – or some of his characters – here.

Cello [S] | 26 | 25 | 24 | $80 |

53 E. 77th St. (bet. Madison & Park Aves.), 212-517-1200

■ "The Yo-Yo Ma" of seafooders, this East Side French wows a "dressy" crowd with Laurent Tourondel's "superlative" cuisine, seamlessly served in an elegant, usually crowded room; if a few find it "self-important", with "small portions" and "obscene" prices, most applaud the "virtuoso performance."

Chanterelle | 28 | 27 | 27 | VE |

2 Harrison St. (Hudson St.), 212-966-6960

■ At once "down-to-earth and awe-inspiring", David and Karen Waltuck's TriBeCa New French still enchants after two decades, ranking No. 2 in NYC for its "flawless" food as well as its "graceful" service, both enjoyed in a "serene", "elegantly simple" room; after "three hours of luxury", a meal here feels like a "vacation" and costs nearly as much (dinner is $79 prix fixe), but it simply "doesn't get much better" and the $38 prix fixe lunch is a deal.

Daniel | 28 | 27 | 27 | $82 |

60 E. 65th St. (bet. Madison & Park Aves.), 212-288-0033

■ For Daniel Boulud's legions of admirers, "a more exquisite dining experience cannot be had" than at his "elegant" East Side French, where "extraordinary" meals ("eloquence in every mouthful") are "masterfully served" in an "opulent", "palace"-like setting; given his reputation and the cost, it's not surprising if a few are "let down" and say "thank God I was treated."

Danube ◐ [S] | 27 | 28 | 26 | $79 |

30 Hudson St. (Duane St.), 212-791-3771

■ David Bouley's TriBeCa "Vienna fantasy" (NYC's No. 1 rated Newcomer) is a "double-rich feast for palate and eye", with "original" food, smooth-flowing service and a "sensual" setting of "new-old-world grandeur" (like "a Klimt dream") that also waltzes off with NYC's top Decor honors; service is "superb" and the wines "unique", and if a few skeptics find it "overdone" and more Bouleynese than Viennese, most declare it "a triumph" – who knew "schnitzel could be so chic?"

Eleven Madison Park [S] | 25 | 25 | 25 | $60 |

11 Madison Ave. (24th St.), 212-889-0905

■ Both architecturally and culinarily "stunning", this latest "Danny Meyer triumph" opposite the renovated Madison Square Park "epitomizes NY swank" thanks to its "soaring" art deco setting, chef Kerry Heffernan's "delicious" New American cuisine and "gracious but not stuffy service" – no wonder it's so popular.

Four Seasons | 27 | 27 | 27 | $73 |

99 E. 52nd St. (bet. Lexington & Park Aves.), 212-754-9494

■ "Aging better than a good French wine", this NY "perennial favorite" achieves "a perfect symphony" of "sublime" Continental cuisine, "impeccable" service and "landmark" design ("the apotheosis of modernism") by Philip Johnson; lunches in the Grill Room afford "great power broker–watching", and the "stunning" Pool Room "never misses" for "special occasions."

Gotham Bar & Grill [S] | 27 | 25 | 25 | $60 |

12 E. 12th St. (bet. 5th Ave. & University Pl.), 212-620-4020

■ Still on the "cutting edge" and "deserving all its accolades", this "elegant" Village New American, a perennial Most Popular top-placer in the *NYC Survey* (No. 3 this year), remains a "mecca of fine dining" where "everything clicks" – to wit, Alfred Portale's "spectacular", "vertically presented" cuisine, "flawless" service and the "beautiful", "airy" setting; P.S. for those who "can't afford dinner", the $20 prix fixe lunch is a best bet.

Gramercy Tavern [S] | 27 | 26 | 26 | $63 |

42 E. 20th St. (bet. B'way & Park Ave. S.), 212-477-0777

■ Danny Meyer's take on American tavern dining (No. 2 in the *NYC Survey* for Popularity) just "keeps getting better"; Tom Colicchio's American cuisine sets a standard of "culinary grace" matched by Claudia Fleming's "flawless" desserts, and the "elegantly" "rustic" Flatiron/Gramercy space is manned by a "superb" staff that defines the difference between good service and true hospitality; while such "exquisite" meals don't come cheap, the no-reservation-needed "tavern room" in front is "easier on the pocket."

Il Mulino ◐ | 27 | 20 | 23 | $65 |

86 W. Third St. (bet. Sullivan & Thompson Sts.), 212-673-3783

■ Irregulars "dream of being regulars" at this "dark" Villager that perennially ranks as NY's No.1 Italian even though it's "harder to get a reservation than an audience with the Pope"; those who do squeeze in should "bring a line of credit" and "come hungry" to savor both the "eating orgy" and service as "enthusiastic" as "Roberto Benigni's Oscar speech"; to avoid waiting, even with reservations, "go for lunch, when it's quiet and really shines."

Jean Georges [S] | 28 | 26 | 27 | $82 |

Trump Int'l Hotel, 1 Central Park West (bet. 60th & 61st Sts.), 212-299-3900

■ This "special place for special times" is a nearly "flawless" "class act" courtesy of star French chef Jean-Georges Vongerichten; "everything" from his "inventive" open kitchen is "sublime" and delivered by a "superb" staff in a "serene" setting off Columbus Circle; "you may pay a king's ransom", but the less formal front room, Nougatine, and the terrace are "incredible buys" at the $20 prix fixe summer lunch; N.B. they also do a super business breakfast, which is making it the Regency West.

La Caravelle 27 25 26 $72

33 W. 55th St. (bet. 5th & 6th Aves.), 212-586-4252

■ Celebrating its 40th anniversary, André and Rita Jammet's Midtown French classic from a "more gracious era" still "sails along in quiet luxury" with former sous-chef Eric Di Domenico at the helm; keys to its enduring appeal include "superlative" food, "sure service" and a "lovely" muraled room that together exemplify "formal dining at its best"; prix fixe only: dinner $68, lunch $38.

La Côte Basque [S] 27 26 26 $72

60 W. 55th St. (bet. 5th & 6th Aves.), 212-688-6525

■ "*Magnifique*" sums up Jean-Jacques Rachou's "classic-to-the-core" Midtown French beauty, a bastion of "old-world" excellence on every level, from its "superb" food and "dignified" service to its "transporting" murals and handsome private rooms upstairs; if it's "a bit of a squeeze", at least you're in swell company, and the $36 prix fixe lunch is an haute-rageous "deal" (dinner is $68).

La Grenouille ◐ 27 27 27 VE

3 E. 52nd St. (bet. 5th & Madison Aves.), 212-752-1495

■ The epitome of "everlasting elegance", the Masson family's "gorgeous" Midtown Classic French is "top-of-the-line" all the way, catering to a glamorous "money crowd" ("real jewelry") with "extraordinary food and service" and "dazzling flowers"; steep prices (prix fixe only, $45 lunch, $90 dinner) are a given at one of NY's premier places "to impress" or "celebrate"; P.S. the upstairs party room doesn't come cheap either, but it may be NY's best.

Le Bernardin 28 27 28 $80

155 W. 51st St. (bet. 6th & 7th Aves.), 212-489-1515

■ "NY is lucky to have" this "swimmingly" "exquisite" French temple of seafood, again rated NYC's No. 1 both for chef Eric Ripert's culinary "artistry" ("da Vinci with fish") and for its "unparalleled service"; add a "luxurious" Midtown setting and it "surpasses expectations in every category"; in fact – "when you need a sure thing", there's "none better" (prix fixe only: $45 lunch, $77 dinner).

Le Cirque 2000 [S] 26 26 25 $79

NY Palace Hotel, 455 Madison Ave. (bet. 50th & 51st Sts.), 212-303-7788

◪ "Made for NY", Sirio Maccioni's Midtown French is like the city itself: "glamorous" and "upbeat", "star-studded" yet "touristy", at times "arrogant" but "always exciting"; while the departure of pastry wiz Jacques Torres is a loss and there's still debate over Adam Tihany's "giddy", colorful decor, the bottom line is that it feels like "*the* place to be", with a $25 "prix fixe bar lunch that's NY's best-kept secret" and wonderful private party rooms for when you have something serious to celebrate; whatever you hear, don't reject an invitation to come here.

Lespinasse 27 28 27 $85

St. Regis Hotel, 2 E. 55th St. (bet. 5th & Madison Aves.), 212-339-6719

■ There's "no better place" for "elegant, formal dining" than this "unforgettable" Midtown French "temple of gastronomy", which surveyors report is "like eating in Versailles" thanks to "stunning" Louis XV accommodations, "impeccable" white-glove service and the "masterpieces" emerging from chef Christian Delouvrier's kitchen; "sky-high prices" seem fitting if "this is heaven."

Lutèce 26 | 24 | 26 | $75

249 E. 50th St. (bet. 2nd & 3rd Aves.), 212-752-2225

◪ "Still thriving", this "grande dame of French haute cuisine", set in an "elegant" East Midtown townhouse, "has kept its good manners" and its lofty status as one of NY's "premier dining experiences"; however, the recent departure of talented chef Eberhard Mueller and an upcoming redo put our ratings in doubt; prix fixe only: $38 lunch, $65 dinner.

Manhattan Ocean Club ◐[S] 25 | 22 | 23 | $60

57 W. 58th St. (bet. 5th & 6th Aves.), 212-371-7777

■ "Others come and go", but this "exceptional" Midtown "fish mecca" "deserves its rep" as a dependable "port in a storm" and an "elegant" lifesaver when you need to "impress clients"; no matter how you slice it, be it food, wine, decor or service, when you come here you can count on "first-class dining all the way."

March [S] 26 | 25 | 26 | $77

405 E. 58th St. (bet. 1st Ave. & Sutton Pl.), 212-754-6272

■ "When you want to impress" somebody special, this "gracious" New American set in a "tony", recently renovated and expanded Sutton Place townhouse is the "ultimate romantic hideaway"; chef Wayne Nish "has a way with flavors" and demonstrates "impeccable attention to detail" that carries over to his staff; in sum, if you're looking for a "heavenly experience", march on over.

Mercer Kitchen, The ◐[S] 23 | 23 | 19 | $52

Mercer Hotel, 99 Prince St. (Mercer St.), 212-966-5454

◪ "Go for the vibe" – it "couldn't be hipper" than at this "spiffy" SoHo New American via Jean-Georges Vongerichten; set in a handsome, "underground", "old-brick-meets-high-tech" space, it has "wonderful" food and "famous" folks ("is that Matt Damon?"), despite "staff too cool to wait tables."

Milos, Estiatorio ◐[S] 26 | 23 | 22 | $65

125 W. 55th St. (bet. 6th & 7th Aves.), 212-245-7400

■ It's "worth refinancing your yacht" for "seafood beyond compare" ("perfectly cooked" and "so fresh" it might swim off your plate) at this modern Midtown Greek piscatory "paradise"; "hefty", "by-the-pound pricing" for entrees can be mitigated by sticking to the less expensive first courses.

Montrachet 26 | 21 | 25 | $64

239 W. Broadway (bet. Walker & White Sts.), 212-219-2777

■ "All it's cracked up to be", this "relaxing" TriBeCa "perfect retreat" from Drew Nieporent "hasn't lost its edge" over the years, still seamlessly serving "fine-tuned" food and one of the "best wine lists in the city"; bargain-hunters tout Friday's "unbeatable $20 prix fixe lunch."

Nobu [S] 28 | 24 | 24 | $66

105 Hudson St. (Franklin St.), 212-219-0500

■ "Walk in and float out" is the norm at Nobu Matsuhisa's "better-than-sex" TriBeCa Japanese-Peruvian that "lives up to all the hype", especially if you "let the chef surprise you" (say *omakase*, i.e. Japanese for 'I leave it up to you'); add super servers, David Rockwell's "whimsical" decor and "celebs galore", and it's no wonder that you must "set the phone to redial" if you hope to get in; P.S. its annex, Nobu, Next Door, offers "easier access."

Oceana 27 | 25 | 25 | $67

55 E. 54th St. (bet. Madison & Park Aves.), 212-759-5941

■ "First class all the way", this Midtown "marine mecca" offers "phenomenal fish" in a posh, "double-decker" setting with "ocean-liner decor" and a crew that treats you like you've been onboard "100 times even on your first visit"; while not cheap (prix fixe only: $45 lunch, $65 dinner), it "never disappoints."

Oyster Bar 22 | 18 | 16 | $42

Grand Central, lower level (42nd St. & Lexington Ave.), 212-490-6650

■ "One of NY's treasures", this "bustling" "classic" in Grand Central serves "amazingly fresh" seafood and "wines to match" in a "vast" vaulted setting that literally "*is* NY"; even given "echo-chamber" noise and "assembly-line service", eating at the counter or raw bar makes one hope that it will last "forever."

Palm 25 | 16 | 20 | $57

837 Second Ave. (bet. 44th & 45th Sts.), 212-687-2953

Palm Too [S]

840 Second Ave. (bet. 44th & 45th Sts.), 212-697-5198

Palm West ◐[S]

250 W. 50th St. (bet. B'way & 8th Ave.), 212-333-7256

■ "Still among the best steak joints in NY", this trio wins kudos for its "fantastic" beef and "incredibly large" lobsters that are worth the "hustle and bustle" and "pricey" tab; while old-timers favor the original East Midtown location, the new Theater District branch is less cramped, with the same "gruff" "old-school" waiters and "interesting" "celebrity caricatures" covering the walls.

Park Avenue Cafe [S] 25 | 23 | 23 | $59

100 E. 63rd St. (bet. Lexington & Park Aves.), 212-644-1900

■ Neil Murphy continues to turn out "witty", "inventive" New American fare that draws a smart crowd to this East Side "oasis of comfort and elegance" with an "upscale" Americana look; though costly, it clicks on all fronts, with "pro" service, a "beautiful brunch", "masterful" desserts and even a "memorable bread basket"; try the chef's table for an "A+" experience.

Peter Luger Steak House [S]⊘ 28 | 15 | 19 | $58

178 Broadway (Driggs Ave.), Brooklyn, 718-387-7400

■ "The best porterhouse in America", "unbelievably juicy" and "flavorful", has kept this cash-only Williamsburg meat mecca the *NYC Survey's* No. 1 steakhouse for 17 years; "German beer-hall" ambiance, "gruff but humorous" waiters and "great sides" are part of the tradition, and for a cholesterol climax, "bring on the *schlag!*"

Picholine [S] 26 | 24 | 24 | $67

35 W. 64th St. (bet. B'way & CPW), 212-724-8585

■ Terry Brennan's masterful modern Med is "one of NY's best" restaurants of any kind and clearly the top spot near Lincoln Center, but "never mind the opera" – it's a "bravissima" show in its own right, with "glorious" food, sharp service, "elegant" decor and showstopping samplings from "chairman of the cheeseboard" Max McCalman's cart; crowded at night, it's quieter and cheaper for wonderful weekday lunches.

River Cafe ◐[S] 25 | 27 | 24 | VE

1 Water St. (Brooklyn Bridge), Brooklyn, 718-522-5200

■ "Nothing can compare" to "the ultimate view of the Downtown skyline" offered at Buzzy O'Keeffe's East River American, though the food is absolutely "delectable", "if you can swallow the price" ($70 prix fixe only dinner); still, "you can bet the Brooklyn Bridge" that everything from the "seamless service" to the swoon-worthy "romantic" setting will be "stunning" and far less expensive at the peaceful à la carte lunch.

Russian Tea Room ◐[S] 18 | 25 | 20 | $62

150 W. 57th St. (bet. 6th & 7th Aves.), 212-974-2111

◪ Warner LeRoy's much "ballyhooed" remake of this legendary Midtown Russian splits voters: while there's general agreement that the "glitzy", "over-the-top" "Ivana Trump" goes to "Las Vegas" redo is "dazzling", more conservative diners call it "a monument to vulgarity"; and while some find the food "wonderful", others consider it a "disappointment"; whichever side one ends up on, the bottom line is that it's as crowded as Disneyland on the 4th of July.

71 Clinton Fresh Food [S] 26 | 17 | 22 | $47

71 Clinton St. (Rivington St.), 212-614-6960

■ "Hype, hype, hurray" for this "unique" Lower East Side New American freshman, a "tiny" storefront that lives up to its big "buzz" thanks to the "bold", "exciting" food of Wylie Dufresne (ex Jean Georges), enhanced by "smart wines, smart service" and fair prices; it's "cramped" and "noisy" but "hip" and hot – behold, "a star is born."

Shun Lee Palace ◐[S] 24 | 22 | 22 | $49

155 E. 55th St. (bet. Lexington & 3rd Aves.), 212-371-8844

■ "It's hard to imagine takeout" after a visit to Michael Tong's "high-echelon" East Midtown flagship that's like "dining at the Chinese Embassy"; its "dramatic", "intriguing menu combos" ("mouthwatering sea bass", "perfect" prawns), black-tie service (follow the maitre d's advice) and handsome Adam Tihany–designed space "set the Sino standard" with delighted diners declaring "nothing compares" to this.

Smith & Wollensky ◐[S] 23 | 18 | 20 | $56

797 Third Ave. (49th St.), 212-753-1530

■ Now with outposts nationwide, Alan Stillman's "top-tier" flagship Midtown steakhouse, aka "Atkins spa", remains a cacophonous "big boy's club" that's perfect "for bachelor parties" and other "macho" rites of passage, and, as a result, is prime man-hunting territory for women; look for "damn good" "slabs of meat" matched with "big cabernets" delivered by "harried" career waiters; make sure you're "hungry, carnivorous – and flush."

Sugiyama 28 | 21 | 25 | $81

251 W. 55th St. (bet. B'way & 8th Ave.), 212-956-0670

■ This tiny Midtown Japanese has catapulted to the No. 4 Food ranking in the *NYC Survey* thanks to "talented chef" Nao Sugiyama, who makes "unbelievable use" of "exotic" ingredients in his "sheer-joy-on-the-tongue" kaiseki dishes; his "unrivaled attention to detail" extends to the "impeccable service" and "amazing china" – "even the rest rooms are works of art."

Sushisay
25 | 18 | 20 | $50

38 E. 51st St. (bet. Madison & Park Aves.), 212-755-1780

■ Highly "skilled chefs" slice "serious" sashimi and sushi at this "austere" modern Midtown "Japanese power-lunch" spot that attracts "big bucks" types; but every solvent sushi savant seeks to sample its seductive seafood since it's surely "among the best in NY."

Sylvia's 🅂
18 | 13 | 17 | $29

328 Lenox Ave. (bet. 126th & 127th Sts.), 212-996-0660

■ Harlem's "Soul Food landmark" continues to be an "accessible", "fun" way to sample "plentiful portions" of "lard-laced" classics and a bona fide destination for its legendary jazz (Saturday) and gospel (Sunday) brunches; "forget the cholesterol count" and dig in.

Tabla 🅂
25 | 26 | 25 | $60

11 Madison Ave. (25th St.), 212-889-0667

■ "Wonderfully conceived" and "truly different", Danny Meyer's Madison Square New American has it all: "thrilling", Indian-accented dishes via chef Floyd Cardoz, "exceptionally caring service" from a "knowledgeable" staff and a "gorgeous", colorful setting; while the $54 prix fixe satisfies big spenders, those with smaller spending habits head for its simpler, separately run downstairs sib, Bread Bar.

Tavern on the Green 🅂
17 | 25 | 18 | $54

Central Park West (bet. 66th & 67th Sts.), 212-873-3200

🗹 A "NYC classic", Warner LeRoy's Central Park "wonderland" is a "must-stop for visitors" and a special-occasion "treat for locals", mainly due to its "glitz-and-gala" setting, especially the wonderful Crystal Room and outdoor garden; critics call it "a feast for the eyes only" but they are easily outnumbered by boosters who insist the American fare is "better than reported"; consensus calls this "landmark" definitely "worth visiting" and possibly the city's best site for a large party.

'21' Club
22 | 23 | 23 | $61

21 W. 52nd St. (bet. 5th & 6th Aves.), 212-582-7200

■ NY's most celebrated former speakeasy still "sets the standard" for "clubby" fine dining thanks to the utmost in service (from the greeter at the front door to the black-tie waiters and even the men's room attendant) and to star chef Erik Blauberg's "dependably good" and consistently improving American kitchen; with a historic setting that includes a legendary wine cellar, the place "oozes of money", power and pulchritude.

Union Pacific
26 | 26 | 25 | $69

111 E. 22nd St. (bet. Lexington Ave. & Park Ave. S.), 212-995-8500

■ "Rocco [DiSpirito] rules" at this Gramercy New American, turning out "bold" food that's a "feast for the palate, eye and soul" ("gives new meaning" to the phrase *"Architectural Digest"*); "superb" service, "great wines by the glass" and "elegant", "soothing decor" combine to make this an "instant classic" and a "definite destination" for any serious food lover.

F	D	S	C

Union Square Cafe [S] 27 | 24 | 26 | $58

21 E. 16th St. (bet. 5th Ave. & Union Sq. W.), 212-243-4020

■ "Gourmet food without the attitude" – and at comparatively modest prices – might be the motto of Danny Meyer's "congenial" Union Square New American, voted NYC's Most Popular restaurant for the fifth year in a row; despite a few protests, Michael Romano's cuisine "keeps on pleasin'" and is served by a "fabulously friendly", "customer-oriented" staff in a choice of three "civilized" settings.

Veritas [S] 26 | 23 | 25 | $71

43 E. 20th St. (bet. B'way & Park Ave. S.), 212-353-3700

■ The "sensational", "fairly priced" wine list "gets the publicity", but this Flatiron oenophile's opus is also "a foodie heaven" thanks to chef Scott Bryan's "superb" New American fare; add "helpful" sommeliers and "sleek", "classy" decor, and it's understandable why few blow their cork over the cost (dinner is $68 prix fixe only).

Windows on the World [S] 21 | 27 | 22 | $61

1 World Trade Ctr., 107th fl. (West St., bet. Liberty & Vesey Sts.), 212-524-7000

◪ While the "awesome" view will always be "the main course", and tourists the main observers, at the WTC's 107th-floor New American, executive chef Michael Lomonaco has "greatly improved" the food, and when you factor in "professional service" and a wine list that nearly "matches" the scenery, the whole package "lives up to its name – WOW"; the early-bird prix fixe is the most economical way to enjoy this "NY must" where on a clear day you can see forever.

Orange County

TOP 10 FOOD RANKING

Restaurant	Cuisine Type
27 Aubergine	Californian/French
Troquet	French
Pascal	French Provençal
Pinot Provence	French Provençal
26 Five Feet	Asian/French
Ritz, The	Continental
Pavilion	Californian/Med.
Gustaf Anders	Swedish/Continental
Ritz-Carlton	New French
Hobbit, The	Eclectic

ADDITIONAL NOTEWORTHY PLACES

Antonello	N/S Italian
Bistango	New American
Cellar	Classic French
Five Crowns	Continental
French 75	French Bistro
Mr. Stox	Traditional American
Riviera at the Fireside	Continental
Roy's	Eurasian
21 Oceanfront	Seafood
Zov's Bistro	Mediterranean

F	D	S	C

Antonello
26	24	26	$43

S. Coast Plaza Village, 1611 Sunflower Ave. (Plaza Dr.), Santa Ana, 714-751-7153

☑ "If you want to impress, this is the place" say patrons who relish being "treated royally" at this Santa Ana Italian graced with a "romantic" faux "Tuscan villa setting"; though naysayers describe it as an "overpriced" "letdown" full of "credit cards and first dates", many feel the "scrumptious, fancy" fare leads to "an unforgettable power-dinner experience."

Aubergine
27	25	26	$62

508 29th St. (Newport Blvd.), Newport Beach, 949-723-4150

■ Voted Orange County's No. 1 for Food, this "jewel" showcases chef (and co-owner) Tim Goodell's "sublime" Cal-French cooking, "exquisitely executed" to reveal "brilliant flavors, textures and a pure love of food"; a recent remodeling "ups the ante" further by adding more space and style to the "sophisticated" Newport bungalow setting; it's "expensive", of course, but this is a "very special treasure" and definitely "worth it."

Bistango S
24 | 24 | 23 | $37

19100 Von Karman Ave. (bet. Campus & Dupont Drs.), Irvine, 949-752-5222

■ "Always busy and rightfully so", this "fun yet elegant" "boomer habitat" in Irvine continues to pack them in for "inventive" New American cuisine, enhanced by a display of modern art and live jazz; it's long been a haunt for a "hip" after-work crowd.

Cellar, The
26 | 23 | 24 | $44

Villa del Sol, 305 N. Harbor Blvd. (Wilshire Ave.), Fullerton, 714-525-5682

■ It's "easy to miss – but don't" urge disciples of the "premier restaurant in North Orange County", renowned for its "rich and old-fashioned" Classic French cuisine matched with an "impressive" wine roster; the "romantic" subterranean "wine-cave" setting is made to feel even more "exclusive" by the "immaculate" service, leading devotees to exclaim that it "deserves its nationwide acclaim" for "old elegance."

Five Crowns S
24 | 25 | 24 | $39

3801 E. PCH (Poppy St.), Corona del Mar, 949-760-0331

■ "Dark and atmospheric", this Continental "throwback" may be "long in the tooth", but it "still sets the standard" in Corona del Mar for "consistently excellent" "slabs of prime rib" as "only a Lawry's operation can deliver"; "refined" service from "pretty wenches" adds to the appeal that makes this one of Orange County's favored "dress-up" destinations for "celebration dinners", especially during the Christmas holiday.

Five Feet S
26 | 20 | 22 | $41

328 Glenneyre St. (bet. Forest Ave. & Mermaid St.), Laguna Beach, 949-497-4955

■ "Laguna's answer to Chinois on Main" remains the place to be for Asian-French "fusion at its best", including a "not-to-be-missed whole catfish" signature dish and "over-the-top", "clever entrees" served in "gigantic" portions; the "always-packed" "scene" is "casual", "funky and loud" and the quarters are notoriously "cramped", but still, many would be happy to "drive 100 miles" for such "complex flavors that work."

French 75 S
24 | 24 | 22 | $45

1464 S. PCH (Mountain St.), Laguna Beach, 949-494-8444

■ This "dark and sexy" '40s-style French bistro in Laguna has "romance written all over it", spurred on by "live piano music" and "private booths", as well as "sophisticated" indulgences like "excellent" champagne cocktails and "fabulous" chocolate soufflés; the menu is both "traditional" and "playful", and perfectly in tune with the room's "fun atmosphere of liberated Paris."

Gustaf Anders S
26 | 23 | 25 | $46

S. Coast Plaza Village, 3851 S. Bear St. (Sunflower Ave.), Santa Ana, 714-668-1737

■ "Unique to California", this slice of Scandinavia in Santa Ana garners raves for its "authentic" Swedish and Continental dishes prepared and served with "subtle perfection" in an "ultramodern" setting; regulars gush over "breads beyond compare", "gravlax to die for" and "herrings with no equal", and "splurge" on the holiday smorgasbords that easily "substitute for a trip to Stockholm" because "you won't find better than this in Sweden itself."

Hobbit, The S
26 | 25 | 27 | $58

2932 E. Chapman Ave. (Malena St.), Orange, 714-997-1972

■ Followers know to "reserve in advance" for a coveted table at this old hacienda in the City of Orange because there's only one seating each night and the prix fixe Eclectic feast is "superb"; the dinner begins with "appetizers and champagne" in the "fabulous wine cellar" and ends with "first-rate desserts"; this "enchanting" evening makes for a "once-in-a-lifetime" "special occasion."

Mr. Stox S
25 | 23 | 23 | $39

1105 E. Katella Ave. (bet. Lewis St. & State College Rd.), Anaheim, 714-634-2994

■ "A star in North County" rave admirers of this Anaheim "landmark", a "dependably elegant" destination for Traditional American food (accompanied by a "fantastic" wine list) turned out in a "classy but warm" setting and enhanced by an "impeccable" staff that "goes overboard to please"; whether for a "business meal" or a "special" event, it promises an "enjoyable experience."

Pascal
27 | 22 | 24 | $48

1000 N. Bristol St. (Jamboree Rd.), Newport Beach, 949-752-0107

■ "Talented" chef-owner "Pascal Olhats does Provence proud" with his enduringly "*magnifique*" homage to the cooking of the "French countryside", executed with "unfailing perfection" and proffered in a Newport venue "stunningly" "decorated with roses" "everywhere"; despite grumbles about "haughty" service, devotees promise you'll have "a night to remember" because this "true winner" is "head and shoulders above the rest."

Pavilion S
26 | 26 | 26 | $46

Four Seasons Hotel, 690 Newport Ctr. Dr. (Santa Cruz Dr.), Newport Beach, 949-760-4920

■ "Another Four Seasons gem" purr partisans of this symbol of "elegance" in Newport, where patrons are pampered with "exceptional" Californian cuisine (with a dash of Med flair) turned out by a "professional" staff in a "beautiful" space with a "relaxing" ambiance; the "prix fixe dinner is outstanding" and, considering the pedigree, the price is "surprisingly reasonable"; this is "what every hotel dining room should be" like.

Pinot Provence S
27 | 26 | 25 | $46

Westin S. Coast Plaza, 686 Anton Blvd. (Bristol St.), Costa Mesa, 714-444-5900

■ "Another Joachim Splichal masterpiece", this "top-notch" Costa Mesa outpost for "luxurious meals" provides a "sumptuous escape to the French countryside", where diners can savor "inventive" Provençal bistro fare that's "often brilliant"; along with an "impressively elegant yet homey" interior and "stellar" service, it adds up to a piece of "French heaven in Orange County."

Ritz, The
26 | 26 | 27 | $48

Fashion Island, 880 Newport Ctr. Dr. (Santa Barbara Ave.), Newport Beach, 949-720-1800

■ Again ranked No. 1 in Orange County for its "polished" service, this "formal" Newport "hangout" for the "old-money crowd" dazzles with "lavish" trappings that make it one of the "finest" choices for a "special occasion"; the "impressive" menu is "classic Continental at its best", and the famous "Christmas goose" extravaganza is not to be missed.

Ritz-Carlton Laguna Niguel 26 | 28 | 27 | $52

Ritz-Carlton Laguna Niguel, 1 Ritz-Carlton Dr. (PCH), Dana Point, 949-240-5008

■ "Luxuriate" in "divine dining" in "Shangri-la" at this "world-class" Dana Point destination, another "Ritz effort that shines" thanks to "an astonishing choice" of dishes ("each a delight") from a "major-league" New French menu, served in "the prettiest place on earth" (it rates No. 1 for Decor in Orange County yet again) by an "impeccable" staff; niceties such as "an awesome wine list" and a "wonderful" formal tea in the library only enhance its appeal.

Riviera at the Fireside 25 | 21 | 26 | $35

13950 Springdale Ave. (#405 Frwy.), Westminster, 714-897-0477

■ "A throwback to a bygone era" and still a "marvelous" spot for "nostalgic" Continental standards like "absolutely the best steak tartare around" and veal Oscar, this enduring Westminster darling of mature diners pampers its followers with "soothing", "supper-club elegance" and "old-world" service from a "tuxedoed" staff that "has worked here for decades"; "yes, it's a dinosaur, but with food this good, who cares?"

Roy's [S] 24 | 22 | 23 | $44

Fashion Island, 453 Newport Ctr. Dr. (San Miguel Dr.), Newport Beach, 949-640-7697

◪ What may be "the toughest reservation in Orange County" rewards determined diners with "fond memories of Roy's in Hawaii" thanks to Eurasian meals judged by fans to be "incomparable" (capped by "the best chocolate soufflé in the world"), delivered by an "attentive" staff amid "classy island decor"; while critics call the hip Newport package "too loud" and "trendy to an extreme", for those looking for "Hawaii on the mainland" it can't be matched.

Troquet 27 | 23 | 24 | $47

S. Coast Plaza, 3333 Bristol St. (Town Ctr. Dr.), Costa Mesa, 714-708-6865

◪ This "fabulous" Costa Mesa "oasis" features "imaginative", "spectacular" French fare "masterminded" "with élan" by Tim and Lisa Goodell (the duo behind top-rated Aubergine) and delivered in a "gorgeous" room; though detractors complain about the "weird mall location", "eyedropper" portions and "service that should be better", the majority proclaims this a "winner."

21 Oceanfront [S] 26 | 25 | 24 | $42

2100 W. Oceanfront (Newport Pier), Newport Beach, 949-673-2100

■ "Old-fashioned, club-style" stalwart that remains a "hoity-toity" favorite for "celebration" dinners over "fancy food" like "excellent oysters" and choice abalone (even if "you need to finance it"); add on "excellent service" and a "beautiful view of the ocean" and it's clear why it continues to endure.

Zov's Bistro & Bakery Cafe 25 | 19 | 21 | $29

Enderle Ctr., 17440 E. 17th St. (Yorba St.), Tustin, 714-838-8855

■ "Always pleasing", with an "always full house", this "real find" in Tustin with "delightful decor" earns "high marks" for its "exceptional" way with "unique" Mediterranean dishes; "caring" chef-proprietor "Zov does it all", offering an "extraordinary variety" of treats – "incredible" "pastries in the morning, great sandwiches and salads at lunch, sophisticated" specialties at dinner; this is "a feast" for all the senses.

Orlando

TOP 20 FOOD RANKING

Restaurant	Cuisine Type
28 Victoria & Albert's	Traditional American
La Coquina	New World
Del Frisco's	Steakhouse
Le Coq au Vin	Country French
27 California Grill	Californian
Flying Fish Cafe	Seafood
26 Chatham's Place	Continental
Manuel's on the 28th	Eclectic/New American
Morton's of Chicago	Steakhouse
Artist Point	Pacific Northwestern
Atlantis	International/Seafood
Yachtsman Steakhouse	Steakhouse
Enzo's Restaurant on the Lake	Northern Italian
Shiki	Japanese
Cypriana Cafe	Greek
Maison et Jardin	Continental
Arthur's 27	International
Le Provence	New French
Ruth's Chris*	Steakhouse
Thai House	Thai

ADDITIONAL NOTEWORTHY PLACES

Antonio's La Fiamma	N/S Italian
Bahama Breeze	Caribbean
Bravissimo Wine Bar Cafe	N/S Italian
Brio Tuscan Grille	Northern Italian
California Cafe Bar & Grill	Pacific Rim/Southwestern
Chez Vincent	Classic French
Citricos	Mediterranean
Delfino Riviera	Northern Italian
Dexter's	Eclectic/International
Emeril's Restaurant Orlando	Cajun/Creole
Fulton's Crab House	Seafood
Harvey's Bistro	New American/European
Johnny Rivers'	Barbecue
Louis' Downtown	Southern
Park Plaza Gardens	Continental/Eclectic
Pebbles	New American
Peter Scott's	Continental
Rolando's	Cuban
Schafer's Caffeehaus	Continental/German
Winnie's Oriental Garden	Chinese

---

* Tied with the restaurant listed directly above it.

Antonio's La Fiamma　　　　25　22　22　$26
611 S. Orlando Ave. (Maitland Ave.), Maitland, 407-645-1035
■ Expect "an evening of pampering" from this immensely popular Maitland Italian with "an excellent deli downstairs and fine dining upstairs"; the "authentic" cuisine is served "with an emphasis on keeping the customers happy" by a "knowledgeable staff" in a "lovely", albeit "painfully noisy", setting; some say the wine list is reason enough to go; N.B. the deli is open on Sundays.

Arthur's 27 🆂　　　　　　26　26　25　$48
Wyndham Palace Resort & Spa, 1900 Buena Vista Dr. (Hotel Plaza Blvd.), Lake Buena Vista, 407-827-3450
■ For "the ultimate" indulgence, this lovely, "romantic" International perched on the top floor of the Wyndham Palace delivers "terrific food", "beautiful views of the Disney parks" (and their fireworks) and the "best atmosphere in Central Florida"; all this comes at a price to match the altitude, but for "special occasion dining" with "lots of elegance", it's "worth every penny"; insiders advise "try to time your reservations for sunset."

Artist Point 🆂　　　　　　26　26　24　$30
Disney's Wilderness Lodge, 901 W. Timberline Dr. (World Dr.), Lake Buena Vista, 407-824-1081
■ "Deliciously unique Pacific Northwest food" is the specialty of this rustic yet "breathtaking" room at Disney's Wilderness Lodge that's "like eating at Frank Lloyd Wright's house"; "still undiscovered by the crowds", it draws kudos for its "great salmon, wild game" and extensive regional wine list; for those seeking a "dining adventure, not a quick meal", this is a "hands-down favorite."

Atlantis　　　　　　　　　26　25　26　$48
Renaissance Orlando Resort, 6676 Sea Harbor Dr. (International Dr.), 407-351-5555
■ "Fine dining at its best" is the province of this "innovative" International seafooder that's "out of the Disney path", although close to another area attraction, SeaWorld; it might be "a bit pricey", but few mind when a "gourmet meal" (try the signature lobster bisque) and "service that's 100 on a scale of one to 10" are the payoffs; "it's at the top, even though it's on the first floor" enthuse admirers.

Bahama Breeze ●🆂　　　　22　24　20　$17
8849 International Dr. (1 mi. south of Sand Lake Rd.), 407-248-2499
499 E. Altamonte Dr. (Palm Springs Blvd. & State Rd. 436), Altamonte Springs, 407-831-2929
■ This "peppy" Caribbean-flavored chain garners acclaim for its "creative", "inexpensive" food and "islandish", "party atmosphere"; though a few say it "reeks of franchise" and can be "too too too much", nonetheless it's "always crowded", so "go early or wait forever" to get in.

Bravissimo Wine Bar Cafe 🆂　　－　－　－　M
337 N. Shine Ave. (Livingston St.), 407-898-7333
Proof that good things come in small packages, this trendy Italian tucked in a residential area near Downtown is looked after by a warm and gracious staff serving delectable homemade soups and pizzas; the tiny wine bar inside is as popular as the six tables under the outside canopy, so reserve ahead.

Brio Tuscan Grille S
| – | – | – | M |

Winter Park Village, 480 N. Orlando Ave. (Canton Ave.), Winter Park, 407-622-5611

Go without a reservation at your own risk: two-hour waits are common on weekends at this bustling Tuscan hot spot that's a focal point of Winter Park Village's burgeoning dining district; the salon set keeps coming back for wood-grilled salmon with citrus pesto, flatbread pizzas and the like, as well as a rambling wine list that perhaps is best explored from one of the prized cafe tables outside.

California Cafe Bar & Grill S
| – | – | – | E |

Florida Mall, 8001 S. Orange Blossom Trail (Sand Lake Rd.), 407-816-5555

Sophisticated, swanky and fun, this recent Florida Mall arrival tempts the well-heeled with provocative Pacific Rim–Southwestern fusion fare (think grilled mahi mahi with mango–scotch bonnet sauce); it's an epicurean adventure set in a bold, contemporary space, and while not cheap it's more affordable than Walt Disney World's unrelated California Grill, with which it's often confused.

California Grill S
| 27 | 27 | 25 | $36 |

Disney's Contemporary Resort, 4600 N. World Dr., Lake Buena Vista, 407-824-1576

■ One of Disney's "finest", this "superb" Californian atop the Contemporary Resort has it all: an "adventuresome", "sophisticated" menu by chef Clifford Pleau, an "exciting wine program" with many by-the-glass choices and an "awesome" view, all of which come together so well that it's voted Orlando's Most Popular restaurant; no surprise, it "can be difficult to get into", so reserve far in advance and "time your dinner for the Magic Kingdom fireworks."

Chatham's Place S
| 26 | 22 | 25 | $33 |

Phillips Pl., 7575 Dr. Phillips Blvd. (Sand Lake Rd.), 407-345-2992

■ Although the Chatham family no longer owns it, this Continental remains a local favorite (despite its proximity to touristy International Drive) for a "really delightful evening"; admirers like the fact that you can "dress up or down" and that everyone "is treated with the same attention as frequent guests"; regulars recommend the signature pecan-crusted grouper, calling it simply "world-class."

Chez Vincent
| 24 | 21 | 21 | $28 |

533 W. New England Ave. (Park Ave.), Winter Park, 407-599-2929

☑ "Sharp, sophisticated and intimate", chef Vincent Gagliano's Classic French in Winter Park's redeveloped West End might be on the "wrong side of the tracks", but many call this "perfect little bistro" a "great addition to the restaurant scene" (though a few hedge that the "food is *almost* there"); though the "slaphappy" service takes some blows, the consensus seems to be that it's "trying hard and should get even better."

Citricos S
| 25 | 26 | 26 | $40 |

Disney's Grand Floridian Resort & Spa, 4401 Grand Floridian Way, Lake Buena Vista, 407-824-1379

■ "Chef Roland Muller's innovative food" draws applause at this Disney Mediterranean at the Grand Floridian Resort, where the "stunning", "eclectic decor" and "very attentive service" also impress; though it might be a bit "noisy" and "a little pricey", the word on the boardwalk is that it's a "great restaurant to try."

Cypriana Cafe

F	D	S	C
26	16	21	$12

505 Semoran Blvd. (Fern Park Blvd.), Casselberry, 407-834-8088

■ For "wonderful, homestyle Greek that's like the real thing", this Casselberry yearling has attracted a lot of admirers who laud its "friendly, intimate appeal" and "reasonable prices"; as their digs are small, insiders caution "there's sometimes a wait, even with reservations"; "don't miss" the grape leaves and the tzatziki.

Delfino Riviera

F	D	S	C
–	–	–	VE

Portofino Bay Hotel, 5601 Universal Blvd., 407-503-1415

Anticipate gourmet dining at this luxe Northern Italian in a Universal Studios hotel that emphasizes fresh seafood (lobster risotto, yellowtail tuna carpaccio, roasted sea bass in Chianti sauce); service is attentive and professional, but the real draw is its lush, quiet-as-a-whisper surroundings.

Del Frisco's Steakhouse

F	D	S	C
28	22	24	$37

729 Lee Rd. (1½ blocks west of I-4), 407-645-4443

■ "Steaks are the signature", but "everything from appetizers to desserts is exquisite" say the many supporters of this "very special" Lee Road "guy place" with "dark wood" decor and a "clubby atmosphere" (the guys think it's "a great place to close a deal"); the few who "wish there were more nonbeef items" seem to miss the point: it's aimed at carnivores who "don't care about prices" given "humongous portions" of "excellent food."

Dexter's of Thornton Park [S]

F	D	S	C
22	18	18	$16

808 E. Washington St. (Hill Ave.), 407-648-2777

Dexter's of Winter Park [S]

F	D	S	C
22	16	18	$15

558 W. New England Ave. (Pennsylvania Ave.), Winter Park, 407-629-1150

■ These "hip" Eclectic-International bistros are always "hopping", thanks to their "all-time wonderful wine lists" and "imaginative, innovative food"; though critics complain of "too many yuppies", everyone allows that it can be "hard to find a seat or a parking spot"; ultimately, the consensus seems to be "for what they do, nobody is better"; N.B. a change of address at the Winter Park outpost outdates its decor rating.

Emeril's Restaurant Orlando [S]

F	D	S	C
–	–	–	E

Universal Studios Escape, Universal CityWalk, 407-224-2424

Superchef Emeril Lagasse's Cajun-Creole is the hands-down culinary star of Universal's CityWalk, thanks to resourceful cooking that showcases basic ingredients in unusual combinations; its techno-industrial setting, reflecting its New Orleans warehouse roots and featuring an open kitchen, is jammed with locals who have displaced tourists who didn't think of making reservations.

Enzo's Restaurant on the Lake

F	D	S	C
26	24	23	$33

1130 S. Hwy. 17-92 (State Rd. 434), Longwood, 407-834-9872

■ "Enzo Perlini is hands-on" at his eponymous, "high-end" Longwood Northern Italian that some say is the "closest thing to a trattoria in North America"; young lovers sigh it's a "first-rate first-date place" as "there's passion in the food and staff", even if others claim nonregulars are "treated like they crashed a party"; most concur, however, "you'd swear you're in Italy having a meal in the country", thanks to its "beautiful location" on Lake Fairy.

Flying Fish Cafe 🅂
27 | 26 | 25 | $34

Walt Disney World Boardwalk Resort, 2101 N. Epcot Resorts Blvd.
(Buena Vista Dr.), Lake Buena Vista, 407-939-2359

■ "Disney outdid itself" at this Boardwalk seafooder where "cutting-edge cuisine" served amid "fantastic decor" makes it "too good to pass up"; especially notable is the open-kitchen view ("get a seat at the bar and watch them in action") and a "not-to-be-missed" chocolate lava cake that will "knock your socks off."

Fulton's Crab House 🅂
21 | 21 | 20 | $27

Downtown Disney, 1670 Buena Vista Dr., Lake Buena Vista,
407-934-2628

☑ "Terrific oysters without the fear" can be found at this Downtown Disney seafooder that prides itself on freshness and "good variety"; a few nonbelievers say "leave it to the tourists" and everyone warns "hold onto your wallet" as the tab can be "ridiculous", yet the "stunning" location (it's housed on an old paddle wheeler) and knowledgeable staff sway many.

Harvey's Bistro
24 | 23 | 22 | $23

Bank of America Bldg., 390 N. Orange Ave. (Livingston St.),
407-246-6560

■ It might be the Downtown "office building location", but this New American–European bistro has a "big city feel" that's "unlike Orlando" and helps make it popular "after work" or "before a basketball game" or the theater; the "inventive menu" utilizing fresh seasonal ingredients also earns respect, as does the "great ambiance and service."

Johnny Rivers' Smokehouse 🅂
– | – | – | M

5370 W. Colonial Dr. (Kirkman Rd.), 407-293-5803

Owner Johnny Rivers has converted an abandoned Red Lobster into an upscale barbecuerie in West Orlando and is packing in locals who come to sample a creative menu that includes BBQ ribs, pulled pork and crunchy fried cornbread; make sure to save room for the Hershey bar bread pudding.

La Coquina 🅂
28 | 27 | 27 | $41

Hyatt Regency Grand Cypress, 1 Grand Cypress Blvd. (State Rd. 535),
407-239-1234

■ "A class act that's hard to follow", this "very elegant" New World restaurant in the Grand Cypress Resort delivers a "romantic, special experience" in a "fairy-tale setting for grown-ups"; its "artistically presented" food and "top-shelf" service make it arguably "the most wonderful" dining adventure in Orlando, but just don't try to visit during summer – it closes for the season; P.S. try the "best Sunday brunch on Planet Earth."

Le Coq au Vin 🅂
28 | 22 | 25 | $29

4800 S. Orange Ave. (Holden Ave.), 407-851-6980

■ Chef-owner Louis Perrotte's "tried-and-true" South Orlando bistro is "where Orlando's chefs dine" on their nights off, and with good reason: its Country French cuisine is so "affordable and unpretentious" and the setting so "warm" that you'll "hate to leave"; though the menu changes every two months, some go "just for the crème brûlée" or the "must-have soufflés", but everyone concurs "do not miss this" – "it's popular, so make reservations."

Le Provence

| 26 | 23 | 23 | $33 |

50 E. Pine St. (bet. Magnolia & Orange Aves.), 407-843-1320

■ "The food gets better every year" declare devotees of this Downtown New French that's called "consistently delightful", with "attentive service" and "stylishly updated" cuisine presented with "real flair" in an "intimate and serene" atmosphere; for a "romantic evening", "*c'est si bon.*"

Louis' Downtown 🖪

| – | – | – | E |

135 N. Lucerne Circle (East-West Expy.), 407-648-4688

Chef Louis Chatham is back in town, much to the delight of fans who jockey for reservations at Downtown Orlando's newest power-dining mecca, a circa 1893 B&B on Lake Lucerne; its Nouvelle Southern cuisine is creatively rendered in dishes like fried green tomatoes laced with lump crabmeat and hollandaise sauce; the stunningly scenic backdrop makes its steep prices easier to digest.

Maison et Jardin 🖪

| 26 | 27 | 26 | $37 |

430 S. Wymore Rd. (½ mi. south of I-4 & State Rd. 436), Altamonte Springs, 407-862-4410

■ This "romantic" Altamonte Springs Continental in an "older house" with a "lovely garden setting" is "of another time and place", serving flaming desserts and "beef Wellington that dreams are made of"; "impeccable service" and an "exciting wine list" complement the "wonderful" though "pricey" menu, and while a tad "stuffy" for some (jackets requested), most say dining at the 'Mason Jar' (as it's known locally) is a "don't miss" experience; N.B. it's open for brunch on Sundays from fall through spring only.

Manuel's on the 28th

| 26 | 28 | 27 | $49 |

Bank of America Bldg., 390 N. Orange Ave. (Livingston St.), 407-246-6580

■ Considered by some "the top restaurant in Florida" (and not just because of its 28th-floor location in Downtown Orlando), this "sophisticated" Eclectic–New American serves "world-quality" cuisine and "creative specials" in a "stunning" yet "intimate" room with a "view so good you'll forget the prices"; "attentive" "service teams" are the final touch that makes it "spectacular all the way around" – this is "Orlando at its best."

Morton's of Chicago 🖪

| 26 | 23 | 24 | $45 |

Goodings Mktpl., 7600 Dr. Phillips Blvd. (Sand Lake Rd.), 407-248-3485

☑ This "top-notch" chain steakhouse near Universal Studios serves beef that's "as close to perfect as you can get", topped off by the likes of a "Godiva hot chocolate cake to die for"; a "classy place for local execs", it exudes "a big-city feeling" (i.e. it's "noisy" and filled with "cigar smoke") and can be "very expensive"; some say "go if you're not paying."

Park Plaza Gardens 🖪

| 22 | 25 | 21 | $33 |

319 Park Ave. S. (New England Ave.), Winter Park, 407-645-2475

☑ Bringing the outdoors indoors, the "beautiful" covered-courtyard setting of this Winter Park Continental-Eclectic makes it "absolutely the prettiest dining room in Central Florida"; N.B. veteran chef Valentin Schwaegerl is back in the kitchen, earning applause for his seafood and wild game specialties.

Pebbles   24 | 22 | 22 | $20

17 W. Church St. (Orange Ave.), 407-839-0892 S
Saks Fifth Ave., Florida Mall, 8001 S. Orange Blossom Trail (Sand Lake Rd.), 407-816-5354
Crossroads Plaza, 12551 State Rd. 535 (I-4), Lake Buena Vista, 407-827-1111 S
2110 W. State Rd. 434 (Douglas Ave.), Longwood, 407-774-7111 S
2516 Aloma Ave. (State Rd. 436), Winter Park, 407-678-7001 S

■ "A touch of California cuisine in a town of Disney dining", this New American chain offers what some call the "best total package for the money", thanks to its "gourmet-on-the-cheap" philosophy; fans rave about its "unusual", "always-changing" menu, "great wine list" and "creative" salads (ask for the zucchini dressing); throw "reasonable prices" and good service into the mix and you have the "best 'every night' restaurant" in town.

Peter Scott's   25 | 25 | 24 | $41

Longwood Village, 1811 W. State Rd. 434 (I-4), Longwood, 407-834-4477

■ An "elegant dinner club with entertainment, dancing" and "'40s flair", this Longwood "lovers' retreat" is the "perfect place to propose" almost anything; Dover sole and Châteaubriand are highlights on a Continental menu that pleases an "older crowd" at this "expensive" (some say "overpriced") "special-occasion spot."

Rolando's S   24 | – | 20 | $13

870 E. State Rd. 436 (Red Bug Lake Rd.), Casselberry, 407-767-9677

■ Some of the "best Cuban food north of Havana" is served at this Casselberry "local favorite", a "wonderful, family-operated restaurant" with "homestyle" cooking in a "neighborhood cafe atmosphere"; the dining area is elegant enough for special occasions following a post-*Survey* makeover, but you'll still feel like "part of the family" as it's so "very friendly."

Ruth's Chris Steak House S   26 | 24 | 24 | $38

610 N. Orlando Ave. (Webster Ave.), Winter Park, 407-622-2444

■ "Nobody does it better" than this chain steakhouse that's moved from Altamonte Springs to Winter Park; it might have a "stupid name" but you get "magnificent dining", even if "everything's à la carte" and "so expensive" ("toothpicks are extra"); "serious steak lovers" claim it's "worth every cent" – the "perfect all-around place for the red-meat eater."

Schafer's Caffeehaus S   – | – | – | M

535 W. New England Ave. (Pennsylvania Ave.), Winter Park, 407-740-7782

More than just a coffeehouse, this Continental with a German accent is the kind of place where both goulash and quiche share equal billing; its offbeat decor (i.e. triangular tables) echoes the eclectic, daily-changing menu of this engaging, chef-owned entry in Winter Park's West End.

Shiki S   26 | 17 | 18 | $20

525 Park Ave. S. (bet. Comstock & Fairbanks Aves.), Winter Park, 407-740-8018

■ This "longtime favorite" Winter Park Japanese earns kudos for its "always-fresh sushi" and the "best cooked salmon and tuna in town"; though some say you "pay upscale prices" for the fashionable Park Avenue address, others reason "it's kind of pricey, but you get what you pay for."

Thai House 🅂

26 | 13 | 20 | $15

2117 E. Colonial Dr. (bet. Bumby & Mills Aves.), 407-898-0820

■ Promoters of this East Colonial Drive Thai like its "pleasant" setting, "gracious" staff and "very fresh" food; you can "eat in or take out", but if it's in, "come early" because long waits are "usual"; N.B. decor ratings do not reflect a recent move down the block to larger quarters.

Victoria & Albert's 🅂

28 | 29 | 29 | VE

Disney's Grand Floridian Resort & Spa, 4401 Grand Floridian Way, Lake Buena Vista, 407-939-7707

■ This American "crown jewel of fine dining" in Disney's Grand Floridian takes Metro Orlando's triple crown, placing No. 1 for Food, Decor and Service; the "best dress-up place in town", it offers "luxury" in the form of chef Scott Hunnel's "flawless" seven-course feast that includes "your own personalized menu" and "a rose for milady"; you must "book way in advance" (especially for the coveted chef's table in the kitchen) and though "you'll be treated like royalty, it costs a king's ransom."

Winnie's Oriental Garden 🅂

23 | 22 | 21 | $19

1346 Orange Ave. (Hwy. 17-92), Winter Park, 407-629-2111

■ The "most upscale fine-dining" Chinese around is how fans describe this Winter Park favorite serving "exquisite, jewel-like food" that's evidence of a "delicate touch in the kitchen"; add "gracious hosting" and "stark, clean decor" to the mix and you have one of the "classiest" dining experiences in town; P.S. "check out the sinks in the bathrooms."

Yachtsman Steakhouse 🅂

26 | 24 | 25 | $33

Disney's Yacht Club Resort, 1700 Epcot Resorts Blvd., Lake Buena Vista, 407-939-3463

■ This Yacht Club Resort chophouse is "the best place on Disney property for steaks" and features a refrigerated glass case where diners can select their own cut of meat (regulars say that the "lamb chops are so good you have to pick them up with your fingers to clean the bones"); there might be "better values around", but if you "want to be pampered" with "superb service", this is a "good choice."

Palm Beach

TOP 10 FOOD RANKING

	Restaurant	Cuisine Type
28	Four Seasons	New American
27	Maison Janeiro	New French
	La Vieille Maison	New French
	Kathy's Gazebo	Classic French/Continental
26	Morton's of Chicago	Steakhouse
	Cafe L'Europe	International
	Chez Jean-Pierre	New French
	Cafe Chardonnay	New American
25	Ruth's Chris	Steakhouse
	La Petite Maison	French Bistro/Med.

ADDITIONAL NOTEWORTHY PLACES

Cafe Mazzarello's	N/S Italian
Capri Blue	N/S Italian
Echo	Asian
La Finestra	Northern Italian
La Tre	Vietnamese
Mark's at the Park	Mediterranean
Max's Grille	New American
100 South Ocean	Continental
32 East	New American
Zemi	New American

F	D	S	C

Cafe Chardonnay Ⓢ
26 | 22 | 25 | $44

Garden Sq. Shoppes, 4533 PGA Blvd. (Military Trail), Palm Beach Gardens, 561-627-2662

■ Atmosphere buffs say sit upstairs at this contemporary art–filled Palm Beach Gardens New American, which features "professional service", cuisine that's "a joy for the palate" and an "enormous", 500-label wine selection; while it's a "great dining experience" any time, a visit is especially appealing off-season (May–October) when flights, vin-focused dinners and a prix fixe menu are available.

Cafe L'Europe Ⓢ
26 | 26 | 25 | $53

331 S. County Rd. (Brazilian Ave.), 561-655-4020

■ "Dress up" to mingle with "Palm Beach jet-setters" ("society with a capital S") at this "classy" International with a wide variety of "wonderful food", "outstanding service" and "plush" surroundings, which include a "great" caviar bar with a baby grand piano (music nightly); it's a delightful "piece of old Europe" "and one of Florida's best."

Cafe Mazzarello's [S] – | – | – | VE

425 Clematis St. (Quadrille Blvd.), West Palm Beach, 561-655-9878
More Mulberry Street than Downtown WPB, this cozy gangsta chic–themed newcomer features Italian home cooking, black-attired waiters, gangster movie posters, TV sets looping Mafia flicks and Ol' Blue Eyes (who else?) crooning in the background; the daily-changing menu is orally presented, so listen up! – although it would be hard to go wrong, given the delectable (albeit pricey) pastas, seafood, veal chops, ricotta cheesecake and more.

Capri Blu ◐ ▽ 22 | 18 | 18 | $34

116 N. Dixie Hwy. (bet. Banyan Blvd. & Clematis St.), West Palm Beach, 561-832-4300
■ "A good Italian menu" that boosters call the "best in the Clematis Street area" offers well-executed preparations of fine classic dishes at this casual but upscale WPB eatery; it doesn't attract huge crowds, but those who've tried it think it deserves a following.

Chez Jean-Pierre 26 | 23 | 24 | $52

132 N. County Rd. (bet. Sunrise & Sunset Aves.), 561-833-1171
■ This always-busy Palm Beach New French bistro has a "cozy" first floor highlighted by "a lovely" long bar (smoking permitted), mirrors, trompe l'oeil paintings and an eat-in wine cellar; upstairs is distinguished by pecky-cedar ceilings and collages on the walls, but no matter where you sit there's "great food" "served well."

Echo [S] – | – | – | VE

230 Sunrise Ave. (County Rd.), 561-802-4222
It's been a long time since Palm Beach had a new top-notch Asian restaurant, but this stunning entry from the Flagler Group (The Breakers) was worth the wait, thanks to a comprehensive, au courant menu of Japanese, Thai, Vietnamese and Chinese specialties presented in a stylish, ultramodern environment that's a visual delight, even down to the tableware; exceptional service is further justification for the pricey tabs.

Four Seasons Restaurant ◐[S] 28 | 28 | 26 | $57

Four Seasons, 2800 S. Ocean Blvd. (Lake Ave. Bridge), 561-582-2800
■ Everything is "taken to another level" at this North Palm Beach "special-occasion" venue where chef Hubert Des Marais' "magnificent" New American cuisine earns the No. 1 Food ranking in the county, pastry chef Tom Worhach's desserts are off the chart ("fabulous"), the staff "pampers" and the "glamorous" formal dining room, with white tablecloths, velvet upholstered chairs and a "beautiful view", is rated No. 1 for Decor; bottom line: you can bank on an overall "great experience."

Kathy's Gazebo Cafe [S] 27 | 23 | 22 | $48

4199 N. Federal Hwy. (Spanish River Rd.), Boca Raton, 561-395-6033
◪ This "formal", chandelier-filled Boca Raton destination continues to serve "excellent" Classic French–Continental cuisine from an open kitchen fronting the bar; even though most feel this is one of "the best restaurants in Florida", impatient types warn that "reservations mean nothing."

La Finestra S
22 | 21 | 21 | $42

171 E. Palmetto Park Rd. (Mizner Blvd.), Boca Raton, 561-392-1838
■ "It's dress-up time" for diners heading to this regally appointed Boca Raton Northern Italian sporting Belle Époque lithographs, starched linen tablecloths, fresh red roses on every table and nightly piano music to complement its "serious food and service"; signature items include chicken and pork with wild mushrooms and a seafood crêpe stuffed with eggplant.

La Petite Maison
25 | 22 | 24 | $45

366 E. Palmetto Park Rd. (bet. SE 3rd & 4th Aves.), Boca Raton, 561-750-7483
■ Reviewers gush that chef Guy Augier and his wife Sylvia "make you feel like part of their family" at this "small", "charming" Boca Raton French-Mediterranean bistro set in a lovely, yellow-trimmed old house with an enclosed patio; look for such "serious" signature dishes as escargots with spinach au gratin, broiled lobster with aioli and duck with red wine sauce, as well as the "reasonably priced" summertime prix fixe.

La Tre Vietnamese S
24 | 15 | 22 | $29

249 E. Palmetto Park Rd. (east of US 1), Boca Raton, 561-392-4568
■ "Glad they're back" declare fans of this relocated and renamed (fka Le Truc) family-run Vietnamese operating out of an unassuming Boca Raton storefront, where an "eager-to-please" staff serves "medium-priced" French-inspired presentations of "excellent" dishes such as boneless duck with spicy eggplant, tamarind squid and curry shrimp; locals add "we need more ethnic restaurants" like this one.

La Vieille Maison S
27 | 28 | 27 | $56

770 E. Palmetto Park Rd. (2½ mi. east of I-95), Boca Raton, 561-737-5677
■ "Romantics" say "try for a private room" when dining at this 25-year-old New French "standby" in a "charming", Mizner-era "old mansion" in Boca Raton; with "beautiful" surroundings (flowers, Impressionist-inspired art, antiques, reproduction furniture), "excellent" cuisine, "superb service" (rated No. 1 in the Palm Beach *Survey*) and "a fine wine list", it's not surprising that this is once again the county's Most Popular restaurant; P.S. it's "pricey", but there's a "great prix fixe" during the summer.

Maison Janeiro
27 | 26 | 25 | $57

191 Bradley Pl. (bet. Oleander & Seminole Aves.), 561-659-5223
■ Tuxedo-clad waiters serve renowned chef Gerard Reuther's "excellent" New French fare "on Versace-designed plates" at this Palm Beach young-and-old, high-society "place to be seen", which is "beautifully" decorated with tomato soup–colored walls, zebra-patterned banquettes and vintage Gallic posters; N.B. an 850-label wine list means oenophiles should plan ahead.

Mark's at the Park S
– | – | – | E

Mizner Park, 344 Plaza Real (Mizner Blvd.), Boca Raton, 561-395-0770
This Boca Raton Mediterranean from superchef Mark Militello has unusually shaped booths and is decorated with offbeat materials such as rice paper, which create a futuristic feel; while the menu changes daily, signature dishes such as the lobster pizza are always available.

Max's Grille 🅂 23 20 21 $34
Mizner Park, 404 Plaza Real (N. Federal Way), Boca Raton,
561-368-0080
■ "Try the meat loaf" and pork chops declare surveyors about
the "wide range" of "solid", "hearty", "upscale" New American
"comfort food" that emerges from the open kitchen of this stylishly
"casual" Boca Raton "old favorite", with a cozy, brown-wood
dining room and an attractive outdoor patio that's ideal for "people-
watching"; P.S. with no reservations except for six or more, expect
"big crowds" and "long waits" ("busy, busy, busy").

Morton's of Chicago 🅂 26 24 24 $50
5050 Town Ctr. Circle (Military Trail), Boca Raton, 561-392-7724
777 S. Flagler Dr. (bet. Chase St. & Lakeview Ave.), West Palm Beach,
561-835-9664
■ "Plentiful portions" of "terrific" prime, aged beef ("wonderful
NY strip") and lip-smacking, succulent chops are the hallmarks of
this high-end steakhouse chain's outlets in West Palm Beach and
Boca; expense-accounters can expect "fine service" and an
attractively appointed, "clublike" ambiance that will impress
even the most picky.

100 South Ocean 🅂 – – – E
Ritz-Carlton Palm Beach, 100 S. Ocean Blvd. (E. Ocean Ave.), Manalapan,
561-533-6000
"Elegant dining" defines this Manalapan Ritz-Carlton destination
where chef Stefan Kauth's frequently changing menu of Continental
cuisine takes advantage of local seasonal products, the impeccable
staff works gracefully and the intimate, European-style dining room
comes with an ocean view and huge fresh flower arrangements.

Ruth's Chris Steak House 🅂 25 21 23 $45
661 US 1 (Lighthouse Dr.), North Palm Beach, 561-863-0660
■ Despite heavy competition, this "dependable" New Orleans–
based steakhouse chain is considered by many carnivores to serve
South Florida's "finest combination of steaks and sides"; though a
few find it "too stuffy", most laud its "serious approach to food and
professional service"; P.S. "all items are à la carte", so expect the
tab to build up.

32 East 🅂 24 21 21 $42
32 E. Atlantic Ave. (bet. 1st & Swinton Aves.), Delray Beach,
561-276-7868
■ "There's a new menu every day" based upon what's good at the
market at this two-story Delray Beach New American where chef
Nick Morfogen takes "food to another level"; the mahogany dining
room is cosmopolitan, and the crowd oozes "sophistication."

Zemi 🅂 – – – VE
Boca Ctr., 5050 Town Center Circle (S. Military Trail), Boca Raton,
561-391-7177
A spartan, high-tech design and monochromatic color scheme
permit chef-owner John Belleme's exceptional New American
cooking with Asian and Mediterranean accents to command center
stage at this pricey Boca newcomer; the clean, uncomplicated
flavors of his finely wrought dishes are complemented by superb
desserts (including tropical fruit sorbets) from pastry chef Steve
O'Leary and served ably by an enthusiastic staff.

Philadelphia

TOP 20 FOOD RANKING

Restaurant	Cuisine Type
29 Le Bec-Fin	Classic French
Fountain	New French/New American
28 Le Bar Lyonnais	Classic French
27 Swann Lounge	Trad. American/French
Susanna Foo	Chinese
Deux Cheminées	Classic French
Jake's	New American
Dilworthtown Inn	New American
Vetri	N/S Italian
Striped Bass	Seafood
26 Dmitri's	Mediterranean
Brasserie Perrier	New French
Prime Rib	Steakhouse
La Famiglia	N/S Italian
La Bonne Auberge	Classic French
Mainland Inn	New American
Monte Carlo Living Rm.	N/S Italian
Tacconelli's Pizzeria	Pizza
Buddakan	Asian
25 Ciboulette	New French

ADDITIONAL NOTEWORTHY PLACES

Audrey Claire	Mediterranean
Bistro St. Tropez	French Bistro
Blue Angel	French Bistro
DiPalma	N/S Italian
Fork	New American
La Jonquille	Classic French
Nan	Thai/French
Opus 251	New American
Overtures	New French/Mediterranean
¡Pasion!	Nuevo Latino
Passerelle	New French/New American
Rouge 2000	Continental
Saloon	N/S Italian
Sansom St. Oyster House	Seafood
Savona	N. Italian/Seafood
Tangerine	Moroccan/New French
333 Belrose	New American
20 Manning	New American
White Dog Cafe	Eclectic
Yangming	Chinese

Audrey Claire [S] 🚫💳
22 | 17 | 19 | $28

276 S. 20th St. (Spruce St.), 215-731-1222

■ Reservations are now available Tuesday–Thursday and on Sunday, but at other times it pays to "go early" to snare a table at this Center City Mediterranean; admirers know it as an "airy", "minimalist" corner storefront where the "creative", "beautifully presented" food is "as delicious" as the crowd is "hip"; N.B. BYO.

Bistro St. Tropez
23 | 20 | 20 | $34

Mktpl. Design Ctr., 2400 Market St., 4th fl. (23rd St.), 215-569-9269

■ Though newcomers may "need a guide" to find this "hip", "delightful" "jewel" of a French bistro "buried" in the Marketplace Design Center, the "magnificent" Schuylkill views and "head-swirling menu" are apt to make Francophiles "feel far from Philadelphia"; most sigh the results are "romantic, to say the least."

Blue Angel, The [S]
24 | 25 | 23 | $39

706 Chestnut St. (7th St.), 215-925-6889

■ "Another Starr in the heavens" is what surveyors say about Stephen Starr's "smashing" "Paris bistro" in the Historic District; those who claim the "noise makes you vibrate" may actually be quivering in anticipation of the "sumptuous" fare, "attentive service" and prime "people-watching" – either way, the scene is undeniably "happening."

Brasserie Perrier [S]
26 | 25 | 24 | $52

1619 Walnut St. (bet. 16th & 17th Sts.), 215-568-3000

■ "Ooh-la-la" squeal surveyors over Georges Perrier's "less stuffy Le Bec-Fin sib" (aka "Le Bec-Fin Lite") on Restaurant Row; "inventive" New French food with "wonderful flavors", "attentive service", "trendy" surroundings and "gorgeous" people "at the bar" make it *très* chic and "top-notch in every category."

Buddakan [S]
26 | 27 | 22 | $46

325 Chestnut St. (bet. 3rd & 4th Sts.), 215-574-9440

■ "Lamborghini-driving divorcees" and "black-clad" "beautiful people" pack Stephen Starr's "sexy" Old City Asian powerhouse in pursuit of "out-of-this-world" "fusion" fare served in a "striking" room dominated by a "giant golden Buddha" and a running waterfall; faced with the "see-and-be-seen" atmospherics, demure diners warn of a "noisy", "intimidating" time ("bring earplugs").

Ciboulette
25 | 23 | 23 | VE

Bellevue Bldg., 200 S. Broad St. (Walnut St.), 215-790-1210

■ Statesiders feel "transported to Europe" at Bruce Lim's "gorgeous" dinner-only New French in the Bellevue, a bastion of "civilized dining" where the "opulent" room sets the scene for "delicious and daring" cuisine; expect "stiff but professional" service in keeping with the "classy" digs; N.B. $45 prix fixe, or $65 for a six-course tasting menu.

Deux Cheminées
27 | 27 | 26 | VE

1221 Locust St. (bet. 12th & 13th Sts.), 215-790-0200

■ "Step back in time to a grander era" at Fritz Blank's Classic French "class act" in an "elegant" Center City brownstone; ever a "very romantic" experience, it "exhilarates all the senses" with "fabulous food", "stunning decor" and an "attentive" staff – just beware of "attitude" and try to "forget the cost"; N.B. dinner only, $80 prix fixe.

Dilworthtown Inn, The 🟥
27 | 27 | 26 | $48

1390 Old Wilmington Pike (Brinton Bridge Rd.), West Chester, 610-399-1390

■ For "candlelit dining" "in the 'burbs", this "romantic", "button-down" West Chester New American is an acknowledged "class" act where the room's "elegance" is matched with "exquisite cuisine", a "superb wine list" and "unobtrusive" service; in sum, it's a chance to "feel special" – but be sure to "bring lots of dough"; N.B. jackets and reservations are required.

DiPalma 🟥
21 | 22 | 20 | $44

114 Market St. (bet. Front & 2nd Sts.), 215-733-0545

☑ Chef-owner Salvatore DiPalma's "high-end" Old City Italian can claim a following that finds the "sophisticated" cooking "first-rate" and the "spacious" surroundings just plain "beautiful"; hedgers cry "too expensive" and remain cautious with the kudos ("promising, but not there yet").

Dmitri's 🟥
26 | 13 | 19 | $25

2227 Pine St. (23rd St.), 215-985-3680
225 S. 12th St. (Locust St.), 215-627-9059
795 S. Third St. (Catharine St.), 215-625-0556 ⊟

■ Namesake Dmitri Chimes recently changed the monikers and menus of his other establishments (fka Pamplona in Center City and Stix in Fitler Square) to tally with this truly "fantastic" Queen Village Mediterranean "gem" where patrons put up with "long lines", "no reservations" and "noisy", "cramped" conditions to enjoy "amazingly fresh seafood", including "sublime" squid and octopus and "wonderful", "unadulterated" whole fish.

Fork 🟥
24 | 23 | 22 | $37

306 Market St. (bet. 3rd & 4th Sts.), 215-625-9425

■ This airy, banquette-lined Old City entry can claim a "cultlike following" among a "young crowd" that admires its "elegant", "snappy" decor, "delicious combinations" of "inspired" New American cuisine and "attentive", "gracious" staff; it can get "hectic" and feel "cramped", but overall it's "exciting" and "deserving of its success"; P.S. if dinner reservations are scarce, "try Sunday brunch."

Fountain Restaurant 🟥
29 | 29 | 29 | $66

Four Seasons Hotel, 1 Logan Sq. (Benjamin Franklin Pkwy. & 18th St.), 215-963-1500

■ Voted No. 1 for Decor in the *Philadelphia Survey* (and No. 2 for Food and Service), this Logan Square "special-occasion" favorite is a "dining fantasy come true", lauded for Jean-Marie Lacroix's "superb" New French–New American cuisine, "flawless service" from a "thoughtful" staff and a "luxurious" (but "not stuffy") setting that defines "simple elegance"; if dinner is beyond your budget, there's always the "awesome" brunch and prix fixe lunch.

Jake's 🟥
27 | 22 | 24 | $45

4365 Main St. (bet. Grape & Levering Sts.), 215-483-0444

■ Bruce Cooper's "high-powered" storefront New American wins praise for its "beautiful presentations" of "outstanding" fare ("amazing lobster mashed potatoes"), "conscientious" staff and "classy" art-filled dining room; the bottom line: it's "the place to dine in Manayunk"; P.S. the "sumptuous" brunch is a standout.

La Bonne Auberge [S] 26 | 27 | 25 | $64

Village 2 Apt. Complex (Mechanic St.), New Hope, 215-862-2462

◪ The "ultimate" "romantic hideaway", this "beautiful country inn" in New Hope sets "the standard" for "special-occasion dining" with its "wonderful" Classic French cooking; devotees deem it "worth every penny", though those unenchanted by the "small portions" grumble it's "all fluff and no substance."

La Famiglia [S] 26 | 23 | 24 | $54

8 S. Front St. (bet. Chestnut & Market Sts.), 215-922-2803

■ For "marvelous", "authentic" Italian cuisine matched with "great wines" in a "luxurious" room, it's hard to top the Sena clan's Old City "classic", a long-running "favorite" for "elegant", "unrushed" dining; it's a "pricey" package, but one of "the best" – this "family knows food and hospitality."

La Jonquille – | – | – | VE

840 Lancaster Ave. (west of Rte. 476), Devon, 610-964-8600

The name means 'the daffodil' and not 'gild the lily', as neophytes must be reminded upon entering this jaw-droppingly ornate Classic French in Devon; Le Bec-Fin alum Michael Kanter's superb cuisine is complemented by an 8,500-bottle assortment of wines and capped off with fellow ex Bec-Finner Marianne Cobaugh's dessert cart; N.B. dinner only, prix fixe starting at $65.

Le Bar Lyonnais 28 | 25 | 26 | $50

1523 Walnut St. (bet. 15th & 16th Sts.), 215-567-1000

■ Anyone looking for a "way to enjoy Le Bec-Fin for less" can grab a "tiny table" at Georges Perrier's "cozy", "sophisticated" "grotto" in a space beneath his Restaurant Row powerhouse; here's a chance to "feel like an insider" while savoring "fabulous" Classic French food in "the lap of luxury."

Le Bec-Fin 29 | 28 | 29 | VE

1523 Walnut St. (bet. 15th & 16th Sts.), 215-567-1000

■ "It's all been said before", but it bears repeating: Georges Perrier's "world-class" Classic French "gastronomic temple" on Walnut Street remains Philly's Most Popular restaurant (and No. 1 for Food and Service) on the strength of its "incomparable" cuisine, "gorgeous" setting, "servers who anticipate your every move" and a dessert cart "to die for"; though "cheaper than flying to France for dinner (barely)", it's even more tempting "if someone else pays"; N.B. $36 lunch prix fixe, $118 dinner.

Mainland Inn [S] 26 | 24 | 25 | $45

17 Main St. (Sumneytown Pike), Mainland, 215-256-8500

■ "Country dining with sophistication" sums up the scene at this "bucolic" New American near Lansdale, which wins raves for its "superior" food, "great" French-Californian wine list, crackerjack staff and "intimate", candlelit rooms; N.B. a more casual, English-style grill is now open downstairs.

Monte Carlo Living Room, The [S] 26 | 23 | 24 | $55

150 South St. (2nd St.), 215-925-2220

◪ "World-class" dining is alive and well at this "special-night-out" Italian on South Street, where "superb" chef Nunzio Patruno is famed for his "exquisitely flavored" fare; the "impressive" setting and "formal" service are "elegance in action" and come at prices to break the bank.

Nan
25 17 20 $30

4000 Chestnut St. (40th St.), 215-382-0818

■ "Long may he cook" – chef Kamol Phutlek dazzles diners with "wonderful", "stylish" dishes and "unbelievable", "synergistic" sauces at his Thai-French BYO in University City; an amiable staff and "reasonable" tabs help offset a "minimalistic" space that can get "chaotic" on weekends (reserve ahead).

Opus 251 🅂
24 23 22 $45

Philadelphia Art Alliance, 251 S. 18th St. (Rittenhouse Sq.), 215-735-6787

■ Sited in a "handsome" mansion on Rittenhouse Square whose "splendor is matched" by "innovative" New American cuisine courtesy of certified master chef Alfonso Contrisciani, this "hidden jewel" is ideal for that "romantic", "special-occasion" meal or for a "wonderful" weekend brunch; nature lovers appreciate the "delightful outdoor garden" too.

Overtures 🅂
25 23 24 $42

609-611 Passyunk Ave. (bet. Bainbridge & South Sts.), 215-627-3455

■ "Go, Peter, go!" rave fans of Peter Lamlein's "wonderful" BYO off South Street, which features "fabulous" New French–Med food, "gracious" service from a "thoughtful staff" and a romantic, "European atmosphere"; in sum, it's a "classy" establishment and *the* place to "bring your best wine."

¡Pasion! 🅂
25 25 23 $46

211 S. 15th St. (bet. Locust & Walnut Sts.), 215-875-9895

■ Chef Guillermo Pernot's "melt-in-your-mouth" Nuevo Latino cuisine and a "lush", "tropical" setting ensure this Center City entry's status as a "must-go"; from the "outstanding seviches" to the "superb" sea bass, enthusiasts evince passion aplenty for the "unique" "gourmet" fare, proclaiming this a "hot spot" that "lives up to the hype."

Passerelle 🅂
25 26 24 $48

175 King of Prussia Rd. (Lancaster Ave.), Radnor, 610-293-9411

☑ "Bliss in the 'burbs" awaits at this "romantic" Radnor New French–American with a "gorgeous setting and food to match"; it's a "can't-wait" destination for "inspired" cuisine served in a "beautiful", "formal" setting ("look for the swans" in the pond), though nonpartisans pass on the "small portions" and "uptight" airs.

Prime Rib, The 🅂
26 26 25 $54

Warwick Hotel, 1701 Locust St. (17th St.), 215-772-1701

■ The "lavish decor", "perfectly cooked meats" and "impeccable" service qualify this "old-school", "manly place" in the Warwick as a "fantasy of a clubby steakhouse"; a link in a DC–area chain, it claims legions of loyalists who relish the "sophisticated" style and "enormous quantities" of "outstanding" food, though a few say it "overdoes it."

Rouge 2000 ●🅂
23 24 19 $39

Rittenhouse Claridge Apt. Bldg., 205 S. 18th St. (bet. Locust & Walnut Sts.), 215-732-6622

☑ With its "electric" mood and "delicious" Continental food, Neil Stein's "chic", "crowded" "jewel box" on Rittenhouse Square is a magnet for the "cell phone" and "Rolex" set; it's the "place to be seen", though foes oppose the "dieter's" portions and service that "defines the word 'attitude.'"

Saloon
24 | 22 | 22 | $53

750 S. Seventh St. (bet. Catharine & Fitzwater Sts.), 215-627-1811
☑ "Fat cats" drop "big bucks" for "hearty portions" of "excellent" Italian ("best veal chops") at this "classy" South Philadelphia "oldie but goodie" where a "good-natured" staff works the "dark" room; a post-*Survey* chef change may address gripes that they're "resting on their laurels"; P.S. "oops, they only take Amex."

Sansom Street Oyster House
21 | 16 | 19 | $28

1516 Sansom St. (bet. 15th & 16th Sts.), 215-567-7683
■ It's seen a chef change and a remodel, but this "old-fashioned", family-owned Center City "pearl" continues to be a "mainstay for fresh, well-prepared" "comfort seafood" at "reasonable prices"; it's a local fave for happy hour–priced "oysters and a glass of steely sauvignon blanc."

Savona S
25 | 26 | 23 | $56

100 Old Gulph Rd. (Montgomery Ave.), Gulph Mills, 610-520-1200
■ "Commendably serious", this Main Line Ligurian seafooder is "full of minks" and "expense-account" types savoring "absolutely fabulous" food and a "dreamy", "elegant" setting with terra-cotta tiles, Venetian banquettes and mahogany furniture; the generally "excellent" staff comes off as "pretentious" to a laid-back few.

Striped Bass S
27 | 28 | 24 | $59

1500 Walnut St. (15th St.), 215-732-4444
☑ Neil Stein's "swank", "over-the-top" Restaurant Row seafooder "lives up to its stellar rep" for "mouthwatering", "decadent" cuisine and an "exquisite" "NYC" environment; but skeptics style it "stuffed shirt" and scold "it's just fish – get those prices under control!"

Susanna Foo S
27 | 25 | 25 | $54

1512 Walnut St. (bet. 15th & 16th Sts.), 215-545-2666
■ "Culinary nirvana" sums up the sentiment on Ms. Foo's Chinese fusion house on Restaurant Row, where the "Jag and Mercedes" crowd lines up for "intoxicatingly" "innovative cuisine"; each dish is a "delicate" "work of art" in keeping with the "elegant" setting (and "expense-account" prices).

Swann Lounge & Cafe S
27 | 27 | 27 | $47

Four Seasons Hotel, 1 Logan Sq. (bet. Benjamin Franklin Pkwy. & 18th St.), 215-963-1500
■ "If you don't feel like dressing up for the Fountain", its "sophisticated" yet "comfortable" Traditional American-French neighbor in the Four Seasons is a "spectacular" alternative; patrons "feel like royalty" at "afternoon tea" or the "amazing brunch", or when listening to jazz "by the fireplace."

Tacconelli's Pizzeria S⊘
26 | 9 | 16 | $15

2604 E. Somerset St. (bet. Almond & Thompson Sts.), 215-425-4983
■ "Get your dough orders in early" at this BYO Port Richmond pizza "legend", so popular that patrons are obliged to reserve their own hunks of dough; the payoff is the "extraordinary", "crispy-crust" pies ("white pizza is better than sex") served amid "nonexistent" decor; N.B. dinner only, Wednesday–Sunday.

Tangerine S
_____ | M

232 Market St. (bet. 2nd & 3rd Sts.), 215-627-5116

Moor is more at Stephen Starr's slick Moroccan–New French
fusion fantasy in Old City, one of Downtown's hottest spots; trendy
types traipse through a theatrical space to enjoy adventurous
food presented to the table for sharing by a professional staff.

333 Belrose
23 | 20 | 18 | $36

333 Belrose Lane (King of Prussia Rd.), Radnor, 610-293-1000

■ Chef-owner Carlo deMarco's "super" New American set in the
former Carolina's in Radnor has "instantly" become a "see-and-be-
seen" scene; credit "top-notch" fare served in "attractive" (albeit
"noisy") digs, though some bristle at "impertinent" service.

20 Manning S
_____ | M

261 S. 20th St. (bet. Locust & Spruce Sts.), 215-731-0900

Audrey Claire's sexy, Asian-influenced New American has wowed
the Rittenhouse Square crowd from day one with excellent cuisine
(try the tuna sashimi or crispy-skin salmon on shiitake chive bun)
and a casual, nonstuffy setting, which features gray banquettes,
a purple glass–backed bar and a communal metal table.

Vetri
27 | 22 | 25 | $54

1312 Spruce St. (bet. Broad & 13th Sts.), 215-732-3478

■ "Bellissimo!" cheer champions of Marc Vetri's "intimate",
"romantic" Italian in the "pedigreed" former Center City digs of
Le Bec-Fin; the "classy atmosphere" sets the tone for "delicious"
cuisine "lovingly served" by a "warm" staff, and if a few flinch at
the cost, most find the "fabulous" experience "worth every penny."

White Dog Cafe S
24 | 21 | 20 | $34

3420 Sansom St. (34th St.), 215-386-9224

■ "Innovative" cuisine mixes with "socially minded" (some say
"hippie") values at Judy Wicks' "bustling" Eclectic "perennial"
on the Penn campus; it's one of this town's "top dogs" for "trendy
but tasty" "organic" cooking, and the room's usually "crowded"
with "noisy" intellectuals; P.S. "check out the bar for cheap eats
and a varied crowd."

Yangming S
24 | 22 | 22 | $34

1051 Conestoga Rd. (Haverford Rd.), Bryn Mawr, 610-527-3200

■ "Not your strip mall" chopstick house, Michael Wei's Main
Line Chinese is an "outstanding" "mainstay" for "creative",
"delicious" food, served in a "classy space" by a "courteous",
"knowledgeable" staff; the "bustling" scene makes it "a winner"
worth "showing off to friends."

Phoenix/Scottsdale

TOP 10 FOOD RANKING

Restaurant	Cuisine Type
28 Mary Elaine's	New French
27 Marquesa	Mediterranean
Vincent Guerithault	Classic French/Southwestern
26 T. Cook's	Mediterranean
RoxSand	New American
Pizzeria Bianco	Pizza
La Hacienda	Mexican
Coup Des Tartes	Classic French/Eclectic
Morton's of Chicago	Steakhouse
Michael's at the Citadel	New American

ADDITIONAL NOTEWORTHY PLACES

Christopher's	French Bistro
Convivo	New American
Franco's Trattoria	Northern Italian
Gregory's Grill	New American
Lon's at the Hermosa	New Amer./Southwestern
Rancho Pinot	New American
Razz's	International
Restaurant Hapa	New American/Asian
Restaurant Oceana	Seafood
Ruth's Chris	Steakhouse

F	D	S	C

Christopher's Fermier Brasserie S | 23 | 22 | 20 | $36 |
Biltmore Fashion Park, 2584 E. Camelback Rd. (N. 24th St.), Phoenix, 602-522-2344
☑ This "exciting" Biltmore Fashion Park French brasserie from chef Christopher Gross has a "more informal" setting than his previous place, punctuated by an "excellent" wine bar run by his wife Paola (100 selections by the glass, plus house-brewed beer); otherwise, expect the same "hip crowd" and such "exquisite" signature dishes as truffle-infused sirloin; still, some say this incarnation "needs some edges polished."

Convivo | 25 | 19 | 25 | $33 |
Walgreen's Shopping Ctr., 7000 N. 16th St. (E. Glendale Ave.), Phoenix, 602-997-7676
■ Surveyors give the big thumbs up to this "low-key, mom-and-pop" venue that serves "creative" New American cuisine (try the "excellent veggie platter") in a "small", "out-of-the-way" Phoenix strip mall setting that, nevertheless, "feels like home"; moreover, there's also a "wonderful wine list" and "impeccable service" from a "great" staff.

Coup Des Tartes 26 | 20 | 24 | $32

4626 N. 16th St. (E. Highland Ave.), Phoenix, 602-212-1082

■ This Midtown Phoenix cottage, "reminiscent of grandma's house", features a monthly-changing menu of "excellent" Classic French–Eclectic fare and the "personal attention" of the owner; while the "small" space might seem "cramped" at first, by the end of the evening you'll agree that this is a "charming" "jewel" and one of the best places in the city to BYO.

Franco's Trattoria 25 | 19 | 23 | $34

Village at Hayden, 8120 N. Hayden Rd. (Vie De Ventura), Scottsdale, 480-948-6655

■ "The next best thing to being in Tuscany" declare fans of this genteel Northern Italian in Scottsdale, which serves a "wonderful" pre-dinner cheese nibble, "exquisite" seafood, meat ("especially the veal") and the "best pasta in the Valley"; N.B. before leaving, peek into the kitchen to catch a glimpse of apprentice chef and ex-governor Fife Symington, who's now taking orders for a change.

Gregory's Grill ▽ 26 | 17 | 25 | $34

Papago Plaza, 7049 E. McDowell Rd. (N. Scottsdale Rd.), Scottsdale, 480-946-8700

■ Enthused diners say "you've got to love a place like this" South Scottsdale New American that, despite being "small", "plain" and "tucked away in a neighborhood of fast-food" joints, "puts a lot of effort" into its "wonderful", "innovative" fare; a "friendly" husband-and-wife team and BYO policy (though there is a corkage fee) further enhance its rep as a "great find."

La Hacienda [S] 26 | 24 | 22 | $39

Fairmont Scottsdale Princess, 7575 E. Princess Dr. (bet. Pima & N. Scottsdale Rds., north of Bell Rd.), Scottsdale, 480-585-4848

■ "They do things right" claim boosters of this "elegant but comfortable" Scottsdale hotel Mexican, whose beamed ceilings, tiled floors and crooning mariachi trio transport diners, especially those who go "for a date"; foodwise, the "authentic" offerings include a roast suckling pig that's a showstopper.

Lon's at the Hermosa Inn [S] 25 | 26 | 23 | $38

Hermosa Inn, 5532 N. Palo Cristi Rd. (E. Stanford Dr.), Paradise Valley, 602-955-7878

■ Set in a "beautiful" adobe built by artist Lon Megargee in the '30s, this "romantic" retreat oozes "authentic old Arizona" right down to its "great patio" with views of Camelback Mountain; as the "last of the small resorts" with "great service" and "superior" SW-influenced New American combos ("best brunch in town"), it's no surprise this is also Phoenix/Scottsdale's Most Popular restaurant.

Marquesa [S] 27 | 27 | 27 | $47

Fairmont Scottsdale Princess, 7575 E. Princess Dr. (bet. Pima & N. Scottsdale Rds., north of Bell Rd.), Scottsdale, 480-585-4848

■ Housed in one of North Scottsdale's plushest resorts, this "world-class" Mediterranean serves up an "imaginative" menu ranging from paella and pan-flashed loup de mer to "creative desserts"; moreover, as the name implies, guests are "treated royally" and the "elegant setting" – with paintings of princesses – is sure to impress; P.S. despite being "expensive", there's a more affordable brunch on the patio every Sunday.

Mary Elaine's

| 28 | 29 | 27 | $57 |

The Phoenician, 6000 E. Camelback Rd. (N. 60th St.), Scottsdale, 480-423-2530

■ Rated No. 1 for Decor and No. 2 for Food and Service in Arizona, it's no surprise that "everything is superb" at this New French "special-occasion" spot in The Phoenician; expect "incredible" cuisine from chef James Boyce, a "great wine list", "impeccable service", "outstanding valley views" and the soothing voice of singer Nancy Gee; so bring your jacket and "expense account" and be prepared for a "five-star" experience.

Michael's at the Citadel S

| 26 | 25 | 24 | $39 |

The Citadel, 8700 E. Pinnacle Peak Rd. (Pima Rd.), Scottsdale, 480-515-2575

☑ "As comfortable as being at home with much better food" is the high praise surveyors bestow upon Michael DeMaria's "plush" Scottsdale New American, a "grown-up" spot with a 23-foot indoor waterfall, "inventive" dishes, "good wines by the glass" and "seductive desserts"; P.S. try to reserve the "great" chef's table overlooking the kitchen.

Morton's of Chicago S

| 26 | 23 | 23 | $49 |

Camelback Esplanade, 2501 E. Camelback Rd. (N. 24th St.), Phoenix, 602-955-9577
15233 N. Kierland Blvd. (N. Scottsdale Rd.), Scottsdale, 480-951-4440

■ Suspender-wearing "manly men" flock to these top-tier chain steakhouses for their "woody atmosphere", "large portions" of solid sides and "excellent" beef ("best porterhouse for two"); more delicate sensibilities could do without "the smell of cigars" and say it's "hard to justify the price" if you're not on an expense account.

Pizzeria Bianco S

| 26 | 23 | 21 | $19 |

Heritage Sq., 623 E. Adams St. (N. 7th St.), Phoenix, 602-258-8300

■ When it comes to "the best wood-fired pizza in Phoenix, maybe anywhere", "nobody does it better" than Chris Bianco and his "wonderful staff", who use "only the best ingredients" to achieve their "awesome" results; handily located Downtown, this pizzeria draws a "great crowd" that can't get enough of the "big-city decor" and transcendent tastes; N.B. lunch is no longer served, but the owners have opened a wine bar/waiting area a few steps away.

Rancho Pinot Grill

| 25 | 22 | 24 | $36 |

Lincoln Village, 6208 N. Scottsdale Rd. (E. Lincoln Dr.), Scottsdale, 480-443-0680

■ With decor that's a cross between "funky cowboy" and "rancher chic", it's hard not to "love" this Scottsdale New American, which also has an "excellent" menu of "creative" "comfort food" (from a wood-burning oven and mesquite grill), delicious desserts, a "great" 5,000-bottle wine list and a "pleasant staff"; truth be told, it's "what a restaurant should be" and "the Valley is lucky to have it."

Razz's Restaurant & Bar

| 25 | 19 | 24 | $35 |

10315 N. Scottsdale Rd. (E. Shea Blvd.), Scottsdale, 480-905-1308

■ Popular chef Razz Kamnitzer "cooks with pizazz" and "comes around to schmooze" too at this North Scottsdale International where loyalists lap up the "welcoming" service and "very creative" combos such as cashew-encrusted salmon with hibiscus-and-lime sauce; a few don't warm to his "strange recipes", but more find this a "happy place."

Restaurant Hapa | 25 | 21 | 24 | $38 |

Lincoln Village, 6204 N. Scottsdale Rd. (E. Lincoln Dr.), Scottsdale, 480-998-8220

■ "Exciting", "interesting" Asian-influenced New American fare served on "beautiful" Japanese-style plates, a minimalist, mirrored dining room and a sushi bar and lounge with rattan furniture generate high scores and praise for James and Stacey McDevitt's "great little" Scottsdale spot; signature dishes include carmelized Chinese-mustard beef tenderloin.

Restaurant Oceana ▽ | 24 | 19 | 24 | $40 |

La Morada, 8900 E. Pinnacle Peak Rd. (Pima Rd.), Scottsdale, 480-515-2277

◪ "Great fish in the desert" is not an oxymoron, thanks to this "small", "friendly" North Scottsdale seafooder whose wide variety of aquatic offerings is given a "sophisticated" treatment and then paired with a strong wine list; whimsical decor (colorful ceramic fish on every table) enlivens this "expensive" experience.

RoxSand [S] | 26 | 24 | 24 | $36 |

Biltmore Fashion Park, 2594 E. Camelback Rd. (N. 24th St.), Phoenix, 602-381-0444

■ This "hip", "bi-level" global-accented New American is called "a true cut above" the competition, thanks to chef-owner RoxSand Scocos' "wonderful" food served in a "sophisticated", "stark" setting that's "the closest thing to NYC in Phoenix"; P.S. don't leave without ordering from the "wonderful" "dessert walk", a glass-enclosed case that features probably "the most chocolate choices in the Southwest."

Ruth's Chris Steak House [S] | 26 | 23 | 25 | $42 |

2201 E. Camelback Rd. (N. 24th St.), Phoenix, 602-957-9600
Scottsdale Seville, 7001 N. Scottsdale Rd. (E. Indian Bend Rd.), Scottsdale, 480-991-5988

■ The No. 2 steakhouse in Arizona, this top-tier chain's branches are praised for their "big-city ambiance", superb sides and "melt-in-your-mouth steaks" ("best filet mignon ever"), served sizzling hot with a pat of butter (known as "the widow-maker"); while many customers are "businessmen" on "expense accounts", if you're paying your own way "share and the price drops dramatically."

T. Cook's [S] | 26 | 28 | 25 | $43 |

Royal Palms Hotel & Casitas, 5200 E. Camelback Rd. (bet. N. Arcadia Dr. & N. 56th St.), Phoenix, 602-808-0766

■ "Spectacular" Mediterranean housed in a "beautiful", historic Phoenix hotel that boasts "excellent" rustic dishes, a "fantastic" romantic bar – antiques, overstuffed chairs, leather-floor cigar room – and an inviting dining room with a hunter's lodge fireplace used to spit-roast meats; in short, a "wow from beginning to end."

Vincent Guerithault on Camelback | 27 | 24 | 25 | $45 |

3930 E. Camelback Rd. (N. 40th St.), Phoenix, 602-224-0225

■ Chef-owner Vincent Guerithault pairs classic Gallic technique with "Southwestern ingredients" to produce "exceptional" dishes at this candlelit, "old-time favorite" on Camelback Road, which is reminiscent of a Country French inn; despite an occasional gripe that this former trendsetter "needs some new tricks", the majority says it's "still one of the best."

Portland

TOP 10 FOOD RANKING

Restaurant	Cuisine Type
29 Genoa	N/S Italian
28 Paley's Place	Northwestern
27 Couvron	New French
Heathman	New French/Northwestern
Tina's	Northwestern
26 Caprial's Bistro	Northwestern
Restaurant Murata	Japanese
3 Doors Down Café	N/S Italian
Cafe des Amis	Northwestern/French Bistro
Wildwood	Northwestern

ADDITIONAL NOTEWORTHY PLACES

Assaggio	N/S Italian
Bluehour	Mediterranean
Cafe Azul	Mexican
Caffe Mingo	N/S Italian
Castagna	New French/Italian
Higgins Restaurant & Bar	Eclectic
Jake's Famous Crawfish	Seafood
Pazzo Ristorante	N/S Italian
Saucebox Cafe & Bar	Pan-Asian
Typhoon!	Thai

F	D	S	C

Assaggio

23	22	21	$24

7742 SE 13th Ave. (Lambert St.), 503-232-6151

☑ "Outstanding" Italian fare and a "great wine bar" bring crowds to this "hip and stylish" Sellwood spot where the "pasta sampler is a good bet" (*assàggio* translates as 'little taste'); foes fuss it's "noisy" and "overpriced", and even devotees concur that the "major drawback" is the "no-reservations" policy that results in "long waits."

Bluehour Restaurant & Bar

—	—	—	VE

Weiden & Kennedy Bldg., 250 NW 13th Ave. (NW Everett St.), 503-226-3394

Floor-to-ceiling translucent black curtains and a long, white marble bar fuel the millennium-cool atmosphere at this airy, new Pearl District Mediterranean from perfectionist restaurateur Bruce Carey; foodwise, talented chef Kenny Giambalvo dazzles diners with a seasonal menu highlighted by gnocchi with fontina and black truffles.

Cafe Azul
25 | 23 | 23 | $30

112 NW Ninth Ave. (bet. Couch & Davis Sts.), 503-525-4422

☒ There's "no compromising" at this "sophisticated" Pearl District Mexican where the kitchen turns out "creative cuisine and sauces" ("the best mole on earth") and "lots of organics"; critics carp that it's "extraordinarily overpriced" "for what you get", but many call it close to "perfect."

Cafe des Amis
26 | 24 | 27 | $35

1987 NW Kearney St. (20th Ave.), 503-295-6487

■ "From pâté to dessert", everything's "fabulous, darling" at this "classy" NW–French bistro that's distinguished for its extraordinary service (voted No. 2 in Portland); loyalists love the "great romantic" setting and are amazed by the cuisine's "consistency" – "this good for this long is astonishing!"

Caffe Mingo 🅂
25 | 20 | 22 | $24

807 NW 21st Ave. (bet. Johnson & Kearney Sts.), 503-226-4646

■ "Delicious, simple fare" is the forte of this "excellent" NW District Italian trattoria that also offers a "relaxed atmosphere", "knowledgeable waiters" and "reasonable prices"; it's no surprise that this "small, intimate space" can get "too crowded" and it's "irritating" there are "no rezzies" for parties less than six, but even though fans "wish it weren't so tough to get a table", they "keep coming back."

Caprial's Bistro & Wine
26 | 19 | 22 | $27

7015 SE Milwaukie Ave. (Bybee Blvd.), 503-236-6457

■ "Local celebrity" Caprial Pence – author and cooking show host – might "greet you at the door" of her Northwestern bistro in Westmoreland; "inspired meals" that are a "feast for the eyes" thrill enthusiasts, while "low wine prices" win the hearts of penny-pinching oenophiles; N.B. an expansion has doubled the dining area and added an open kitchen, thus outdating the above decor score.

Castagna
– | – | – | E

1752 SE Hawthorne Blvd. (18th Ave.), 503-231-7373

Expect fresh, seasonal ingredients prepared New French–Italian style at this Hawthorne newcomer where minimalism informs both the presentation and the decor; husband-and-wife owners Kevin Gibson and Monique Siu's great attention to detail is displayed in everything from the cork-and-limestone floors to the signature seared scallops with mushrooms.

Couvron
27 | 23 | 25 | $53

1126 SW 18th Ave. (Madison St.), 503-225-1844

■ "World-class ambitions" inform everything about this "upscale" West Side New French that offers "unusual presentations" of "outstanding" cuisine, along with "very attentive" service that's "perfect for a special occasion"; though the "too-small space" and "spendy" tabs leave some gasping for air, most take a deep breath and declare "it's worth saving up for."

F D S C

Genoa
29 24 28 $55

2832 SE Belmont St. (bet. 28th & 29th Aves.), 503-238-1464

■ Rated No. 1 for Food and Service in the *Portland Survey*, this Italian "treasure" in Southeast is also voted the city's Most Popular restaurant, and stalwarts say "everything is impeccable", from the "inspired", seven-course prix fixe menu to the "intimate atmosphere" and "unsurpassed" staff; though a minority moans it's "too dark" and "very spendy", the majority agrees that "quality has never faltered" at this "still-special experience."

Heathman, The [S]
27 24 26 $36

Heathman Hotel, 1001 SW Broadway (Salmon St.), 503-241-4100

■ Chef Philippe Boulot unveils "superb" New French–NW cuisine at this "sublime" Downtown hotel dining room that's "class all the way"; a "top-notch wine list", "casual but sharp" service and a "sophisticated" setting gladden its "gourmet guests", and despite a few who mumble "overrated", the majority considers this a "truly adult experience."

Higgins Restaurant & Bar [S]
25 23 24 $34

1239 SW Broadway (Jefferson St.), 503-222-9070

■ "Greg Higgins is the man", for his Eclectic with a pronounced French accent elates acolytes with "fresh, smart" dishes that make for a "premier food experience"; though faultfinders fuss there's "sometimes too much happening on one plate", most call it "absolute perfection", especially "Portland's art elite", who make the bar their own after the theater lets out.

Jake's Famous Crawfish [S]
23 21 22 $29

401 SW 12th Ave. (Stark St.), 503-226-1419

◪ Some dub this "timeless" Downtown seafooder "old faithful", as it's been serving "consistently excellent" fin fare since 1892, and the hooked "love the crawfish dishes" and "super gumbo"; dissenters hedge "when it's good, it's great, but it's good only half the time" and add that the "tired" scene could use "a breath of fresh air."

Paley's Place [S]
28 25 26 $36

1204 NW 21st Ave. (Northrup St.), 503-243-2403

◪ "Outstanding", "refined" Northwestern cuisine using local and organic ingredients awaits diners at Vitaly and Kimberly Paley's "intimate" bistro in a turn-of-the-century NW home; expect some of the "most personal service in town" and more spacious and stylish digs, thanks to a nifty redo that added "cozy banquettes", a "charming" bar, "great vintage posters" and five points to the decor rating; N.B. the sweetbreads and crème brûlée are a must.

Pazzo Ristorante [S]
23 23 22 $27

Hotel Vintage Plaza, 627 SW Washington St. (Broadway), 503-228-1515

◪ "Grab a barstool" at the counter – "the best seat in the house" – for "great theater" and "free cooking lessons" provided by the open kitchen at this "warm" Downtown Italian with its "great, garlicky food"; it's a "favorite" for "entertaining" or a "business lunch."

Restaurant Murata
26 | 18 | 21 | $27
200 SW Market St. (bet. 2nd & 3rd Aves.), 503-227-0080
■ Surveyors report "huge slices" of "beautifully presented", "excellent sushi" from master chef Ryoshiro Murata at this Downtown Japanese in a "traditional" setting (i.e. a "bit formal"); to get a sense of how "unusual and authentic" his offerings are, call 48 hours in advance for the *kaiseki ryori,* a multicourse dinner whose price you set ($45 minimum).

Saucebox Cafe & Bar
22 | 21 | 19 | $22
214 SW Broadway (Burnside St.), 503-241-3393
■ "Very chic", "dark" and "narrow", this Downtown Pan-Asian appeals to both the "beautiful people" who "drip coolness" while sipping cocktails and "hip" foodies who appreciate the "assortment of fresh fish and noodle dishes", especially the "fantastic Javanese salmon"; those who don't fit in find it "too trendy."

3 Doors Down Café
26 | 22 | 24 | $25
1429 SE 37th Ave. (Hawthorne Blvd.), 503-236-6886
■ Fans gush "three thumbs up" for the "perfectly cooked pasta", "intimate" setting and "informed" "servers who are glad to see you" at this Hawthorne Italian; sure, there's "always a line" and "no reservations", but the price is a "value" and to some it's "consistently the best meal in town."

Tina's S
27 | 21 | 25 | $30
760 Hwy. 99 W. (opp. fire station), Dundee, 503-538-8880
■ Renovations at this French-accented Northwestern in the Wine Country have doubled the size of the dining area and added a fireplace and "cute little bar"; while the atmosphere's "clearly better", the kitchen has always turned out "superb", "creative" dishes and the "outstanding staff" deftly knows its way around the vino list, which is heavily weighted toward local pinot noir treasures.

Typhoon! S
25 | 19 | 20 | $21
2310 NW Everett St. (23rd Ave.), 503-243-7557
Typhoon! on Broadway S
Imperial Hotel, 400 SW Broadway (Stark St.), 503-224-8285
■ "The most creative", "gorgeous" Thai food in Portland, served on "cool plates", can be found at this top-rated "yuppie haven" with a branch in the Imperial Hotel; while portions can be "small" and prices "high", this "amazing experience" is "breaking new ground", and the Broadway location reputedly has the largest tea selection (150 choices) of any restaurant in the country.

Wildwood S
26 | 23 | 23 | $34
1221 NW 21st Ave. (Overton St.), 503-248-9663
☑ "Like a San Francisco restaurant" is the big-city tribute pros pay to this "trendy" "exponent of Northwestern" cuisine, known for chef-owner Cory Shreiber's "bold" seasonal food, "snappy service" and "avant-garde" decor; the "cramped seating" and "noisy" room annoy a few of the "pretty people", but overall it's still a "favorite."

Salt Lake City & Mountain Resorts

TOP 10 FOOD RANKING

	Restaurant	Cuisine Type
27	Fresco Italian Cafe	Northern Italian
	Grapevine	Continental
	Mariposa	New American
26	New Yorker	Trad. American/Continental
	Glitretind	New American
	Martine	Med./New American
	Spencer's	Steakhouse/Trad. American
	Chez Betty	Trad. American/Continental
	Ichiban Sushi	Japanese
	Metropolitan	New American

ADDITIONAL NOTEWORTHY PLACES

Bambara	New American
Grappa	N/S Italian
La Caille	Classic French
Log Haven	New American/Eclectic
Mandarin	Chinese
Market Street Grill	Seafood
Red Iguana	Mexican
Sundance Tree Room	Regional American
Tuscany	Northern Italian
Wahso	Asian/New French

F | D | S | C

Bambara [S] – | – | – | M

Hotel Monaco, 202 S. Main St. (W. 200 South), Salt Lake City, 801-363-5454

Set in a trendy Downtown hotel, this hip SLC New American yearling boasts a smashing art deco interior and up-to-the-minute Scott Blackerby–created cuisine; since it's across the street from the Capitol Theatre, check out the pre-performance menu.

Chez Betty [S] 26 | 20 | 23 | $41

Copperbottom Inn, 1637 Short Line Rd. (Deer Valley Dr.), Park City, 435-649-8181

■ It may take a map to find this Continental–Traditional American in a Park City hotel, but its "excellent" food and "polished service" offset the "gloomy decor"; surveyors say its the "most pleasing and least pretentious" eating experience in Utah.

Fresco Italian Cafe S
| 27 | 24 | 25 | $34 |

*1513 S. 1500 East (bet. Emerson & Kensington Aves.), Salt Lake City,
801-486-1300*

■ Rated No.1 for Food in the Utah *Survey,* this SLC "perennial
favorite" serves "excellent" and "delicious" Northern Italian food
in a "lovely setting" (an adjoining bookstore adds ambiance);
"dining on the patio [and garden] in summer is preferred", but in
any season it's "an intimate pleasure that never disappoints",
thus "reservations are a must."

Glitretind Restaurant S
| 26 | 26 | 25 | $45 |

Stein Eriksen Lodge, 7700 Stein Way (Royal St.), Deer Valley, 435-645-6455

■ At this "sophisticated but not stuffy" New American in Deer
Valley, the "outstanding" "food is as gorgeous as the mountain
setting" ("what a view!"); sure, it's "pricey" and the "place to see
and be seen" ("look for Stein [Eriksen] wanna-bes"), but "it's great
for a special occasion."

Grapevine, The
| 27 | 25 | 26 | $33 |

129 N. 100 East (bet. 100 & 200 North), Logan, 435-752-1977

■ "An unbelievable find" tucked away in a historic Victorian home
surrounded by gardens filled with lavender and grapevines, this
chef-owned-and-operated Logan "gem" steals the crowds from
Cache Valley and beyond "given no competition" when it comes
to the "always excellent" Continental cuisine; limited hours (dinner
only, Wednesday–Saturday) mean it's "almost always full."

Grappa Italian Restaurant S
| 24 | 27 | 22 | $46 |

151 Main St. (Swede Alley), Park City, 435-645-0636

☑ The "place to be in Park City", particularly for a "romantic
supper date", is the take on this "atmospheric" Italian filled with
"beautiful people"; while opponents opine it's "overpriced" and
"overrated", most maintain "freshness reigns" here, making for
an "unforgettable meal" that's "worth every penny."

Ichiban Sushi & Japanese Cuisine S
| 26 | 25 | 20 | $29 |

336 S. 400 East, Salt Lake City, 801-532-7522

■ Even if "you think you don't like sushi, the Japanese-trained
female chef will teach you" to ("try the Funky Charlie"– just one
of the "very creative" "killer" offerings here); while regulars
"thank God" this longtime Park City spot moved to a spiffed-up
Downtown SLC location in an old church, several respondents
specify that you take a "seat at the sushi bar" because service can
be "slow" elsewhere in the room.

La Caille S
| 20 | 29 | 23 | $53 |

*Little Cottonwood Canyon, 9565 S. Wasatch Blvd. (3500 East), Sandy,
801-942-1751*

☑ "One of the most beautiful restaurants in the country" and voted
No.1 for Decor in the Utah *Survey* is this "idyllic" Sandy Classic
French "château retreat"; while critics carp about the sky-high tab
("you pay for the ambiance and bosoms" – i.e. the waitresses'
"revealing period uniforms"), atmosphere addicts insist this
"exceptional special-occasion place" deserves attention, while
business types tout it as "great for the expense-account crowd."

Log Haven [S] 25 | 27 | 23 | $37

6451 E. 3800 South (Wasatch Blvd., 4 mi. up Millcreek Canyon), Salt Lake City, 801-272-8255

■ Its "unsurpassed", "spectacular" "mountain setting" – a "revived" lodge nestled in thick pines and wildflowers accented by a lily-pad pond – is "worth the trip" up Millcreek Canyon; almost as highly rated is the "innovative" and "delicious" New American–Eclectic cuisine; all in all, for "celebrations and romance", it's one of the "best dining experiences" in the area.

Mandarin 25 | 19 | 20 | $18

348 E. 900 North, Bountiful, 801-298-2406

■ A trip to Bountiful could bring you to the "best Chinese ever", an "always crowded" stalwart with a "vast" menu, "consistently fresh, flavorful, quality ingredients" and "fab-o food"; some insiders advise "order the Peking duck 48 hours ahead – it's the only way to get a reservation" and avoid the "much too long wait."

Mariposa, The [S] 27 | 26 | 25 | $47

Silver Lake Lodge, Deer Valley Resort, 7600 Royal St., Deer Valley, 435-645-6715

■ This "great retreat" at Deer Valley Resort's Silver Lake Lodge is a "class act" offering "imaginative" New American dishes that are "as good as it gets", an "elegant" ambiance and "amazing service"; it may "flatten your credit card", but that doesn't stop a "clientele of beautiful people" from packing the place; N.B. open December–mid-April.

Market Street Grill [S] 25 | 22 | 22 | $25

54 Market St. (Main St., bet. 300 & 400 South), Salt Lake City, 801-322-4668

■ Seafooder and "Salt Lake mainstay" – anchor of the successful Gastronomy Inc. group – that some label a "neighborhood wonder" for "fresh fish", the "best blackened chicken plate (and it's not even on the menu)" and "good breakfasts"; yes, it's "noisy", "but that's the fun" and locals rely on it for "regular dinners out."

Martine 26 | 23 | 24 | $30

22 E. 100 South (bet. Main & State Sts.), Salt Lake City, 801-363-9328

■ "Just what SLC needs – a hip, delicious place Downtown" say boosters of this Med–New American success story where the "imaginative", "unusual dishes" include "fun-to-graze-on tapas", while the "pub menu at lunch is a proven winner"; devotees declare that they do "things right" and are "consistent enough to recommend" anytime.

Metropolitan 26 | 26 | 23 | $51

173 W. Broadway (300 South, bet. 200 West & W. Temple St.), Salt Lake City, 801-364-3472

◪ "Someone brought an urbane New York bistro and dropped it" in Downtown Salt Lake say admirers of this "beautiful" New American with "exquisite food" (albeit presented in "dime-size portions") and an "unforgettable tasting menu"; the less-than-sophisticated snipe that the "pretentious" atmosphere means you "must wear black – or sit behind the fern", and wallet-watchers warn that the tab may require "a second mortgage", but sybarites simply shrug that the "big splurge is worth it."

New Yorker, The   26 | 26 | 25 | $43
60 W. Market St. (Main St., bet. 300 & 400 South), Salt Lake City,
801-363-0166
■ Longtime "chef Will Pliler is a master" at this Downtown SLC
Traditional American–Continental that, despite a basement setting,
remains Gastronomy Inc.'s "ritzy" "crown jewel"; the "consistently
excellent food", "gracious service" and "great wine list" set a
"benchmark for excellence" and draw the "pretty people", making
it a place "to go to close a deal" or when "you're feeling romantic."

Red Iguana, The 🟦   25 | 13 | 18 | $14
736 W. North Temple St., Salt Lake City, 801-322-1489
■ This Downtown "gastronomic gem" may be a "hole-in-the-wall",
but many surveyors say it's the "best Mexican" in SLC, serving
"great moles" and other "authentic" entrees that always draw a
crowd; despite the "kitschy", "very east LA decor" and "lack of
seating", devotees decree that it's the place for "killer food" – "I
crave it in my sleep."

Spencer's for Steaks & Chops 🟦   26 | 24 | 23 | $39
Hilton Salt Lake City Center, 255 S. West Temple St. (bet. 200 & 300 South),
Salt Lake City, 801-238-4748
■ "Classic", "very upscale" Downtown SLC Traditional American
whose "good, high-end steaks" are dubbed the "best Chicago beef
in the region"; a "cigar-friendly bar" and a "great selection of
martinis" make this "unique for Utah" steakhouse a "place where
you can remember what being on an expense account was like."

Sundance Tree Room 🟦   25 | 26 | 22 | $40
Sundance Resort, 6 mi. up Provo Canyon (North Fork Canyon Rd.),
Sundance, 801-223-4200
■ There's a "gorgeous mountain ski resort setting" for this
Sundance American with a Western accent that's co-owned by
Robert Redford; offering "very creative food" and a "comfortable",
"inviting" ambiance, it's the "best of the best" ("only the tree is
dead – the rest is a true treasure").

Tuscany 🟦   23 | 27 | 22 | $33
2832 E. 6200 South (Holladay Blvd.), Holladay, 801-277-9919
■ "Impress out-of-towners with SLC chic" at this "favorite"
Holladay destination, which showcases "romantic Northern Italian
dining" with a "luxurious setting" in which to savor "innovative"
food, accompanied by a "wonderful wine list" and served by an
"impeccable" staff; "though it's quite big", it's a "gorgeous" "place
to be seen", so prepare for a "mob scene."

Wahso 🟦   – | – | – | E
577 Main St. (5th St.), Park City, 435-615-0300
Park City restaurateur Bill White (Grappa) strikes gold once again
on highly competitive Main Street at this elegant upstairs venue
offering a sophisticated Asian fusion menu with New French
underpinnings in intimate dining spaces adorned with Far Eastern
furnishings reminiscent of Shanghai in the '30s; toss in impeccable
service and it's no wonder oddsmakers predict another bonanza
for this already successful organization.

San Diego

TOP 10 FOOD RANKING

Restaurant	Cuisine Type
28 El Bizcocho	Classic/New French
27 WineSellar & Brasserie	New French
Mille Fleurs	New French
Sushi Ota*	Japanese
Azzura Point	Californian/Med.
Pamplemousse Grille	Californian/New French
26 Rancho Valencia	Californian/Continental
George's at the Cove	New American
Belgian Lion	Belgian/French
Laurel	New French

ADDITIONAL NOTEWORTHY PLACES

Bertrand at Mister A's	New American
Cafe Japengo	Asian/Japanese
Cafe Pacifica	Californian
Marine Room	New French
Morton's of Chicago	Steakhouse
Prado	Cal./Southwestern
Rainwater's on Kettner	Steakhouse
Star of the Sea	Seafood
Tapenade	French Bistro/Seafood
Vignola	New French

F	D	S	C

Azzura Point S | 27 | 26 | 25 | $45 |

Loews Coronado Bay Resort, 4000 Coronado Bay Rd.
(Silver Strand Blvd.), Coronado, 619-424-4477
■ This airy room with "smashing" decor on the second floor of the view-endowed Loews Coronado Bay Resort is where "serious" foodies join hotel guests for chef Michael Stebner's "innovative" Cal-Med fare; it's a "special-occasion vacation in our hometown."

Belgian Lion, The | 26 | 21 | 23 | $36 |

2265 Bacon St. (W. Point Loma Blvd.), 619-223-2700
☑ "Expensive but very good" Belgian-French in Ocean Beach that reminds some of "grandma's parlor" with its lace doily–strewn setting, "wonderful cassoulet" and other "hearty" fare; though some claim service isn't always doting, regulars revel in "personal attention" and find this Coulon family veteran "still great"; open Thursday–Saturday, dinner only.

---

* Tied with the restaurant listed directly above it.

Bertrand at Mister A's 🖪

– | – | – | VE

Fifth Ave. Financial Ctr., 2550 Fifth Ave., 12th fl. (Laurel St.), 619-239-1377
Given the location and sublime views atop the Fifth Avenue
Financial Centre near Balboa Park, the takeover of the venerable
Mister A's by Bertrand Hug of Mille Fleurs fame would seem a
marriage made in heaven, and this sleek, French-accented New
American with chef Todd Davies in the kitchen almost certainly
will become a top expense-account destination; despite a few
growing pains, reservations are already essential.

Cafe Japengo 🖪

25 | 24 | 20 | $29

*The Aventine, 8960 University Ctr. Ln. (bet. La Jolla Village & Lebon Drs.),
858-450-3355*
☑ Emphatically "too noisy", this "yuppie heaven" at the epicenter
of the Golden Triangle offers "excellent", "artistic sushi" and
other Asian-inspired food in an "elegant Japanese setting" that's
such a "place to be seen" among singles, those over 30 head to
quieter tables in the back; while staffers are "great for viewing",
they can be "slow", which fuels critics who say "overrated."

Cafe Pacifica 🖪

25 | 22 | 22 | $31

2414 San Diego Ave. (Old Town Ave.), 619-291-6666
■ "Tremendous seafood" with an "innovative" edge is the specialty
of this "consistently strong" performer on the border of historic
Old Town, which "never disappoints" the knowledgeable locals and
tourists who come here for "great sunsets" and a well-priced menu
that draws on solid Californian cuisine traditions; while undeniably
"charming", it "could use more space around the tables."

El Bizcocho 🖪

28 | 26 | 26 | $44

*Rancho Bernardo Inn, 17550 Bernardo Oaks Dr.
(Rancho Bernardo Rd.), Rancho Bernardo, 858-675-8550*
■ The last bastion of black-tie service in town, this grand hotel
dining room in Rancho Bernardo may be "far, far" from Downtown,
but it takes top honors for its "world-class" Classic and New
French cuisine (voted No. 1 for Food in San Diego); the "sublime"
service (also rated No. 1) and "elegant decor" add to the appeal,
and while it's "pricey" (especially the wine list), most agree the
raves are "well deserved."

George's at the Cove 🖪

26 | 26 | 25 | $37

1250 Prospect Pl. (bet. Cave & Ivanhoe Sts.), La Jolla, 858-454-4244
■ This "real La Jolla tradition" is consistently voted SD's Most
Popular restaurant, but these days the culinary accolades go to the
New American cuisine and sterling seafood specialties of new chef
Trey Foshee; the triple-tiered setting still offers "romantic", "less-
expensive" dining "on the roof terrace under a full moon", a pricier
ground-floor main room that "can't miss for business" meals and
a bar in between where singles mingle and nibble on light bites.

Laurel Restaurant & Bar 🖪

26 | 26 | 22 | $38

505 Laurel St. (5th Ave.), 619-239-2222
☑ "The place to take guests who think SD is a hick town" is this
"sleek, sexy", dinner-only New French near Balboa Park with a
"big-city feel" that gives an extra edge to Douglas Organ's "superb"
cuisine; as you'd expect from the younger sister of WineSellar &
Brasserie, there's an "excellent wine list", so even if some find it
noisy, with uneven service, more "wish they were open for lunch."

Marine Room 🄂   23 26 22 $37
2000 Spindrift Dr. (Torrey Pines Rd.), La Jolla, 858-459-7222
■ "Right on the ocean (and sometimes in it)", this "elegant" New French on the surf in La Jolla is "unsurpassed" for its "famous view", and with chef Bernard Guillas working "wonders with the food", there's "life" in the kitchen; well-dressed "out-of-towners" and local "beautiful people" enjoy the "rich, rewarding" "special-occasion" atmosphere, which combined with the excellent, if "stuffy" service makes it "always an experience – especially for your wallet."

Mille Fleurs 🄂   27 27 26 $54
Country Squire Courtyard, 6009 Paseo Delicias (Avenida de Acacias), Rancho Santa Fe, 858-756-3085
☑ Set in a blissfully beautiful Mediterranean-style villa in Rancho Santa Fe, this "big-bucks" New French "for the horsey set" features "wonderful" food served in a "romantic" setting that "looks like France"; while some find the service "pompous" and the "small portions" "grossly overpriced", the majority maintains that owner Bertrand Hug's discreet retreat is "the ideal special-occasion spot."

Morton's of Chicago 🄂   26 24 25 $48
285 J St. (bet. 2nd & 3rd Aves.), 619-696-3369
■ Meat lovers would gladly "take out a second mortgage" to finance a trip to this "dark", "woody", casually elegant Downtown steak palace serving notoriously "huge portions" of the "best beef this side of Chicago"; of course, cost isn't an issue for the expense-account crowd that heads here for "first-class" food and service.

Pamplemousse Grille 🄂   27 24 25 $43
514 Via de la Valle (Jimmy Durante Blvd.), Solana Beach, 858-792-9090
■ "Beautiful people" and horse-racing types (in season) jockey for a table at this "noisy", art-filled, understatedly elegant Cal–New French near the sea, where former NYer Jeffrey Strauss' "talent and imagination" fuel an "exceptional, exciting" menu that's "a treat", right down to "the best tarte Tatin in San Diego"; still, some label it "overpriced."

Prado, The 🄂   – – – E
Balboa Park, 1549 El Prado, House of Hospitality (Plaza de Panama), 619-557-9441
The show-stopping, museum-like interior and outdoor terrace with grand Balboa Park views percolate at this lavish redo of the former Cafe del Rey Moro by restaurateurs Lesley and David Cohn; tourists and locals (as well as ticket-holders for the nearby Old Globe Theatre) happily pay plenty to dine on chef Jeff Thurston's imaginative Cal–Contemporary SW cooking that's backed up by friendly, competent service.

Rainwater's on Kettner ●🄂   25 22 24 $38
1202 Kettner Blvd. (B St.), 619-233-5757
☑ "Our version of Morton's of Chicago but better" say some locals of this homegrown steakhouse, a spacious, clubby "power location" "for a business lunch" near the Downtown waterfront; it pleases expense-account "big shots" with "delicious beef" and a "wine room for parties", but foes find it "stuffy" and "overrated."

Rancho Valencia S

26 | 29 | 25 | $44

Rancho Valencia Resort, 5921 Valencia Circle (Rancho Diegueno Rd.), Rancho Sante Fe, 858-759-6216

■ Surveyors say "you can't beat the ambiance" at this smashingly "beautiful" room (voted No. 1 for Decor in San Diego) near Rancho Santa Fe; besides "superb" Cal-Continental fare with Pacific Rim accents, it boasts a "great view", "leisurely service" and the "prettiest patio" on which to "lose the day"; in sum, it's well "worth the drive."

Star of the Sea S

23 | 22 | 23 | $39

(fka Anthony's Star of the Sea)
1360 N. Harbor Dr. (Ash St.), 619-232-7408

☑ Locals relish chef Brian Johnston's imaginative seasonal seafood menus, heavy on local fish and lobster, and love the glass-walled views of the bay, but some bemoan the new informal dress policy at this "classic" place to "impress" on the Downtown waterfront; although now 33 years old, the recently redecorated, expense-account seafooder still seems young compared to the Star of India, the 1850s-vintage merchantman that raises its sails a few yards away on San Diego Bay.

Sushi Ota S

27 | 13 | 17 | $26

4529 Mission Bay Dr. (Balboa Ave.), 858-270-5670

■ Despite an "odd location" near the freeway at the back side of Pacific Beach, this Japanese shrine is "always crowded" because the chef is an "artist with a knife", turning out "creative" sushi that's "the best in San Diego"; the food is so good that "visitors from Tokyo specifically request" a visit here, and it more than makes up for "lunch-counter decor" and "inconsistent service."

Tapenade S

– | – | – | E

7612 Fay Ave. (bet. Kline & Pearl Sts.), La Jolla, 858-551-7500

Jean-Michel and Sylvie Diot left behind successful restaurants in NY for sunny SD, and their French venture in La Jolla has drawn raves from day one, offering a seafood-heavy bistro menu in a breezy South of France–like setting; it's fairly "pricey", but the well-heeled clientele doesn't seem to mind.

Vignola

▽ 26 | 20 | 24 | $34

828 Sixth Ave. (bet. E & F Sts.), 619-231-1111

■ Simply decorated, this Gaslamp Quarter New French earns raves for its "awesome foie gras" and "innovative fare" from "hot" chef Fabrice Poigin, who is warmly remembered from previous stints around town; "reasonable prices" and a smoothly trained young staff are pluses.

WineSellar & Brasserie

27 | 20 | 25 | $42

9550 Waples St. (bet. Mira Mesa Blvd. & Steadman St.), 858-450-9557

■ Douglas Organ is too old now to be the *enfant terrible* of San Diego chefs, but his casually chic New French "hidden gem" in Sorrento Mesa remains a true "original" that's "worth a trip to the warehouse district", offering "the best marriage of food and wine", as well as "attentive service"; some find it "too expensive for the decor", but with 3,000 wines to choose from and a six-variety tasting every Saturday (lunch optional), it's "heaven" for oenophiles.

San Francisco Bay Area*

TOP 20 FOOD RANKING

Restaurant	Cuisine Type
29 French Laundry/N	New American
28 Gary Danko	Classic French/New Amer.
Chez Panisse/E	Californian
Masa's	Classic French
Ritz-Carlton Dining Room	New French
La Folie	New French
Elisabeth Daniel	New French
27 Terra/N	Californian/New French
Fleur de Lys	New French
Erna's Elderberry/S	Californian/New French
Charles Nob Hill	Californian/New French
Boulevard	New American
Sent Sovi/S	New French/New Amer.
Le Papillon/S	New French
Chez Panisse Cafe/E	Californian/Mediterranean
Aqua	Seafood
26 Fifth Floor	New French
Jardinière	Californian/New French
Acquerello	N/S Italian
Postrio	Cal./Asian/Med.

ADDITIONAL NOTEWORTHY PLACES

Auberge du Soleil/N	Classic French/Med.
Azie	New French/Asian
Bistro Jeanty/N	French Provençal
Campton Place	French Provençal
Eos	Asian/Fusion
Farallon	Californian
Fringale	French Bistro
Hawthorne Lane	Californian
Kokkari Estiatorio	Greek
Lark Creek Inn/N	New American
La Toque/N	New French
Oliveto Cafe & Restaurant/E	Northern Italian
Ondine/N	French/Japanese
Pisces/S	Seafood
Rose Pistola	N. Italian/Seafood
Rubicon	Californian/New French
Slanted Door	Vietnamese
Spago Palo Alto/S	Californian
Tra Vigne/N	N/S Italian
Zuni Cafe	Italian/Mediterranean

---

* E=East of San Francisco; N=North of San Francisco; and
  S=South of San Francisco.

Acquerello   26 | 23 | 25 | $56 |
1722 Sacramento St. (bet. Polk St. & Van Ness Ave.), 415-567-5432
■ Fans feel this "romantic", "hidden gem" in Van Ness/Polk may be the "best" Italian in the city, with "food and service to suit a king" and a "superb (albeit expensive) wine list" to match; despite the "spare", some say "stuffy", interior, most maintain this "converted church" makes for a "divine restaurant."

Aqua   27 | 26 | 24 | $58 |
252 California St. (bet. Battery & Front Sts.), 415-956-9662
■ Michael Mina's trendy, sleek-as-a-shark Downtowner continues to "set the standard for seafood" with "soaring architectural presentations", "amazing sauces" and "whimsical desserts"; the "understated" dining room, filled with "dazzling flowers", attracts a "power crowd" out "to close that deal"; a small school of critics complains about the "noisy" setting, "snooty service" and the need to "bring your corporate card", but they're outvoted.

Auberge du Soleil S   25 | 28 | 25 | $58 |
Auberge du Soleil Inn, 180 Rutherford Hill Rd. (Silverado Trail), Rutherford, 707-967-3111
■ It's just "a joy to be" at this "romantic" Rutherford "destination restaurant" where everything is "stunning": the "beautiful view of the Napa Valley" ("remember to request outdoor seating"), the "fabulous" Classic French–Mediterranean fare ("just put your finger anywhere on the menu"), the vino selection (the "best list in California for American wines") and the "pleasant staff"; N.B. new chef Richard Reddington is expected to maintain the same high standards.

Azie S   22 | 25 | 19 | $51 |
826 Folsom St. (bet. 4th & 5th Sts.), 415-538-0918
◪ "High-tech meets SoMa" at this trendy newcomer where owner Jody Denton dazzles diners with "brilliant" New French–Asian fusion in "inspired" presentations rivaled only by the room's "alluring decor"; the "über-hip" hold court at the bar while "curtained booths" and a DJ keep the mood "darkly dreamy"; however, skeptics warn of a "pretentious" and "pricey" scene.

Bistro Jeanty S   26 | 22 | 23 | $41 |
6510 Washington St. (Yount St.), Yountville, 707-944-0103
■ "Philippe Jeanty works his magic and the crowds come and come" to this "welcoming", "laid-back", Provençal bistro in Yountville, which serves "incredibly delicious" Country French classics at relatively "reasonable" prices; followers insist "forget the fancy places" because this is one very "convincing" "slice of France" and the "place in Napa Valley to come back to."

Boulevard S   27 | 26 | 25 | $51 |
1 Mission St. (Steuart St.), 415-543-6084
■ "Paradise found" sums up this "high-energy" Downtown New American that's the No. 1 Most Popular restaurant in the *SF Survey* ("I send everyone here – they always get it right"); "all the raves are well earned" for Nancy Oakes' "outstanding food", Pat Kuleto's "art-nouveau Parisian bistro" setting and a "truly professional staff" that "never fails to impress" the "well-heeled" crowd; insiders suggest "sit toward the back" or "go early and eat at the counter."

Campton Place 🖸
26 | 25 | 25 | $56

Campton Pl. Hotel, 340 Stockton St. (bet. Post & Sutter Sts.), 415-955-5555

■ "Amid the maddening crowd of Union Square", this Downtown oasis provides "what every hotel restaurant should" – "subdued elegance", "flawless service" and "sumptuous food"; chef Laurent Manrique's "interesting" French Provençal dinner menu complements the long-renowned "great breakfasts", ensuring its status as "a special place for special occasions."

Charles Nob Hill 🖸
27 | 25 | 26 | $67

1250 Jones St. (Clay St.), 415-771-5400

■ Chef Ron Siegel is famed for "winning on the *Iron Chef*" Japanese TV show, but these days his audience is Nob Hill "blue bloods" who offer his "sensational" Cal-French fare as "exhibit A for why being civilized matters"; since the "rarified" room and "stellar service" are "luxurious", it's "worth every penny – and plenty of pennies it will be."

Chez Panisse
28 | 25 | 26 | $65

1517 Shattuck Ave. (bet. Cedar & Vine Sts.), Berkeley, 510-548-5525

■ Disciples of "the Church of Alice" Waters beat a path to this "high altar of food" in Berkeley to "pay homage" to the "reigning matriarch of California cuisine", savor the "simple" yet "sublime" seasonal organic fare and be coddled by "superb service"; some wonder "what's all the fuss?", but they're drowned out by a choir of believers who vow "heaven must be something like this"; P.S. the only potential downside (aside from snagging reservations) is playing "prix fixe roulette" – what they serve is what you get.

Chez Panisse Cafe
27 | 23 | 24 | $41

1517 Shattuck Ave. (bet. Cedar & Vine Sts.), Berkeley, 510-548-5049

■ "There is nothing second class" about Alice Waters' "relaxed and casual" upstairs cafe; followers feel it's "just as good" but "a lot cheaper" than its downstairs "sister" and appreciate the fact that it is "less intense", "easier to get into" and offers "more choices" of "seasonally fresh" Cal-Med cuisine (e.g. a particularly noteworthy pizza); N.B. the cafe now accepts reservations up to one month in advance for lunch and dinner.

Elisabeth Daniel, Restaurant
28 | 24 | 25 | VE

550 Washington St. (bet. Montgomery & Sansome Sts.), 415-397-6129

■ City slickers are being wowed by this "great" Downtown newcomer with "fancy shmancy" New French fare ("sweetbread ravioli from heaven") and "amazing" "choreographed service"; "talented chef" Daniel Patterson presents a three-course prix fixe menu at lunch ($35) and six courses at dinner ($68), while his wife, Elisabeth Ramsey, presides over the refined but unpretentious room.

EoS Restaurant & Wine Bar 🖸
25 | 20 | 21 | $42

901 Cole St. (Carl St.), 415-566-3063

■ Oenophiles and foodies "flock from all over" to this cacophonous Cole Valley bistro for chef Arnold Eric Wong's "delicious, inventive" Asian-Fusion fare, "exceptional wine list" and "desserts to die for" – don't miss the bananamisu; the "architecturally presented" dishes rise to "distressingly tall heights" (and so have the prices), but most maintain that it's "worth looking for parking"; N.B. walk-ins can opt to eat at the adjoining wine bar.

Erna's Elderberry House S

27 26 27 $70

48688 Victoria Ln. (Hwy. 41), Oakhurst, 559-683-6800

■ For those lucky enough to "find it and afford it" (it's in Oakhurst, "close to Yosemite"), this Cal–New French is "unforgettable in every way", with its "absolutely flawless service", dreamy "castle-like atmosphere" and "exquisite" cuisine that'll put you in "culinary heaven"; since Erna conveniently owns the equally lavish Château du Sureau resort next door, visitors are fully equipped for "a romantic weekend away."

Farallon S

24 28 23 $53

450 Post St. (bet. Mason & Powell Sts.), 415-956-6969

◪ Dazzled diners Downtown would swim upstream just to eye Pat Kuleto's "over-the-top" "*20,000 Leagues Under the Sea*" decor (swirling with "jelly fish and sea-urchin lamps" and "cast-iron seaweed stair railings") and to eat chef Mark Franz's "inventive" Cal creations; while the unimpressed won't take the bait, calling the coastal cuisine "too splashy for my taste", they're outvoted by surveyors who shout "there's nothing fishy about this place!"

Fifth Floor S

26 28 27 VE

Hotel Palomar, 12 Fourth St. (Market St.), 415-348-1555

■ A "palace for the palate" that "seems closer to heaven than just the Fifth Floor" is what surveyors say about this "sensational New French newcomer" in Downtown's Hotel Palomar; chef George Morrone's "sophisticated food" is complemented by a "clubby setting" ("Sinatra could be at the next table"), "polished service" and "phenomenal wine list"; the menu is pricey, but the experience is most "exceptional."

Fleur de Lys

27 27 26 $70

777 Sutter St. (bet. Jones & Taylor Sts.), 415-673-7779

■ Hubert Keller "puts his heart and soul into his food and it shows" swoon fans of this Downtown New French where a "sumptuous" canopied setting serves as the backdrop for "creative" cuisine that's "first-rate" (the "vegetarian tasting menu is awesome"); some sniff at the "stuffy service", but most agree with the romantic who rhapsodized "this is a restaurant to propose in, and I did."

French Laundry S

29 27 27 VE

6640 Washington St. (Creek St.), Yountville, 707-944-2380

■ Once again voted No. 1 for Food in the *SF Survey* and moving up to No. 2 for Popularity and Service, Thomas Keller's New American legend in Yountville is "more of an event than a meal", from scoring reservations (doled out no more or less than two months in advance) to "taking out a mortgage" to pay for the "perfectly presented", sublime" tasting menu, delivered by an "impeccable" staff; an "unforgettable experience", it may be "without equal in the culinary firmament."

Fringale

26 19 22 $41

570 Fourth St. (bet. Brannan & Bryant Sts.), 415-543-0573

■ *C'est* "magnifique" exclaim fans of this "timeless" SoMa French bistro featuring Gerald Hirigoyen's "consistently awesome" cuisine; the space-invaded complain "if the tables were any closer, it would be communal dining" and wish the "tiny restaurant" were "larger so I could get a reservation", but many maintain that it's the "best meal for the money in SF."

Gary Danko [S] 28 | 27 | 27 | VE
800 North Point St. (Hyde St.), 415-749-2060
■ "Gary's back and better than ever" at this Fisherman's Wharf French–New American, whipping up "sublime" creations while his old Ritz-Carlton crony, Nick Peyton, oversees a staff that "can't do enough to please"; a "mix-and-match tasting menu" that offers "the best of both worlds", an "elegant room" and an "impressive wine list" add up to "the epitome of what fine dining should be" – no wonder the reservationless lament: "let us in."

Hawthorne Lane [S] 26 | 25 | 24 | $52
22 Hawthorne St. (bet. 2nd & 3rd Sts.), 415-777-9779
■ "Hidden away" in SoMa, Annie and David Gingrass' "chichi" Cal delivers a "deft blend of all the elements for a memorable culinary experience": "imaginative" creations (starting with "wonderful" homemade breads), a "modern", "understated interior" filled with art and ironwork, "excellent", "friendly" service and "marvelous energy", courtesy of a "yuppie expense-account crowd."

Jardinière [S] 26 | 26 | 24 | $56
300 Grove St. (Franklin St.), 415-861-5555
■ "Beautiful people", pre-concert culture vultures and devotees of fine dining make the pilgrimage to this "pricey" Hayes Valley "gastronomical mecca" for "seriously talented" chef Traci Des Jardins' "inventive" Cal–New French cuisine ("amazing scallops") and Pat Kuleto's "gorgeous" interior, which is dominated by a dramatic center bar and a balcony that provides "great people-watching"; P.S. save room for the "wonderful" cheese course.

Kokkari Estiatorio 24 | 27 | 23 | $46
200 Jackson St. (Front St.), 415-981-0983
■ "Gorgeous" Downtown taverna where the well-connected Greek community and "beautiful people" lap up "excellent", "rustic" Hellenic fare highlighted by a "killer meze platter", "unbelievable moussaka" and "don't-miss" lamb; reservations are hard to score, but if you can't get a seat "in the front room by the fireplace" or at the "big community table", the "convivial" bar is nice consolation.

La Folie 28 | 23 | 26 | $68
2316 Polk St. (bet. Green & Union Sts.), 415-776-5577
■ Chef-owner "Roland Passot continues to make magic" at this "cozy" Van Ness/Polk New French, which "rises above" its Gallic rivals; true, it's "a real budget buster", but citing the "beautiful presentations" of "memorable" dishes and "impeccable" yet "friendly" service, most agree it's "worth" the beaucoup bucks.

Lark Creek Inn [S] 24 | 25 | 23 | $46
234 Magnolia Ave. (Madrone Ave.), Larkspur, 415-924-7766
■ Although Bradley Ogden has scattered his New American "comfort food" all around the Bay Area, his original Larkspur establishment – located in a "storybook" "Victorian home" – "maintains its well-earned reputation" as the "most elegant and delicious" place in Marin for "special occasions"; so, go on a lark and "dine under the redwoods on the patio" surveyors urge – "it doesn't get more adorable than this."

La Toque ●S
25 | 23 | 26 | $74

1140 Rutherford Cross Rd. (Hwy. 29), Rutherford,
707-963-9770

■ "Wonderful tasting menus" showcase top toque Ken Frank's "superb" cooking at this New French, which surveyors claim is "almost as good as [its mighty neighbor] the French Laundry – and without the booking pains"; add in "personable service" and the result is "a drop-dead dinner" in a "romantic" Rutherford setting.

Le Papillon S
27 | 24 | 25 | $55

410 Saratoga Ave. (Kiely Blvd.), San Jose, 408-296-3730

■ "Catering to Silicon Valley money", this South Bay butterfly isn't cheap, but it does offer some "superb haute New French cuisine" (the "herb-crusted halibut is amazing") and a sense of "cosseted comfort"; although some say "the atmosphere can be a little stuffy", to most it's "one of San Jose's best."

Masa's
28 | 25 | 27 | VE

Hotel Vintage Court, 648 Bush St. (bet. Powell & Stockton Sts.),
415-989-7154

☑ Judging from ratings, the "departure of [former chef] Julian Serrano has not hurt" this Downtown Classic French destination where chef Chad Callahan continues the tradition of "astonishingly creative", "outstanding" cuisine (in four- and five-course menus) and the staff "makes you feel like royalty"; for those who are less impressed with the "dark", "gloomy" and "formal" setting, a scheduled renovation should help lighten things up.

Oliveto Cafe & Restaurant S
24 | 21 | 21 | $45

5655 College Ave. (Shafter Ave.), Oakland, 510-547-5356

☑ "The subtle flavors of Tuscany come to life" at "master chef" Paul Bertolli's "outstanding" Oakland trattoria where he presents "extraordinary, rustic" Northern Italian fare in a "spartan setting"; while many feel it's as "good as anything in Italy", critics complain the portions are "too small" for the "high prices"; perhaps they should try the more casual, moderately priced cafe downstairs.

Ondine S
25 | 27 | 23 | $56

558 Bridgeway (Princess Ave.), Sausalito, 415-331-1133

■ "A classic reborn" is the consensus on this Sausalito waterfront spot resuscitated by chef Seiji Wakabayashi's "highly sophisticated fusion" of French and Japanese cuisines whose flavors and presentations are as "striking" as the "drop-dead views of San Francisco"; while a few find it "too expensive", fans warn "when word of this place gets out, it will be difficult to get a reservation."

Pisces S
26 | 21 | 23 | $50

1190 California Dr. (Broadway), Burlingame, 650-401-7500

■ "Another Charles Condy success" declare devotees, who are already calling this "great newcomer", with its "amazing seafood creations", "the Aqua of the South Bay" (which Condy owns, along with SF's Charles Nob Hill); although they deplore the "crowded, noisy" room ("should be in a larger space" – already!), locals "thank God" there's "finally an upscale restaurant in Burlingame."

Postrio [S] 26 | 26 | 24 | $53

Prescott Hotel, 545 Post St. (bet. Mason & Taylor Sts.), 415-776-7825

■ Wolfgang Puck's Downtown Californian is still the "gold standard" of SF dining, dishing up just the right mix of "beautiful people", "professional service" and "consistently great food"; who doesn't "feel like a movie star descending the staircase" into the "dramatic dining room" and supping on Steve and Mitchell Rosenthal's "remarkable" Asian-accented Mediterranean fare and "amazing desserts"?; although "the bar is a total meat market", it's still one of the best spots for "fun, late-night dining."

Ritz-Carlton Dining Room 28 | 28 | 28 | $68

Ritz-Carlton Hotel, 600 Stockton St. (bet. California & Pine Sts.), 415-773-6198

■ Expect the "transcendental" at this "blow-the-bank" Nob Hill "grande dame" featuring Sylvain Portay's "outstanding" New French cuisine; since the staff is among the "finest in the USA" (rated SF's No.1 for Service) and the "elegant" ambiance is that of a "great European hotel", "it doesn't get any better than this"; N.B. jacket required.

Rose Pistola [S] 22 | 20 | 18 | $40

532 Columbus Ave. (bet. Green & Union Sts.), 415-399-0499

◪ "The energy is palpable" at Reed Hearon's "hip-and-happening" North Beach North Italian–seafooder, which continues to be packed nightly with out-of-towners and locals who consider themselves lucky to get in; while less-trendy types are tired of the din ("I've been in quieter steel plants") and "hype", fans feel that "it's got everything going for it" ("delicious food" and a "vibrant" atmo), so "sit up front for less noise and more people-watching."

Rubicon 24 | 21 | 22 | $49

558 Sacramento St. (bet. Montgomery & Sansome Sts.), 415-434-4100

◪ "Classy" Downtowner that's a top "choice for impressing clients", thanks to chef Scott Newman's "superb" Cal-French fare and master sommelier Larry Stone's "incredible" "world-class wine list"; although detractors dis "the corporate power vibe", oenophiles insist the "food-and-wine pairings are mind-blowing" and "suggest you settle in, pay the money and enjoy."

Sent Sovi [S] 27 | 22 | 24 | $61

14583 Big Basin Way (5th St.), Saratoga, 408-867-3110

■ Chef-owner David Kinch's "romantic" Saratoga "jewel" features "beautifully presented, creative" New French–American cuisine and employs a "knowledgeable staff" that "treats you very well"; a copper-topped bar and Oriental rugs add to this "heaven-sent" choice that you may "never want to leave."

Slanted Door, The [S] 26 | 18 | 19 | $34

584 Valencia St. (17th St.), 415-861-8032

■ Charles Phan's "outstanding", "inventive Vietnamese" creations served in "cool digs" have "yuppies slumming in the Mission", hitting "automatic redial to get a reservation" at this "trendy" place that's "hell to get into"; patrons overlook the "deafening din" for the "brilliant flavors" of the small dishes and "the perfect wines to complement" them.

Spago Palo Alto S
24 | 24 | 22 | $51

265 Lytton Ave. (Bryant St.), Palo Alto, 650-833-1000

■ "Another home run in the Wolfgang Puck Spago series", this "big, high-style" Californian (featuring an original Rauschenberg) is a perfect fit for the "powerful" "Silicon Valley crowd" that "comes to network" and to show off their "trophy wives"; despite the hype, surveyors concede chef Michael French's "inventive" fare is "fabulous" and the staff "treats you like royalty" ("and charges you like it too").

Terra S
27 | 24 | 25 | $54

1345 Railroad Ave. (bet. Adams & Hunt Sts.), St. Helena, 707-963-8931

■ Chef-owner "Hiro is a hero" in the kitchen and his wife Lissa works small miracles in the "romantic", "stone-walled" dining room; together they keep this "just about perfect" St. Helena Cal–New French (with strong Asian accents) on terra firma, although reviewers report they "feel like they're eating in heaven"; professional service and a formidable wine list also prompt patrons to rate it "one of the best anywhere."

Tra Vigne S
25 | 26 | 22 | $43

1050 Charter Oak Ave. (Hwy. 29), St. Helena, 707-963-4444

■ Surveyors smitten with Michael Chiarello's "gorgeous" St. Helena Italian swear it's "like eating in a villa", with its "vaulted ceilings to the sky", "sublime" food that's "always scaling new heights" and "idyllic" outdoor space; although you may have to "brave the lines" and some "attitude" to enjoy this "wine-country classic", amici admit that it was "so wonderful we bought the cookbook"; N.B. don't miss the Cantinetta, an Italian-style deli/gourmet shop on the premises.

Zuni Cafe ●S
24 | 20 | 19 | $38

1658 Market St. (bet. Franklin & Gough Sts.), 415-552-2522

■ More than 20 years after it opened, this "legendary" Italian-Mediterranean mainstay on the edge of Hayes Valley "maintains the hip vibe" that still attracts the city's rich and famous ("you just feel cool eating here"); loyalists swoon "ah, the Caesar salad, the oven-roasted chicken, the burgers" – Zuni standards that "set the standard" for all others; despite a few of the inevitable "overrated" comments, it remains the "quintessential SF" scene.

TOP 10 FOOD RANKING

Restaurant	Cuisine Type
27 Old House	Continental/Southwestern
Geronimo	Eclectic/Southwestern
26 Santacafe	Southwestern
Cafe Pasqual's	Southwestern
Ristra	Southwestern/New French
Anasazi	Southwestern
25 Julian's	N/S Italian
24 Bistro 315	French Bistro
Il Vicino	N/S Italian
La Casa Sena	Southwestern

ADDITIONAL NOTEWORTHY PLACES

Andiamo!	Northern Italian
Bull Ring	Traditional American
Coyote Cafe	Southwestern
El Farol	Spanish/New Mexican
Gabriel's	Mexican
Guadalupe Cafe	New Mexican
Il Piatto	Northern Italian
Pink Adobe	Continental/New Mexican
Rancho de Chimayo	New Mexican
Rancho de San Juan	Eclectic/International

F	D	S	C

Anasazi Restaurant S

25	27	24	$42

Inn of the Anasazi, 113 Washington Ave. (bet. Marcy St. & Palace Ave.), 505-988-3236
■ Reviewers rave about the "gorgeous presentation" of "creative" Southwestern cuisine and the "superb decor" at this Downtowner in the Inn of the Anasazi; a minority maintains it's an "overpriced hotel dining room" that "suffers from changing staffs and chefs", but they're clearly outvoted.

Andiamo! S

24	19	20	$28

322 Garfield St. (bet. Guadalupe & Sandoval Sts.), 505-995-9595
■ "Terrific" Northern Italian food is the hallmark of this popular little bistro near the Rail Yard, which also gets high marks for its "friendly" service and "charming" "old bungalow" setting; though some find the atmosphere too "noisy" and "cramped", they're easily assuaged after one bite of the "great crispy duck" and "best polenta."

Bistro 315
24 | 19 | 21 | $37
315 Old Santa Fe Trail (bet. Alameda St. & Paseo de Peralta), 505-986-9190
☑ This "lovely", "intimate" French bistro near the Plaza offers an "interesting", seasonally-changing menu of "excellent" Provençal cuisine, including "delicious duck"; the outdoor patio is touted too, though some find the interior "cramped" and the service – while generally "friendly" – occasionally "uneven."

Bull Ring, The 🖸
22 | 19 | 21 | $33
Wells Fargo Plaza, 150 Washington Ave. (Lincoln St.), 505-983-3328
■ You'll "see Santa Fe's power brokers" shooting the bull over some of "the best steaks in town" at this "old-style political hangout" Downtown, with a "lively", "smoky" bar that's an ideal perch for sipping a sublime martini; wallet-watchers be warned: unless you have an "expense account", you may find the "hearty", "straightforward" Traditional American fare "too expensive" ("everything is à la carte").

Cafe Pasqual's 🖸
26 | 21 | 22 | $24
121 Don Gaspar Ave. (Water St.), 505-983-9340
■ "Fantastic breakfasts" "at the common table" are "a must" for both "tourists" and "locals" at this "loud", "crowded" and "colorful" Southwestern "old reliable", a block south of the Plaza, which still produces "delicious", "unexpected combinations" more than 20 years after its debut; most "go for breakfast and lunch" rather than dinner – just remember to "get there early" to avoid the "long lines" since this "bustling favorite" is hardly a secret.

Coyote Cafe 🖸
23 | 24 | 22 | $40
132 W. Water St. (bet. Don Gaspar Ave. & Galisteo St.), 505-983-1615
☑ Acclaimed chef Mark Miller's classic eatery a block off the Plaza still "lives up to its billing" thanks to endlessly "innovative", "superbly presented" Southwestern dishes sporting "super" flavors; however, many locals feel the "noisy" main dining room (prix fixe only) has become an "overpriced" "tourist cliché" and recommend eating "on the rooftop" of the "festive", lower-priced cantina instead.

El Farol 🖸
19 | 20 | 18 | $27
808 Canyon Rd. (Camino del Monte Sol), 505-983-9912
☑ This "funky" Spanish–New Mexican "hangout" in a historic adobe on Canyon Road serves "tapas from heaven" in a "fun atmosphere" that includes "great live music" and a "late-night" "people-watching" scene; but naysayers note that the bill from all those "cute little" dishes can add up.

Gabriel's 🖸
22 | 22 | 21 | $22
Hwy. 285 N. (2 mi. north of Camel Rock Casino), Cuyamungue, 505-455-7000
■ Mexican "favorite", 12 miles north of Santa Fe, that's known for its "generous portions" of "freshly prepared", "excellent food", including " great guacamole made at your table" that's considered the "best anywhere"; dining here "under clear blue skies" in a "superb outdoor setting" with heart-stopping mountain views makes for a "romantic Mexican getaway without the travel."

Geronimo 🅂　　　　　27 | 28 | 25 | $46

724 Canyon Rd. (Camino del Monte Sol), 505-982-1500

■ Voted New Mexico's Most Popular restaurant and No. 2 for Food and Decor, this "pricey but worth it" Eclectic-Southwestern in a "lovely", "historic" Canyon Road adobe wins applause for chef Eric DiStefano's "extraordinary", "innovative" cuisine; patrons also praise the "romantic", "intimate" interior and the "thoughtful" service; overall, it's a "signature of Santa Fe" and a "must."

Guadalupe Cafe 🅂　　　　22 | 17 | 19 | $16

422 Old Santa Fe Trail (bet. Alameda St. & Paseo de Peralta), 505-982-9762

■ A "favorite" place for "breakfast with the locals", this "standby" on the Old Santa Fe Trail is a "wonderful value" for "traditional" New Mexican fare, although the "great red-and-green chile" may be a bit "too hot" for more tender palates; it's "crowded" and waits can be long, but "monster portions" and a "great outdoor patio" keep it "popular."

Il Piatto 🅂　　　　　23 | 19 | 21 | $27

95 W. Marcy St. (bet. Lincoln & Washington Aves.), 505-984-1091

■ "Consistently good [Northern] Italian food" and a "reasonable wine list" pack in the crowds at this "lively" Downtown trattoria that "never disappoints" and "won't break the bank"; nevertheless, "scrunched up" surveyors say that the "close quarters" are "not for the claustrophobic."

Il Vicino 🅂　　　　　24 | 20 | 18 | $13

321 W. San Francisco St. (bet. Guadalupe & Sandoval Sts.), 505-986-8700

■ One of Downtown's most popular lunch spots for "excellent wood-fired pizza" and lasagna washed down with "awesome microbrews", this "upbeat" Italian is also reasonably priced; a "great hangout after a movie", it tends to get "mobbed."

Julian's 🅂　　　　　24 | 25 | 23 | $38

221 Shelby St. (bet. Alameda & Water Sts.), 505-988-2355

■ A Downtown adobe is the "lovely" setting for this "very romantic", "elegant" spot that some say serves the "best Italian in Santa Fe"; the "high-quality" cuisine and "attentive service" make it a "special-occasion place" that's "worth the splurge."

La Casa Sena 🅂　　　　24 | 25 | 22 | $36

125 E. Palace Ave. (Washington Ave.), 505-988-9232

■ Southwestern stalwart located in a historic adobe near the Plaza that's noted for its "creative" menu, "consistent" cooking, "gorgeous" courtyard and "Santa Fe charm", making it a "great" place to "bring your friends to impress them"; P.S. the adjacent cantina with its "singing waiters" is also "fun and more reasonable."

Old House, The 🅂　　　　27 | 26 | 26 | $41

Eldorado Hotel, 309 W. San Francisco St. (bet. Guadalupe & Sandoval Sts.), 505-988-4455

■ Rated No. 1 for Food in New Mexico, this Downtown Continental-SW in the Eldorado Hotel "consistently exceeds expectations" with chef Martin Rios' "exquisite attention to detail" and "wonderful" cuisine; a "warm", "intimate" atmosphere and "sophisticated" service add to the "world-class" experience; N.B. dinner only.

Pink Adobe [S] | 21 | 24 | 21 | $31 |

406 Old Santa Fe Trail (Alameda St.), 505-983-7712

◪ "You'll meet everyone in town" at this long-standing "landmark" that's the "essential Santa Fe experience" for enthusiasts who come for the "cozy", historic setting, "classic" Continental–New Mexican menu and the "great" Dragon Room bar; naysayers insist that "it doesn't live up to the hype", but they're outvoted by fans of the "steak Dunnigan" and "always-a-joy" atmosphere.

Rancho de Chimayo [S] | 20 | 26 | 21 | $21 |

Santa Fe County Rd. 98 (¼ mi. off Hwy. 76), Chimayo, 505-351-4444

◪ An "institution" in the village of Chimayo, 20 minutes northeast of Santa Fe, this "historic" former hacienda with "authentic atmosphere" is a "romantic" destination for fans of "excellent traditional" New Mexican food and a "must for out-of-towners"; enjoy the "beautiful outdoor patio" while sipping a "great Chimayo cocktail" (a margarita made with cranberry juice instead of lime) or dine inside in the "charming" main house.

Rancho de San Juan | 26 | 29 | 28 | $55 |

Rancho de San Juan, Hwy. 285 (mile marker 340), Española, 505-753-6818

■ Rated No.1 for Decor and Service in New Mexico is this "very special" country inn in a "gorgeous" rural setting 40 minutes north of Santa Fe; the "elegant and charming" decor, "superb" Eclectic-International menu and "wonderful" staff add up to an "exceptional dining experience"; even reviewers who find it "expensive" concur that it's an "out-of-this-world" place for a "fabulous anniversary dinner."

Ristra [S] | 25 | 22 | 24 | $41 |

548 Agua Fria (Guadalupe St.), 505-982-8608

■ "New favorite" in Sanbusco that's the spot for "excellent, imaginative cuisine", a "blend of Southwest and [New] French" fare that's "spectacular", especially the "simply sublime" mussel appetizer; the menu may be "limited", but there's "excellent service", plus a "sophisticated" setting with a "wonderful" patio.

Santacafe [S] | 26 | 26 | 24 | $40 |

231 Washington Ave. (bet. Marcy St. & Paseo de Peralta), 505-984-1788

◪ This "favorite special-occasion spot" near the Plaza "remains an excellent retreat" for pros who praise its "top-notch", "inventive blend" of "Southwestern and cross-cultural" dishes, served either in the "elegant" interior or on the "lovely" patio; some report occasional "disappointment," saying the food is "up and down", but the majority maintains that the experience is "always great."

TOP 20 FOOD RANKING

Restaurant	Cuisine Type
28 Rover's	New French
Campagne	Country French
27 Tosoni's	Continental/Italian
Fullers	Northwestern
Shiro's Sushi	Japanese
Wild Ginger	Pan-Asian
26 Cafe Campagne	French Bistro
Nishino	Japanese
Dahlia Lounge	Northwestern/Asian
Kingfish Café	Southern/Soul
Inn at Langley	Northwestern
Il Terrazzo Carmine	Northern Italian
Szmania's	Northwestern/German
Le Gourmand	Classic French
Cafe Juanita	Northern Italian
Kaspar's	Northwestern
Shoalwater	Northwestern
Toyoda Sushi*	Japanese
25 Cafe Lago	N/S Italian
Canlis	Northwestern

ADDITIONAL NOTEWORTHY PLACES

Brasa	Mediterranean
Cascadia	Northwestern
Chez Shea	New American
El Gaucho	Trad. American/Steakhouse
Etta's Seafood	Seafood
Fandango	Latin American
Flying Fish	Seafood
Harvest Vine	Spanish/Tapas
Herbfarm	New Amer./Northwestern
Lampreia	Northwestern
Le Pichet	French Bistro
Mistral	New Amer./Northwestern
Monsoon	Vietnamese
Nell's	New Amer./Northwestern
Palace Kitchen	Northwestern
Saito's Japanese Café & Grill	Japanese
Sapphire Kitchen & Bar	Pan-Mediterranean
Tango Tapas Bar & Lounge	Pan-Latin
Typhoon!	Thai
Waterfront	Northwestern/Asian

* Tied with the restaurant listed directly above it.

Brasa S

| – | – | – | M |

2107 Third Ave. (Lenora St.), 206-728-4220
This bold Belltown beauty marks the long-awaited return of ex
Campagne chef Tamara Murphy and her contemporary rendition
of Med cuisine, much of it cooked over an open fire; the sensuous
dining room is designed for lingering, and the bar is a prime site
for a pre- or post-event bite.

Cafe Campagne S

| 26 | 23 | 23 | $25 |

Pike Place Mkt., 1600 Post Alley (Pine St.), 206-728-2233
■ "Ooh-la-la!", this "first-class bistro" is Post Alley's own "slice
of Paris", serving French comfort fare that "rivals its big sister
[Campagne] upstairs" for "consistency and quality", amounting
to "champagne food at beer prices"; the Gallic setting is ideal for
a "rainy-day breakfast", "terrific Sunday brunch" or romantic
dinner – this is a "treat" at a cost that "can't be beat."

Cafe Juanita S

| 26 | 20 | 23 | $34 |

9702 NE 120th Pl. (97th Ave.), Kirkland, 425-823-1505
■ "Sometimes forgotten", this "creekside" Kirkland Northern
Italian is a "warm and inviting" "class act" that's "worth the
money" and "the drive" to experience the evolving menu; standouts
include "fantastic lamb shanks"and "wonderful desserts", matched
with "personal service" and "perhaps the best vino list for the
money in town" (the Cavatappi winery is annexed to the cafe).

Cafe Lago S

| 25 | 18 | 21 | $25 |

2305 24th Ave. E. (bet. Lynn & McGraw Sts.), 206-329-8005
■ There are "long lines" and "great smells" at this "intimate and
'in'" Montlake Italian; regulars arrive early to get the most from the
"limited" menu, which includes pizza raised "to an art"; a "friendly"
staff adds to the charm, and if faultfinders grumble "pricey and
crowded", for most "this is the real thing."

Campagne S

| 28 | 25 | 25 | $44 |

Inn at the Market, 86 Pine St. (bet. 1st Ave. & Post Alley), 206-728-2800
■ "Elegant" Country French cooking (voted Seattle's No. 2 for Food)
coupled with "impeccable service" make for a "superb dining
experience" at this Pike Place Market "treasure"; the "intimate
setting" enhances both business and pleasure (even if you have
to "mortgage your house for wine" from the "outstanding" list).

Canlis

| 25 | 27 | 27 | $48 |

2576 Aurora Ave. N. (Halladay St.), 206-283-3313
■ The panoramic view of Lake Union remains "unmatched" and
the "food has really improved" at this "favorite", a "grand old lady"
with a "marvelous" makeover; chef Greg Atkinson gives the Pacific
NW "steak-and-seafood" menu "a '90s twist", and the "superb
service" is rated No. 1 in the *Seattle Survey*; "consistent luxury"
is "expensive", though, and this is still "blue-blood" home turf.

Cascadia

| – | – | – | VE |

2328 First Ave. (bet. Battery & Bell Sts.), 206-448-8884
Belltown's newest showplace features luxe trappings (like an
etched-glass water wall and baby grand) that set the appropriate
tone for chef-owner Kerry Sear's sumptuous Northwestern menu;
delicacies like partridge in wild grasses satisfy the adventurous,
while those seeking more casual nibbles stake out its low-key bar.

Chez Shea [S]

25 | 24 | 24 | $41

Pike Place Mkt., 94 Pike St. (1st Ave.), 206-467-9990

■ It must be the "orgasmic food and decor" – romantics regard this "sexy" Pike Place Market "hideaway" as the "perfect place" to "be proposed to" or "seduce" someone; skinflints flinch at "high prices", but the "adventurous" prix fixe New American menu and "impeccable" service are tops for a "quiet rendezvous"; N.B. chef Amy McCray signed on mid-*Survey*, but the kitchen is known for its consistency.

Dahlia Lounge [S]

26 | – | 23 | $34

2001 Fourth Ave. (Virginia St.), 206-682-4142

■ Chef-restaurateur Tom Douglas' firstborn is in full bloom, with a menu of "flavorful, Asian-influenced" Northwestern cuisine that extends the "food as art" philosophy from "innovative entrees" to "incredible daily specials"; since the "top-notch" staff pays "amazing attention to detail", it's "one classy joint" that can deliver "a sublime experience"; N.B. the move to a new home has been a happy one, providing more space, while retaining the charm of the original.

El Gaucho ◐[S]

23 | 23 | 24 | $46

2505 First Ave. (Wall St.), 206-728-1337

◪ "Power steaks" coalesce with martinis and a piano bar in a "sexy" "supper club" setting with "unparalleled" service to make this Belltown Traditional American a favorite for "show-off dinners"; the scene strikes some as "pretentious", though, and the penny-wise warn "better be on an expense account" – "El Gouge-o is more like it."

Etta's Seafood [S]

25 | 21 | 22 | $30

2020 Western Ave. (bet. Lenora & Virginia Sts.), 206-443-6000

■ "Tom Douglas does seafood" at this "upbeat" eatery that's noted for its "innovative approach" and "first-class ingredients" – the salmon is "exquisite" and crab cakes are "unsurpassed"; too "trendy" for some, its proximity to Pike Place Market makes it "hard to get in" and, inevitably, "touristy."

Fandango [S]

– | – | – | E

2313 First Ave. (bet. Battery & Bell Sts.), 206-441-1188

Less than a block from her still-soaring Flying Fish, chef-owner Christine Keff has another hit on her hands with this dinner-only Latin American; housemade tortillas, full-flavored cooking, colorful cocktails and a lively setting make this a simpatico Belltown addition where the people-watching is prime and the rear tables get a peek-a-boo view over Elliott Bay.

Flying Fish ◐[S]

25 | 22 | 21 | $33

2234 First Ave. (Bell St.), 206-728-8595

◪ "Fish from all over the world" surface at this "super-trendy", "high-energy" Belltown seafooder where chef-owner Christine Keff works "Asian-inspired culinary magic" to create "crowd-pleasers" like whole fried snapper, wok-seared "crab by the pound" and other "magnificent" presentations of "superbly prepared" aquatics; it's a "fun and sophisticated" scene, but phobes frown on "uneven quality", "slow service" and "the din" – "what's the big deal?"

Fullers 27 25 25 $46

Sheraton Hotel & Towers, 1400 Sixth Ave. (bet. Pike & Union Sts.), 206-447-5544

■ It's an "art gallery" exhibiting "top-flight" food say admirers of this Downtowner's "exquisite" style; celeb chef Monique Barbeau has passed the toque to her sous, Tom Black, but surveyors remain enthusiastic about the "dramatic" Northwestern menu and "gracious service"; a minority grumbles it's too "expensive" and "stuffy", but it remains "a must for the self-respecting gourmet."

Harvest Vine – – – M

2701 E. Madison St. (27th Ave. E.), 206-320-9771

Order a bottle of Pesquera to pass the time while you wait for a table at this minuscule Madison Valley tapas bar where regulars hold out for a seat at the copper-topped counter since the show is too good to miss; anticipate authentic little dishes from Spain (fresh grilled sardines, lamb, octopus, blood sausages, even baby eels) and impressive paellas, along with some mighty fine desserts.

Herbfarm, The [S] – – – VE

195 NE Gilman Blvd. (Front St.), Issaquah, 206-784-2222

"Legendary and awesome but not yet rebuilt" after a fire destroyed its original farm site in 1997, this fabled outpost is now occupying a 40-seat wine-aging room at the Hedges Cellars Winery in Issaquah; here, chef Jerry Traunfeld is creating his "exquisite" "once-in-a-lifetime experience for the palate" for the few lucky gourmands who "can get a reservation" to indulge in a "superb" NW-accented New American prix fixe feast; N.B. a new luxe location in Woodinville is scheduled to open in early 2001.

Il Terrazzo Carmine 26 24 24 $38

411 First Ave. S. (bet. Jackson & King Sts.), 206-467-7797

■ Owner Carmine Smeraldo, "the godfather of Seattle's Italian food scene", is "always there to greet" the "sophisticated" patrons that frequent this "stylish", "festive" "standout" near Pioneer Square; expect "white-glove treatment all the way" and "few compromises on the authentic" menu, composed of "first-class" Northern specialties like "great venison farfalle"; "important dinner coming up and want to impress? – go here."

Inn at Langley 26 25 25 $48

Inn at Langley, 400 First St. (Park Ave.), Langley, Whidbey Island, 360-221-3033

■ Open for a one-seating dinner Friday–Saturday only, this relaxed Whidbey Island inn provides an "incredible" "adventure for palate and soul"; reserve at least two months in advance and hope for a seat at "the communal table", though all diners in the small room "get a cooking lesson" while watching talented chef Stephen Nogal prepare a "fabulous" five-course prix fixe Northwest feast in the exhibition kitchen.

Kaspar's 26 22 24 $39

19 W. Harrison St. (1st Ave. W.), 206-298-0123

■ Chef Kaspar Donier creates "artistically arranged" and "exceptional" NW cuisine for his eponymous Queen Anne spot, a renovated room in a "classy" locale that feels even more welcoming due to the "warm hospitality" of the "professional" staff; P.S. the "fabulous wine bar" is "an excellent deal" with its short menu of small bites.

Kingfish Café 🅂⊄
26 | 23 | 21 | $22

602 19th Ave. E. (Mercer St.), 206-320-8757

■ The "beautiful" "Coaston sisters have taken Soul Food to another level" at their Capitol Hill hitter where "big portions" and "lovely interpretation of Southern standards" help make this spot "as good as its buzz"; "get there a half-hour before the place opens" say those who "hate the wait."

Lampreia
25 | 21 | 22 | $48

2400 First Ave. (Battery St.), 206-443-3301

⬛ Chef Scott Carsberg is a "near perfectionist" whose seasonal NW menu features "absolutely simple" but "exquisite" food; loyalists like the "refined service" and "elegant, romantic" atmosphere, but a minority calls the setting "sparse", claiming this "overpriced" Belltowner is "the most pretentious restaurant in Seattle."

Le Gourmand
26 | 20 | 24 | $46

425 NW Market St. (6th Ave. NW), 206-784-3463

■ "Caring, intelligent" chef-owner Bruce Naftaly is a "treasure" who "prepares everything with love" at this "fine" Ballard French Classic where "the freshest ingredients" often come from the chef's own trees, vines and garden; "great sauces" are key to his seasonal, prix fixe menu, which is "unbeatable for the money – hell, almost unbeatable, period."

Le Pichet 🅂
– | – | – | M

1933 First Ave. (Virginia St.), 206-256-1499

Just steps from the Pike Place Market, this cozy French bistro features chef-partner Jim Drohman's (ex Campagne) unpretentious, fully satisfying fare, from fresh-baked pastries to housemade charcuterie; affordable wines (mostly French) are a highlight, most of them available by the trademark *pichet* (pitcher).

Mistral
– | – | – | VE

113 Blanchard St. (1st Ave.), 206-770-7799

Chef-owner William Belickis (ex Fullers) marches to the beat of his own drummer at this Belltown newcomer, creating refined New American–Northwestern dishes and offering them in a prix fixe format (patrons choose the price point, which determines the number of courses) sans a printed menu; it's all about seasonality and execution, though the prices may knock the wind out of some.

Monsoon 🅂
– | – | – | M

615 19th Ave. E. (E. Mercer St.), 206-325-2111

In a sleek Capitol Hill dining room dominated on one end by a boisterous kitchen, the Banh family is busy pleasing crowds with compelling Vietnamese fare; the biggest complaints are about the wait at this popular place, but they quickly fade away after patrons peruse the seasonally influenced menu.

Nell's 🅂
– | – | – | E

6804 E. Greenlake Way N. (1st Ave.), 206-524-4044

Last year, Saleh Joudeh handed over the reins to his long-loved Saleh al Lago to his former sous chef, Philip Mihalski, who changed the name and the concept, but kept the same concern for quality; the New American menu emphasizes NW ingredients, but retains several of his predecessor's Italian-accented classics; patrons continue to get the best of both worlds, since Saleh still makes the rounds of the redecorated Green Lake dining room most nights.

Nishino [S] — 26 | 22 | 22 | $33

3130 E. Madison St. (Lake Washington Blvd.), 206-322-5800

■ Tatsu Nishino (ex LA's Matsuhisa) serves "creative", "cutting-edge" cuisine at this "graceful" Madison Park Japanese; his "beyond description chef's-choice dinner" and "great sushi bar", where everything is "beautifully presented", are "impressive"; though some complain about "tiny", "overpriced" portions, most feel the food is "wonderful" and "can't wait to return."

Palace Kitchen ◐[S] — 23 | 22 | 21 | $31

2030 Fifth Ave. (Lenora St.), 206-448-2001

◪ "Tom Douglas' restaurants are always fabulous" and this Downtown NW (his third) is no exception; the "flashy and fun" U-shaped bar is the center of the Palace's universe, where the "self-consciously hip" "cocktail set" comes to see and "be seen" in a "cool" setting; while fans feel the cooking's "worthy of adulation" and that Douglas and company are "not afraid to lead food trends", foes find the menu too meat-y, the room "very noisy" and the seats "hard and uncomfortable."

Rover's — 28 | 24 | 27 | $65

2808 E. Madison St. (28th Ave.), 206-325-7442

■ "Gifted chef" Thierry Rautureau presides over "the best special-occasion place in the Northwest", where you can "indulge all your senses" with "impeccable everything"; "is there an award he hasn't won?" ask surveyors who voted his "romantic" Madison Park New French hideaway No. 1 for Food in Seattle; "always superb", the "world-class" prix fixe only menu is "spendy", but well worth the "splurge" for "ambrosia on a plate."

Saito's Japanese Café & Bar — – | – | – | M

2122 Second Ave. (bet. Blanchard & Lenora Sts.), 206-728-1333

Even busy Belltown has room for more great Japanese dining, and here chef-owner Yutaka Saito slices sashimi like an artist while giving equal attention to sushi and other crowd-pleasers; the list of 50 sakes makes for a most authentic accompaniment.

Sapphire Kitchen & Bar [S] — – | – | – | M

1625 Queen Anne Ave. N. (Blaine St.), 206-281-1931

This sexy little spot – with its crimson booths, deep blue walls and overall lively vibe – is one of the most interesting venues atop Queen Anne; the frequently changing Pan-Med menu is peppered with local seasonal ingredients, while the wine list focuses on the Iberian Peninsula.

Shiro's Sushi [S] — 27 | 17 | 21 | $31

2401 Second Ave. (Battery St.), 206-443-9844

■ Celebrated sushi chef Shiro Kashiba's eponymous Belltowner delivers "sushi from heaven", making it Seattle's No. 1 choice for Japanese; "sit at the counter and watch an artist in action", but "get there when they unlock the door or you'll have to give people the evil eye" as you wait; the decor is "simple and classy", though "elbow-to-elbow" tables and "paper napkins disappoint."

Shoalwater 🄢   26 | 23 | 23 | $37
Shelburne Inn, 4415 Pacific Hwy. (45th St.), Seaview,
360-642-4142
■ For a "very special" meal at Ann and Tony Kischner's "warm, cozy" restaurant in the 1896 Shelburne Inn, it's "worth a trip" to the Pacific Coast; though it's close to the beach, there's "no view" from the formal dining room, but the "NW ingredients are skillfully prepared" and the wine list is carefully composed.

Szmania's 🄢   26 | 23 | 25 | $36
3321 W. McGraw St. (34th Ave.), 206-284-7305
■ "Out-of-the-way" Magnolia affords a chance to get "away from the trendy scene" and into chef Ludger Szmania's "fabulous food" at this "NW treasure" with a German accent; the "delectable entrees" (the "half-portion concept is brilliant"), "romantic atmosphere" and "highly professional" service mean this "gem" "has it all."

Tango Tapas Bar & Lounge 🄢   – | – | – | M
1100 Pike St. (Boren Ave.), 206-583-0382
Riding the wave that's bringing vibrant Pan-Latin flavors to town, this Capitol Hill newcomer leans heavily on tapas augmented by a menu of mains like the signature paella with housemade chorizo; the short walk to Downtown and the Paramount adds to the appeal.

Tosoni's   27 | 15 | 25 | $34
14320 NE 20th St. (bet. 140th & 148th Aves.), Bellevue,
425-644-1668
■ "A slice of Europe in Bellevue?"; chef-owner Walter Walcher and his wife Wendy prove it can be done, wowing crowds at this "Eastside sleeper" with an "ambitious" Continental menu that leans on Italy for inspiration; the fare is weighted toward "great meats", the service toward personal attention.

Toyoda Sushi 🄢   26 | 14 | 19 | $24
12543 Lake City Way NE (125th St.), 206-367-7972
■ There's "never a dull moment" and patrons can count on "a smile from Mr. T", who slices and dices in person at this "relaxed", "crowded" Lake City sushi bar; the "high standards" and "no-fuss setting" add up to "consistently fine value", making it a strong all-around contender for "best sushi in town."

Typhoon! 🄢   – | – | – | M
Bella Botega, 8936 161st Ave. NE (NE 90th St.), Redmond,
425-558-7666
1400 Western Ave. (Union St.), 206-262-9797
Set in spreading-like-wildfire Redmond, this newcomer draws devotees from near and far for Thai cuisine that breaks the mold; a liquor license is still pending, but meantime there's a list of 150 teas to tempt you; N.B. a new sib recently opened on Western Avenue in Seattle.

Waterfront S

– | – | – | E

2801 Alaskan Way, Pier 70 (Broad St.), 206-956-9171

The team of restaurateur Paul Mackay (El Gaucho) and chef Vicky McCaffree makes a big splash with a menu focused on Northwestern seafood and Asian-inspired preparations; with its wide view of Elliott Bay, the perch at the end of Pier 70 is a major draw, and no detail is overlooked, including the piano player who serenades each evening; N.B. there's even a free shuttle to nearby El Gaucho.

Wild Ginger S

27 | – | 22 | $30

1401 Third Ave. (Union St.), 206-623-4450

■ "Oh the flavors, the smells, the crowds!"; the "definitive Seattle Pan-Asian" with the booming satay bar remains the city's Most Popular restaurant – and possibly the noisiest; James Beard Award winner Jeem Han Lock has a "wicked way with spice" and continues to conduct "a concert of flavors without a clash of cultures"; N.B. the move to bigger, brighter digs doesn't seem to have alleviated the crowds or the cacophony.

Southern New York State

TOP 20 FOOD RANKING

Restaurant	Cuisine Type
29 Xaviar's	New American
Xaviar's at Piermont	New American
28 Freelance Cafe	New American
La Panetière	New French
27 La Crémaillère	Classic French
Il Cenàcolo	Northern Italian
Escoffier	Classic French
Buffet de la Gare	Classic French
Maxime's	Classic French
26 American Bounty	New American
Azuma Sushi	Japanese
Rest. X & Bully Boy Bar	New American
Zephs'	Eclectic
Caterina de Medici	Northern Italian
Harralds	International
Le Canard Enchainé	French Bistro
25 Arch	Eclectic/New French
Calico	New American
Crabtree's Kittle House	New American
McKinney & Doyle	New American

ADDITIONAL NOTEWORTHY PLACES

An American Bistro	New American
Auberge Maxime	New French
Bear Cafe	New American
Belvedere Inn	New American
Bistro Twenty-Two	Eclectic/New French
Bois d'Arc	Regional American
Cafe Mezé	Mediterranean
Cafe Tamayo	New American
Citrus Grille	Cal./New American
DePuy Canal House	New American
Equus	New French
Harvest on Hudson	Mediterranean
Hunan Village	Chinese
Inn at Pound Ridge	New American
Iron Horse Grill	New American
Le Château	Classic French
Lusardi's	Northern Italian
Old Drovers Inn	French/New American
Purdys Homestead	Regional American
Terrapin	New American

F D S C

American Bounty Restaurant 26 | 25 | 25 | $41

Culinary Institute of America, 1946 Campus Dr. (opp. W. Dorsey Ln.),
Hyde Park, 845-471-6608

■ Considered "an excellent showcase for the CIA", this student-run Hyde Park New American garners praise for its "outstanding" food and "lovely setting" that "feels like a country inn"; "careful" service from "sweet and eager to please" pupils (all "gunning for an A") adds to the "bountiful experience" that's "worth the trip."

An American Bistro S 25 | 14 | 21 | $34

174 Marbledale Rd. (bet. Fisher Ave. & Main St.), Tuckahoe,
914-793-0807

■ "Please don't tell everyone" plead fans who'd like to keep this "tiny" New American "gem" tucked away in an "unlikely" industrial area of Tuckahoe a secret; but "plentiful" portions of "superior" and "imaginatively" presented food at "value" prices along with "courteous owners and servers" have already made it a "favorite", despite "long waits" and "noisy", "cramped quarters."

Arch S 25 | 25 | 25 | $54

Rte. 22N (end of I-684), Brewster, 845-279-5011

■ "To eat on the patio under the rhododendrons is heaven" swoon fans of this "very special" Brewster Eclectic–New French boasting a "beautiful countryside setting" and a "changing menu but unchanging excellence" in everything from the greeting to the dessert ("get the soufflés"); even critics admit it's "pretentious but deservedly so" and "worth the dollars" for "fine dining at its best"; P.S. "lunch [Wednesday–Friday] is a bargain."

Auberge Maxime S 25 | 25 | 24 | $53

721 Titicus Rd. (Rtes. 116 & 121), North Salem, 914-669-5450

☑ "A treat in the country", this North Salem gem is "top-notch", serving "wonderful" New French fare (such as the famed duck) in a "beautiful setting" where "everything is special, including the grounds"; "expensive but worth it" is the consensus, although a minority sniffs "be sure to wear your jewels for good service."

Azuma Sushi S 26 | 15 | 20 | $35

219 E. Hartsdale Ave. (Central Ave.), Hartsdale, 914-725-0660

■ Partisans swear that "the best sashimi and sushi in the world" is found at this small, "spartan" Hartsdale sushi parlor that's "always filled with Japanese" and "city folk" who find it "absolute heaven" despite long waits and "zero ambiance"; but it's "too bad" about the "snippy" service; N.B. aside from some appetizers, no cooked dishes are served.

Bear Cafe S 24 | 21 | 21 | $33

295A Tinker St. (Rte. 212), Bearsville, 845-679-5555

■ "You wouldn't believe such good food in the wilds of Bearsville", but raves abound for this "innovative" New American just west of Woodstock offering "top-notch" fare in a "casual", "streamside" setting; while quibblers find the menu "a little overambitious" and add that the place can get "busy and loud", scan the crowd carefully – "you might see Todd Rundgren, Dave Matthews" or other music stars here.

	F	D	S	C
Belvedere Inn [S]	22	28	22	$41

10 Old Rte. 9 (County Rte. 84), Staatsburg, 845-889-8000

■ "Excellent in all respects" and voted No. 1 for Decor in the *SoNY Survey*, this Dutchess County restaurant and inn is set on 20 verdant acres and offers top-quality lodgings as well as "imaginative" French-inspired New American fare; there are "beautiful views of the river" from the dining room or any of the six terraces of this "lovely old house", so insiders recommend you "go for the sunsets."

	F	D	S	C
Bistro Twenty-Two [S]	25	23	24	$49

391 Old Post Rd. (east of I-684), Bedford, 914-234-7333

■ "First-rate" Eclectic–New French food is matched by an "elegant modern setting" and "superb service" at this "serene" Bedford "gem" that's popular with a "well-heeled older crowd"; although "pricey", it's "always terrific" and the Sunday prix fixe is a relief to the wallet.

	F	D	S	C
Bois d'Arc [S]	25	20	22	$40

29 W. Market St. (Rte. 9), Red Hook, 845-758-5992
424 Zena Rd. (Sawkill Rd.), Kingston, 845-679-5995

■ And then there were two: "clever chef" Jim Jennings expanded last year, bringing his "unique" East Texas cooking to the west side of the Hudson; fans of the "intimate" Red Hook original ("some of the best food in the Hudson Valley", "excellent service") have high expectations for its sibling that's just outside of Woodstock; a few naysayers insist it's "too contrived", but they're outvoted.

	F	D	S	C
Buffet de la Gare	27	21	23	$50

155 Southside Ave. (Spring St.), Hastings-on-Hudson, 914-478-1671

■ "So French, *so* great" gush admirers of this "charming" family-run favorite serving "exquisite" Classic French fare in a "small", "romantic" room; though "expensive", most believe it's "worth every penny" for an experience that's "comparable to anything NYC has"; some comment that service can be "snooty, but every so often they smile."

	F	D	S	C
Cafe Mezé [S]	23	20	21	$38

20 N. Central Ave. (Hartsdale Ave.), Hartsdale, 914-428-2400

■ Experience shows at this Hartsdale Mediterranean from the Livanos restaurateur family, where their professional touch has created a hot spot with "creatively presented" "imaginative food"; "consistently good service" is another boon, but friends and foes alike pan the "excruciating noise when full."

	F	D	S	C
Cafe Tamayo [S]	25	21	22	$33

89 Partition St. (Main St.), Saugerties, 845-246-9371

■ "Shouldn't all restaurants make you feel this good, well fed and taken care of?" demand fans of this Saugerties New American delivering "one of the best dining experiences in the Valley"; chef-owner James Tamayo's "impeccable", "star-studded" cuisine is matched by a "welcoming" staff, presided over by wife Rickie, and the "pretty" 1864 tavern even provides "flattering lighting"; it's "worth the drive."

Calico Restaurant & Patisserie [S] 25 | 16 | 24 | $31

9 Mill St./Rte. 9 (opp. Beekman Arms), Rhinebeck, 845-876-2749

■ Pastry connoisseurs adore Rhinebeck's "sweet hole-in-the-wall", claiming its "only competition is [Manhattan's] Payard"; most also like the "creative" New American food, although some think "the menu needs a revamp", and with just a few tables, many find it "better for lunch than dinner"; but surveyors offer no qualifiers about the exceptional desserts: it's the "best pastry between Montreal and NYC."

Caterina de Medici 26 | 22 | 24 | $37

Culinary Institute of America, 1946 Campus Dr. (opp. W. Dorsey Ln.), Hyde Park, 845-471-6608

■ It's "like being in Firenze at half the price" rave admirers of this Hyde Park Northern Italian, which they consider "the best value at the CIA"; the student chefs and waiters "do a great job" providing both "wonderful food" and "willing" service (but go "when you have lots of time"); some say it "misses the mark for authenticity", but they are overruled.

Citrus Grille [S] 24 | 20 | 22 | $40

430 E. Saddle River Rd. (bet. Lake St. & Rte. 59), Airmont, 845-352-5533

■ "One of the best in Rockland County", this Californian–New American is showered with compliments for its "imaginative", "artfully prepared" cuisine that includes "innovative seafood", and the "good staff" earns nods too; but its rep draws crowds, making it "noisy on weekends" and "difficult to get a table."

Crabtree's Kittle House [S] 25 | 25 | 24 | $45

Crabtree's Kittle House Inn, 11 Kittle Rd. (Rte. 117), Chappaqua, 914-666-8044

■ "Romantic and elegant", this Northern Westchester colonial inn (circa 1790) is a true "place for celebration", providing a "stately", "soothing" setting for "excellent" New American food that's bolstered by a staff that "makes you feel special" and an "extensive wine list" (some suggest you "stay overnight" so you can freely sample); although "pricey", most agree it's "worth every penny" and the weekend jazz is "a treat."

DePuy Canal House [S] 25 | 25 | 23 | $52

Rte. 213 (Lucas Ave.), High Falls, 845-687-7700

■ For over 30 years, chef-owner John Novi has been wowing "open-minded" foodies with his "marvelous", "very innovative" New American cooking, providing a "total dining experience" in a "charming" "antiques"-laden 1797 stone house with "many fireplaces" (plus overnight accommodations); although the food combos are "too outrageous" for a few, most agree "prices are high, but the result is worth it."

Equus [S] 24 | 28 | 23 | $54

Castle at Tarrytown, 400 Benedict Ave. (Rtes. 9 & 119), Tarrytown, 914-631-3646

◪ "You feel like royalty" at this "dignified" Tarrytown New French in a "lovely old mansion" with beautiful views of a 10-acre landmark estate, and chef Fabrizzo Salerni creates suitably "grand" dishes to match the "special-occasion" setting; but it's all "a bit pretentious" to some, and the tab may rival a king's ransom ("bring two wallets"); N.B. the Castle is a member of the tony Relais & Châteaux hotel group.

Escoffier, The
27 | 26 | 25 | $47

Culinary Institute of America, 1946 Campus Dr. (opp. W. Dorsey Ln.), Hyde Park, 845-471-6608

■ Plan to "call months ahead" to enjoy the "pampering dining experience" offered at this "flagship of the CIA", where "superb" Classic French cuisine is complemented by "fine student service" and "beautiful" surroundings; it's pricey but "outstanding" and definitely "worth the trip", particularly for a "long Saturday lunch."

Freelance Cafe & Wine Bar S ≠
28 | 21 | 24 | $39

506 Piermont Ave. (Ash St.), Piermont, 845-365-3250

■ Setting the "standard for all others", this "little sister to Xaviar's" uses the Piermont kitchen it shares with its tonier sibling to turn out "excellent", "innovative" New American fare; as for hospitality, maitre d' Ned Kelly (brother of highly regarded chef-owner Peter) is simply "the best"; the only drawback is the no-reservation policy and the resulting "wait."

Harralds ≠
26 | 25 | 26 | $61

3760 Rte. 52 (bet. Durrschmidt & Mountain Rds.), Stormville, 845-878-6595

◪ "Expect to be treated royally" at Harrald and Eve Boerger's venerable Dutchess County retreat, a "charming" Tudor cottage where a "sweet staff" serves "magnificent" International food in a "gorgeous" setting; cons call it "pretentious and overpriced", but devotees declare it "worth the trip" as it "can't be beat."

Harvest on Hudson S
22 | 27 | 19 | $41.

1 River St. (opp. Hastings-on-Hudson RR station), Hastings-on-Hudson, 914-478-2800

■ The site for this Hastings-on-Hudson yearling is a "converted oil-company warehouse", and with its "breathtaking" river views and soaring interior, it's a "spectacular" showcase for "interesting", "innovative" Med-style cuisine; those who found the former shared-plate concept "annoying" will welcome the fact that new chef Michael Smith serves only individual portions.

Hunan Village S
24 | 18 | 20 | $27

1828 Central Park Ave. (Slater Ave.), Yonkers, 914-779-2272

■ "Simply the best", this "surprising jewel in central Yonkers" remains No. 1 for Chinese in the *SoNY Survey;* the "creative" menu ensures there's "always something new and intriguing", and a "knowledgeable staff" is on hand to offer guidance; it's "pricey" and can get "crowded", but why quibble?; P.S. the Chinese New Year banquet is "not to be missed."

Il Cenàcolo S
27 | 21 | 24 | $48

228 S. Plank Rd. (Rte. 300), Newburgh, 845-564-4494

■ "What are they doing here?" marvel admirers of this top-rated Newburgh Northern Italian, an outpost of "Manhattan flair and expertise" that's also "like being in Tuscany"; the "creative but traditional" food "never misses", and though a minority detects "attitude", most celebrate the "enthusiastic, professional service" and agree this one's "worth the drive" – "costs a fortune, but we enjoyed every penny."

Inn at Pound Ridge [S] 24 | 26 | 23 | $47

258 Westchester Ave./Rte. 137 (Rte. 172), Pound Ridge, 914-764-5779

■ Starry-eyed surveyors say it's "heaven on earth" at this "classic country inn" in Northern Westchester, where the fireside is a perfect place to "fall in love"; the 19th-century ambiance is matched with "top-notch", French-accented New American cuisine, and the only clouds are the "large catered affairs" that may result in "lackluster service."

Iron Horse Grill 24 | 22 | 23 | $41

20 Wheeler Ave. (Manville Rd.), Pleasantville, 914-741-0717

■ Chef-owner Philip McGrath (ex Equus) is off and running with this Pleasantville New American set in a historic train station, where "wonderful food", including game in season, is coupled with "great service" for "an outstanding experience"; locals would buy tickets if they could – it's "hard to get in" (although outdoor dining expands seating in warm weather).

La Crémaillère [S] 27 | 27 | 26 | $58

46 Bedford-Banksville Rd. (Merritt Pkwy., exit 31), Banksville, 914-234-9647

■ Everything is "*magnifique*" at this "ultimate special-occasion" "jewel" in Northern Westchester that feels like a "hideaway in rural France"; its "bucolic setting" is matched by "beautifully presented food" that's "haute cuisine at its peak", "served with grace and panache" and complemented by a "great wine collection"; despite a few growls about "haughty" staff, most agree it's "pure heaven – but this heaven costs plenty."

La Panetière [S] 28 | 27 | 26 | $59

530 Milton Rd. (Oakland Beach Ave.), Rye, 914-967-8140

■ "Check the real world at the door – it feels like heaven inside" this "sublime" Rye New French that's No. 1 for Popularity in the *SoNY Survey;* raves abound for the "unusual menu", "excellent food", the "beautiful country house" setting and the "outstanding" staff; while critics call it "pretentious" and "overpriced", most maintain it's "a true masterpiece" that's "worth every penny."

Le Canard Enchainé [S] 26 | 22 | 23 | $35

276 Fair St. (bet. John & Main Sts.), Kingston, 845-339-2003

■ "The good things we heard are true" report ecstatic visitors to this Kingston French bistro that's "like a visit to Paris" "without the airfare"; admirers cite the "lovely presentation" of "yummy", "interesting" food, as well as the "beautiful decor and wonderful service", and note that while "dinner is expensive, lunch is reasonable" – "what a find!"

Le Château [S] 25 | 27 | 25 | $54

Rte. 35 (Rte. 123), South Salem, 914-533-6631

◪ It's not quite a castle, but this "great mansion" built by J.P. Morgan in South Salem is a "four-season scenic winner" with views of "woods and grazing deer", along with "attentive service" and "fine dining" on Classic French food; it's "very expensive", so most "save it for a special occasion" (but unless it's yours, "don't go when there's a wedding on").

Lusardi's S   24   20   21 $43
1885 Palmer Ave. (bet. Chatsworth Ave. & Weaver St.), Larchmont, 914-834-5555

■ Larchmont Northern Italian "cousin of the East Side Manhattan eatery of the same name" that's a "favorite nightspot" for legions who rate it a "consistent winner"; a few naysayers judge it "overpriced", and even fans agree it's "noisy" and "bustling", but the "brilliant cooking" and "professional service" make it "hard to get reservations."

Maxime's S   27   25   26 $56
11 Old Tomahawk St. (Rte. 118N), Granite Springs, 914-248-7200

■ "Give it the Maxime-um rating" swoon fans of this ultimate "special-occasion" "oasis" where chef-owner Maxime Ribera's Classic French cuisine is "delightful" and "delicious" "perfection"; the "romantic", "beautiful country setting" in Northern Westchester and the "upper-class treatment" are more reasons ardent admirers swear it's "well worth the steep price", although a few hungry types lament "small portions."

McKinney & Doyle Fine Foods Cafe S   24   19   21 $29
10 Charles Coleman Blvd. (Main St.), Pawling, 845-855-3875

Corner Bakery S   25   18   22 $35
10 Charles Coleman Blvd. (Main St.), Pawling, 845-855-3707

■ Surveyors sing the praises of this "delightful" Pawling cafe and adjacent bakery ("best north of Manhattan"); at breakfast, the bakery's "superb" baked goods can be eaten in the cafe, which later serves "consistently fine", "inventive" New American fare in a "casual, friendly atmosphere"; a few gripe about "too many tables", but legions agree it's still "worth the trip"; P.S. the cafe now has a full bar.

Old Drovers Inn S   25   26   24 $50
Old Rte. 22 (E. Duncan Hill Rd.), Dover Plains, 845-832-9311

☑ "What a hideaway should be" and a "terrific destination for a Sunday drive", this "charming" Relais & Châteaux property in an 18th-century Dover Plains inn features "low-beamed ceilings", candlelit tables, "giant drinks" (consider the "guestrooms if you have more than two") and "exceptional" French–New American food; budget-watchers warn: be prepared to spend "big money."

Purdys Homestead S   –   –   –   E
100 Titicus Rd. (Rtes. 22 & 116), North Salem, 914-277-2301

A charming renovation has created a dining room that is both early American and sleekly contemporary in feel at this Regional American in northern Westchester; similarly, the short seasonal menu has country touches but reflects the cosmopolitan skills of chef-owner Charles Steppe (who honed his skills in some of NY's top restaurants) and his wife, pastry chef Maureen Brown-Steppe; asserting its own personality, the 1775 farmhouse has successfully shaken off the ghost of The Box Tree, its former occupant.

Restaurant X & Bully Boy Bar S   26 | 25 | 25 | $48

117 Rte. 303 (bet. Lake Rd. & Rte. 9W), Congers, 845-268-6555

■ Xaviar's and Freelance Cafe chef-owner Peter Kelly has "another hit" in this New American in Rockland County, with "fabulous", "updated comfort food", "professional yet casual" service and a "scenic", "comfortable" setting "by a duck pond"; P.S. the "large" multiroom space means it's "easier to get into" than its siblings.

Terrapin Restaurant S   ▽ 26 | 18 | 24 | $31

250 Spillway Rd. (Rte. 28A), West Hurley, 845-331-3663

■ "Deep in the sticks" lies this "spectacular" Ulster County New American where chef-owner Josh Kroner wows diners with "perfectly conceived and executed" cooking; his wife Tamara Hunter runs the front of the house and together they've created a place for "country dining par excellence."

Xaviar's S⊅   29 | 26 | 28 | $62

Highlands Country Club, Rte. 9D (Rte. 403), Garrison, 845-424-4228

■ "Heaven would have difficulty topping" this New American in Garrison that's rated No. 1 for Food and Service in the *SoNY Survey;* superlatives abound for the "wonderful" "all-round dining experience", from the prix fixe dinner (Friday and Saturday only) to the "best [buffet] brunch in the USA", all served in a "country-club chic" setting with gentle harp music; in sum, "it doesn't get any better than this."

Xaviar's at Piermont S⊅   29 | 25 | 27 | $60

506 Piermont Ave. (Ash St.), Piermont, 845-359-7007

■ "More intimate than its big sister" (and right on its heels with the No. 2 SoNY ranking for Food and Service), Peter Kelly's "cozy" "romantic treasure" in Rockland County is a "magical place" where "gastronomic feasts" and "gracious service" are the norm, with an "exquisite prix fixe" dinner served Wednesday–Sunday, as well as lunch on Fridays and the acclaimed Sunday brunch; it's "worth the wait for reservations" – "book early and enjoy!"

Zephs' S   26 | 18 | 24 | $41

638 Central Ave. (bet. Nelson Ave. & Water St.), Peekskill, 914-736-2159

■ An "unlikely setting" does not dampen enthusiasm for this "very likeable" Peekskill Eclectic "in an old building" "in a strange neighborhood"; boosters say it deserves "more recognition" for its "experimental but consistently good food" and praise the "warm and accommodating service"; not everyone likes the "almost austere decor", but most say it's "worth seeking out."

St. Louis

TOP 10 FOOD RANKING

Restaurant	Cuisine Type
28 Fio's La Fourchette	Classic French/Swiss
Tony's	N/S Italian
27 Trattoria Marcella	N/S Italian
Dominic's	N/S Italian
Café de France	Classic French
Giovanni's	N/S Italian
Sidney Street Cafe	New American
26 Faust's	New American
Malmaison	Classic French
Zinnia	New American

ADDITIONAL NOTEWORTHY PLACES

Bar Italia Ristorante	Northern Italian
Cafe Balaban	New American
Cafe Mira	New American
Cafe Provençal	French Bistro
Cardwell's at the Plaza	New American
Eddie's	Steakhouse
Harvest	New American
Park Avenue Bistro	New American
Remy's Kitchen & Wine Bar	Mediterranean
Shiitake	Pacific Rim

F	D	S	C

Bar Italia Ristorante 🖪 | 24 | – | 20 | $23 |

13 Maryland Plaza (Euclid Ave.), 314-361-7010

■ "Simple, stylish and fresh", this Central West End trattoria is "as good as a trip to Northern Italy without the jet lag", and its move to larger quarters a while back is deemed "a blessing"; "slow service" is a drag for a few, but most say this "underrated" spot is the "only St. Louis restaurant that could make it in NY."

Cafe Balaban 🖪 | 24 | 21 | 21 | $30 |

405 N. Euclid Ave. (McPherson Ave.), 314-361-8085

☑ "Consistently high standards" keep this "Central West End anchor" an "old reliable" "year in and year out"; though there are complaints that the "tables are too close together" and suggestions that the New American "menu needs updating", the majority deems this "soigné" spot a "rock-solid adult dining experience."

F	D	S	C

Café de France
27	24	25	$42

410 Olive St. (4th St.), 314-231-2204
■ "Uncompromising excellence" is to be found at this "classy" Downtown Classic French "gem" that "runs like a well-oiled machine", thanks to chef-owner Marcel Keraval's "beautifully presented" menu that's "full of surprises" and a "helpful" staff that "isn't all over you"; of course, you should "plan on haute prices" ("whew!"), but it's "worth every penny (and calorie)" when you want "a fancy night out."

Cafe Mira
25	23	22	$36

12 N. Meramec Ave. (Forsyth Blvd.), Clayton, 314-721-7801
◪ "Every dish is a work of art" at this "avant-garde" Clayton New American courtesy of Mike Johnson, "one of the best chefs in town"; his "very trendy tall food" ("nothing you could ever make at home") arrives in a "chic" but "noisy" space populated by a "stylish" crowd who keeps busy "air-kissing" one another; overall, it's "superb – if money is no object."

Cafe Provençal
24	20	22	$27

34 N. Central Ave. (bet. Forsyth Blvd. & Maryland Ave.), Clayton, 314-725-2755 [S]
427 S. Kirkwood Rd. (Clinton Ave.), Kirkwood, 314-822-5440
■ These "delightful" French bistros win uniform raves for their "Parisian feel", "wonderful prix fixe" menu, "solid wine list" and "passionate service", though the newer Kirkwood branch seems to have the edge: it's "easier on the ears" and not "overcrowded" like its Clayton sibling (where you just might need to "bring a shoehorn" to squeeze in); either way, fans call them the "best fine dining value in St. Louis."

Cardwell's at the Plaza [S]
25	23	22	$27

94 Plaza Frontenac (Clayton Rd. & Lindbergh Blvd.), 314-997-8885
■ "After a tough morning at the spa", the ladies who lunch head for this "trendy" New American that's "the best thing to happen to Plaza Frontenac"; it's also just the ticket "after shopping" (Neiman Marcus is next door) or for "business dinners" thanks to its "innovative" menu served in a "relaxing atmosphere"; however, snobs sniff it's "too good for its [mall] location."

Dominic's
27	25	26	$43

5101 Wilson Ave. (Hereford Ave.), 314-771-1632
■ "In a league of its own", this "quintessential" "old-world Italian" where "limos double-park nightly" just might be the "classiest restaurant on the Hill"; "dazzling" cooking and "truly lovely decor" "make you feel special", though a few say that the otherwise impeccable service verges on being "almost too much"; sure, it's costly, yet most "don't mind paying the price" for this exercise in "pure class."

Eddie's
–	–	–	E

40 N. Central Ave. (Maryland Ave.), Clayton, 314-725-1661
Restaurateur Eddie Neill's Clayton steakhouse on the former site of Cafe Provençal offers St. Louis diners remarkable steaks, chops and roasts, along with a high-style wine list with a modest markup and an overall mellow mood complemented by relaxingly calm service.

Faust's [S] 26 | 26 | 24 | $41

Adam's Mark Hotel, 112 N. Fourth St. (Memorial Dr.), 314-342-4690

■ Named for 19th-century St. Louis restaurateur Tony Faust, this "cosmopolitan" New American in the Adam's Mark maintains his high standards with "superb dining", one of the "best wine stewards"and a "beautiful view of the Arch"; "underappreciated by locals" but "adored by travelers", it's just the place for "a long, sensuous meal" and "elegance without ostentation."

Fio's La Fourchette 28 | 26 | 28 | $49

7515 Forsyth Ave. (Jackson Ave.), Clayton, 314-863-6866

■ This "consistently superb" Classic French–Swiss "pearl in Clayton" has garnered "*très* formidable" ratings in the *St. Louis Survey* (voted Most Popular, No. 1 for Food and No. 2 for Service), causing many to sigh it's the closest they'll come to Paris "without TWA's help"; special kudos go to the "heart-safe menu items", the "free seconds" on "any part of the meal" and the "pure romance" of the setting; as for the pricing, it's "well worth the arm and the leg."

Giovanni's 27 | 24 | 25 | $41

5201 Shaw Ave. (Edwards Ave.), 314-772-5958

■ "Great for a special event", this "outstanding" Italian vet in the heart of the Hill offers a "beautiful dining room" and equally "beautiful food"; it might be "high-priced" (so "eat *all* your pasta"), but the enraptured sigh it's worth it for an "always perfect evening" at what some deem the "best all-around restaurant in St. Louis."

Harvest [S] 26 | 24 | 23 | $36

1059 S. Big Bend Blvd. (Clayton Rd.), 314-645-3522

◪ "The menu changes with the season" at this "hip, happening" New American in Richmond Heights, where diners reap the benefits of an "incredible, varied" array of "vertical food", topped off by "heavenly bread pudding"; hairsplitters hedge it "can be too loud" and "a little pretentious", but the majority finds it simply "amazing" or, at least, "never boring"; P.S. "reserve well in advance."

Malmaison [S] 26 | 27 | 25 | $42

St. Albans Rd. (off Hwy. T), St. Albans, 636-458-0131

■ "It's a long drive" to this Classic French in St. Albans, but fans say it's "worth the effort" for an "outstanding dining experience" in the "most romantic place" around (the "best fireplace in St. Louis" helps); Marseilles-born chef Simone Andujar uses herbs grown by the front door in her "superb" wild game dishes, causing devotees to sigh "it doesn't get any better than this."

Park Avenue Bistro – | – | – | E

1917 Park Ave. (Mississippi Ave.), 314-231-7275

Restaurateur Dana Ruben recently opened this seasonal New American bistro in the picturesque Lafayette Square area to rave reviews; much of the credit goes to chef Erick Brown (ex Cardwell's at the Plaza), who performs miracles with crab cakes, horseradish-encrusted salmon and veal dressed in the best lemon vinaigrette in town; classy atmospherics (exposed-brick walls, fresh flowers, a patio) don't hurt either.

Remy's Kitchen & Wine Bar   25 | 22 | 22 | $26
222 S. Bemiston Ave. (Bonhomme Ave.), Clayton, 314-726-5757
■ Lisa Slay is cooking in the kitchen of this "chic" yet laid-back Mediterranean cafe (from restaurateur Tim Mallett) in Clayton, turning out a "creative" "mix-and-match" menu of "small and large plates" backed up by "always interesting wine flights"; it's "understandably packed" and "noisy" – and the fact that it's "open fairly late" keeps night owls alert.

Shiitake   – | – | – | E
7927 Forsyth Blvd. (Central Ave.), Clayton, 314-725-4334
Part of the Del Pietro group of high-style restaurants, this splendid, dinner-only venue is among the latest entries in the burgeoning Clayton restaurant scene; chef Thom Zoog produces a pricey but ingenious Pacific Rim menu from which gingery, lemongrass dining dreams come true.

Sidney Street Cafe   27 | 24 | 25 | $32
2000 Sidney St. (Salena St.), 314-771-5777
■ When you feel like going "gourmet all the way", savor this "unique" South Side New American where "wonderful meals" arrive in "charming" surroundings with "zero attitude" ("if you can get in", that is); the only debate involves its "chalkboard menus" – some "love" them, while others say they should "spring for" printed versions.

Tony's   28 | 26 | 28 | $52
410 Market St. (Broadway), 314-231-7007
◪ "Still the standard for the others to shoot for", this longtime Downtown Italian "landmark" has been voted No. 1 for Service (as well as No. 2 for Food and Popularity) in the *St. Louis Survey*, and you can plan on being "pampered" with "food so luscious you can't describe it"; while a few nitpickers shrug it's "the most overrated", many more feel that "no one else even comes close."

Trattoria Marcella   27 | 18 | 24 | $29
3600 Watson Rd. (Pernod Ave.), 314-352-7706
■ "St. Louis Italian has never been better" than at this South Sider with a "stellar reputation" for food that "looks and tastes different" from the competition (especially the "riveting" lobster risotto); despite "plain" decor and a sometimes "noisy" room, "decent prices" keep it "popular", and although it has "recently expanded", it's "still hard to get in" – so "reserve ahead."

Zinnia 🅂   26 | 21 | 24 | $30
7491 Big Bend Blvd. (Shrewsbury Ave.), Webster Groves, 314-962-0572
■ "Cozy" Webster Groves New American that "continues to outperform itself" with "fresh ideas" on the menu matched by "fresh flowers on every table"; "don't let the purple building throw you off" (or "the fact that it used to be a gas station") – this is "unpretentious elegance", where everything's "well executed" and "very imaginative."

Tampa Bay/Sarasota

TOP 10 FOOD RANKING

	Restaurant	Cuisine Type
28	Mise en Place	New American
	Beach Bistro	New American/Med.
27	Bern's Steak House	Steakhouse
	Blue Heron	Eclectic
	Euphemia Haye	Eclectic
	Bijou Café	Continental/New American
	Michael's on East	New American
26	Ophelia's	Eclectic
	Morel	Eclectic/New American
	Armani's	Northern Italian

ADDITIONAL NOTEWORTHY PLACES

Bonefish Grill	Trad. American/Seafood
Café L'Europe	Continental
Caffe Paradiso	Northern Italian
Lafite	Continental/Reg. American
Maritana Grille	Floribbean
Oystercatchers	Seafood
Ritz Carlton	Classic French
Salt Rock Grill	Steakhouse/Seafood
SideBern's	Asian/Mediterranean
Zoria	Eclectic

	F	D	S	C
Armani's	26	28	27	$46

Hyatt Regency Westshore, 6200 Courtney Campbell Causeway (Hwy. 60), Tampa, 813-874-1234

■ "Just the place to wear a little black dress", this "elegant" Northern Italian in Tampa's Hyatt Regency Westshore has it all: "terrific food", "classy atmosphere", "wonderful service" and "views to the nth degree"; but "don't forget your wallet", as this "premier dining experience" comes at a steep price – though the consensus is it's "worth it" for a "top-of-the-line" evening at one of the Gulf Coast's finest.

	F	D	S	C
Beach Bistro [S]	28	23	26	$41

6600 Gulf Dr. (66th St.), Holmes Beach, 941-778-6444

■ Foodies from Anna Maria and beyond can't resist this "intimate" New American–Mediterranean, a "restaurant with charisma" that offers "outstanding service", "fabulous" sunset views and "always remarkable" fare; true, it's "pricey" and "limited seating" might make it "too crowded", but the majority feels it's "worth it" to enjoy one of the area's "best overall", a place that "would make it in Paris or NY."

Bern's Steak House 🖫
27 | 22 | 27 | $42

*1208 S. Howard Ave. (bet. Marjorie & Watrous Sts.), Tampa,
813-251-2421*

■ Since 1956, this "national treasure for beef" in Tampa's Hyde Park has been gathering accolades for its "famous, fabulous" steaks and the "best wine list in the world"; while not everyone likes its "bordello-like", "red-flocked wallpaper" decor, most give all-around high marks to this "dining event" and recommend you "tour the kitchen and wine cellar, then feast in the dessert room."

Bijou Café
27 | 23 | 24 | $34

1287 First St. (Pineapple St.), Sarasota, 941-366-8111

■ This "elegant little" Theater District place is Sarasota's "most sophisticated" cafe despite its unlikely location in a former "1930s service station"; "they work hard at" their "inventive" Continental–New American menu, serving "perfect food" that's enhanced by "excellent" wines and "gentle service"; though "jammed on opera nights", it manages a "lovely", "laid-back" atmosphere.

Blue Heron, The 🖫
27 | 22 | 24 | $33

*Shoppes at Clover Pl., 3285 Tampa Rd. (bet. Lake St. George & US 19),
Palm Harbor, 727-789-5176*

■ "A rare combination of food and sauces" distinguishes the Eclectic mix served by this posh Palm Harbor veteran, whose post-*Survey* renovation is not reflected in its already respectable decor score; devotees adore the "high-quality" cuisine so fervently that they beg "please open for lunch", but for now it's dinner only.

Bonefish Grill 🖫
– | – | – | M

5901 Fourth St. N. (59th Ave.), St. Petersburg, 727-521-3434

Currently the darling of hip St. Pete piscatorians is this casual traditional American seafooder turning out creative eats amid chic, cream- colored environs, complete with an open kitchen and a sexy bar; while its reasonable prices make for great values, the rub is its no-reservation policy, which means there's often a wait.

Café L'Europe 🖫
26 | 25 | 24 | $37

431 St. Armands Circle (Hwy. 41), Sarasota, 941-388-4415

■ The "grande dame of Sarasota", a Continental "fixture on St. Armands Circle", is more than a quarter-century old and is "still tops", a "model dining spot for food, wines, decor and service"; this "haven" can seem "a bit fussy" and "expensive" (some call lunch "a better value"), but most think it's "worth it" for one of the "most romantic" experiences in town.

Caffe Paradiso
– | – | – | M

*4205 S. MacDill Ave. (bet. Knights & Wallcraft Aves.), Tampa,
813-835-6622*

An intimate hideaway in South Tampa, this dinner-only Northern Italian is the brainchild of Paolo Tini, son of restaurateur Cesare Tini; partisans praise exotic offerings like the salmon-stuffed ravioli and say the more traditional dishes are just as heavenly.

Euphemia Haye S
27 | 23 | 23 | $41

5540 Gulf of Mexico Dr. (Gulf-to-Bay Rd.), Longboat Key, 941-383-3633

■ It's "hard to beat" this "classy" Longboat Key Eclectic for "world-class dining" in a "romantic" setting; it can be "cramped downstairs" ("hope you like your neighbors"), but claustrophobes can opt for the upstairs Haye Loft piano bar, where a "light menu" or a "wonderful choice of desserts" awaits; up or down, there's a "wine list that touches all bases", as well as "attentive service."

Lafite
– | – | – | VE

Registry Resort, 475 Seagate Dr. (Vanderbilt Beach Rd.), Naples, 941-597-3232

Housed in one of the tonier properties in the swank resort town of Naples, this Continental-Regional American resplendent with crystal chandeliers and beveled mirrors is the embodiment of elegance; its sumptuous cuisine is simply excellent and its service the utmost in professionalism, but its break-the-bank prices mean for most it's best as a special-occasion spot.

Maritana Grille S
▽ 27 | 28 | 25 | $47

Don CeSar Beach Resort, 3400 Gulf Blvd. (Pinellas Bayway),
St. Petersburg Beach, 727-360-1882

■ Experience "nirvana" at this Floribbean gem, the signature dining room of St. Pete's historic Don CeSar Resort, where beachside panoramas from the terrace and indoor saltwater aquariums make it one of the most striking rooms on the Gulf Coast; the "fabulous, creative" fare, prepared over a pecan and cherrywood grill, gives the view a run for its money.

Michael's on East
27 | 26 | 25 | $40

Midtown Plaza, 1212 East Ave. S. (bet. Bahia Vista & Prospect Sts.),
Sarasota, 941-366-0007

■ Again voted the Gulf Coast's Most Popular restaurant, this "posh" New American was "redesigned" and its "drop-dead gorgeous" look has "greatly improved the noise level"; the "superb", "up-to-date" menu attracts a "very glitzy crowd" in search of "a special night on the town" and though it can be "a little pricey", most say it's "well worth it" to savor Sarasota's "brightest star."

Mise en Place S
28 | 24 | 24 | $35

442 W. Kennedy Blvd. (Grand Central St.), Tampa, 813-254-5373

■ "Incredibly inventive cuisine" at "fair prices" attracts gourmands to this Downtown New American, rated No. 1 for Food on the Gulf Coast; its "state-of-the-art combinations", "creative presentation" and "great wine selection" make this "as good as it gets in Tampa."

Morel
26 | 20 | 24 | $33

3809 S. Tuttle Ave. (north of Bee Ridge Rd.), Sarasota, 941-927-8716

■ This "tiny" Sarasota Eclectic–New American thrills fans with its "memorable" cuisine and "superb preparation and presentation" ("smooth service" doesn't hurt either); though in an "unlikely location for such a fine restaurant" – a "tacky storefront" "in a strip mall" – this "lovely little bistro" is always "pleasant" and "friendly"; dinner only.

Ophelia's S
26 | 25 | 24 | $35

9105 Midnight Pass Rd. (south of Turtle Beach), Sarasota, 941-349-2212
■ "Sit outside if you can" at this "pretty spot" on Siesta Key and enjoy its "romantic atmosphere" and "views galore", plus an "exciting" Eclectic menu "presented in an appealing way" with "different choices" and "wonderful desserts"; it can get "pricey", but for "elegantly served, inspired cuisine", the majority agrees that this "A-1" place is "worth it."

Oystercatchers S
26 | 26 | 25 | $35

Hyatt Regency Westshore, 6200 Courtney Campbell Causeway (Hwy. 60), Tampa, 813-281-9116
■ "A beautiful water view" of Old Tampa Bay and "very good" seafood that some rate "best in the area" await at this Hyatt Regency Westshore fish palace where the open kitchen is proudly on display; a "great brunch" and one of the "best breakfast buffets" around are more reasons why fans dub this "special-occasion" place simply "wonderful."

Ritz-Carlton Dining Room S
– | – | – | VE

Ritz-Carlton Naples, 280 Vanderbilt Beach Rd. (bet. Gulfshore Dr. & US 41), Naples, 941-598-6644
In the best tradition of the Ritz-Carlton, this beautifully appointed hotel dining room provides comfortable opulence with its fine Classic French cuisine (the eight-course blind tasting menu is a popular choice), pampering service and wine selection of nearly 700 labels; meals here are consumed in tempo with the mellow tones of a live jazz duo.

Salt Rock Grill S
▽ 26 | 28 | 23 | $33

19325 Gulf Blvd. (¼ mi. north of Park Blvd.), Indian Shores, 727-593-7625
■ Truly a "place to be seen", this "superb" surf 'n' turfer offers a "diverse", "interesting" menu from its open kitchen, a "great wine list" and stunning decor (including a cigar bar) that all merge to form the quintessential "yuppie hangout"; it's "good and noisy", but what else would you expect from one of Tampa Bay's most "popular" spots?

SideBern's S
– | – | – | M

2208 W. Morrison Ave. (S. Howard Ave.), Tampa, 813-258-2233
This SoHo offspring of Bern's Steak House offers a fusion menu that draws inspiration from both Asia and the Mediterranean, with the former represented by some stellar dim sum; though the wine list is not as encyclopedic as its parent's, the pared-down choices still impress, and its airy modern interior includes an 18-seat communal table that's a good spot to make new friends.

Zoria S
– | – | – | E

1934 Hillview St. (Tamiami Trail), Sarasota, 941-955-4457
Imaginative preparation is the order of the day at this Sarasota Eclectic helmed by two chefs formerly with Ophelia's; ignore the poor acoustics and concentrate instead on scrumptious goodies like the savory duck breast or flourless chocolate tart.

Tucson

TOP 10 FOOD RANKING

Restaurant	Cuisine Type
28 Ventana Room	New American
27 Dish	Eclectic
Janos	Southwestern/Classic French
25 Cafe Poca Cosa	Mexican
Le Rendez-Vous	Classic French
Tack Room	Regional American
Wildflower	New American
Gold Room	Southwestern/Continental
24 Gavi	N/S Italian
¡Fuego!	Southwestern

ADDITIONAL NOTEWORTHY PLACES

Anthony's/Catalinas	Continental
Arizona Inn	Continental
Cafe Terra Cotta	Southwestern
Daniel's	Northern Italian
J-Bar	Mexican/Caribbean
Kingfisher	New American/Seafood
Le Bistro	French Bistro
McMahon's	Steakhouse
Mi Nidito	Mexican
Pastiche Modern Eatery	New American

F	D	S	C

Anthony's in the Catalinas 🅂

22	26	23	$41

6440 N. Campbell Ave. (E. Skyline Dr.), 520-299-1771
◪ Nestled in the Catalina foothills, this "special-occasion" spot receives a plethora of plaudits for its "million-dollar" patio and dining room views of the city lights and one of the "best wine lists in the Southwest" (over 1,400 choices); but while pros praise the "consistently good" Continental food, others opine that it's "dull."

Arizona Inn 🅂

22	25	24	$32

Arizona Inn, 2200 E. Elm St. (bet. N. Campbell Ave. & N. Tucson Blvd.), 520-325-1541
◼ Set in a "classic" hotel where "finger bowls" and "beautiful gardens" create the kind of "lovely refined atmosphere" that captures "old Tucson", this "sedate" Continental attracts a clientele of "blue-blooded" seniors and celebrities; the "conservative" menu may not excite cutting-edge diners, but the "lovely" ambiance "reeks of class."

Cafe Poca Cosa 25 | 22 | 22 | $21

Clarion Santa Rita Hotel, 88 E. Broadway Blvd. (S. Scott Ave.), 520-622-6400

■ "Cheerful", "bustling" Downtown Tucson Mexican where the inventive menu changes twice a day and the words "unique" and "creative" apply to both the brightly colored "trendy decor", which includes Oaxacan folk art masks, and the "huge portions" of "glorious" "gourmet" cooking ("chicken mole so good you'll weep").

Cafe Terra Cotta [S] 24 | 22 | 22 | $27

St. Philip's Plaza, 4310 N. Campbell Ave. (E. River Rd.), 520-577-8100

◪ While it's seen the birth of many imitators, this "polished", earth-toned Tucson favorite has "maintained its edge after all these years" and continues to be a "wonderful place to bring guests" for "fun selections" of "original Southwestern" cuisine, good wines by the glass, a "delightful patio" and popular outdoor jazz; N.B. while it will retain its current phone number, the restaurant is scheduled to move three miles away, to 3500 E. Sunrise Drive, early next year.

Daniel's Restaurant & Trattoria [S] 23 | 24 | 23 | $36

St. Philip's Plaza, 4340 N. Campbell Ave. (E. River Rd.), 520-742-3200

◪ "Stately", beige-toned decor, a "formal" but "restful" ambiance, "delicious" cuisine ("marvelous Caesar salad prepared tableside") and a "good wine list" make this bi-level Northern Italian an "upscale" choice for "gracious", "special-occasion" dining; though some find it "pretentious" and "overrated", more say that it's "worth a return", especially on an "expense account."

Dish, The 27 | 22 | 26 | $34

3200 E. Speedway Blvd. (N. Country Club Rd.), 520-326-1714

■ So "cozy" "it feels like coming home", this "jewel box" "hidden" behind Rum Runner Wine & Cheese is lauded as a "sparkling experience" because of its "first-class" Eclectic food, "extensive wine list" (30 by the glass) and "pampering" service; N.B. with only 12 tables, reservations are recommended.

¡Fuego! Restaurant, Bar & Grill [S] 24 | 20 | 22 | $32

Santa Fe Sq., 6958 E. Tanque Verde Rd. (N. Sabino Canyon Rd.), 520-886-1745

■ Wild game such as Rocky Mountain elk and Alaskan caribou are some of the "daring" choices on the "creative" menu of this Tucson Southwestern, which also serves "wonderful", tamer meat and seafood dishes and has a warm, comfortable setting highlighted by a large hearth; oenophiles will want to take advantage of the award-winning, California-oriented wine list.

Gavi 24 | 16 | 20 | $23

Foothills Mall, 7401 N. La Cholla Blvd. (W. Ina Rd.), 520-219-9200 [S]
6960 E. Sunrise Dr. (N. Kolb Rd.), 520-615-1900
7865 E. Broadway Blvd. (N. Pantano Rd.), 520-290-8380

■ Go "early" or expect a "long wait" for a table at these "lively", "casual" "family-run" Italians, which serve "big portions" of "cheap", "phenomenal" dishes ("pasta par excellance") in "lively" dining rooms, some of which are soccer themed; signature dishes include spicy calamari and satisfying tiramisu.

Gold Room 🅂   25 | 26 | 24 | $40

*Westward Look Resort, 245 E. Ina Rd. (bet. N. 1st Ave. & N. Oracle Rd.),
520-297-1151*

■ "Beautiful views" of Downtown Tucson from a "lovely" patio
and brightly colored dining room attract aesthetes to this "elegant"
resort dining venue where the menu is divided between SW dishes
using herbs from the chef's garden and Continental entries such
as filet mignon; P.S. try to make it for the "great Sunday brunch",
which features a jazz trio.

Janos   27 | 25 | 25 | $48

*Westin La Paloma, 3770 E. Sunrise Dr. (bet. N. Campbell Ave. &
N. Swan Rd.), 520-615-6100*

◪ Now firmly established in its "marvelous setting", "great chef"
Janos Wilder's "spectacular" space in the foothills enhances his
"imaginative SW–Classic French food" with an "outstanding view",
as well as with "excellent wines" and "solicitous" service; it's an
"original" that pleases the palate as much as it "hits the wallet",
and if nostalgists "miss the old location", Wilder's disciples declare
he "sets the standard" no matter where he sets up shop.

J-Bar   ▽ 23 | 23 | 23 | $27

*Westin La Paloma, 3770 E. Sunrise Dr. (bet. N. Campbell Ave. &
N. Swan Rd.), 520-615-6100*

■ Bright and tourist-friendly, Janos Wilder's newest operation
(right next to Janos) features Mexican specialties – sometimes
spiced with a Caribbean accent – that come off as a "creative
take on old friends"; noting that it shares a patio overlooking the
city lights with its tony neighbor, wallet-watchers ask "how can
you beat Janos at half the price?"

Kingfisher ●🅂   22 | 17 | 21 | $30

2564 E. Grant Rd. (N. Tucson Blvd.), 520-323-7739

◪ "Loved it" even though the "decor could be updated" – so says
the conflicted clientele of this New American fish house, known
for "super seafood" and freshly shucked "oysters to die for" served
in a "barnlike room"; the "lively atmosphere" and "thoughtful wine
list" make it a popular "late-night spot" among "singles" and
"Generation Xers" who find the "weird" digs "cool" and "retro hip."

Le Bistro 🅂   23 | 20 | 22 | $32

2574 N. Campbell Ave. (bet. E. Glenn St. & E. Grant Rd.), 520-327-3086

■ Laurent Reux is a "wonderful" "chef-owner who cares", and
the proof is in the "dependable, excellent" "French food" and
"sumptuous desserts" that make this "cozy" bistro an area "fave";
the menu takes a seafaring slant ("best steamed mussels in town"),
and insiders intimate it's especially "great for lunch."

Le Rendez-Vous 🅂   25 | 21 | 22 | $37

3844 E. Ft. Lowell Rd. (N. Alvernon Way), 520-323-7373

■ It's "Paris in the desert" at this Classic Gallic "gem", home to
the "best Dover sole in the state", a *magnifique* Grand Marnier
soufflé and other "traditional" fare served in an atmosphere "thick"
with "romantic charm"; if the sauces seem a bit "rich", that's one
measure of their "real French flavor"; N.B. the five-course prix
fixe menu is priced at $70 for two.

McMahon's S
24 | 26 | 22 | $48

2959 N. Swan Rd. (bet. E. Ft. Lowell Rd. & E. Glenn St.), 520-327-2333

✍ Surveyors are split on whether this "elegant" steakhouse is "just like dining in New York" or "much ado about nothing", but carnivores concur the "excellent" beef "does not disappoint"; faced with a widespread observation that it's "way overpriced", regulars advise "take friends and split orders" or get yourself an "expense account."

Mi Nidito S
24 | 16 | 19 | $16

1813 S. Fourth Ave. (E. 29th St.), 520-622-5081

■ "President Clinton ate here", giving official credence to this "authentic", "homey" cantina's standing as "possibly the best Sonoran in town"; no doubt POTUS skipped the "long wait", but local VIPs cheerfully "stand in line" for "a great meal" amid "Mexican ambiance to the max."

Pastiche Modern Eatery ●S
22 | 21 | 23 | $28

3025 N. Campbell Ave. (E. Ft. Lowell Rd.), 520-325-3333

✍ "Inventive" New American bistro that's "on the way up", thanks to a menu of "unusual combinations" that are often "quite good" (the "option of half-portion" entrees allows for "mixing and matching"); it's known for its "pleasant", "well-trained" staff and "great atmosphere" emanating from a room embellished with plenty of "local art and color."

Tack Room S
25 | 25 | 26 | $49

7300 E. Vactor Ranch Trail (E. Tanque Verde Rd.), 520-722-2800

✍ A "longtime staple" for "top-notch food with a Western accent", this revered Regional American makes patrons "feel important" with its "formal" setting, "superb service" and "excellent food and wine"; modernists dismiss the "stuffy" style as "out of date", but the many who reckon it one of "Arizona's finest" "applaud the resistance to change"; N.B. dinner only.

Ventana Room S
28 | 28 | 28 | $47

Loews Ventana Canyon Resort, 7000 N. Resort Dr. (N. Kolb Rd.), 520-299-2020

■ Tucson's Most Popular restaurant is also No. 1 in the state for Food and Service and No. 2 for Decor, and its champions crown it "best in the West" for its "spectacular views" and "supreme", "beautifully presented" New American fare; defying expectations for a "hotel setting", it complements its "lovely" atmosphere with "impeccable service" (and a harpist) to make for a "special occasion" "every time"; N.B. dinner only.

Wildflower S
25 | 21 | 22 | $29

Casas Adobes, 7037 N. Oracle Rd. (W. Ina Rd.), 520-219-4230

✍ Even advocates admit this "busy" "NY bistro–style" source of "adventurous" New American cuisine is "noisy", but they put up with "poor acoustics" to enjoy a "good wine list" and "trendy" food that's "always tasty" and "sometimes great"; if a few contrarians contend the performance is "inconsistent", the majority simply sigh "oh, that warm lobster salad!"

Washington, DC

TOP 20 FOOD RANKING

Restaurant	Cuisine Type
29 Inn at Little Washington	New American
28 Makoto	Japanese
27 Kinkead's	New American
Citronelle	New French
Gerard's Place	New French
Obelisk	Northern Italian
L'Auberge Chez François	Classic French
Melrose	New American
L'Auberge Provencale	Classic French
Marcel's*	Classic French/Belgian
26 Galileo/Il Laboratorio	N/S Italian
Vidalia	New American
Prime Rib	Steakhouse
Prince Michel	Classic French
1789	New/Trad. American
Seasons	New American
Nora	New American
25 Kaz Sushi Bistro	Japanese
Morton's of Chicago	Steakhouse
Rabieng	Thai

ADDITIONAL NOTEWORTHY PLACES

Bis	French Bistro
Black's Bar & Kitchen	Seafood
Bombay Club	Indian
Bread Line	Bakery
Butterfield 9	New American
Carlyle Grand Cafe	New American
DC Coast	New American
Duangrat's	Thai
Equinox	New American
Etrusco	N/S Italian
Five Guys	Hamburgers
Georgia Brown's	Southern/Soul Food
Jaleo	Spanish
Johnny's Half Shell	Seafood
Maloney & Porcelli	Steakhouse
Old Ebbitt Grill	Traditional American
Pizzeria Paradiso	Pizza
Red Sage	Southwestern
Taberna del Alabardero	Spanish
Timothy Dean	New American

* Tied with the restaurant listed directly above it.

F | D | S | C

Bis S
25 | 24 | 22 | $44

Hotel George, 15 E St., NW (1st St.), 202-661-2700
■ "Political electricity" sparks this "stunning" French bistro, a strong "vote-getter on Capitol Hill" whose "superb" American-influenced Gallic classics (like escargot "bursting with flavor"), "chic bar" and "seductive lighting" have made it a "trendy", "star-watching" destination; the bottom line: "this one's a real comer."

Black's Bar & Kitchen S
22 | 17 | 19 | $35

7750 Woodmont Ave. (bet. Cheltenham Dr. & Old Georgetown Rd.), Bethesda, MD, 301-652-6278
☑ Jeff and Barbara Black "do it again" at this "energetic" Bethesda newcomer with "innovative" Gulf Coast–influenced American seafood dishes (especially "ethereal" fish), an "upbeat" oyster bar, a nicely appointed room and some of the most desirable patio and deck seating around; but as might be expected of an 'in' place, it's usually "crowded."

Bombay Club S
25 | 26 | 25 | $38

815 Connecticut Ave., NW (bet. H & I Sts.), 202-659-3727
■ "You don't need a sari to be treated like a rani" by the truly "impeccable" staff at this "sophisticated Indian" near the White House, a "quiet", "civilized" "power lunch" haunt with "well-spaced tables" and a "British colonial" club feel that make for an "elegant" backdrop for the "wonderful" cuisine (the tandoori salmon is terrific).

Bread Line
21 | 12 | 14 | $12

1751 Pennsylvania Ave., NW (bet. 17th & 18th Sts.), 202-822-8900
■ Mark Furstenberg is a "perfectionist" who brings "four-star talent" to the "$10 lunch" trade, and his "astronomically good" breads and sandwiches have "revolutionized the White House–area lunch scene"; his bakery is "a bit frenzied" and "minimalist", but the "long lines are testimony" to DC's "appreciation of quality."

Butterfield 9
– | – | – | E

600 14th St., NW (F St.), 202-289-8810
Calling power players, theatergoers and trendsetters, this svelte new Downtown sophisticate (carved out of the defunct Garfinkel's department store) inspired by the classic flick *The Thin Man* is run by real pros (notably restaurateur Umbi Singh) who showcase what's billed as New American cuisine with a classic twist (think lamb chops with figs and tapenade); already, cell phones all over town have been working overtime trying to snag one of DC's hottest reservations.

Carlyle Grand Cafe S
24 | 21 | 21 | $29

4000 S. 28th St. (Quincy St.), Shirlington, VA, 703-931-0777
■ This "classy" New American surely "put Shirlington on the culinary map" thanks to its "consistently" "excellent" seasonal menu, "beautiful" surroundings and "affordable" tabs; the service is "fast paced", but it draws such big crowds that there are often "long waits", so call ahead to get on the waiting list.

Citronelle

27 | 25 | 25 | $61

(aka Michel Richard's Citronelle)

Latham Hotel, 3000 M St., NW (30th St.), 202-625-2150

■ "Michel stays – we win"; chef-owner Michel Richard's full-time dedication to his Georgetown "splurge" destination ensures patrons that this is "everything a restaurant should be"; indulge in "exceptional", "cutting-edge" New French cuisine (ranked tops in DC) that's based on "classical" techniques and accompanied by a "superb wine list"; the "elegant yet understated" approach comes off as "cool" to some, though not to those dining stoveside at the chef's table in the spectacular glass-walled kitchen.

DC Coast

25 | 24 | 23 | $44

1401 K St., NW (14th St.), 202-216-5988

■ The "hip Downtown place" for "A-list" "young pros", this "stylish" New American makes "sophisticated dining" fun with "wonderful" seafood dishes, "great energy", "stargazing potential" and a "soaring" space with striking sight lines; it's also one of DC's toughest reservations, but be forewarned that if you don't nab a table on the "quieter" balcony, the "only way to have a conversation will be over your cell phone."

Duangrat's 🖫

25 | 21 | 22 | $27

5878 Leesburg Pike (Glen Forest Rd.), Falls Church, VA, 703-820-5775

■ This dressed-up Thai featuring "elegant" costumed waitresses and "soothing" "pastel"-painted rooms offers "terrific, authentic" regional dishes, drawing crowds to its Northern Virginia locale; the cognoscenti advise "forget the pad Thai and explore" the rest of the menu (notably the three-flavored fried flounder) or try the "interesting specials"; N.B. on most weekends, there's classical dancing upstairs.

Equinox

24 | 19 | 22 | $45

818 Connecticut Ave., NW (I St.), 202-331-8118

☑ "Rising star" chef-owner Todd Gray is in the kitchen at this Farragut Square New American – a most "welcome addition" to the neighborhood – creating "exciting" but "unpretentious" seasonal dishes, while his wife, Ellen, works the front of the house and attends to "Washington's power" elite.

Etrusco

– | – | – | E

1606 20th St., NW (bet. Q & R Sts.), 202-667-0047

Chef Francesco Ricchi "is back in DC where he belongs" at this soothing Dupont Circle Italian newcomer whose "great room" (a barrel-vaulted atrium) beautifully complements his personalized take on the cuisine of the red, white and green; early reports suggest that "this could be a favorite", so keep an eye on it.

Five Guys 🖫⇗

25 | 9 | 17 | $8

4626 King St. (Beauregard St.), Alexandria, VA, 703-671-1606
107 N. Fayette St. (King St.), Alexandria, VA, 703-549-7991
6541 Backlick Rd. (Old Kingmill Rd.), Springfield, VA, 703-913-1337

■ "Incredible" "big bad burgers" "stacked high with fixin's" and teamed with "fantastic" fresh-cut Cajun fries are why these Northern Virginia "kids-and-guys" patty places win accreditation as the *DC Survey*'s top Bang for the Buck; sure, the grease may "drip off your elbows" and it's counter service only, but these eats are actually "worth a drive around the Beltway in rush hour."

Galileo 🖪   26   24   24 $57
1110 21st St., NW (bet. L & M Sts.), 202-293-7191
Il Laboratorio
1110 21st St., NW (bet. L & M Sts.), 202-293-7191
■ "Elegant", if "a little stuffy", Roberto Donna's primo "power" destination has long been considered the "best of the best for that important lunch or dinner" Downtown, thanks to "outstanding" Italian cuisine and "top-notch" service; he's earning even more applause at hot, hot Laboratorio (his "spectacular" showcase restaurant within Galileo) where several nights a week he crafts a tasting menu "extravaganza", an "out-of-this-world" experience.

Georgia Brown's 🖪   23   23   21 $35
950 15th St., NW (bet. I & K Sts.), 202-393-4499
■ "Stunning" and "sophisticated", this Downtown Southerner entices "Washington insiders" and "celebrities" with its "y'all-come"-by hospitality; even if its "delectable" Soul Food "clogs some arteries", the staff's "energy" and professionalism "warm" all hearts; P.S. "loosen your belt" in advance and check out the "great jazz brunch."

Gerard's Place   27   23   25 $59
915 15th St., NW (bet. I & K Sts.), 202-737-4445
■ "Simple elegance" distinguishes this Downtown knockout where eponymous chef Gerard Pangaud masterminds a "brilliant" New French menu; his "gourmet" innovations are proffered by a highly "knowledgeable" staff in a "quiet", "intimate" environment that's ideal for power meals and romantic rendezvous alike; of course it's "pricey", but it's "outstanding in every regard" and "well worth the splurge"; P.S. on "Monday nights you can bring your own bottle" of wine and there's "no corkage" fee.

Inn at Little Washington 🖪   29   29   29 $90
Main & Middle Sts., Washington, VA, 540-675-3800
■ "In a class of its own" and once again the *DC Survey*'s No. 1 restaurant for Food, Decor and Service, this "national treasure" in the Virginia countryside epitomizes a "sybaritic dining experience" with "exquisite" New American cuisine that's the "gastronomic equivalent of sex"; the "extravagant" "gold mine of an interior" beautifully enhances a special dinner, as does the "phenomenal" staff; given its high visibility, it's a tribute to owners Patrick O'Connell and Reinhardt Lynch that so many "salute" this inn as an "absolutely" "unforgettable" destination.

Jaleo 🖪   23   20   19 $28
480 Seventh St., NW (E St.), 202-628-7949
■ The "food and atmosphere pulse with excitement" at this Penn Quarter Spanish "scene" where the "sangria's a must", as are the "scrumptious" tapas; though the limited-reservation policy and "waits" at prime times are drawbacks, the majority thinks that this is a seriously "fun" "place to gather with friends"; P.S. it tastes even more "like Spain" now that chef-owner Jose Andres is spending most of his time here.

Johnny's Half Shell 24 | 18 | 21 | $32

2002 P St., NW (bet. 20th & 21st Sts.), 202-296-2021

■ A "rising star" in Dupont Circle, this "hip" but "completely unpretentious" bistro is creating quite a buzz with its "sparkling" fresh, "creatively" prepared seafood, matched by a "first-rate" wine list; but be warned that it doesn't take reservations and it's "too small" to squeeze in all comers, so "get there early" or try to snag a seat at the white marble bar.

Kaz Sushi Bistro 25 | 20 | 21 | $32

1915 I St., NW (bet. 18th & 20th Sts.), 202-530-5500

■ Chef-owner Kaz Okochi delights the "eye and the palate" with "fresh, creative appetizers", "terrific, imaginative" raw fish creations ("waiter, there's a mango in my sushi") and delightful desserts (the green tea tiramisu is "to die for") at this "minimalist" Japanese near the World Bank; it pulls in a "hip, young crowd" and major "foodies" and chefs who overlook the occasionally "slow" service as they anticipate the "exciting choices."

Kinkead's [S] 27 | 24 | 25 | $49

Red Lion Row, 2000 Pennsylvania Ave., NW (I St., bet. 20th & 21st Sts.), 202-296-7700

■ Bob Kinkead's "very original" seafood-oriented New American cooking has made this power-central destination the *DC Survey*'s Most Popular restaurant and one of the toughest reservations in town; its "no-kinks" perfectionism makes it a "special-occasion" site that "instantly impresses" with "stylish" brass-and-cherrywood surroundings, a "knowledgeable" (if "arrogant") staff and "superb fish dishes" (ranked among "the best" in DC); the bottom line: this is "a treat" "not to be missed."

L'Auberge Chez François [S] 27 | 27 | 27 | $55

332 Springvale Rd. (2 mi. north of Georgetown Pike), Great Falls, VA, 703-759-3800

■ "Who doesn't love this woodsy outpost of Alsatian cooking" in Great Falls, with its "adorable Provençal decor, warm and unstuffy" ambiance and utterly "romantic" garden?; the Haeringer family is to be commended for its "elegant restraint in leaving well enough alone" by continuing to offer a "glorious" five-course prix fixe Classic French menu (top-ranked in the *DC Survey*) that may be the "best fine dining value" around; in sum, it's an "unparalleled experience" that's definitely "worth the drive."

L'Auberge Provencale [S] 27 | 26 | 26 | $63

13630 Lord Fairfax Hwy. (Rte. 340), White Post, VA, 540-837-1375

■ Chef-owner Alain Borel and his wife, Celeste, are "delightful" hosts, and their antiques-filled pre–Revolutionary War manor house in the Virginia Hunt Country is a "hopelessly romantic" destination for Classic French dining; whether you linger over an "absolutely fabulous" five-course prix fixe dinner in the "beautiful" garden room or out on the patio, it promises to be "lovely all the way."

Makoto ▣

28 | 23 | 26 | $49

4822 MacArthur Blvd., NW (Reservoir Rd.), 202-298-6866

■ "Wear respectable socks" when taking "visiting dignitaries" and businesspeople to this top-rated, painfully "authentic" Japanese in the Palisades, where patrons sit shoeless in a "tiny", "exquisitely simple" "traditional" dining room as a "charming" staff serves "outstanding", "dramatically presented" tidbits that amount to "food as art"; P.S. if "little cubes at little tables" aren't your thing, there's also a little "gem" of a sushi bar.

Maloney & Porcelli ●▣

∇ 23 | 22 | 23 | $45

601 Pennsylvania Ave. (Indiana Ave.), 202-478-8300

■ "Be ready to really eat" when you arrive at this Penn Quarter beef house, a NYC transplant boasting huge steaks, "excellent" duck and a legendary crackling pork shank; its "lively", illuminated onyx bar, lovely blond woods, open kitchen and patio arouse "great expectations", but be certain to bring the corporate card, as it's "maybe a little rich for the DC crowd."

Marcel's

27 | 24 | 24 | $58

2401 Pennsylvania Ave., NW (24th St.), 202-296-1166

■ "Talented" chef Robert Wiedmaier's "wonderful" West End French-Belgian quickly rocketed "into an elite class" (it's in the Top 10 for food) shortly after it opened in the space that formerly housed Provence; anticipate a "gracious maitre d'", "hearty" and "adventurous" cuisine ("the duck is a treat") paired with "outstanding" wine service, "mouthwatering desserts" and a "romantic" (albeit sometimes "loud") ambiance; in sum: "a winner."

Melrose ▣

27 | 25 | 26 | $51

Park Hyatt Hotel, M & 24th Sts., NW, 202-955-3899

■ Overcome your "anti–hotel" dining room bias at this "spacious", "classy" West End "refuge" that showcases "wonderful", "refined" New American cuisine, museum-worthy art, an "elegant" outdoor courtyard and "gracious" service; extraordinarily versatile, it's "a good business restaurant", a "classy spot" for celebratory weekend dining and dancing, a "standard"-setting Sunday brunch pick and a smart choice for "super" holiday dinners.

Morton's of Chicago ▣

25 | 22 | 23 | $51

Washington Sq., 1050 Connecticut Ave., NW (L St.), 202-955-5997
3251 Prospect St., NW (Wisconsin Ave.), 202-342-6258
Fairfax Sq., 8075 Leesburg Pike (Aline Rd.), Tysons Corner, VA, 703-883-0800

■ "Unreconstructed beef eaters" laud the "fantastic" porterhouse and other "decadent" portions of prime meats served at these clubby steakhouses; patrons also enjoy being treated like a "power broker and insider" by the "knowledgeable" staff and don't mind signing the expense-account voucher, but they can skip "being introduced to their entree" as part of the pre-ordering ritual.

Nora

26 | 24 | 24 | $51

2132 Florida Ave., NW (R St.), 202-462-5143

■ Nora Pouillon sure knows how to make "all-organic" dining taste "so much better than it sounds" at this "exceptional" New American set in a "romantic" carriage house above Dupont Circle; it's "very big with official Washington" and many discerning diners, even if a few quibblers call it "too politically correct" and "costly."

Obelisk [S] 27 22 26 $57

2029 P St., NW (bet. 20th & 21st Sts.), 202-872-1180

■ For a "superb" experience that's like "eating fine food at someone's home", indulge in this "gem" off Dupont Circle that captures Northern Italian sensibility with its "simple, pure and satisfying" seasonal cuisine (top-rated in its category); admirers urge "be open-minded" and let the chef's "creative prix fixe menus stimulate your palate"; just as "wonderful" as the fare are the wines and a staff that's intent on making each meal "special."

Old Ebbitt Grill ◐ [S] 20 22 20 $31

675 15th St., NW (bet. F & G Sts.), 202-347-4801

■ DC's big, handsome, neo-Edwardian "public club" (think dark paneling, "period" gas lamps and leather-lined booths) set in a prime Downtown locale provides a highly Washingtonian backdrop for everything from "power breakfasts" to "late-night oysters"; its "huge bar scene" draws plenty of "politicos", as does the "classic" American food and "helpful" staff, but even if they falter "it's the atmosphere, stupid."

Pizzeria Paradiso [S] 25 16 18 $20

2029 P St., NW (bet. 20th & 21st Sts.), 202-223-1245

■ "Perfectly" named, the "eternal winner" of the *DC Survey*'s top pizza honors gets it just right – a "flavorful", "crisp" "wood-smoked" crust judiciously covered with "top-notch ingredients" (some say the sandwiches are "even better"); a "charming little place" off Dupont Circle filled with "happy clatter", its "paramount" pies and "well-chosen" wines often lead to peak-hour "waits."

Prime Rib 26 25 25 $53

2020 K St., NW (bet. 20th & 21st Sts.), 202-466-8811

■ Rated the top steakhouse in DC and the "classiest of the power meateries", this gilt-edged Downtown American supper club attracts lawyers and lovelies who "dress up" to feast on the "finest" prime rib and "superb" crab imperial, accompanied by a "wonderful wine list"; the elegant surroundings exude a "coat-and-tie" "dignity" that simply "can't be duplicated", making all diners "feel important."

Prince Michel [S] 26 22 26 $59

Rte. 29 S. HCR4, Box 77, Leon, VA, 540-547-9720

■ High scores signal the "excellence" of this posh haute French destination in Leon, where the kitchen's "exquisite" updated classics and the staff's "subtle" pampering leave patrons only wishing it weren't "so far out" of town; the elegant venue offers prix fixe tasting menus, as well as à la carte courses (Thursdays–Saturdays), and the extravagant midday Sunday repast makes for a "fun getaway."

Rabieng [S] 25 17 20 $24

Glen Forest Shopping Ctr., 5892 Leesburg Pike (Glen Forest Dr.), Falls Church, VA, 703-671-4222

■ "Incredible Thai country food from the owners of Duangrat's" earns this "reserved" Falls Church favorite "top" honors; in a "smaller" space with a "more down-to-earth" atmosphere than its citified sibling, diners will find gutsy, "spicy" "peasant" dishes infused with a "wonderful blend of flavors"; P.S. you "must try" the "novel" Thai-style dim sum offered at the weekend brunch.

F | D | S | C

Red Sage [S] 21 | 24 | 20 | $38

605 14th St., NW (F St.), 202-638-4444

◪ A big tourist attraction, this "eye-popping" Southwestern "original" lassoes in Downtown lawyers and lobbyists for "short orders" and "fantastic happy hours" in the frenetic upstairs chile bar accented with "cloud and lightning" motifs; for "real food", expense-account types entertain in the downstairs room (a "sight to see" itself) where the kitchen, which has a "way with chiles", keeps "reinventing" its dishes; if there are critics who feel it has "fallen off some", at least it's now easier to "get a table."

Seasons [S] 26 | 26 | 26 | $55

Four Seasons Hotel, 2800 Pennsylvania Ave., NW (28th St.), 202-944-2000

■ The early-morning limo lineup outside this major "breakfast player" in Georgetown attests to the "reliably elegant" pampering and near-"perfect" orchestration of "classy" special events at this "serene" New American showcase with a "gorgeous" garden terrace; overlooking the C&O canal, it's also a "first-rate" site for lunch or dinner, as well as for afternoon tea or Sunday brunch.

1789 [S] 26 | 26 | 25 | $53

1226 36th St., NW (Prospect St.), 202-965-1789

■ Open the door of this historic Federal townhouse in Georgetown and "enter the world of blue blazers" and patrons celebrating a "dressy occasion", all warmed by wintertime "fires burning" in "private"-feeling period dining rooms; Ris Lacoste's "wonderful" American cooking is served in "classically" "elegant" surroundings imbued with a "gracious ambiance", making it "a place you can take both your mother and your daughter and love yourself."

Taberna del Alabardero 25 | 25 | 24 | $50

1776 I St., NW (18th St.), 202-429-2200

■ As "sensuous" as Spain itself, this "expensive" Downtown Iberian classic "transports" guests to the "old world" "in grand style" with "world-class" cooking, an "exhaustive" wine list and "impeccable service"; the "extravagant" setting is apt for "entertaining clients" or "someone you really like", thus it's not hard to see why "the King of Spain" once dined here; P.S. "strolling serenaders" play classical Spanish music Friday–Saturday nights.

Timothy Dean [S] – | – | – | E

St. Regis Hotel, 923 16th St., NW (K St.), 202-879-6900

Hometown hero Timothy Dean (ex NYC's Palladin) brings his acclaimed French-accented New American cooking to the palatial site near the White House once occupied by Lespinasse; amid updated decor that's as opulent as ever, savor fresh, light dishes based on local products (e.g. corn soup with bone-marrow flan) at prices not quite as luxe as its predecessor's.

Vidalia [S] 26 | 23 | 24 | $49

1990 M St., NW (bet. 19th & 20th Sts.), 202-659-1990

■ The "luscious" Southern-accented New American comfort food turned out at this Dupont Circle South expense-account "treat" has nouveau and native Southerners alike cheering the "great" kitchen that "performs magic"; though claustrophobes clamor about the "basement" location and not everyone cottons to the staff's "Deep South" tempo, the "warm" ambiance and "personable" service convey a stylish "hospitality" that's "classy in every way."

AREA ABBREVIATIONS

AC	Atlantic City	MI	Miami
AT	Atlanta	MN	Minneapolis/St. Paul
BA	Baltimore/Annapolis	NJ	New Jersey
BO	Boston	NO	New Orleans
CH	Chicago	NY	New York City
CI	Cincinnati	OC	Orange County, CA
CL	Cleveland	OR	Orlando
CO	Columbus	PB	Palm Beach
CT	Connecticut	PH	Philadelphia
DA	Dallas	PO	Portland, OR
DC	Washington, DC	PS	Phoenix/Scottsdale
DE	Denver Area	SA	Santa Fe
FL	Fort Lauderdale	SC	Salt Lake City Area
FW	Fort Worth	SD	San Diego
HO	Honolulu	SE	Seattle
HS	Houston	SF	San Francisco Area
KC	Kansas City	SL	St. Louis
LA	Los Angeles	SN	So. New York State
LI	Long Island	TB	Tampa Bay/Sarasota
LV	Las Vegas	TC	Tucson

CUISINES

Afghan
Helmand, BA

American (New)
Abacus, DA
Acacia, NJ
American Bounty, SN
American Restaurant, KC
Anago, BO
An American Bistro, SN
Angeluna, FW
Antrim 1844, BA
Aria, AT
Astor Place, MI
Atlantic, MI
Aujourd'hui, BO
Aureole, LV
Aureole, NY
Bacchanalia, AT
Bambara, SC
Barney's, LI
Bayona, NO
Beach Bistro, TB
Bear Cafe, SN
Beehive, DE
Belvedere Inn, SN
Bernards Inn, NJ
Bertrand at Mister A's, SD
Biba, BO
Bijou Café, TB
Bistango, OC

Bistro Mezzaluna, FL
Blackbird, CH
BluePointe, AT
Boulevard, SF
Brown Dog Cafe, CI
Buckhead Diner, AT
Buffet at the Kimbell, FW
Butterfield 9, DC
Cafe Allegro, KC
Cafe Aspen, FW
Cafe Balaban, SL
Cafe Chardonnay, PB
Cafe Mira, SL
Cafe on the Green, FW
Cafe Sebastienne, KC
Cafe Tamayo, SN
Calico, SN
Cameron's, CO
Canoe, AT
Cardwell's at the Plaza, SL
Carlyle Grand Cafe, DC
Carole Peck, CT
Charles Court, DE
Charlie Trotter's, CH
Chez Shea, SE
Citrus Grille, SN
Convivo, PS
Courtright's, CH
Crabtree's Kittle House, SN
Daily Review Cafe, HS

Daniel's on Broadway, NJ
Daveed's at 934, CI
DC Coast, DC
DePuy Canal House, SN
dick & harry's, AT
Dilworthtown Inn, PH
Dining Room, NJ
Ebbitt Room, NJ
Eleven Madison Park, NY
Elms, CT
Emeril's, NO
Emeril's Delmonico, NO
Equinox, DC
Esty Street, NJ
Fat Cats, CL
Faust's, SL
510 Restaurant, MN
Flagstaff House, DE
Focaccia Grill, LI
Food Studio, AT
Fork, PH
Fountain, PH
Four Seasons, PB
Freelance Cafe, SN
French Laundry, SF
Frog & The Peach, CT
Frog & The Peach, NJ
Gary Danko, SF
George's at the Cove, SD
Glitretind, SC
G. Michael's, CO
Goodfellow's, MN
Gotham Bar & Grill, NY
Grace, CH
Gramercy Tavern, NY
Grand Finale, CI
Green Room, DA
Gregory's Grill, PS
Grille on Broadway, KC
Grill Room, NO
Hamersley's Bistro, BO
Hampton's, BA
Harvest, SL
Harvest Moon Inn, NJ
Harvey's Bistro, OR
Herbfarm, SE
Highlands Garden Cafe, DE
Himmarshee B&G, FL
Icarus, BO
Inn at Little Washington, DC

Inn at Pound Ridge, SN
Iron Horse Grill, SN
Iron Horse Inn, CI
Jake's, PH
Jeffrey's, CT
Jeffrey's, NJ
JiRaffe, LA
Joe & Maggie's, NJ
Karen & Rei's, NJ
Kevin Taylor, DE
Keystone Ranch, DE
Kingfisher, TC
Kinkead's, DC
Kosta's, CL
Lark Creek Inn, SF
Lindey's, CO
Linwood's, BA
Little Nell, DE
Log Haven, SC
Lon's at the Hermosa, PS
Loring Cafe, MN
Lucia's, MN
Mainland Inn, PH
Manuel's on the 28th, OR
March, NY
Mariposa, SC
Market Square Bistro, CL
Mark's, HS
Mark's Las Olas, FL
Mark's South Beach, MI
Martine, SC
Max Downtown, CT
Max's Grille, PB
Max's Place, MI
McKinney & Doyle, SN
Melrose, DC
Mercer Kitchen, NY
Meritage, NJ
Metropolis, KC
Metropolitan, SC
Michael's, LA
Michael's at the Citadel, PS
Michael's on East, TB
Mill River Inn, LI
Mise en Place, TB
Mistral, SE
Mitchell's, NJ
Mĸ, CH
Mᴏᴅ., CH
Morel, TB

Moxie, CL
Mumbo Jumbo, AT
Nana Grill, DA
Nell's, SE
Nevis, FL
Nora, DC
Old Drovers Inn, SN
one sixtyblue, CH
One Walnut, CL
Opus 251, PH
Palace, CI
Panama Hatties, LI
Park Avenue Bistro, SL
Park Avenue Cafe, NY
Park 75, AT
Passerelle, PH
Pastiche Modern Eatery, TC
Pebbles, OR
Phoenix, CI
Plaza Cafe, LI
Polo Grill, LI
Postrio, LV
Potager, DE
Radex, DE
Rancho Pinot, PS
Rebeccas, CT
Renaissance, DE
Restaurant Alma, MN
Restaurant Hapa, PS
Rest. X & Bully Boy Bar, SN
River Cafe, NY
Rosemary & Sage, NJ
RoxSand, PS
Rudys' 2900, BA
Sacre Bleu, DE
Saddle Peak Lodge, LA
Saddle River Inn, NJ
Sake Lounge, HS
Seasons, CH
Seasons, DC
Sent Sovi, SF
1789, DC
71 Clinton Fresh Food, NY
Sevy's Grill, DA
Sidney Street Cafe, SL
Sierra Grill, HS
Spago, LV
Splendido, DE
Starker's Reserve, KC
Starr Boggs, LI

Steve's Centerbrook, CT
Stolen Grill, KC
Strings, DE
Sweet Basil, DE
Tabla, NY
Tasca, HS
Tavern on the Green, NY
Terrapin, SN
32 East, PB
302 West, CH
333 Belrose, PH
Tierra Mar, LI
Timothy Dean, DC
Tony Ruppe's, HS
Tremont 647, BO
TRU, CH
28 Oak Street, NJ
20 Manning, PH
Two Chefs, MI
240 Union, DE
208 Talbot, BA
Union Pacific, NY
Union Square Cafe, NY
Urbana, HS
Van Gogh's, AT
Ventana Room, TC
Veritas, NY
Vidalia, DC
Voltaire, DA
Washington Inn, NJ
Waters Edge, NJ
Watershed, AT
West Street Grill, CT
Wildflower, DE
Wildflower, TC
Windows on the World, NY
Wish, MI
Xavier's, SN
Xavier's at Piermont, SN
York St., DA
Zealous, CH
Zemi, PB
Zin, KC
Zinnia, SL

American (Regional)
Alpenglow Stube, DE
Ann Howard's Apricots, CT
Bois d'Arc, SN
Cafe Annie, HS

Crofton on Wells, CH
Grouse Mtn. Grill, DE
Lafite, TB
Mayflower Inn, CT
Milton Inn, BA
Out on Main, CO
Piñons, DE
Polo Grill, BA
Purdys Homestead, SN
Rainbow Lodge, HS
Rowes Wharf, BO
Sundance Tree Room, SC
Tack Room, TC

American (Traditional)

Bang!, DE
Bee & Thistle Inn, CT
Bonefish Grill, TB
Briarwood Inn, DE
Bull Ring, SA
Charleston, BA
Chez Betty, SC
El Gaucho, SE
Golden Lamb, CI
Golden Lamb Buttery, CT
Grill, LA
Harvest, BO
Maidstone Arms, LI
Manhattan Grill, DE
Michael's, LV
Mr. Stox, OC
New Yorker, SC
Old Ebbitt Grill, DC
Palace Arms, DE
Palomino Euro Bistro, HO
Prince Court, HO
Ram's Head Inn, AC
Rotisserie/Beef & Bird, HS
1789, DC
Spencer's, SC
St. Paul Grill, MN
Stroud's, KC
Swann Lounge, PH
'21' Club, NY
Victoria & Albert's, OR
We Oui, DA

Asian

Ambrosia on Huntington, BO
Azie, SF

Belvedere, LA
Benjy's, HS
Blue Ginger, BO
Buddakan, PH
Cafe Blanc, LA
Cafe Japengo, SD
Chaya Brasserie, LA
Chinois, LV
Chinois on Main, LA
Dahlia Lounge, SE
Echo, PB
Eos, SF
Five Feet, OC
OnJin's Cafe, HO
Pacific East, LI
Postrio, SF
Restaurant Hapa, PS
Salamander, BO
Scott Chen's, HS
Second Street Grill, LV
Shiro, LA
Sia's, AT
SideBern's, TB
Wahso, SC
Waterfront, SE

Austrian

Danube, NY

Bakery

BonBonerie, CI
Bread Line, DC

Barbecue

Angelo's Barbecue, FW
East Coast Grill, BO
Fiorella's Jack Stack, KC
Goode Co. Barbecue, HS
Johnny Rivers', OR
Montgomery Inn, CI
Railhead Smokehouse, FW
Sonny Bryan's, DA

Belgian

Belgian Lion, SD
Marcel's, DC

Brazilian

Cafe Brazil, DE
Fogo de Chao, DA
Porcao, MI

Cajun/Creole

Antoine's, NO
Arnaud's, NO
Brennan's, HS
Brennan's, NO
Brigtsen's, NO
Christian's, NO
Clancy's, NO
Commander's Palace, NO
Dee Felice Cafe, CI
Emeril's, NO
Emeril's Delmonico, NO
Emeril's New Orleans, LV
Emeril's Orlando, OR
410 Bank Street, NJ
Galatoire's, NO
Gautreau's, NO
Le Parvenu, NO
Mr. B's Bistro, NO
Sal & Judy's, NO
Upperline, NO

Californian

Aubergine, OC
Azzura Point, SD
Belvedere, LA
Benjy's, HS
Bistro 45, LA
Cafe Blanc, LA
Cafe Pacifica, SD
California Grill, OR
Charles Nob Hill, SF
Chef Shafer's Depot, LA
Chez Panisse, SF
Chez Panisse Cafe, SF
Chinois, LV
Citrus Grille, SN
Devon, LA
Erna's Elderberry, SF
Farallon, SF
Hawthorne Lane, SF
Hotel Bel-Air, LA
Jardinière, SF
JiRaffe, LA
Joe's, LA
Mélisse, LA
Mel's B&G, DE
Napa Valley Grille, CL
Pamplemousse Grille, SD
Patina, LA

Pavilion, OC
Pinot Bistro, LA
Pinot Brasserie, LV
Postrio, LV
Postrio, SF
Prado, SD
Rancho Valencia, SD
Rubicon, SF
Sage, BO
Shiro, LA
Spago Bev. Hills, LA
Spago Palo Alto, SF
Terra, SF

Cambodian

Elephant Walk, BO
Phnom Penh, CL

Caribbean

Bahama Breeze, OR
410 Bank Street, NJ
J-Bar, TC
Ortanique on the Mile, MI
Tupelo Honey, LI

Chinese

Arc-en-Ciel, DA
China Gourmet, CI
Chopstix, AT
Chrysanthemum, MI
Empress, HS
Empress Court, LV
Golden Dragon, HO
Hunan Village, SN
Mandarin, SC
Mayflower Cuisinier, LV
Pacific Moon Cafe, CI
P.F. Chang's, LV
Royal Star, LV
Shun Lee Palace, NY
Susanna Foo, PH
Tropical Chinese, MI
Tung Lai Shun, LA
Winnie's Oriental Garden, OR
Yangming, PH
Yujean Kang's, LA

Continental

Anthony's, HS
Anthony's/Catalinas, TC
Arizona Inn, TC

Baricelli Inn, CL
Bijou Café, TB
Black Orchid Cafe, FL
Briarwood Inn, DE
Brooks, FL
Café L'Europe, TB
Charles Court, DE
Chatham's Place, OR
Chez Betty, SC
Crystal Cafe, MI
Fiore Rotisserie, LV
Five Crowns, OC
Flagstaff House, DE
Forge, MI
Four Seasons, NY
Gold Room, TC
Grapevine, SC
Gustaf Anders, OC
Hôtel St. Germain, DA
Hugo's Cellar, LV
Inn at Perry Cabin, BA
Isis, LV
Jeffrey's, CT
Johnny's Bar, CL
Johnny's Downtown, CL
Kathy's Gazebo, PB
Lafite, TB
La Réserve, HS
Maison et Jardin, OR
Mazzi, LI
Michel's at the Balcony, FW
Mirko's, LI
New Yorker, SC
Old House, SA
100 South Ocean, PB
103 West, AT
Palace Arms, DE
Palm Court/Carltun, LI
Pano's & Paul's, AT
Park Plaza Gardens, OR
Peter Scott's, OR
Pink Adobe, SA
Rancho Valencia, SD
Rib Room, NO
Ritz, OC
Ritz-Carlton Buck. Café, AT
Riviera/Fireside, OC
Rouge 2000, PH
Rudys' 2900, BA
Schafer's Caffeehaus, OR

Seeger's, AT
Stonehenge, CT
Tio Pepe, BA
Tony's, HS
Tosoni's, SE

Cuban
Habana, CT
Rolando's, OR
Versailles, MI

Deli/Sandwich Shop
Brent's Deli, LA
Carnegie Deli, NY
Patisserie Descours, HS
White House, AC
Wolfie Cohen's Rascal, MI

Dessert
Patisserie Descours, HS

Diner
Starliner Diner, CO

Eclectic/International
Alana's Food & Wine, CO
Arch, SN
Arthur's 27, OR
Atlantis, OR
Babette's Cafe, AT
Bayport Cookery, MN
Bexley's Monk, CO
Bistro Twenty-Two, SN
Blue Ginger, BO
Blue Heron, TB
Blue Room, BO
Café Boulud, NY
Cafe L'Europe, PB
Cafe Matisse, NJ
Caspita! Cafe, NJ
Chaya Brasserie, LA
Chef Shafer's Depot, LA
Chez Melange, LA
China Grill, MI
Classic Cafe, FW
Coup Des Tartes, PS
Dexter's, OR
Dish, TC
EatZi's, DA
Euphemia Haye, TB
Geronimo, SA

Grand St. Cafe, KC
Grape, DA
Grape Escape, FW
Handke's Cuisine, CO
Harralds, SN
Higgins Restaurant, PO
Hobbit, OC
Hoku's, HO
Hot Chocolates, FL
La Plage, LI
Laurels, DA
Log Haven, SC
Manuel's on the 28th, OR
Matisse, NJ
Mirepoix, LI
Mirko's, LI
Morel, TB
Nemo, MI
Nomi, CH
Ophelia's, TB
Orchids, HO
Out on Main, CO
Panama Hatties, LI
Park Plaza Gardens, OR
Rancho de San Juan, SA
Randall's, FW
Razz's, PS
Rigsby's, CO
Rue Cler, DE
Salamander, BO
Savaradio, AC
Sergio's, CL
Spago Bev. Hills, LA
Starliner Diner, CO
Tantra, MI
Trio, CH
Tupelo Honey, LI
Tuscany, LI
Upperline, NO
Vesta Dipping Grill, DE
Victoria Park, FL
White Dog Cafe, PH
Zephs', SN
Zoria, TB

Eurasian
Bali-By-The-Sea, HO
Indigo, HO
Roy's, DE
Roy's, HO
Roy's, OC

European
Harvey's Bistro, OR

Floribbean
Maritana Grille, TB

French (Bistro)
Aquitaine, BO
Aubergine Cafe, DE
Bis, DC
Bistro at Maison de Ville, NO
Bistro 45, LA
Bistro St. Tropez, PH
Bistro 315, SA
Blue Angel, PH
Cafe Bizou, LA
Cafe Campagne, SE
Cafe des Amis, PO
Cafe Provençal, SL
Chez Gerard, DA
Chez Nous, HS
Christopher's, PS
Crozier's, NO
D & J Bistro, CH
Floataway Cafe, AT
French 75, OC
Frenchy's Bistro, LA
Fringale, SF
Hamersley's Bistro, BO
La Crêpe Nanou, NO
La Petite Maison, PB
Le Bistro, TC
Le Canard Enchaîné, SN
Left Bank, FL
Le Pichet, SE
Le Soir, LI
Mimosa, LA
Montrachet, NY
OnJin's Cafe, HO
Peristyle, NO
Petit Louis, BA
Pinot Bistro, LA
Pinot Brasserie, LV
Sel de la Terre, BO
Tapenade, SD
Tramontana, DA
Truc, BO
Union League Cafe, CT
We Oui, DA

French (Classic)

Alain Ducasse, NY
American Hotel, LI
Andre's, LV
Antoine's, NO
Auberge du Soleil, SF
Belgian Lion, SD
Buffet de la Gare, SN
Café Boulud, NY
Café de France, SL
Café des Artistes, NY
Cavey's, CT
Cellar, OC
Cello, NY
Chez Alphonse, CI
Chez Catherine, NJ
Chez François, CL
Chez Vincent, OR
Christian's, NO
Coup Des Tartes, PS
Daniel, NY
Da Pietro's, CT
Deux Cheminées, PH
El Bizcocho, SD
Escoffier, SN
Fio's La Fourchette, SL
510 Restaurant, MN
French Room, DA
Fromagerie, NJ
Gary Danko, SF
Hôtel St. Germain, DA
Isis, LV
Janos, TC
Jean-Louis, CT
Kathy's Gazebo, PB
La Belle Vie, MN
La Bonne Auberge, PH
La Cachette, LA
La Caille, SC
La Campagne, NJ
La Caravelle, NY
La Colombe d'Or, HS
La Côte Basque, NY
La Crémaillère, SN
La Grenouille, NY
La Jonquille, PH
La Marmite, LI
La Mer, HO
L'Antibes, CO
La Petite Maison, DE

La Provence, NO
L'Auberge Chez François, DC
L'Auberge Provencale, DC
Le Bar Lyonnais, PH
Le Bec-Fin, PH
Le Château, SN
Le Cirque, LV
Le Cirque 2000, NY
Le Français, CH
Le Gourmand, SE
L'Endroit, LI
Le Rendez-Vous, TC
Les Nomades, CH
Lespinasse, NY
Le Titi de Paris, CH
L'Orangerie, LA
Louis XVI, NO
Lutèce, NY
Maison Robert, BO
Malmaison, SL
Marcel's, DC
Masa's, SF
Maxime's, SN
Nikolai's Roof, AT
NOMI, CH
Prince Michel, DC
Refectory, CO
Ritz Carlton, TB
Ritz-Carlton Buck. Café, AT
Ritz-Carlton Dining Room, BO
Roger Sherman Inn, CT
Saddle River Inn, NJ
Suzette's, LV
Swann Lounge, PH
Tante Louise, DE
Tatsu's, KC
Thomas Henkelmann, CT
Vincent Guerithault, PS

French (Country)

Campagne, SE
Chez Gerard, DA
Copper Beech Inn, CT
Le Coq au Vin, OR
Saint-Emilion, FW

French (New)

Ambria, CH
Ambrosia on Huntington, BO
Arch, SN

Artesia, NO
Auberge Maxime, SN
Aubergine, OC
Aubriot, CH
Aux Delices, CT
Azie, SF
Barney's, LI
Belvedere, LA
Bistro Twenty-Two, SN
Blue Door, MI
Bouley Bakery, NY
Brasserie Jo, CH
Brasserie Le Coze, AT
Brasserie Perrier, PH
Cacharel, FW
Cafe Panache, NJ
Carlos', CH
Castagna, PO
Chanterelle, NY
Charles Nob Hill, SF
Chef Mavro's, HO
Chez Jean-Pierre, PB
Chinois on Main, LA
Ciboulette, PH
Citronelle, DC
Clio, BO
Couvron, PO
DeVille, HS
Diaghilev, LA
Eiffel Tower, LV
El Bizcocho, SD
Elephant Walk, BO
Elisabeth Daniel, SF
Empress, HS
Equus, SN
Erna's Elderberry, SF
Everest, CH
Fifth Floor, SF
Five Feet, OC
Fleur de Lys, SF
Fountain, PH
Frenchtown Inn, NJ
Gabriel's, CH
Gerard's Downtown, NO
Gerard's Place, DC
Heathman, PO
Hotel Bel-Air, LA
Hôtel St. Germain, DA
Jardinière, SF
Jean Georges, NY

Julien, BO
La Colline Verte, CT
La Folie, SF
La Palme d'Or, MI
La Panetière, SN
La Petite Maison, DE
La Toque, SF
LaTour, NJ
Laurel, SD
La Vieille Maison, PB
Le Bernardin, NY
Le Palais, AC
Le Papillon, SF
Le Provence, OR
L'Espalier, BO
Lilac, NJ
Louis XVI, LI
Lumière, BO
Maisonette, CI
Maison Janeiro, PB
Marine Room, SD
Mary Elaine's, PS
Mélisse, LA
Mille Fleurs, SD
Mirabelle, LI
Nan, PH
Napa, LV
Old Drovers Inn, SN
Ondine, CT
Ondine, SF
103 West, AT
Overtures, PH
Pamplemousse Grille, SD
Papillon Cafe, DE
Parker's, CL
Pascal's on Ponce, MI
Passerelle, PH
Patina, LA
Picasso, LV
Radius, BO
Rat's, NJ
Renoir, LV
Restaurant du Village, CT
Ristra, SA
Ritz-Carlton, OC
Ritz-Carlton Buck. Din. Rim., AT
Ritz-Carlton Din. Rm., CH
Ritz-Carlton Din. Rm., SF
Riviera, DA
Rover's, SE

Rubicon, SF
Ryland Inn, NJ
Sans Souci, CL
Sent Sovi, SF
Serenäde Restaurant, NJ
Silks, BO
Stage House Inn, NJ
Stone Creek Inn, LI
Tallgrass, CH
Tangerine, PH
Terra, SF
Troquet, OC
Vignola, SD
Vong, CH
Wahso, SC
WineSellar & Brasserie, SD

French (Provençal)

Bistro Jeanty, SF
Bistro Provence, HS
Cafe Perrier, HS
Campton Place, SF
Drai's, LV
Mistral, BO
Pascal, OC
Pinot Provence, OC

Fusion

Eos, SF
Samba Room, DA
Samba Room, FL

German

Schafer's Caffeehaus, OR
Szmania's, SE

Greek

Black Olive, BA
Cypriana Cafe, OR
Kokkari Estiatorio, SF
Milos, Estiatorio, NY
Samos, BA

Hamburger

Five Guys, DC
Kincaid's, FW
'21' Club, NY

Hawaiian

Alan Wong's, HO
Chef Mavro's, HO
Padovani's Bistro, HO
Pineapple Room, HO

Indian

Bombay Club, DC
Tabla, NY

Italian

(N=Northern; S=Southern;
N&S=Includes both)
Abruzzi, AT (N&S)
Acquerello, SF (N&S)
Andiamo!, SA (N)
Antonello, OC (N&S)
Antonio's La Fiamma, OR (N&S)
Armani's, TB (N)
Assaggio, PO (N&S)
Babbo, NY (N&S)
Bar Italia Ristorante, SL (N)
Barolo Grill, DE (N)
Barresi's, CI (N&S)
Boccaccio, BA (N)
Bravissimo, OR (N&S)
Bravo! Nader, LI (N&S)
Brio Tuscan Grille, OR (N)
Buca di Beppo, MN (N&S)
Cafe Giovanni, NO (N&S)
Cafe Juanita, SE (N)
Cafe Lago, SE (N&S)
Cafe Martorano, FL (N&S)
Cafe Mazzarello's, PB (N&S)
Caffé Abbracci, MI (N&S)
Caffe Mingo, PO (N&S)
Caffe Paradiso, TB (N)
Capri Blue, PB (N&S)
Carbone's, CT (N)
Carpaccio, MI (N)
Casa D'Angelo, FL (N&S)
Castagna, PO (N&S)
Caterina de Medici, SN (N)
Cavey's, CT (N)
Chef Vola's, AC (N&S)
Cousin's, AC (N&S)
Da Marco, HS (N)
Damian's, HS (N&S)
D'Amico Cucina, MN (N&S)
Daniel's, TC (N)
Da Pietro's, CT (N)
Dario, LI (N&S)
Da Ugo, LI (N&S)
Delfino Riviera, OR (N)
DiPalma, PH (N&S)
Dominic's, SL (N&S)

Enoteca il Castello, LI (N)
Enzo's, OR (N)
Escopazzo, MI (N&S)
Etrusco, DC (N&S)
Fat Cats, CL (N&S)
Floataway Cafe, AT (N&S)
Franco's Trattoria, PS (N)
Fresco Italian Cafe, SC (N)
Gabriel's, CH (N&S)
Galileo, DC (N&S)
Garozzo's, KC (N&S)
Gavi, TC (N&S)
Gennaro's, CT (N&S)
Genoa, PO (N&S)
Giovanni's, SL (N&S)
Girasole, AC (N&S)
Giumarello's, NJ (N&S)
Giuseppe's Ritrovo, CO (S)
G. Michael's, CO (N&S)
Grappa, SC (N&S)
Il Capriccio, BO (N)
Il Cenàcolo, SN (N)
Il Mulino, NY (N)
Il Piatto, SA (N)
Il Terrazzo Carmine, SE (N)
Il Vicino, SA (N&S)
Irene's Cuisine, NO (N&S)
Johnny's Bar, CL (N)
Johnny's Downtown, CL (N)
Julian's, SA (N&S)
La Campania, BO (N&S)
La Famiglia, PH (N&S)
La Finestra, PB (N)
La Grotta, AT (N&S)
La Mora Cucina, HS (N)
La Pace, LI (N)
La Piazza, FW (N&S)
La Piccola Liguria, LI (N&S)
La Riviera, NO (N)
La Vista, HS (N&S)
L'Endroit, LI (N)
Lidia's, KC (N&S)
Locanda Veneta, LA (N)
Lombardi Mare, DA (N&S)
Lupo, Trattoria del, LV (N&S)
Lusardi's, SN (N)
Maurizio's, BO (N&S)
Max a Mia, CT (N)
Max Amoré, CT (N)
Mi Piaci, DA (N)

Monte Carlo Liv. Rm., PH (N&S)
Mosca's, NO (N&S)
Navona, LI (N&S)
Nicola's, CI (N)
Nino's, HS (N&S)
Obelisk, DC (N)
Oliveto, SF (N)
Ombra, DE (N&S)
Osteria del Teatro, MI (N)
Pazzo Ristorante, PO (N&S)
Peppercorn's Grill, CT (N&S)
Piccolo, LI (N)
Piccolo Arancio, CT (N&S)
Piero's, LV (N)
Polo Grille, CT (N&S)
Primavera, FL (N&S)
Quattro's, CT (N&S)
Ristorante Luci, MN (N&S)
Rose Pistola, SF (N)
Sage, BO (N&S)
Sal & Judy's, NO (N&S)
Saloon, PH (N&S)
Salvatore's, CL (N&S)
Salve!, DA (N)
Saporito's, BO (N&S)
Savona, PH (N)
Scalea's, CI (N&S)
Scalini Fedeli, NJ (N)
Scali Ristorante, CO (N&S)
Sempre Vivolo, LI (N&S)
Simposio, HS (N)
Spiaggia, CH (N&S)
Stresa, LI (N&S)
Terramia, BO (N&S)
3 Doors Down, PO (N&S)
Tony's, SL (N&S)
Tosoni's, SE (N&S)
Trattoria Diane, LI (N)
Trattoria Marcella, SL (N&S)
Trattoria Roma, CO (N&S)
Tra Vigne, SF (N&S)
Tre Figlio, AC (N&S)
Tuscan Steak, MI (N)
Tuscany, LI (N)
Tuscany, SC (N)
Valentino, LA (N&S)
Valentino, LV (N)
Va Pensiero, CH (N&S)
Veni Vidi Vici, AT (N&S)
Vetri, PH (N&S)

Zelo, MN (N)
Zuni Cafe, SF (N&S)

Japanese
Asanebo, LA
Azuma Sushi, SN
Cafe Japengo, SD
Domo, DE
Ginza, BO
Hashiguchi, AT
Ichiban Sushi, SC
Jo An, CI
Kamogawa, AT
Kaz Sushi Bistro, DC
Kotobuki, LI
Kyo-Ya, HO
Maiko, MI
Makoto, DC
Matsuhisa, LA
Mirai Sushi, CH
Nishino, SE
Nobu, LV
Nobu, NY
Ondine, SF
Origami, MN
Prince Court, HO
Restaurant Japan, CO
Restaurant Murata, PO
Sagami, NJ
Saito's, SE
Sake Lounge, HS
Shiki, OR
Shiro's Sushi, SE
Shuhei, CL
Soto, AT
Sugiyama, NY
Sushi Den, DE
Sushi Huku, AT
Sushi Nozawa, LA
Sushi Ota, SD
Sushisay, NY
Toni's Sushi, MI
Toyoda Sushi, SE
Wild Ginger, NJ
Yohei Sushi, HO

Jewish
Brent's Deli, LA

Latin American
Chino Latino, MN
Fandango, SE

Samba Room, DA
Samba Room, FL
Tango Tapas, SE
Tierra, AT

Louisiana (Contemporary)
Dakota, NO
Gabrielle, NO
Gamay, NO
NOLA, NO
Pelican Club, NO
Peristyle, NO

Mediterranean
Auberge du Soleil, SF
Aubergine Cafe, DE
Audrey Claire, PH
Azzura Point, SD
Beach Bistro, TB
Beehive, DE
Bistro Louise, FW
Bluehour, PO
Brasa, SE
Cafe Mezé, SN
Caffe Bella, BO
Campanile, LA
Chez Panisse Cafe, SF
Citricos, OR
Dmitri's, PH
Eno, AT
Gardens, LA
Harvest on Hudson, SN
Il Sole, DA
La Belle Vie, MN
La Petite Maison, PB
Mark's at the Park, PB
Marquesa, PS
Martine, SC
Maurizio's, BO
Mediterranean Grill, CT
Mediterraneo, DA
Mel's B&G, DE
Moonstruck, NJ
Olives, BO
Olives, LV
Overtures, PH
Palomino Euro Bistro, DA
Palomino Euro Bistro, HO
Palomino Euro Bistro, MN
Pavilion, OC

Picholine, NY
Postrio, SF
Remy's Kitchen, SL
Renaissance, DE
Rialto, BO
Ritz-Carlton Buck. Din. Rm., AT
Riviera, DA
Riviera Grill, HS
Sans Souci, CL
Sapphire Kitchen, SE
SideBern's, TB
Stone Creek Inn, LI
Strings, DE
T. Cook's, PS
Zov's Bistro, OC
Zuni Cafe, SF

Mexican

Border Grill, LV
Cafe Azul, PO
Cafe Poca Cosa, TC
Ciudad, DA
Eduardo de San Angel, FL
Esperanza's, FW
Frontera Grill, CH
Gabriel's, SA
Ixcapuzalco, CH
Javier's, DA
J-Bar, TC
Joe T. Garcia's, FW
La Hacienda, PS
La Montaña, DE
Mi Nidito, TC
Red Iguana, SC
Topolobampo, CH

Midwestern

Dakota B&G, MN
Lola, CL

Moroccan

Tangerine, PH

New Mexican

El Farol, SA
Guadalupe Cafe, SA
Pink Adobe, SA
Rancho de Chimayo, SA

New World

Américas, HS
Chef Allen's, MI
Darrel & Oliver's Cafe, FL

La Coquina, OR
Norman's, MI

Northwestern

Artist Point, OR
Cafe des Amis, PO
Canlis, SE
Caprial's Bistro, PO
Cascadia, SE
Dahlia Lounge, SE
Fullers, SE
Heathman, PO
Herbfarm, SE
Inn at Langley, SE
Kaspar's, SE
Lampreia, SE
Mistral, SE
Nell's, SE
Palace Kitchen, SE
Paley's Place, PO
Shoalwater, SE
Szmania's, SE
Tina's, PO
Waterfront, SE
Wildwood, PO

Nuevo Latino

¡Pasion!, PH

Pacific Rim

Abacus, DA
A Pacific Cafe, HO
California Cafe, OR
Japengo, LV
Jozu, LA
Second Street Grill, LV
Shiitake, SL
3660 on the Rise, HO

Pan-Asian

Bambú, MI
Pacific Moon Cafe, CI
Pacific Time, MI
Saucebox Cafe & Bar, PO
Shuhei, CL
Wild Ginger, SE

Pizza

Figlio Wood-Fired Pizza, CO
Frank Pepe Pizzeria, CT
Pizzeria Bianco, PS

Pizzeria Paradiso, DC
Sally's Apizza, CT
Tacconelli's Pizzeria, PH

Russian
Diaghilev, LA
Nikolai's Roof, AT
Russian Tea Room, NY

Scandinavian
Aquavit, MN
Aquavit, NY

Seafood
Al Biernat's, DA
Aqua, LV
Aqua, SF
AquaKnox, DA
Atlanta Fish Market, AT
Atlantique, CH
Atlantis, OR
Baleen, MI
Beacon, CT
Black Olive, BA
Black's Bar & Kitchen, DC
Blue Pointe Grill, CL
Bo Brooks, BA
Bonefish Grill, TB
Bristol B&G, KC
Burt & Jack's, FL
Buzio's, LV
Cafe Pacific, DA
Capital Grille, DA
Cello, NY
Chops, AT
Doris & Ed's, NJ
East Coast Grill, BO
Etta's Seafood, SE
Flying Fish, SE
Flying Fish Cafe, OR
Fulton's Crab House, OR
Hobo's Fish Joint, FL
Jake's Famous Crawfish, PO
Jasper White's, BO
Jax Fish House, DE
JJ's, KC
Joe's Stone Crab, MI
Johnny's Half Shell, DC
Kincaid's, MN
Kingfisher, TC
KingFish Hall, BO

Le Bernardin, NY
Legal Sea Foods, BO
Lombardi Mare, DA
Manhattan Ocean Club, NY
Market Street Grill, SC
McCormick & Schmick's, KC
Neros, LV
Nine, CH
Oceana, NY
Oceanaire, MN
Orchids, HO
Oyster Bar (Gr. Cent.), NY
Oystercatchers, TB
Pierpoint, BA
Pierpont's, KC
Pisces, SF
Plaza Cafe, LI
Prime, AT
Pyramid Grill, DA
Red Fish Grill, MI
Restaurant Oceana, PS
Rose Pistola, SF
Royal Star, LV
Salt Rock Grill, TB
Sansom St. Oyster House, PH
Savona, PH
Shaw's, CH
Shiro, LA
Star of the Sea, SD
Striped Bass, PH
Sunfish Grill, FL
Tapenade, SD
21 Oceanfront, OC
Water Grill, LA

South American
Américas, HS
Churrascos, HS

Southern/Soul
Aria, AT
Braddock's Grandview, CO
Georgia Brown's, DC
Harvest, AT
Kingfish Café, SE
Louis' Downtown, OR
Ouisie's Table, HS
South City Kitchen, AT
Sylvia's, NY

Southwestern

Anasazi, SA
Armadillo Cafe, FL
Cafe Annie, HS
Cafe Pasqual's, SA
Cafe Terra Cotta, TC
California Cafe, OR
Coyote Cafe, SA
¡Fuego!, TC
Geronimo, SA
Gold Room, TC
Janos, TC
La Casa Sena, SA
La Montaña, DE
La Vista, HS
Lon's at the Hermosa, PS
Mansion on Turtle Creek, DA
Michaels, FW
Nava, AT
Old House, SA
Prado, SD
Reata, FW
Red Sage, DC
Ristra, SA
River Cafe, HS
Ruggles Grill, HS
Santacafe, SA
Sia's, AT
Sierra Grill, HS
Star Canyon, DA
Star Canyon, LV
Vincent Guerithault, PS

Spanish

El Farol, SA
Harvest Vine, SE
Jaleo, DC
Meson Galicia, CT
Picasso, LV
Taberna del Alabardero, DC
Tasca, HS
Tio Pepe, BA

Steakhouse

Al Biernat's, DA
Beacon, CT
Bern's Steak House, TB
Bob's Steak & Chop, DA
Bone's, AT
Brenner's, HS

Brighton Steak House, AC
Bryant & Cooper, LI
Burt & Jack's, FL
C & H Steak Company, HS
Capital Grille, DA
Carmen Anthony, CT
Charlie Palmer Steak, LV
Chops, AT
Churrascos, HS
Del Frisco's, DA
Del Frisco's, DE
Del Frisco's, FW
Del Frisco's, OR
Delmonico, LV
Eddie's, SL
El Gaucho, SE
Fogo de Chao, DA
Gibsons Steakhouse, CH
Grill 23 & Bar, BO
Hugo's Cellar, LV
Hy's Steak House, HO
Hyde Park, CO
Hyde Park Grille, CL
JJ's, KC
Kincaid's, MN
Lawry's, DA
Lawry's the Prime Rib, LA
Lewnes' Steakhouse, BA
Lynn's Steakhouse, HS
Maloney & Porcelli, DC
Manhattan Grill, DE
Manny's Steakhouse, MN
McMahon's, TC
Mitchell's, CO
Morton's of Chicago, AT
Morton's of Chicago, CH
Morton's of Chicago, CI
Morton's of Chicago, CL
Morton's of Chicago, CT
Morton's of Chicago, DA
Morton's of Chicago, DC
Morton's of Chicago, LV
Morton's of Chicago, MI
Morton's of Chicago, OR
Morton's of Chicago, PB
Morton's of Chicago, PS
Morton's of Chicago, SD
Neros, LV
Nick & Sam's, DA
Nine, CH

Palm, LA
Palm, LI
Palm, LV
Palm, MI
Palm, NY
Pappas Bros., HS
Peter Luger, LI
Peter Luger, NY
Pierpont's, KC
Plaza III, KC
Porcao, MI
Precinct, CI
Prime, AT
Prime, LV
Prime Rib, BA
Prime Rib, DC
Prime Rib, PH
Pyramid Grill, DA
Rainwater's on Kettner, SD
Rib Room, NO
River Palm Terrace, NJ
Ruth's Chris, BA
Ruth's Chris, CO
Ruth's Chris, FL
Ruth's Chris, HO
Ruth's Chris, KC
Ruth's Chris, LA
Ruth's Chris, MI
Ruth's Chris, NO
Ruth's Chris, OR
Ruth's Chris, PB
Ruth's Chris, PS
Salt Rock Grill, TB
Smith & Wollensky, NY
Spencer's, SC
Steak House, LV
Sullivan's, DA
Tuscan Steak, MI
Yachtsman Steakhouse, OR

Swedish

Gustaf Anders, OC

Swiss

Fio's La Fourchette, SL

Tapas

Harvest Vine, SE
Jaleo, DC
Tango Tapas, SE

Tearoom

BonBonerie, CI

Tex-Mex

Star Canyon, LV

Thai

Arun's, CH
Basil Leaf, NO
Duangrat's, DC
Nan, PH
Rabieng, DC
Siam Lotus, LI
Siam Palace, MI
Tamarind, AT
Thai House, OR
Typhoon!, PO
Typhoon!, SE
Vong, CH

Vegetarian

Watercourse Foods, DE

Vietnamese

Arc-en-Ciel, DA
Hy-Vong, MI
Kim Son, NO
La Tre, PB
Lemon Grass Rest., NO
Little Saigon, AC
Miss Saigon, MI
Monsoon, SE
Nine Roses, NO
Pasteur, CH
Phnom Penh, CL
Slanted Door, SF

ALPHABETICAL PAGE INDEX

Rating Sheets

To aid in your participation in our next *Survey*

	F	D	S	C

Restaurant Name _____
Phone _____
Comments _____
_____
_____

Restaurant Name _____
Phone _____
Comments _____
_____
_____

Restaurant Name _____
Phone _____
Comments _____
_____
_____

Restaurant Name _____
Phone _____
Comments _____
_____
_____

Restaurant Name _____
Phone _____
Comments _____
_____
_____

Restaurant Name _____
Phone _____
Comments _____
_____
_____

	F	**D**	**S**	**C**

⌐⌐⌐⌐

Restaurant Name _____

Phone _____

Comments _____

_____

_____

⌐⌐⌐⌐

Restaurant Name _____

Phone _____

Comments _____

_____

_____

⌐⌐⌐⌐

Restaurant Name _____

Phone _____

Comments _____

_____

_____

⌐⌐⌐⌐

Restaurant Name _____

Phone _____

Comments _____

_____

_____

⌐⌐⌐⌐

Restaurant Name _____

Phone _____

Comments _____

_____

_____

⌐⌐⌐⌐

Restaurant Name _____

Phone _____

Comments _____

_____

_____

	F	D	S	C

⅃⅃⅃⅃

Restaurant Name _____
Phone _____
Comments _____
_____
_____

⅃⅃⅃⅃

Restaurant Name _____
Phone _____
Comments _____
_____
_____

⅃⅃⅃⅃

Restaurant Name _____
Phone _____
Comments _____
_____
_____

⅃⅃⅃⅃

Restaurant Name _____
Phone _____
Comments _____
_____
_____

⅃⅃⅃⅃

Restaurant Name _____
Phone _____
Comments _____
_____
_____

⅃⅃⅃⅃

Restaurant Name _____
Phone _____
Comments _____
_____
_____

	F	D	S	C

⌐⌐⌐⌐

Restaurant Name _____
Phone _____
Comments _____
_____
_____

⌐⌐⌐⌐

Restaurant Name _____
Phone _____
Comments _____
_____
_____

⌐⌐⌐⌐

Restaurant Name _____
Phone _____
Comments _____
_____
_____

⌐⌐⌐⌐

Restaurant Name _____
Phone _____
Comments _____
_____
_____

⌐⌐⌐⌐

Restaurant Name _____
Phone _____
Comments _____
_____
_____

⌐⌐⌐⌐

Restaurant Name _____
Phone _____
Comments _____
_____
_____

| | **F** | **D** | **S** | **C** |

Restaurant Name _____
Phone _____
Comments _____
_____
_____

Restaurant Name _____
Phone _____
Comments _____
_____
_____

Restaurant Name _____
Phone _____
Comments _____
_____
_____

Restaurant Name _____
Phone _____
Comments _____
_____
_____

Restaurant Name _____
Phone _____
Comments _____
_____
_____

Restaurant Name _____
Phone _____
Comments _____
_____
_____

www.zagat.com

	F	D	S	C
	⌐	⌐	⌐	⌐

Restaurant Name _____
Phone _____
Comments _____
_____
_____

	F	D	S	C
	⌐	⌐	⌐	⌐

Restaurant Name _____
Phone _____
Comments _____
_____
_____

	F	D	S	C
	⌐	⌐	⌐	⌐

Restaurant Name _____
Phone _____
Comments _____
_____
_____

	F	D	S	C
	⌐	⌐	⌐	⌐

Restaurant Name _____
Phone _____
Comments _____
_____
_____

	F	D	S	C
	⌐	⌐	⌐	⌐

Restaurant Name _____
Phone _____
Comments _____
_____
_____

	F	D	S	C
	⌐	⌐	⌐	⌐

Restaurant Name _____
Phone _____
Comments _____
_____
_____

Wine Vintage Chart 1985-1999

This chart is designed to help you select wine to go with your meal. It is based on the same 0 to 30 scale used throughout this *Survey*. The ratings (prepared by our friend **Howard Stravitz**, a law professor at the University of South Carolina) reflect both the quality of the vintage and the wine's readiness for present consumption. Thus, if a wine is not fully mature or is over the hill, its rating has been reduced. We do not include 1987, 1991 or 1993 vintages because they are not especially recommended for most areas.

	'85	'86	'88	'89	'90	'92	'94	'95	'96	'97	'98	'99
WHITES												
French:												
Alsace	24	19	22	28	28	23	27	25	22	23	25	22
Burgundy	23	24	19	25	21	23	22	26	28	25	24	25
Loire Valley	–	–	–	26	25	–	22	24	26	23	22	23
Champagne	28	25	24	26	29	–	–	24	27	24	24	–
Sauternes	22	28	29	25	27	–	–	22	23	24	23	–
California:												
Chardonnay	–	–	–	–	–	–	22	26	22	26	23	26
REDS												
French:												
Bordeaux	26	27	25	28	29	18	24	25	24	23	24	22
Burgundy	24	–	23	26	29	22	21	26	27	25	24	25
Rhône	25	19	25	28	27	15	23	25	22	24	27	25
Beaujolais	–	–	–	–	–	–	–	23	21	24	23	24
California:												
Cab./Merlot	26	26	–	21	28	25	27	26	25	26	23	25
Zinfandel	–	–	–	–	–	–	26	25	24	23	22	23
Italian:												
Tuscany	26	–	23	–	26	–	23	25	19	28	25	24
Piedmont	25	–	25	28	28	–	–	23	26	28	26	25